Limited Liability Partnershi

Third Edition

Limited Liability Partnerships Handbook

Third Edition

Paula Smith (LLB), Partner, EOS Law LLP

Bloomsbury Professional

**Bloomsbury Professional Ltd, Maxwelton House,
41–43 Boltro Road, Haywards Heath, West Sussex, RH16 1BJ**

© Bloomsbury Professional Ltd 2012

Bloomsbury Professional, an imprint of Bloomsbury Publishing Plc

A CIP Catalogue record for this book is available from the British Library.

ISBN: 978 1 84766 715 1

Typeset by Phoenix Photosetting, Chatham, Kent
Printed and bound by Hobbs the Printers Ltd, Totton, Hampshire

Preface

The second edition of this book was published in 2007 by the late Simon Young at a time when LLPs had been in existence for just over six years and the flow of incorporations had been steadily increasing since LLP inception in the UK in 2001. That increasing flow of incorporations has continued over the last five years with LLPs becoming the vehicle of choice not just for professional practices but also for traditional business which might ordinarily have looked to a limited liability company. This is due not only to increasing awareness of the LLP as a trading vehicle but also because of the perceived benefits of trading through a separate legal entity operating with tax transparency, organisational flexibility and of course the protection of limited liability.

Since the previous edition of this book there has been a relative flood of legislative reform, bringing LLPs in line with amendments to company legislation and the Companies Act 2006 in particular. The application of the Companies Act 1985 to LLPs has largely been repealed and new regulations applying various parts of the Companies Act 2006 and related regulations have been introduced. The transition has, to date, appeared smooth, and practitioners have no doubt appreciated the new approach to LLP legislation – publishing much of the legislation as it applies to LLPs, rather than having to cross refer amendments to multiple sources of company law!

The relatively smooth transition probably owes much to the fact that the new legislation is far from a radical overhaul of company and LLP legislation; the legislation has largely been re-ordered, updated and restated, although there have of course been changes, some of which are considered in this edition, including provisions in relation to the registered name of an LLP, trading disclosures and accounting and audit provisions, to name a few.

Notwithstanding the increasing use of and familiarity with LLPs, the entity is still in its relative infancy, and there will no doubt be further developments over the forthcoming years as case law in relation to LLPs inevitably increases. Whilst some recent decisions have helped to clarify supposed uncertainties, eg in relation to the employment status of a fixed share member, others, particularly in relation to what fiduciary duties may be owed by members to the LLP itself, have caused some surprise amongst practitioners and one suspects that there will be further developments in this area. Recent decisions have also confirmed the 'worker' status of a fixed share member with the accompanying rights that that affords and the question of age discrimination in relation to compulsory retirement is still a vexed issue with many partners citing the difficult economic climate as the principal reason for wanting to continue in practice, which is no doubt likely to lead to an increasing number of disputes in this area also.

Whilst the registration of LLPs has increased, almost inevitably, so too has the number of liquidations. This area, and particularly the potential for personal liability for members on insolvency, is likely to be another issue to watch over the coming years. Members may increasingly find that the limited liability that they thought they had acquired does not shield them from every claim.

Notwithstanding these issues, the LLP clearly appeals to many and I am privileged to have worked with many firms in the course of their conversion to LLP or who are setting up in business and choosing the LLP as their vehicle of choice. For those who are looking to convert, or who are already trading as an LLP, I hope this revised edition will be of help.

I would to thank Simon Young, as without his dedication to the area of LLPs and the hard work he put in to preparing the first two editions this excellent work would not have come into existence. I would also like to thank my colleagues at EOS Law LLP for their help and support, in particular Rob Turner, Hugh Clay, Kevin Curry and Amanda Bolton and the accountants who kindly 'volunteered' to give their input to the relevant chapters and who infected me with their enthusiasm for the LLP SORP(!) and finally to Andrew for those endless cups of tea without which writing this book would not have been possible!

The law is, as far as possible, stated as at 1 April 2012.

Paula Smith
June 2012

Contents

Contents

Table of Cases

Table of Statutes

[All references are to paragraph numbers.]

Table of Statutory Instruments

Table of Other Material

Index of Definitions

Definition	Description
2001 Regulations	The Limited Liability Partnerships Regulations 2001 (SI 2001/1090)
2008 Regulations	The Limited Liability Partnerships (Accounts and Audit) (Application of Companies Act 2006) Regulations 2006 (SI 2008/1911)
2008 Large LLP (Accounts) Regulations	The Large and Medium–sized Limited Liability Partnerships (Accounts) Regulations 2008 (SI 2008/1913)
2008 Small LLP (Accounts) Regulations	Small Limited Liability Partnerships (Accounts) Regulations 2008 (SI 2008/1912)
2009 Regulations	The Limited Liability Partnerships (Application of Companies Act 2006) Regulations 2009 (SI 2009/1804)
BIS	UK Department for Business, Innovation and Skills
Business Names (Miscellaneous Provisions) Regulations 2009	The Company and Business Names (Miscellaneous Provisions) Regulations 2009 (SI 2009/1085), as amended by SI 2009/2404
Business Names (Public Authorities) Regulations 2009	The Company, Limited Liability Partnership and Business Names (Public Authorities) Regulations 2009 (SI 2009/2982)
Business Names (Sensitive Words) Regulations 2009	The Company, Limited Liability Partnership and Business Names (Sensitive Words and Expressions) Regulations 2009 (SI 2009/2615)
C(A,I and CE) Act 2004	Companies (Audit, Investigations and Community Enterprise) Act 2004
CA 1985	Companies Act 1985, as amended
CA 1989	Companies Act 1989, as amended
CA 2006	Companies Act 2006, amended
CDDA 1986	Company Directors Disqualification Act 1986
EA 2010	Equality Act 2010

Index of Definitions

Definition	Description
FA 1994	Finance Act 1994
Fee Regulations	The Registrar of Companies (Fees) (Companies, Overseas Companies and Limited Liability Partnerships) Regulations 2009 (SI 2009/2101) as amended by SI 2009/2439 and SI 2011/309
FA 2003	Finance Act 2003
FSMA 2000	Financial Services and Markets Act 2000
HMRC or Revenue	HM Revenue & Customs
IA 1986	Insolvency Act 1986
IA 2000	Insolvency Act 2000
ICTA 1988	Income and Corporation Taxes Act 1988
ITA 2007	The Income Tax Act 2007
ITTOIA 2005	Income Tax (Trading and Other Income) Act 2005
L and T (Covenants) Act 1995	Landlord and Tenant (Covenants) Act 1995
LTA 1954	Landlord and Tenant Act 1954
LLPA 2000	Limited Liability Partnerships Act 2000
LPA 1907	Limited Partnerships Act 1907
PA 1890	Partnership Act 1890
SORP	The Statement of Recommended Practice issued by the Consultative Committee of Accountancy Bodies in relation to accounting by LLPs (latest edition, 31 March 2010)
SRA	Solicitors Regulation Authority
TCGA 1992	Taxation of Chargeable Gains Act 1992
Trading Disclosures Regulations	The Companies (Trading Disclosures) Regulations 2008 (SI 2008/495)
TUPE 2006	The Transfer of Undertakings (Protection of Employment) Regulations 2006 (SI 2006/246)
WTR 1998	The Working Time Regulations Act 1998 (SI 1998/1833)

Chapter 1

The Background and Legislative Development

1.1 This introductory chapter looks at the development of the law of partnership and the ways in which it has spread into other types of business vehicles. It goes on to consider some difficulties with modern partnership practice, and identifies the needs which gave rise to the concept of limited liability partnerships. The progress of the legislation which has created this new entity is reviewed, and in the process a number of the themes which will pervade the discussion of them throughout the book are considered.

The spread of partnership law

1.2 This book concerns itself largely with the *Limited Liability Partnerships Act 2000* (as amended) (*LLPA 2000*), the latest concluded variation in the spread of partnership law across the landscape of British business law. It helps to be able to see this development in the context of the overall development of the law defining the business vehicles which have been available to entrepreneurs over the last two centuries, all of which have derived from partnerships in one way or another, from the inception of joint stock companies, which begat limited companies, through limited partnerships, to the confusingly similarly named but very different limited liability partnerships (LLPs).

This seems likely to be the most important change for some time to come, as on 20 July 2006 the Department for Trade and Industry (now the Department for Business, Innovation and Skills (BIS)) announced that it was not after all going to take forward proposals emanating from the Law Commission and the Scottish Law Commission for reform of general partnerships, although it has introduced some relatively minor amendments to the law on limited partnerships as set out in the *Limited Partnerships Act 1907* by way of *The Legislative Reform (Limited Partnerships) Order 2009 (SI 2009/1940)*. Further amendments may follow, depending on the outcome of further consultation by BIS.

In the beginning was the partnership

1.3 It is perhaps trite to say that, before anyone thought of doing anything else, the only way in which two or more people could operate a business venture was as a partnership. The OED records the use of the term as far back as 1700. What is perhaps remarkable is that the concept has survived largely unchanged in its fundamentals for 300 years, namely that a group of people could combine, with unlimited liability, to operate a business which had no identity of its own separate from the members of that group as combined individuals.

The last major attempt at statutory control was the *Partnership Act 1890*, and it was notable that during the recent progress of the *LLPA 2000* through various Parliamentary stages, whilst the concept underlying it received almost universal support, there were many (ultimately unsuccessful) attempts to incorporate the affectionately viewed mechanism and subsequently developed case law of the *PA 1890*, on the basis of 'If it isn't broke, don't fix it'.

The Companies Acts

1.4   However, the *LLPA 2000* should not be thought of as the first time that the concept of a partnership has been used to spin off a new business vehicle into common use. It was partly the need for partnerships to be able to change to cope with the demands of the Industrial Revolution that led to the passing of the Joint Stock Companies Acts in the middle of the nineteenth century which provided for incorporation upon registration for the first time, and which in turn were the forebears of the positive rash of Companies Acts which continues up to the present day.

Limited partnerships

1.5   The next development was the formation of limited partnerships, in accordance with the *LPA 1907*.

Here, the idea was to allow participation in the business by one or more 'limited' partners, whose role was simply to provide capital but not otherwise to participate in or be liable for the running of the business, which was to be left to the 'general' partner(s). The key to this remaining in the partnership sphere rather than that of a company was, and indeed still is, that the general partners retained unlimited personal liability. These have in practice been of use mainly in particular fields, eg investment, shipping, and other high-value areas.

The restrictions of partnerships

1.6   A constant theme of the development of the business world throughout the twentieth century, and the latter half in particular, has been the relentless growth of the professional services sector. The President of the Institute of Chartered Accountants in England and Wales once said 'The work now shared amongst hundreds of members of the [accountancy] profession will pass to a few big international firms', and that was in 1926!

It is perhaps not surprising therefore that the concept of a partnership being a small group working together has long since ceased to be relevant. It did so in the face of legal restriction, since statute restricted the size of partnerships, to 20, unless the partnership carried on a profession which was exempted either by the *CA 1985* itself (such as chartered accountants and solicitors), or by one of a series of regulations passed under it (such as registered architects or chartered surveyors). That restriction was finally abolished in December 2002 in the face of overwhelming criticism that it was outdated and unnecessary.

For those City professional service firms who now number even their UK partners in hundreds, the attempt to retain the personal concept of partnership has therefore long been something of an irrelevance.

The rise of personal liability

1.7   Going hand in hand with the increase in the size of professional service firms has been an increase in the frequency and size of claims against them, and the consequent risk of an uninsured and uninsurable wipe-out of the partners' personal assets, perhaps even years after their retirement or death. The risk of negligence claims spread beyond previously considered bounds, and caused a measure of panic in the professional ranks.

Introducing the concept of limited liability partnerships

1.8   Whereas the concept of previous types of business vehicle was home grown, that of the limited liability partnership is an import. Bearing in mind that the spread of the litigious approach which gives rise to their perceived need is often considered as migrating here from the US, it is perhaps no surprise that that is where the idea originated. Dr Kern Alexander, in an address to the Institute of Advanced Legal Studies, in June 2001, traced the development of the LLP in the US, from the first statute in Texas in 1991, through to the stage where now all of the US states have introduced LLP legislation. The earliest of these tended to shield partners only from vicarious liability for the negligence of others within the partnership, but not for normal trading debts. Later statutes, including those based upon the *Uniform Partnership Act* (as last revised in 1997) which has been applied in over 40 states, protect against personal liability for business debts as well as contractual debts.

The conversion of a US partnership to a US LLP is a relatively straightforward process, generally arrived at by a partnership vote (seen as the equivalent to an amendment of the partnership agreement) and by carrying out certain administrative formalities. The vote is reversible. There is no creation of a separate, incorporated, entity, and for that reason tax transparency (see 1.13 below) applies, and has come to be partially accepted internationally (eg in the Canadian tax authorities' treatment of US LLPs which has moved to transparency from their previous approach of treating LLPs as incorporated bodies). (Some other countries, especially those outside the common law jurisdictions, are less willing to apply this principle.) As the partnership does not become incorporated, there is no requirement under these statutes for disclosure of partners' financial positions. Some states impose minimum capital and/or insurance requirements.

Bringing the concept to the UK

1.9   The concept of LLPs, in UK terms, was first seized upon by the largest firms of accountants. One reason the accountants fought shy of incorporation, through their US arms, was fear of US-style litigation. As many of these firms were operating on an international level, it was increasingly unpalatable for a partner operating out of, say, the London office to put their personal assets at risk because of an action taken by a fellow partner operating out of the New York office and who they might probably never have met. As they did not initially find support from the UK government for the idea of UK LLPs, they turned their attention to the possibility of offshore incorporation, and even got so far as to commission the drafting of legislation in Jersey.

At that stage the government woke up to the possible loss of revenue and international commercial prestige if the major firms carried out their threat to move their bases offshore, and began to espouse the idea of limitation of liability.

The consultation process

1.10   In 1996, the Common Law team of the Law Commission looked at the possibility of replacing joint and several liability within professional partnerships with a system of proportional liability (and which concluded that the existing law on joint and several liability was fair). This was followed the next year by a consultation paper issued by the DTI itself, entitled *Limited Liability Partnerships: A New Form of Business Association for Professions*. (It is worth noting that at this stage both the DTI and the Law Commission were limiting their consideration to professional partnerships.)

A positive response to the DTI consultation paper led to the publication of a draft Bill and regulations in September 1998, and after further consultation a revised version was published in July 1999.

Progress through Parliament

1.11   The Bill was introduced in the House of Lords in November 1999. One important change from earlier thoughts was that the government now believed that the new opportunity should be available, not just to professional partnerships, but to any business. The explanatory notes, which accompanied the Bill, gave as the reasons for promoting the Bill concerns arising from:

- increased frequency and size of professional negligence claims;

- increased size of partnerships (in which not all partners will be personally known to each other);

- increasing specialisation of partnerships;

- merging of different professions within a firm; and

- the risks to a partner's personal assets when claims exceed assets/ insurance cover.

The principle of the Bill received all-party support, but did not attract universal approbation. In the Lords, Lord Phillips of Sudbury, himself a practising solicitor, described the Bill as 'wholly unnecessary' and as providing 'your two-man cowboy building outfit with a uniquely flexible and light-framed means of screwing the public'. In the Commons, Austin Mitchell MP categorised the supporters of the Bill as painting the 'tear-jerking spectacle of those in accountancy partnerships living in terror in case their yachts, farms, pubs and holiday retreats are suddenly confiscated'. They were however lone voices crying in the wilderness, and the Bill received Royal Assent on 20 July 2000.

The partnership ethos

1.12   Whilst the principle of the Bill was generally accepted, it was not the case that the details had as smooth a passage. The main battleground, which emerged on many occasions and in many guises, was whether the new animal should (as in the US model) look more like a partnership, or a limited company. The government favoured the latter, but others tried hard to preserve both the ethos of the inter-personal relationships of partnerships, and the framework of the *PA 1890* which they saw as embodying that ethos. Those opponents were partially successful, in that in February 2000 a further consultation paper was published proposing a default code (based on selected provisions of the *PA 1890*) to govern by regulation some aspects of the governance of LLPs and the relationships between members. Responses being favourable, these provisions were later incorporated by regulation.

The success was however only partial, and the government did not relent on two central issues: namely the refusal to legislate for a duty of good faith between the members of an LLP as individuals; and the specific disapplication of all partnership law in respect of LLPs to the extent that it is not expressly embodied in the *LLPA 2000* or regulations made under it (or any later statutory provision).

The role of the Inland Revenue

1.13   It was recognised by the government that many professions had for some years had the opportunity, if they disliked partnership status, to incorporate under the *Companies Acts*, but that few had chosen to do so either for cultural or, very often, for fiscal reasons. Imposing on LLPs a tax regime similar to that of limited companies was therefore likely to mean a low take-up rate. An important theme of the legislation has therefore been that LLPs will in effect be taxed as if they were still partnerships, so that it is the individual members rather than the LLP itself which will be taxable. The jargon adopted is that the approach is one of 'transparency', ie that the Revenue will look through the corporate entity to the reality of the underlying membership.

Further, the transfer from partnership to LLP status is intended to be tax neutral.

The protection of the public

1.14   Protecting the public was the other main battleground in the passage of the legislation. The government was adamant that the price to be paid for limitation of liability was that the public should be protected by the publication of information about the LLP's finances akin to that required of limited companies.

Opponents argued that this would place unduly onerous duties of disclosure on the members of LLPs, and place them at a disadvantage in relation to those who chose to remain as partnerships, or (in the case of the 'global' firms) to utilise LLPs operating under the looser US requirements. Their cries were not heard, and there remain duties of disclosure based on company-style provisions which are often referred to as the 'cost' of limited liability. For the most part however they are duties of disclosure of the members' aggregate financial position, rather than that of individuals' positions, as the underlying idea is that a member of the public thinking of doing business with an LLP needs to know how the overall business is doing, and how much the totality of its membership has backed their faith in the business by investing their own capital in it, rather than how its rewards or capital are divided amongst the members.

The main regulations

1.15   As will be seen, the *LLPA 2000* achieves much of its effect through regulations made under it. The key ones are:

- the *2001 Regulations*;
- the *2008 Regulations*;

- the *2008 Small LLP (Accounts) Regulations*;
- the *2008 Large LLP (Accounts) Regulations*;
- the *2009 Regulations*.

To say that the *2001 Regulations* are not easy to understand is an understatement indeed. They do not work as 'stand-alone' regulations, but rather (for the most part) by extremely lengthy schedules which apply, disapply, amend, supplement or replace detailed provisions of the *CA 1985*, the *IA 1986* and sundry other statutes. One member of the Standing Committee considering the draft *2001 Regulations* commented that a reader trying to make sense of them 'will need to have several books open at once to make sense of the legislation, with elbows, staplers and rulers holding pages open at various points'. Perhaps this was a result of the speed at which the LLP legislation was introduced, which was commented on more than once as the Bill made its way through Parliament. Thankfully, the *2009 Regulations* rather more helpfully set out instead the amended text of the relevant statutes as they apply to LLPs, being primarily the *CA 2006*, and which replace the provisions relating to the *CA 85* modifications set out in the *2001 Regulations*.

There was much opposition to the incorporation of so much of the effect of the new law being in secondary legislation, as opposed to being incorporated into the *LLPA 2000* itself and accordingly needing full Parliamentary scrutiny for any amendment. However the only concession the government was prepared to make was to say that the affirmative resolution procedure is used for changes that are made to legislation applying to LLPs, rather than by Ministerial decision alone.

Other regulations

1.16   As one would expect, there is a plethora of other statutory instruments that apply to LLPs in addition to those mentioned at 1.15 above, including those that apply relevant accounting principles to an LLP. These are dealt with in more detail throughout this work.

A comprehensible version

1.17   Anyone wishing to consider the detailed legislative provisions relating to LLPs would do well to read the *LLP Legislation Handbook* written by John Machell, Jennifer Haywood and James Mather.

Commencement

1.18   The whole of *LLPA 2000* came into force on 6 April 2001, together with the initial set of regulations applicable to LLPs namely the *2001 Regulations*. The first LLPs were incorporated on the commencement day, the proud possessor of number OC300001 being Ernst & Young LLP. After a relatively slow start, the number of LLPs is ever increasing and there are now over 75,000 LLPs registered at Companies House.

Application of the Act

1.19   The *LLPA 2000* initially only applied to LLPs and their formation in England, Wales and Scotland but by *Sch 3, Pt 1, para 9* to the *2009 Regulations* the *LLPA 2000* was extended to include Northern Ireland. The provisions for Scottish LLPs (in respect of which there are also separate regulations) are outside the scope of this work.

There is also provision for overseas LLPs, ie those incorporated or established abroad but having some connection with Great Britain.

Chapter 2

What is an LLP?

2.1   This chapter considers in broad terms the concepts applicable to an LLP. In particular, it places the LLP, as a body corporate, in the spectrum of business vehicles, and looks at the consequences of the corporate identity. It considers the prerequisites for the formation and continuity of an LLP. The contrast between the laws applicable to LLPs and partnerships are considered in general.

The definition of an LLP

2.2   Since LLPs are entirely creatures of statute, it follows that the first task of the *LLPA 2000* is to define its subject matter.

The first statement (*LLPA 2000, s 1(1)*) is that an LLP is a new form of legal entity. Although, at first sight, this seems a simplistic observation, it is worth bearing in mind when considering the construction of the legislation, since there is always going to be the temptation to consider an LLP as a sub-species of one of the types of legal entity with which we are familiar, ie a limited company or a partnership. It is not – it is a stand-alone concept which, save insofar as other statutory provisions are specifically applied to it, must be viewed under its own code.

An LLP's corporate personality

2.3   The *LLPA 2000* goes on (in *s 1(2)*) to state that an LLP is a body corporate, and lest there be any doubt it spells out the fact that that means it has legal personality separate from that of its members.

Indeed the very term 'members', which is used throughout the legislation, has presumably been introduced to distinguish the position of the individuals involved in an LLP from that of 'partners' in a partnership, and to reinforce the separate nature of an LLP. In this sense the LLP is much more like a limited company than a partnership. The ways in which this separate personality affects the position of an LLP will pervade the rest of this book, but amongst the most significant are its ability to join in other business ventures as shareholder/member/partner, to own land in its own right, to sue and be sued, issue debentures and grant fixed and floating charges over its assets.

The moment of creation

2.4   *LLPA 2000, s 1(2)* goes on to state that an LLP is formed by being incorporated under that Act. Therefore of course no LLP could be formed under UK law before the commencement of the *LLPA 2000* on 6 April 2001. (That is not to say that no business using the suffix 'LLP' could be trading in the UK before that date – the major law firm 'Clifford Chance LLP' practised as such for some time beforehand, being the UK arm of an LLP registered under the law of New York.)

It is the fact of incorporation which gives birth to the LLP, not the decision to form an LLP or even the documentation, in the shape of a limited liability partnership agreement (to use the term adopted by the legislation – somewhat curiously since it otherwise refers to 'members') (in this work referred to by its more commonly used title of 'members agreement'), which records and details that decision. Again, though this is a simple concept, it has its practical aspects, since the moment of creation will be dependent on an event beyond the control of the members, ie the dating by the Registrar of Companies of the LLP's certificate of incorporation. Results of this timing difficulty are that the dangers of pre-incorporation contracts will need to be guarded against where possible, and that efforts should also be made to avoid the situation where a period of time after incorporation exists during which the LLP has no provisions in place for its internal governance other than the default regulations specified in the *Regulations* (see Chapter 8 below).

Unlimited capacity

2.5   An LLP has unlimited capacity (*LLPA 2000, s 1(3)*). There are therefore no restrictions placed on its operations, and it can do anything any other legal person – natural or incorporated – can do. There is no equivalent either of the distinction between public and private limited companies, or of the doctrine that a limited company may risk operating *ultra vires* if it carries out activities beyond the scope of the objects clauses contained in its memorandum of association if it has an objects clause.

It is worth noting that *CA 2006, s 8* replaced *CA 1985, s 2* and likewise removed the requirement for a limited company to have an objects clause so that, as with an LLP, limited companies incorporated under the *CA 2006* will not have to contend with any actions being *ultra vires*.

As will be seen, there is no obligation for an LLP to define, in its initial documentation, what its business purposes are – merely that it is intended to be a business entity. It is therefore quite at liberty wholly to alter the nature of its business at any time without any external sanction, although the members may place internal restrictions on such actions.

Unlimited maximum size

2.6   There is no restriction on the maximum number of members which an LLP may have.

Minimum size

2.7   The minimum number of members required to form an LLP is two (*LLPA 2000, s 2(1)(a)*). The idea is that this remains a constant minimum throughout the existence of the LLP (though see 2.11 below as to the possible usage of LLPs by what are in reality sole traders).

It is not however an absolute, ie the LLP as an entity does not cease to exist the moment the qualification fails to be met, eg by reason of the death of one of the only two members. Rather, it becomes a reason for someone to apply to have the LLP wound up. It might also be a reason for the Registrar to investigate the possibility of striking it off the register as having ceased to operate (*CA 2006, s 1000* as modified). In the meantime, the LLP continues to exist and can continue to trade. If however it does so for more than a six-month period of grace, then the surviving member, if he/she knows that the LLP is carrying on business with only one member, becomes jointly and severally liable with the LLP for debts incurred during the period in which the LLP has only a single member (*LLPA 2000, s 4A*) (inserted by *2009 Regulations, Sch 3, Pt 1, para 3*). A prudent survivor will therefore arrange that within the six-month period he/she either introduces a new member or ceases to trade, if wanting to avoid personal liability.

Duration and continuity

2.8   Like a limited company, an LLP does not die naturally, though it can be killed off. Thus, its existence is not even terminated by the death of its last surviving member, or by the cessation of a specific reason for which it was brought into life, eg the completion of a joint venture. It has to be brought to an end by a positive act, being either the conclusion of a winding up or a striking off.

The idea is that, like a company, the continuity of existence until that act, eg during the conduct of a winding up, allows for an orderly disposal of the LLP's affairs. This distinguishes it from a partnership at will under the *PA 1890*, which may cease to exist at a moment's notice, by reason of a unilateral act, and thus needs to be wound up under the provisions of that Act since it has no continued existence after that moment. (Such an act would usually be the service by an individual partner of a notice to dissolve the partnership. No such power is conferred on a member of an LLP.)

Disapplication of partnership law

2.9   To emphasise the fact referred to at 2.2 above, to the effect that an LLP is of a unique nature, *LLPA 2000, s 1(5)* specifically states that, except as it or any other statute may specifically require, the law relating to partnerships does not apply to LLPs. It should be noted that this goes further than saying that no statutory provisions shall apply unless otherwise specified: the wording would seem to be apt to exclude case law as well. Consequently, none of the provisions of *PA 1890* will be applicable but, even where the wording of selected parts of them have sneaked back onto the scene by being re-embodied in the *2001 Regulations* as default provisions, it should not be assumed that the case law on the interpretation of them as provisions of *PA 1890* will be used in construing the *2001 Regulations*.

This was affirmed in the case of *F & C Alternative Investments (Holdings) Limited v Barthelemy* [2011] EWHC 1731 (Ch). This High Court case involved, *inter alia*, consideration as to whether members of an LLP owed fiduciary duties to each other and/or to the LLP. The defendants argued that each of the members owed to the others fiduciary duties as co-members in the LLP. The court rejected this submission on the basis that these duties would apply if the LLP were a traditional partnership, but it was not and partnership law was specifically excluded from applying to LLPs by virtue of *LLPA 2000, s 1(5)*. The court concluded that it was essentially a matter for the members to decide what obligations they wished to impose on each other, thereby making it more important than ever to put in place a suitably drafted members' agreement (see Chapter 8 for a more detailed analysis of the issues raised in this case and its impact on the members of an LLP).

The requirements for incorporation

2.10   As noted above at 2.4, an LLP exists by virtue of incorporation. *LLPA 2000, s 2(1)(a)* provides that a prerequisite for incorporation is the completion of the necessary documentation by 'two or more persons associated for carrying on a lawful business with a view to profit'. 'Person' in this sense means legal person, and so those who are associating can be individuals, limited companies, other LLPs or any combination of them. (They cannot at present be partnerships *per se*, although see comments at 6.5 below.)

Association – reality or illusion?

2.11   'Associated' in *LLPA 2000, s 2(1)(a)* (see 2.10 above) is nowhere defined, and should therefore presumably be given its natural, and fairly loose, meaning. The way(s) of association are not therefore seemingly limited. It does not therefore require, for instance, that all members must intend to be active in the operation of the business, and the equivalent of a 'sleeping partner' is possible.

Further, no minimum investment is needed. A sole trader or practitioner could therefore seek the protection of limited liability by persuading another to lend his/her name to the exercise, making a minimal capital contribution, keeping out of the running of the business, and receiving a token reward; since, assuming that the LLP remains solvent, that other would seem to be at minimal risk of personal liability. This is not without risk to the third party, however, if the LLP hits financial difficulties as that member will be treated in the same way as every other member, notwithstanding their limited involvement in the running of the business.

The requirement of a lawful business

2.12   The second limb of the above requirement (see 2.10) is that the association must be for the purpose of carrying on a 'lawful business'. The word 'business' is defined simply (in *LLPA 2000, s 18*) as including every trade, profession and occupation. Thus the availability of LLP status is not in any way limited to professional service firms, as some supporters in Parliament had suggested. It is just as available for a firm of plumbers as it is for a firm of accountants. The take-up rate may nonetheless be higher in the professions, because of the greater perception of vulnerability to negligence claims, but this will be solely a matter of choice.

The term does however appear to connote the carrying on of an actual activity, so that merely an association with a view to profit will not be enough. For instance, it is thought that merely combining to hold investments for members' own benefit would not qualify, though no doubt holding them for others' benefit, as an investment manager, would. Unfortunately, 'lawful' is not defined. It is hoped that it would not be construed so as to prevent the formation of an LLP to carry on a business which would become lawful on the granting of a licence or similar consent, such as a public house, but would not be able to seek that legal sanction until after incorporation.

The requirement for profit

2.13   The business to be carried on by the persons who have associated must be one which is to be carried on with a view to profit. Again, 'profit' is to be given its natural meaning. One class of venture, which is therefore effectively excluded from using LLP status, is that of a charitable or philanthropic enterprise. Such bodies are likely to have to remain either unincorporated associations, or else companies (usually limited by guarantee rather than shares). It is however worth noting that the Charity Commission is introducing a new vehicle, the Charitable Incorporated

Organisation (CIO), which is intended to replace the company limited by guarantee as a more suitable vehicle for incorporated charities. Although CIOs have been mooted for several years, their progress has been slow and Parliament is still to debate the draft regulations which, when approved, will enable the CIO to be implemented.

Although there is nothing to say what the 'profit' is to be used for however, ie it is not required to be for the personal or exclusive benefit of the members, so ostensibly there would be nothing to prevent an LLP being utilised in the same way as trading companies operated by charities, this would not seem possible in practice, since such an operation needs to be 100% owned by the charity, which would preclude its having the necessary two members.

Premature incorporation

2.14 When the *LLPA 2000* came into force, there was a rush of registrations. Some of these came from existing partnerships who had not yet decided whether they actually wanted to trade as LLPs, but who wanted to protect their existing trading names by registration. As pointed out by the previous author and others, this gave rise to two concerns. First, those firms had started the clock running for the purposes of the stamp duty exemption available to new LLPs (strictly limited to one year) (see 9.21 *et seq.* below). Secondly, they must have made a declaration that they were 'associated for carrying on a lawful business', when in fact they had no such completed intention.

The moral is that formation should only follow a definite decision to proceed promptly to use the LLP as a trading vehicle. (A way around the problem for firms in the scenario in question would be to form a limited company with the desired name, since no such requirements as to trading apply thereto, and then if proceeding later with the LLP to change the name of the company immediately before incorporating the LLP.)

Chapter 3

The Process of Formation and Naming

3.1   This chapter looks at the processes required for the formation of an LLP in practical terms. One of the key choices necessary is the name of the LLP, and the restrictions on that choice are considered. Another is the location of the registered office. The forms and fees required are reviewed.

The incorporation document – general

3.2   The primary document required for formation of an LLP is the 'incorporation document'. The document itself must have been subscribed by the requisite 'two or more persons associated for carrying on a lawful business with a view to profit' (*LLPA 2000, s 2(1)(a)*) (see Chapter 2 above).

The registration document is Form LL IN01 (it is worth noting that all LLP forms have the prefix 'LL' –thereafter the forms generally follow the same numbering as apply to limited companies although there are a limited number of forms that retain the prefix 'LLP' – see Appendix 1) which can be delivered to the Registrar electronically or in paper format. It includes (*LLPA 2000, s 2(1)(c)*) a statement that the requisite persons confirm that the requirements of *LLPA 2000, s 2(1)(a)* have been complied with. A requisite person in this case is either any one of the subscribing members, or a solicitor engaged in the formation. Anyone making such a statement which they know to be false, or which they do not believe to be true, is committing an offence (*LLPA 2000, s 2(3) and (4)*).

Many incorporation agents are now able to offer electronic incorporations (for a fee) which makes incorporation a much quicker process with Companies House confirming that they are generally able to process standard applications within 24 hours. Compare this with the turnaround time for paper-based applications which is stated to be around five working days.

No agreement required

3.3   Before turning to the detail of the incorporation document, and the choices which that necessitates, it is worth pausing to emphasise that there is no requirement to file or produce any form of written members' agreement, or even evidence of a verbal agreement, since none needs to exist. This can produce a curious result when it comes to interpretation of the application of other statutes applied to the *LLPA 2000* by the *2001 Regulations*. In the case of reference to the *IA 1986*, reference to the articles of association of a company, is specifically deemed (by *2001 Regulations, reg 5(2)(e)*) to include reference to an LLP's 'limited liability partnership agreement' (ie the members' agreement)(to the exclusion of the incorporation document), even though none may exist. An LLP must also not be registered with a name that is an inappropriate use of indications of legal form or company type, such as including the words 'Plc' or 'community interest company' in the name of the LLP (*Regulation 4* of and *Sch 2* to the *Business Names (Miscellaneous Provisions) Regulations 2009* which apply to LLPs by virtue of *2009 Regulations, reg 10* and the modified *CA 2006, s 65*).

Further, even if such an agreement does exist, there is no need to file it or in any other way make it a public document. Thus the privacy of internal arrangements, which many see as a crucial advantage of partnerships over companies, is preserved for LLPs.

The incorporation document – requirements

3.4   There are only five pieces of information which need to appear on the incorporation document, and none of them is of a financial nature (*LLPA 2000, s 2(2)*). They are:

- the LLP's name;
- whether the LLP's registered office is to be situated in:

  o   England and Wales,

  o   Wales,

  o   Scotland, or

  o   Northern Ireland;

- the address of the registered office;
- the required particulars of all initial members, being, by virtue of *LLPA 2000, s 2(2ZA)*, inserted by *2009 Regulations, Sch 3, Pt 1, para 1(5)*), the information required to be included in the register of members' residential addresses and register of members of the LLP. The requirements as to the contents of those registers are set out in *ss 162 to 165* of *CA 2006* as modified and are:

  o   name and any former name;

  o   a service address or in the case of a corporate member, its registered or principal office;

  o   for an individual member the country or state (or part of the UK) in which he/she is usually resident and their date of birth;

- ○ in the case of a corporate member, its registered number and jurisdiction in which it is registered;

- ○ whether he/she or it is a designated member; and

- either:

  - ○ that all members from time to time will be designated members; or

  - ○ alternatively, which of the initial members are to be so designated if not all of them are.

It is worth noting that an LLP is obliged to keep a register of individual members' addresses and this must state a service address for each individual member. It is the service address which is disclosed on public record whilst the residential address, albeit that it is still included on Form LL IN01, will not appear on public record and must remain confidential other than as set out below. These provisions apply equally to limited companies and were introduced by *CA 2006, s 242* as modified. The only situations where the Registrar may disclose this information is either where it is permitted under *CA 2006, s 243* (as modified) (disclosure to a specified public authority or to a credit reference agency in the specific circumstances as set out in *s 248*), or *CA 2006, s 244* (disclosure pursuant to a court order) (as modified) or where the Registrar communicates directly with the member in question. It is possible pursuant to *CA 2006, s 243(4)* (as modified) for a member to apply to the Registrar to prevent the Registrar from disclosing such information to credit reference agencies in certain circumstances (namely that disclosure may put that member or any person who lives with them at risk).

The scheduled requirements

3.5 The *Schedule* to the *LLPA 2000*, which is given force by *LLPA 2000, s 1(6)*, contains detailed provisions about the requirements as to the naming of the LLP, and the siting etc of the registered office. These requirements will therefore have to be taken into account in making the choices which must be made before completion of the incorporation documents.

The format of names – general

3.6 For any LLP whose registered office is situated in England and Wales, Scotland or Northern Ireland, there is a choice of three suffixes which must be used for the LLP's name (*LLPA 2000, Sch, para 2(1)*). They may either use the full phrase 'limited liability partnership', or one of the abbreviated forms 'LLP' or 'llp'. None of those terms may be used anywhere in the name other than at the end, so that whilst 'Fred Bloggs (Coventry) llp' would be permissible, 'Fred Bloggs llp (Coventry)' would not.

Guidelines on the naming of LLPs (*Limited Liability Partnerships: Incorporation and Names*, GPLLP1, May 2012) are available from Companies House (notes can be downloaded from www.companieshouse.gov.uk).

The format of names – Wales

3.7 For those LLPs which, in their incorporation document, wish to state that their registered office is in Wales, there is an option (*LLPA 2000, Sch, para 2(2)*) for their suffix to be expressed in the Welsh language equivalent of the above.

Thus the suffix must be either 'limited liability partnership', 'partneriaeth atebolrwydd cyfyngedig', or one of the abbreviated forms 'LLP', 'llp', 'PAC' or 'pac'. (The same limitations as to placing such an expression anywhere in the name other than the end will apply.)

The choice of name – avoiding existing names

3.8 The restrictions applying to the choice of name are intended to assimilate the requirements for LLPs' names with those of companies and to avoid any confusion by similarity of names. Thus the Registrar's record-keeping requirements (*CA 2006, s 1099*) include a register of all incorporated LLPs. The name of an LLP must not be the same as one appearing in any section of the registers as kept under *CA 2006, s 1099(1)* (*CA 2006, s 66* as modified).

When determining if a name is the same, there are certain specific factors which need to be disregarded, pursuant to *CA 2006, s 66,* as modified, and certain provisions of the *Business Names (Miscellaneous Provisions) Regulations 2009*. These include:

- use of 'the' (when followed by a blank space) or 'www' at the start of the name;

- the use of the letter 's' at the end of the name or any blank space between characters;

- the use of punctuation;

- any characters after the first 60;

- any distinction between 'and' and '&' or 'Plus' and '+', for instance; and

- use of various designated expressions at the end of the name, including 'company' and 'limited liability partnership' in various forms.

The effect of the last point in particular is that 'Fred Bloggs LLP' would be regarded as being the same as 'Fred Bloggs Limited', and so if the latter already exists, formation of an LLP with the former name would not be permissible unless it was to form part of the same group or unless Fred Bloggs Limited consented, which one would consider unlikely unless it was in fact connected to it in some way.

Companies House offer an availability search for a proposed name. This is free of charge and it is essential for anyone thinking of incorporating an LLP to carry out such a search at the very early stages to ensure that costs are not incurred, ie purchasing letter headed notepaper etc before ensuring that the name is available and thereafter registered.

The choice of name – other restrictions

3.9   Companies House has confirmed that it will not incorporate an LLP with a name that suggests that the primary obligations as set out at *LLPA 2001, s (1)(2)* are not complied with – the argument being that as the members' agreement is not filed with the Registrar, they have no other way of verifying this. Examples given are the use of 'association' or 'trust' in the LLP name and which are often used in the context of 'not for profit' organisations.

As with a company, there are also other restrictions (*CA 2006, ss 53 to 56,* as modified) on an LLP's ability to choose its name. It cannot select any name which would, in the opinion of the Secretary of State, be offensive; or by its very usage constitute a criminal offence; or be likely to be connected in any way with central or local government or a public authority specified in the *Business Names (Public Authorities) Regulations 2009* (unless specific approval is given). Examples of the type of specified public bodies include the House of Lords, the Governor and Company of the Bank of England and the Financial Services Authority.

In addition, the name may not include, without the Secretary of State's consent, any word or expression requiring approval under regulations made pursuant to *s 55* of the *CA 2006* (as modified). These tend to be terms which have association with royalty, or imply a broad base, eg 'international', or have associations with a particular profession, eg 'dental' (the *Business Names (Sensitive Words) Regulations 2009*).

In addition to the requirement to obtain the approval of the Secretary of State under the modified *CA 2006, s 54* (name suggesting connection with government or public authority) or *s 55* (other sensitive words or expressions) (both sections as modified), both the *Business Names (Public Authorities) Regulations 2009* and the *Business Names (Sensitive Words) Regulations 2009* provide that (pursuant to the power contained in *CA 2006, s 56,* as modified), in connection with the application for the approval of the Secretary of State, the view of a specified government department or other body must be sought. For instance, when making an application to the Secretary of State for approval to use a name that would be likely to give the impression of the LLP being connected with the Law Commission, the view of the Ministry of Justice must be sought, and equally, for an application to use a name including the word 'Nursing', the view of the Nursing & Midwifery Council must be sought.

Regulation 2 of and *Sch 1* of *Business Names (Miscellaneous Provisions) Regulations 2009* which apply to LLPs by virtue of the *CA 2006, s 57* as modified, contain an exhaustive list of characters that may be used in the name of an LLP, and also specifies that the name of the LLP can be no longer than 160 of the permitted characters.

In addition to and notwithstanding the above specific restrictions, the LLP should ensure that its name is not so similar to that of another party's trademark (registered or unregistered) as to risk a claim of passing off or trademark infringement from that third party. A search of the Trade Mark Register of the UK Intellectual Property Office (which is currently free of charge) is, therefore, always advisable for those intending to incorporate an LLP at the very early stages of that process.

In addition to the Registrar refusing to register a name or requiring a name change (see 3.10 below), any person may apply to the Company Names Adjudicator (introduced by *CA 2006, s 70* and who resides at the UK Intellectual Property Office) to object to a registered LLP name if it is the same as or similar to a name associated with the applicant in which he/she has goodwill (*CA 2006, s 69* (as modified)). It should be noted that in these circumstances the complainant does not have to be the owner of a registered company. If, having considered the defences available (including that the name was registered in good faith before the complainant commenced its own activities etc), the Company Names Adjudicator upholds a complainant then he/she can made an order to force the respondent LLP to change its name (*CA 2006, s 73, as modified*). The ability to bring such proceedings, effectively to protect rights of goodwill in a name, is a welcome move that will enable parties to challenge trademark infringements or passing off at a very early stage.

Names that are 'too like' others

3.10   It is even possible for an LLP to be required to change its name, after it has been formed, and the initially chosen name has been approved by the Registrar.

If the name is 'too like' a name which appears (or should have appeared) in the register at the time of formation, the Secretary of State may direct the LLP that it must, within such period as he/she may specify, change its name (*CA 2006, s 67, as modified*). Normally, that direction must be given to the LLP within one year of its incorporation. The period is extended to five years, however, if the Secretary of State believes either that misleading information has been given to secure the LLP's registration under a particular name, or that undertakings or assurances given in order to obtain such registration have not been fulfilled (*CA 2006, s 75*, as modified).

Misleading names

3.11   Another possible cause for a direction from the Secretary of State to change a name is if he/she believes that the LLP's registered name gives so misleading an indication of the nature of its activities as to be likely to cause harm to the public *CA 2006, s 76(1)* as modified.

There is no time limit for when such a direction may be given. The LLP must comply with the court's directions within 6 weeks of the date of the direction unless it has made an application to set aside the direction (see 3.12 below) (*CA 2006, s 76(3)* as modified).

Application to set aside Secretary of State's direction

3.12   Any LLP in respect of which the Secretary of State issues such a direction in accordance with 3.11 has the right to apply, within three weeks of the direction, to court to have the direction set aside.

The court can either set the direction aside or confirm it. In the latter case it must set a period for compliance (*CA 2006, s 76(5)*, as modified).

Failure to comply with direction

3.13   If an LLP fails to comply with any such direction as is mentioned in 3.10 or 3.11 above, within:

- the required time limit; or
- any extension of the time limit granted by the Secretary of State; or
- (if it has been confirmed by the court as above on an application to set aside) within the time prescribed by the court;

then an offence has been committed.

Those liable for that offence are both the LLP itself, and any designated member in default (*CA 2006, ss 68(5), 75(5), 76(6)*, as modified). Anyone so convicted is liable to a fine (*CA 2006, ss 68(6), 75(6), 76(7)*, as modified).

The registered office

3.14   The modified *s 86* of the *CA 2006* requires that an LLP shall at all times have a registered office situate in one of the four possible locations referred to at 3.4 above, to which communications and notices may be addressed. As with a company, it does not have to be a trading address.

The initial registered office is that specified in the incorporation document (*CA 2006, s 86(2)*, as modified). This can be changed at any time, on the filing (normally by a designated member) of form LL AD01. Form LL AD05 is appropriate if the new registered office is to be in Wales. Such a change will take effect on delivery of the above form. However, third parties have a 14-day period of grace within which they can still serve documents at the old address (*CA 2006, s 87(2)*, as modified).

Note also that solicitors' LLPs are required to have a practising address for their registered office, and to notify the Solicitors Regulation Authority of any change in the registered office (Solicitors Practice Framework Rules 2011).

Incorporation fees

3.15   The fee payable on incorporation (as set out at *Sch 1, Pt 2, para 9* of the *Fees Regulations)* is £40 where documents are delivered in paper form (or £100 if same-day registration is requested), or £14 where documents are delivered by electronic means (or £30 for same day registration). This includes the provision of the LLP's certificate of incorporation. Electronic communication is currently only available through formation agents or those with software which is compatible with that of Companies House. The fees of the agents will be in addition to those stated here.

Publication of the LLP's name

3.16   Each LLP must display its name outside its registered office and every location at which it keeps LLP records (which it is required to keep) available for inspection or place of business (other than a location which is primarily living accommodation), in conspicuous and legible fashion. If it does not do so, the LLP and every designated member will be in default and be liable to a fine and, potentially, a daily default fine (*CA 2006 s 82*, as modified and the *Trading Disclosures Regulations 2008* as applied to LLPs by *2009 Regulations, reg 14*). Further, again at risk of a fine for default, it must print its name legibly (*CA 2006, s 82* (as modified) and the *Trading Disclosure Regulations* as applied to LLPs by *2009 Regulations, reg 14*) on all:

- business letters;
- notices and official publications;
- cheques, bills of exchange, promissory notes, and endorsements;
- orders for money, goods or services;
- invoices or other demands for payment, receipts, letters of credit and bills of parcels;
- applications for licences to carry on an activity or a trade;

- all other forms of business documentation and correspondence (hard copy and electronic ie emails); and

- its website(s).

Consequences of default

3.17 There are two consequences of default in respect of the above provisions as to documents. One is, as mentioned above, a fine. The second is that the protection of limited liability status may be put at risk if it is not clear to a third party dealing with the LLP that, indeed, it is an LLP and not, as it might seem, that that third party is dealing with an individual or alternatively an unincorporated partnership.

It can often come as a surprise to members of an LLP that operating as a limited liability partnership does not offer total protection from personal liability. Poor internal governance that allows its members or employees to correspond with third parties without reference to the limited liability status of the business in which they operate could readily remove the protection that the member sought to invoke by choosing to convert in the first place.

LLP seal

3.18 An LLP may choose to have a seal. If so, it is required by *CA 2006, s 45*, as modified to have its name legibly shown on that seal, and failure to comply with this will render the LLP and every member in default liable to a fine. The use of, or authorising the use of, a seal purporting to be that of the LLP but which does not have its name legibly shown, by a member or other person acting on behalf of the LLP is also an offence committed by that person, who is liable to a fine.

Particulars in correspondence

3.19 Certain details must appear on all business letters, order forms and websites of the LLP (*CA 2006, s 82*, as modified and the *Trading Disclosures Regulations* as applied to LLPs by the *2009 Regulations, reg 14*). These are:

- the LLP's place of registration;

- its registered number;

- its registered office address;

- if its name ends in an abbreviation (ie 'LLP', 'llp', 'PAC', or 'pac') the fact that it is a limited liability partnership, or a partneriaeth atebolrwydd cyfygedig.

Failure to comply renders both the LLP, and any designated member in default, liable to a fine.

In the event that an LLP's business letter includes the name of any member (other than as signatory or in the text of the letter itself), then the name of every member of the LLP must be disclosed in the letter, other than where the LLP has more than 20 members and it has a list of its members' names available for inspection at its principal place of business (to which such letter must refer) (the *Companies (Trading Disclosures Regulations, reg 8* as applied to LLPs and amended by the *2009 Regulations, reg 14* and *CA 2006, s 82* as modified).

Business names

3.20   The provisions of *Pt 41* of *CA 2006* will take effect in relation to any LLP that uses a business name that is not its corporate name, without any addition. *CA 2006, Pt 41*, contains restrictions and requirements in relation to the use of a business name similar to those in effect in relation to the choice of an LLP name itself, including provisions relating to the use of names indicating a connection with government, local authority or certain specified public bodies, the use of other sensitive words or expressions and using a name containing an indication of its legal form that is inappropriate.

Professional requirements for letterhead

3.21   In addition to the statutory requirements, it is worth noting that LLPs from certain professions may have additional requirements. Several will have the requirement that the professional body which regulates them is named and stated as their regulator. Solicitors' LLPs also have to comply with the Solicitors Regulation Authority Code of Conduct, so that they state on letterhead, websites and e-mails that they are 'authorised and regulated by the Solicitors Regulation Authority', and include the LLP's registered name and number.

Chapter 4

Post Formation Administration

Change of name

4.1   Like a company, an LLP may change its name at any time (*LLPA 2000, Sch, para 4(1)*). Exactly the same obligations and restrictions apply to the choice of the new name as applied to it upon formation, and exactly the same powers are vested in the Secretary of State to direct a subsequent change of the new name (see 3.6 to 3.13 above).

There is no provision in the legislation requiring any special decision-taking process for the name change, so it can, unless the members' agreement provides otherwise, be determined upon by simple majority. Upon change, a notice of the change, in Form LL NM01, must be signed by a designated member, and delivered to the Registrar (*LLPA 2000, Sch, para 5*, as amended, by the *2009 Regulations*). A fee of £10 for paper filing (£50 for same day registration) or £8 for electronic filing (£30 for same day registration) is payable in accordance with the *Fees Regulations*. There is no time limit for delivery, because the change is ineffective until the Registrar has checked the register (ie the one kept under *CA 2006, s 1099(1)*) entered the new name in it and issued a certificate of the change of name.

English LLPs can file this form electronically via an incorporation agent or those with compatible software. Currently Welsh LLPs are not able to take advantage of this process.

The difference in turnaround time for non-same day applications is again substantial with online forms usually being processed within 24 hours, whilst the turnaround time for the paper forms is currently approximately five days.

Effect of change of name

4.2   Such a change of name has no effect on the rights or duties of the LLP (*LLPA 2000, Sch, para 6(a)*).

There is no effect either upon any legal proceedings which may have been started by it or commenced against it, and any such proceedings simply continue against it in its new name (*LLPA 2000, Sch, para 6(b)*).

Change of registered office

4.3   Likewise, the members of an LLP can at any time resolve, by ordinary means, to change its registered office. Notice must be given to the Registrar in Form LL AD01, signed by a designated member (or, if appropriate, by any relevant insolvency practitioner who has assumed control of the LLP's affairs). No fee is payable. As with change of name, there is normally no time limit for filing the notice, since the change is not effective until registered.

As noted on the form (see also 3.14 above), for a period of 14 days from the date of registration, service of legal proceedings upon the LLP at its old registered office remains valid (*CA 2006, s 87* as modified).

Note that for solicitors' LLPs the Solicitors Regulation Authority must be notified of any change under the *Solicitors Practice Framework Rules 2011*.

Any change in the situation of the registered office of an LLP from England and Wales to Wales or from Wales to England and Wales (as the case may be) should be notified to the Registrar on Form LL AD05.

Steps to follow changes

4.4   Whenever an LLP effects either of the changes noted at 4.1 and 4.3 above, ie in respect of its name and registered office, it should act promptly in changing various items to reflect the new situation, and to comply with the relevant statutory requirements.

Thus the signage outside all offices will need to be changed, the correspondence, websites and other stationery will need updating, and the common seal (if any) will need renewing (*CA 2006, s 82*, as modified and the *Trading Disclosures Regulations* as applied to LLPs by the *2009 Regulations*).

Joining/leaving members

4.5   Upon any person either becoming a member of an LLP, or ceasing to be a member of an LLP, then notice of that change must be given to the Registrar within 14 days (*LLPA 2000, s 9(1)(a)*). No fee is payable.

The details required are those which the LLP is required to include in the LLP's register of members and register of residential addresses namely, for new individual members his/her name, address, service address (if any), date of birth and country of residence. For corporate members the details are the corporate or form name and registered or principal office, registration number and place of registration (*LLPA 2009, s 9 as amended by the 2009 Regulations*).

The notice, in Form LL AP01 (for an individual member) or Form LL AP02 (for a corporate member) (for appointments) or Form LL TM01 (for terminations) must be signed by a designated member. For appointments, the form must also be signed by the incoming member whose details appear upon the form, to confirm his/her consent to act (*LLPA 2000, s 9(3)*, as amended by the *2009 Regulations*). Forms LL AP01 and LL AP02 also provide for an indication as to whether the new member is or is not to be a designated member, though strictly speaking that latter element of notification is not necessary if the LLP is one where all members from time to time are designated members. Form LL TM01 makes no similar provision, since if a person ceases to be a member that automatically means he/she ceases to be a designated member (*LLPA 2000, s 8(6)*).

Changes in designated members

4.6   If a person is and is continuing to be a member, but either becomes a designated member when he/she was previously not one, or ceases to be a designated member, then again notice to the Registrar must be given within 14 days (*LLPA 2000, s 9(1)(a)*). The notice of appointment is Form LL CH01 (for an individual member) and Form LL CH02 (for a corporate member) and which must be signed by or on behalf of the member and also a designated member. If the LLP either on incorporation or at a later date chooses either to have all members as designated members or only specified members, and the position is changed so that only specified members or all of the members (as the case may be) are to be designated members, then Form LL DE01 must be filed to notify Companies House of the change. At the same time, Form LL CH01 or Form LL CH02 will need to be filed for any member that is not already a designated or who ceases to be a designated member. No fee is payable.

Change of members' details

4.7   If any member changes his/her name or address, notice must be given to the Registrar.

Again Form LL CH01 (for an individual member) and Form LL CH02 (for a corporate member) is used, and must be signed by a designated member. No fee is payable. The relevant period for filing is within 14 days of the change (*LLPA 2000, s 9(1)(b)* as amended by the *2009 Regulations*).

Enforcement of notice requirements

4.8   Failure to comply with any of the above requirements for notification of changes in relation to members at 4.5, 4.6 or 4.7 above, is an offence on the part of the LLP, and of every one of the designated members (*LLPA 2000, s 9(4)*). It is, however, a defence for any designated member who may be charged with such an offence to prove that he/she took all reasonable steps to ensure compliance (*LLPA 2000, s 9(5)*).

In practice, the difficult issues are likely to be changes in members' names (eg on marriage) and (more commonly) addresses. When a person becomes a member, or ceases to be one, it tends to be an event of relative significance, and minds will tend to be directed towards the consequent administrative issues. The same will hopefully apply when someone becomes or ceases to be a designated member, though this may be regarded as less significant for the business.

A change in a member's residential address does not however touch upon the business at all and, unless the member remembers to notify the appropriate administrator, may not even be communicated to the LLP at all. It, however, and potentially any designated member, will still be liable for breach of this statutory obligation. Prudence dictates therefore that there should be a positive obligation placed on members by the members' agreement to report such changes, and that whoever is responsible for preparation of the annual return (see 4.9 below) should make positive enquiries of all members as to their current addresses. Anyone guilty of an offence under this section is liable to a fine (*LLPA 2000, s 9(6)*).

Annual returns

4.9   Annual returns are provided for by the modified *ss 854, 855, 855A* and *858* of the *CA 2006*. Each LLP will have a 'return date'. This will normally be the anniversary of the date of incorporation (*CA 2006, s 854(2)(a)*, as modified). If, however, when making any return, the LLP opts to deliver its next return on a different date, then the anniversaries of that date will subsequently apply, until any similar future alteration (*CA 2006, s 854(2)(b)* as modified).

The annual return is Form LL AR01. Companies House no longer sends out a pre-prepared annual return for approval and signature. Instead, the onus is on the LLP to ensure that it files the annual return within the prescribed time period (28 days from the return date). This is to encourage the move away from paper filing to electronic filing. The filing fees accord with this as the filing fee for paper filing of an annual return is £40, whereas the fee for online filing is a much reduced £14.

Contents of returns

4.10   The return provides the following information (*CA 2006, s 855*, as modified):

•   the registered office address;

- the address of any place other than the registered office at which there may be kept any records of the LLP (known as the Single Alternative Inspection Local or SAIL address);

- in respect of any member of the LLP being an individual:
  - name (and in certain circumstances, former names) and service address;
  - country or state of usual residence;
  - date of birth;
  - whether the member is a designated member;

- in respect of any member of the LLP being a body corporate or a firm that is a legal person:
  - registered or principal office and corporate or firm name;
  - whether the member is a designated member;
  - for EEA companies or firms to which the *First Company Law Directive (68/151/EEC)* applies, details of the register where the company file is kept (including relevant state) and the registration number;
  - and for all others, particulars of the legal form of the firm or company and the law by which it is governed and, if applicable, its registered number and the register in which it is registered.

Limitations on usefulness of the return

4.11   Any applicable changes in details relating to the situation of the registered office, accounting reference date, the members or the SAIL address should still be given on the appropriate form.

In other words, though the return is a useful reminder to administrators, and a good opportunity to catch up on omissions from the last year, it does not of itself take the place of the obligation to file notification of individual changes.

Failure to file returns

4.12   A failure to file such a return within 28 days of the return date is an offence (*CA 2006, s 858*, as modified). It continues until such time as a valid return is delivered to the Registrar.

The offence is committed not only by the LLP, but also by every designated member, unless any such member can show that he/she took all reasonable steps to avoid the commission or continuation of the offence (*CA 2006, s 858(4)*, as modified). Any person committing such an offence is liable on summary conviction to a fine.

Ensuring internal compliance

4.13   Again, therefore (because of the point made in 4.8 above) it behoves all designated members to ensure that the system for the filing of the return, and the lines of responsibility in this regard, are clearly delineated.

There is no requirement in the legislation for anyone to have a post equivalent to that of a company secretary, but this is a clear example of the need for someone within the LLP to know that they have tasks of an administrative or secretarial nature delegated to them, and preferably for someone else to be designated to check upon the performance of those duties. This may be clarified in the members' agreement, or documented elsewhere, but it is advisable for it to be clearly and widely known who has such tasks.

Companies House

4.14   Reference is made throughout this work of the electronic filing of documents with the Registrar of Companies. Currently there are two methods of such online filing; namely using the Companies House WebFiling service, which is free of charge (although it is not currently possible to process all forms through this service) or, where using the WebFiling service is not possible, using software which is compatible with Companies House software and which is offered by many of the incorporation agents (for a fee).

Companies House is continually updating the list of forms that can be filed via the WebFiling service and those presenting forms at Companies House should refer to the guidance on its website (www.companieshouse. gov.uk).

Chapter 5

The Transfer of Business

5.1 This chapter deals with the processes involved in transferring an existing business into an LLP, and looks at the documentation which will be required. It refers to later chapters dealing with the tax effects of transfer. In considering transfers, it indicates factors which may tend to make transfer, and hence LLP status, attractive or otherwise, for businesses with particular features. The chapter also indicates factors which may affect individuals who either cease to be involved, or join initially, at the time of conversion.

The concept of transfer

5.2 Matters to be considered on a transfer will relate primarily to an existing business which is being transferred to an LLP (a process which is commonly known as 'conversion'), rather than where an LLP is used as the vehicle for an entirely new business. It is likely to be less commonplace for there to be a conversion from an existing limited company to an LLP, as the tax structures affecting the two are so different, and the government, when bringing in the legislation, refused to make amendments in such a way as to make such a conversion attractive. It is not necessarily the case however that the conversion will automatically be from an existing partnership. It might well be from the business of a sole trader, if one or more new owners of the business were at that time being taken in.

The matters which need consideration will in many instances be familiar to professional advisers who are accustomed to dealing with transfers occurring upon incorporation of an existing business.

The extent of transfer

5.3 The first question which needs to be considered is whether it is the whole of the existing business which is to be transferred into the LLP, or merely a selected part or parts. There would, for instance, be nothing to stop a business transferring into an LLP a part of the business which was perceived to be particularly risk sensitive, but retaining as a partnership other areas for which they wished positively to avoid LLP status, eg to avoid public financial disclosure. Such a partial transfer will obviously be more complex than a total one, since there will be a need

31

to define precisely what is or is not to pass into the LLP and whether, because of the partial transfer, the two separate businesses will need to share any services.

Conversely, if it is to be the whole of the business, and if that business in turn owns one or more subsidiaries, it is important to ensure that the transfer agreement picks that up as well. For instance, if a partnership has created a separate company (in which, for example, its employees may be employed), the shares in which are held in trust for the partners for the time being in the firm by a nominated party, then the transfer should be clear as to the passing of the legal and beneficial interest in those shares to the LLP.

In most cases, however, it is envisaged that the transfer will be of the whole business.

Cessation of the existing business

5.4   Another matter which will fall to be determined early on is what is to happen to the existing business. Upon the transfer being implemented, will the existing partnership fall to be dissolved immediately? Alternatively, will an interim period be allowed during which the partnership will continue to exist, albeit no longer as an active trading entity, whilst any transitional problems are allowed to work their course, so that it is only formally dissolved after a set period?

In broad terms, the simpler the business, the less there is likely to be a need for such a transitional stage.

One area where such a transitional phase was considered by a number of firms was in relation to solicitors' practices which had adopted the practice of getting testator clients to appoint two un-named partners in the firm, or any successor firm, to be the executors of their wills. The probate registrars took the view that an LLP could not be a 'firm', and so the members of an LLP which had succeeded to the practice of a solicitors' partnership could not take the envisaged grant of probate. One suggested solution was for the partnership to remain in shadow form, with the partners simply taking out grants as necessary and then instructing the LLP to carry out the legal work.

There were, however, two snags with this course. The first was that the shadow association could probably not have been interpreted, at law, as being any longer a partnership, since such a body is, by definition, a relationship between 'persons carrying on a business in common with a view of profit' (*PA 1890, s 1*). The shell would neither have been a business, nor conducted with a view to (its) profit. The second was that, under the rules applying to solicitors' professional indemnity insurance, the LLP could not have been a 'successor practice' to the partnership, which would have required its own insurance, with an element therefore of potentially expensive double cover.

Fortunately, the matter was the subject of a case where Lightman J exercised a considerable amount of common sense, and held that, for such purposes, profit-sharing members of an LLP who were entitled to participate in the profits of that business were in just the same position as profit-sharing partners in a general partnership – *In the estate of Edith Lilian Rogers dec'd* [2006] EWHC 753 (Ch). This removed a practical barrier to the conversion of many solicitors.

Advantages of transitional provisions

5.5   Matters which might dispose a business to making such transitional arrangements would include the following circumstances:

- If it were decided (because perhaps of changes in profit-sharing arrangements) that rather than transferring the right to bill existing work in progress and the right to collect outstanding bills to the new LLP, it was to be the case that the old partnership should render interim bills for all work outstanding at the transfer date, and collect those from debtors direct.

- If there were a need for continuity whilst appointments (eg as auditors or insolvency practitioners) were to be transferred.

- If there were outstanding litigation in which the partners were involved.

- If there were a need for arrangements to be made for freehold or leasehold property, in the names of the partners, which for some reason is not to be transferred into the beneficial ownership of the LLP.

Disadvantages of transitional provisions

5.6   One straightforward snag with transitional provisions (as mentioned in 5.4 above) is that they are likely to be more cumbersome to operate administratively than a clean break. There will be two businesses running in parallel, each having its own legal and accounting requirements and more than likely using the same or a very similar name.

Another drawback, which may have a particular impact for professional service firms, is the risk, as contemplated in 5.4 above, that the newly created LLP will not, in terms of its professional indemnity insurance, be able to be classed as the 'successor practice' to the existing partnership if, in fact, the partnership is still in existence in one form or another.

Dissolution agreement

5.7   Depending on the assessment of the need for transitional provisions, there may need to be a dissolution agreement, as well as the transfer of business agreement. If so, it will need to make clear that no new commitments can be entered into during this period except for the purpose of effecting an orderly winding up, so that there is no danger of a trading phoenix rising from the ashes.

There will need to be a degree of discretion as to unforeseen circumstances. The agreement will need to deal with such post-termination issues as would have been appropriate before transfer, eg matters arising on the death of a partner. There should be a long-stop date at which dissolution is deemed to occur come what may, and provision for earlier agreement as to dissolution if all transitional arrangements can be completed earlier than expected.

Transfer agreement

5.8   Precisely when the transfer is made will depend on individual circumstances. Businesses may find that they incorporate their LLP first and then, perhaps some months later (eg to suit their year end), effect the transfer. Alternatively they may wish to transfer as soon as the certificate of incorporation is received, so that they want all documentation in place and ready to bind all parties either the moment the LLP comes into legal existence or at a pre-determined date thereafter.

The latter circumstances are provided for by the *LLPA 2000, s 5(2)*. This states that a pre-incorporation agreement, between the persons who subscribe their names to the incorporation document, may impose obligations upon the nascent LLP, even though it does not itself exist at the time of the agreement, so that the obligations come into effect at any time after its incorporation.

The effect of personnel changes

5.9   One apparent problem with the wording of the *LLPA 2000, s 5(2)* is however the requirement that such an agreement (as is referred to in 5.8 above) be made 'between the persons who subscribe their names to the incorporation document'. It is arguable that by implication words to the effect of 'and no others' need to be read into the end of this phrase, since the statute does not refer to the possibility of any other signatories, and actually says that the agreement must be 'made ... between' such persons, and not just be signed by them (which would allow the possibility of others).

The potential difficulty caused is if not all the partners in the old partnership wish to become members of the new LLP. To make the transfer agreement effective from the partnership side, it may well need to have all partners as parties to it. If one or more of them is not also a subscriber to the incorporation document, does this then invalidate the agreement, since it does not comply with s 5(2)? It may seem that in practice the point will never be relevant, since those involved will only sign if they are happy in any event. However, what if things do not in practice work out as intended, and there are unhappy individuals? Can they claim that the agreement was a nullity because it did not comply with s 5(2)? In order to avoid having to test the point in court, it may well be sensible, where it is intended that the transfer agreement will take effect upon or soon after incorporation, to try to ensure that all partners do indeed become members of the LLP, even if it is known that they will be so only for a very limited period, and that means putting the transfer into place at a time other than the natural time for adding or removing members, ie the financial year end. Alternatively, if partnership changes cannot be avoided, it would be wise not to rely on the provisions of s 5(2) and for the LLP to enter into the agreement after its incorporation.

The scope of the transfer agreement

5.10   It is not of course possible to prescribe a 'one-size-fits-all' list of contents for a transfer agreement, as so much will depend on the individual circumstances. Matters which will however most often need to be dealt with are listed below, and each is developed in the following paragraphs:

- obligations to former partners and their estates (see 5.11);

- obligations owed by former partners under restrictive covenants (see 5.12);

- valuation of assets (see 5.13);

- novation of continuing contracts (see 5.14);

- personal appointments (see 5.15);

- how work in progress is to be dealt with (see 5.16);

- assignment of book debts and liabilities (see 5.17);

- professional indemnity insurance (see 5.18 and 5.19);

- transfer of real property (see 5.20–5.25);

- banking matters (see 5.26);

- transfer of partners' financial balances (see 5.27);

- external finance agreements and rental arrangements (see 5.28);

- staff employment contracts and rights (see 5.29);

- VAT consequences of transfer (see 5.30);

- intellectual property ownership and obligations (see 5.31); and

- provision for goodwill (see 5.32).

Obligations to former partners

5.11   Many partnerships will have outstanding obligations to former partners, or perhaps even to their families and estates. These may be straightforward and defined, eg where a former partner's capital account is being paid off over a set period, by known instalments. Others may be more complex, such as the provision of annuities for former partners and spouses, where the extent of the obligation is unlikely to be capable of definition, other than by obtaining an actuarial valuation or, more finitely, by purchasing an open market annuity to convert the firm's liability into capital terms. Further, these obligations may not yet be capped if, for instance, senior partners, who are to continue for a while as members of the LLP, have a legitimate expectation under existing arrangements of receiving such annuities upon their own retirements.

The transfer agreement will need to deal with all issues relating to future liability for such obligations, so that it is clear whether the LLP is to be obliged to take them on for the future, and to indemnify individual partners against any claims by the annuitant. The more difficult it is to quantify these obligations, the less the LLP is likely to wish to take these over, and the greater the scope for disagreement. The problem is exacerbated by the fact that the change to company-style accounting will mean that the full balance of all such obligations must appear at their true cost in the balance sheet of the LLP. If large, this may make the business appear to third parties to be unattractive. This is an area which is perceived as one of the most common disincentives to conversion, if the above problems cannot easily be resolved.

Obligations of former partners

5.12   Often former partners will continue to owe obligations to the partnership they have left, either as a matter of general partnership law or, more usually, as a consequence of express obligations arising from the partnership agreement and/or a retirement agreement. Commonly, these would be duties of confidentiality, and the obligation to observe restrictive covenants.

The original documents will need to be checked to see whether the benefit of such obligations can be passed to the LLP. If so, they will need to be assigned, and can presumably be included in the clauses which assign the generality of obligations owed to the former business, unless they need to be picked out and treated differently for any reason.

Whilst the LLP may wish for the existing partners who have the benefit of those covenants to enforce those covenants, depending on the construction of the relevant clause, they could face great difficulty in doing so as the partnership which has the benefit of the covenant will have ceased to trade or exist and so would query if there can be any loss from any breach of the covenant in any event. If the covenants are sufficient important to protect the goodwill of the business, the LLP would probably be well advised to wait until such covenants (which will be of limited duration) have expired before the transfer is completed.

Valuation of assets

5.13   It may well be the case in many instances that valuation of assets is not a major issue. This is because the closing balances for the valuation of assets in the books of account of the partnership, arrived at by applying the same policies as previously (eg as to depreciation), will simply become the opening balances of the LLP, which will continue to apply the same policies. There may be difficulty in special cases if the accountants advise that they are obliged, by the accounting standards applicable to LLPs, to apply policies which are different from those applied in respect of the partnership.

In some circumstances it may in any event be the case that the transfer agreement needs to treat the issue in greater detail. This could be so if, for example, freehold properties are shown in the accounts of the partnership at their original cost, with no adjustment for any subsequent change in value. There may also be matters for which no true value has ever needed to be ascribed, but now need to be provided for.

Novation of current contracts

5.14   Third parties with whom the partnership has had dealings, either as suppliers or as clients/customers, may not be bound to accept a change in the identity of the party with whom they have contracted. In other words the business may not be able to insist on novating their contracts, so as to substitute the LLP's obligations and rights for the partnership's.

In many cases the third party will agree, and the LLP may have a draft novation agreement for standard use; but the transfer agreement should also provide for the circumstances where this is not possible. In terms of suppliers to the business, where there are continuing contractual obligations, the agreement should provide for the continuing performance of the obligations by the partnership in dissolution, upon its being indemnified by the LLP against the cost of such performance. Any resultant benefits should be held in trust for the LLP. Care will need to be taken to check that the making of such arrangements do not however constitute a breach of the third-party agreement.

With regard to clients and customers, again novation may be needed, and new terms of engagement letters etc should in such cases be sent for agreement where possible. In many instances, however, partnerships have worked on the basis that they merely need to inform the clients of the change in their circumstances, rather than actually secure agreement to new terms of engagement (although some have done so in order to use the opportunity to modernise their applicable terms). It stands to reason that the consent of any key clients to the conversion to LLP should be obtained before the conversion process begins in earnest, although in practice many firms have found that their clients are understanding of the desire to convert as they themselves will normally be operating by way of a limited liability vehicle.

One special case which has been of concern to solicitors is that of conditional fee agreements, and their associated insurance policies. Many such agreements are silent as to the possibility of assignment. The case of *Jenkins v Young Brothers Transport Ltd* [2006] EWHC 151 (QB) appears to suggest that it is sufficient for the solicitors to give notice of the assignment to the client, thus fulfilling the requirements of *s 136* of the *Law of Property Act 1925*, but the court there was careful to restrict its judgment to the facts of that case. Affected firms will need to check carefully the terms of all such agreements and associated policies.

In some cases where it is not possible to novate or assign the benefit of a contract to the LLP, it may be necessary for the partnership effectively to sub-contract the performance of the obligations to the LLP, in return for indemnifying it against the costs of so doing, and holding receipts for post-transfer work upon trust for the LLP although, again, care will need to be taken to ensure such arrangements do not constitute a breach of the contract.

Personal appointments

5.15   There may be some appointments which, though legally personal to the appointee, are in effect appointments of the business in which the appointee is a partner/member. An example would be appointments of insolvency practitioners, as liquidators, receivers, supervisors of voluntary arrangements etc.

Since they are personal, the appointments themselves will need no alteration, but the transfer agreement should provide for them to continue for the benefit of the LLP.

Treatment of work in progress

5.16   The issue of work in progress has been referred to a number of times above. The transfer agreement will need to indicate clearly how this is to be dealt with as between the partnership and the LLP. Options will include the following:

- All work in progress is billed by the partnership, on an interim basis, as at the transfer date. This might be appropriate if the LLP was not going to be taking over the benefit of pre-transfer book debts or the burden of pre-transfer liabilities.

- All work in progress is valued, as at the transfer date, by the LLP, upon the basis that pre- and post-transfer work is apportioned on the first post-transfer bill delivered. Again, this would not be appropriate if the LLP was to take over all book debts and liabilities. In this instance, provision should be made for resolving any disputes as between the partnership in dissolution, and the LLP, as to the amounts to be billed (especially in cases of work which is for a fixed fee, or which is not to be identified on the basis of recorded time and hence needs somehow to be apportioned).

- The LLP takes over all rights to bill for and to receive monies for such work in progress as may have existed. This may well be applicable if the LLP is taking over all book debts and liabilities, and will be more attractive if there are not likely to be any outgoing or incoming members of the LLP over the period for which receipts are envisaged from the partnership's work.

Book debts and liabilities

5.17   The issue of book debts and liabilities follows on from that of work in progress. Essentially what needs to be resolved is whether the LLP simply steps into the shoes of the partnership and takes over the benefit of all debts owed to the partnership and the burden of all liabilities owed by it, without needing to separate or quantify them. In many instances this will be the simplest and preferred way forward. (Even so, it may be necessary for some specific exclusions to be provided for, eg professional indemnity claims.)

If the above method is adopted, the partnership will need to retain the right to inspect and copy the records which will be passed over to the LLP. If, however, perhaps because of differences in the make-up of the LLP from that of the partnership, this is not suitable, then the agreement may need to provide that the partnership, as part of its dissolution process, collects the debts due to it, and pays the monies that it owes. Again, the issue of who has possession of the books and records, and who has the right to inspect and copy them, needs to be dealt with.

An incidental reason why the destiny of book debts needs to be dealt with clearly, is that an LLP can create a charge over them, and any prospective chargee will no doubt wish to ensure that such debts have been properly vested in the chargor LLP in the first place.

Professional indemnity claims

5.18   Two types of professional negligence claims will need to be dealt with. The first, and easier, will be those claims which are already known of, and probably the subject of negotiations and/or litigation. They should already have been notified to the partnership's insurers. If liability for the uninsured excess in respect of such claims is to be transferred to the LLP, then it will pass with the general liabilities. If not, however, then special provision will need to be made.

More difficult will be those claims which have not yet emerged, and which may lie dormant for some years. To insurers, the LLP will probably be a successor practice to the partnership (though this should be checked with them). The claimant may however still sue the old partnership, so that again it is the issue of the uninsured element of any claims which the agreement needs to deal with.

Dealing with gaps in insurance cover

5.19   There may, however, be other instances of unexpected lack of insurance cover which also need to be resolved.

What if, for instance, negligence occurs in a matter being conducted across the bridge between the periods of the partnership and the LLP, where the LLP has different insurers from those of the partnership, and the matter should have been reported to insurers before the transfer but was not? It is possible that the partnership's insurers may refuse cover because the claim was not notified to them at the right time. The LLP's insurers may likewise disclaim because the claim or circumstances were not reported to them at the inception of cover.

Consideration may need to be given to whether the agreement should provide both a warranty from the partners that they have revealed all claims, or circumstances which might give rise to a claim, which are known to them; and an indemnity to the LLP against liability for any breach of that warranty. Clearly the future owners of the LLP may benefit from this; but may the founding members (who will be in command of the process of transfer) want to protect their personal positions by excluding such liability so far as they legally can? The fact that there is no real definition, of what constitutes 'circumstances' which mean that a potential claim should be reported, could give rise to some genuine disagreement in this area, and the transfer agreement should be clear as to the consequences of the various possible outcomes.

Transfer of real property

5.20   One of the distinguishing differences between a partnership and an LLP is that the latter, as a separate legal entity, can hold real property, whether freehold or leasehold, in its own right; whereas partnerships have always had to rely upon the holding of land by nominees or trustees.

Often, this issue has caused problems in practice, especially where land has been included in the partnership's books on tax accountants' advice, or at the behest of bankers to bolster the balance sheet, with no thought being given to whether it was really intended that the land should thus become a partnership asset, held upon similar shares to the rest of the partnership capital, rather than the often different trusts which may appear on the face of the conveyancing documentation. A classic instance of this is in family farming partnerships where land, put in the accounts at low historic cost, may apparently become an asset of a partnership which changes over the generations, and may have no written partnership agreement, without any consideration of underlying ownership issues. With an LLP being created, the chance arises to put this beyond doubt.

Keeping land out of the LLP

5.21   It will not always be desirable or possible to transfer property into the LLP.

For one thing, those partners who own the land may prefer to retain it as a private asset, marketable outside the scope of the LLP, especially if they have viewed it as a 'pension fund'. This will be less commonly so where it is formally held upon trust for the existing partnership, but even in such circumstances it might be desired to retain it personally if, for instance, expansion of the number of members was contemplated and the existing owners wished to retain the benefit of future increases in value. There might also be a wish to retain it if the land is disproportionately high in value to the remainder of the business's capital, and it is feared that the high consequent capital contributions required for new members to acquire equal shares in the LLP will prove off-putting to prospective members.

The impact of deferred gains

5.22   There will normally be no tax consequences inherent in the transfer of property into the LLP, in terms either of capital gains tax or stamp duty land tax provided, in the case of the latter, that the transaction is completed within a year of incorporation and that conditions as to underlying ownership are complied with.

One instance, however, where tax may prove a disincentive to transfer is if there are significant deferred gains already locked into the property, eg because roll-over relief has been obtained on the acquisition of the property. A problem may however arise if the LLP ceases trading and goes into formal liquidation, since at that time the deferred liabilities revert to the transferring members, regardless of actual disposal of the asset (*TCGA 1992, s 156A*, as imported by the *LLPA 2000, s 10(4)*) (see 9.16).

Third-party consents

5.23   Even if it is desired to transfer land into the name of the LLP, it may not be possible to do so.

In many cases third-party consents will be needed, either from mortgagees or landlords. In cases where consent cannot be refused unreasonably, it is suggested that it would normally be unreasonable to refuse consent to a transfer to the LLP, subject to a requirement to give personal guarantees. In such cases, the documentation (comprising the property transfer or assignment, the necessary licences and consents, the transfer agreement and the members' agreement) will need to deal with issues such as an indemnity from the LLP to those members giving personal guarantees, the right of outgoing guarantor members to seek release from their guarantees, and the right of the LLP to require the mortgagee or lessor to accept substitute guarantors.

Landlords may also require the original tenant partners to enter into an authorised guarantee agreement in accordance with s 16 of the *L&T (Covenants) Act 1995*.

Some tenants are believed to have had to accept that their landlords will only agree to a sub-lease to the LLP, rather than an assignment, in order to retain the original personal covenants. This is hopefully unusual, however.

Unavailability of consent

5.24   There may, however, be some instances where the requirement for the consents means that it is not possible for the property to be transferred to the LLP. For example, this could be because an unwilling landlord has the benefit of an unqualified covenant against assignment. Alternatively, if it is known that attempting to transfer will provoke a long and bitter battle with a third party, even if it is thought the battle is winnable, it may simply be felt not worth incurring the cost and anguish of the attempt.

Further, it may be the case that such restrictions in practice prevent the use of the property by the LLP at all, and hence force either abandonment of the idea of forming the LLP, or a move. This would be the case if a mortgagor or lessor was able to refuse consent, and there was a covenant against parting with possession of the property which would be breached by operating the LLP from the premises. Alternatively, it might be the case that, even if the occupation by the LLP was not a breach of covenant, it might mean that the tenants under the lease, ie the former partners, were no longer the occupiers, and so protection under *Pt 2* of the *LTA 1954* might be lost.

Ascertaining whether any consents will be needed and, if so, whether they are likely to be forthcoming without undue difficulty, should thus be one of the first tasks for the prospective LLP or its advisers to undertake.

Occupation of property by the LLP

5.25   If for any reason it is undesirable, or impossible, for the property to be transferred into the LLP, but it is possible for it to be occupied by the LLP (as, for instance, where partners wish to retain an uncharged property as a personal asset), then thought needs to be given as to the formal recording of the arrangements for that occupation, ie by the creation of a lease to the LLP.

This may provide an opportunity for financial planning not previously open to partners, eg if the property is owned by all of them, and they had not previously been able to grant a lease to themselves, thus creating a freehold reversionary interest which would be potentially saleable as an investment property at some future date.

Banking matters

5.26   In most cases the bank accounts of the partnership will cease to be operated as at the transfer date, and new ones will be opened in the name of the LLP, with balances simply being transferred from one to the other on that date. Even better, some banks will allow the continuance of the existing accounts and numbers, with a simple change in the account titles, if they are given appropriate indemnities.

Care should be taken to ensure that arrangements are made sufficiently well in advance with the business's bankers for that to happen, since, for example, it will be an offence for the LLP to continue to use the partnership's cheque books (*CA 2006, s 82* as modified, relevant provisions of which incorporates the Trading Disclosures Regulations (see 3.16)).

In some cases however the transfer may, in respect of all or some of the accounts, be deferred, eg because the partnership under the dissolution agreement is to continue to collect pre-transfer book debts. In any event the transfer agreement should make clear what is to happen, and deal with any rights the LLP may require, eg to pay into its accounts any cheques made payable to the partnership. The members' agreement should deal in the normal way with such issues as the mandates to be given to the bank, and with issues arising from the possible need for personal guarantees to be given to the bank, eg an indemnity, a right to contribution from other guarantors, and arrangements for the provision of guarantors in substitution for outgoing members.

Partners' financial balances

5.27 There will normally be no need for any changes in the accounting structure of the business insofar as the balances attributable to individuals are concerned. All that the transfer agreement will need to record is that the closing balances of the partners' accounts will be the opening balances of the members' accounts. This will be so insofar as capital accounts, current accounts, loan accounts, and deferred tax accounts are concerned. Note, however, the provisions of 11.5 *et seq* below as to the detailed accountancy treatment of the various types of members' interests.

It was originally suggested by some commentators that, in order to preserve loan relief where partners had borrowed as individuals in order to invest in their capital accounts, it would be necessary for partners to withdraw that capital, repay their lenders, and then borrow afresh to invest in their members' capital account. Fortunately, that cumbersome mechanism seems to have been rendered unnecessary by HMRC's agreement to allow the continuation of relief for the original loan (see 9.9 below).

Finance and rental agreements

5.28 Many partnerships will have a range of finance and rental agreements, relating chiefly to such items as cars, computers, etc. The transfer agreement should deal with such issues.

Many of the problems referred to in 5.23 and 5.24 above, in the context of property transfers, will be relevant for this purpose, eg:

- the necessity for consents;
- the requirement for guarantees; and
- the possibility of breaches of agreement.

In practice these are less likely to be of sufficient importance to jeopardise the concept of the transfer to an LLP, though it may be necessary in some arrangements for alternative arrangements to be made, eg by paying off an agreement from an un-cooperative supplier and refinancing it elsewhere.

Staff matters

5.29 For most partnerships they will themselves be the employers of all staff. There should not be any particular staff issues arising out of the transfer of employment to an LLP, as all staff will be protected by TUPE 2006, (as amended). The transfer agreement need therefore only briefly record that all staff are to be transferred, unless some are to be made redundant at the time of transfer, in which case liability for consequent payments, which by TUPE 2006 will normally fall upon the LLP in the first instance, will need to be allocated between the partnership and the LLP. Care should however be taken to comply with the requirements of TUPE 2006 as to consultation with staff.

There are some partnerships which utilise a service company for the purpose of employing their staff, in which case no transfer of service arrangements will apply, though the transfer of ownership of the service company itself will need to be addressed. The transfer agreement may deal with how and when staff are to be told of the change, and what notification of continuity of employment is to be given. (Businesses, which are amongst the significant minority that still do not have written contracts of employment, may wish to use the opportunity of transfer to put their affairs in order in this regard!)

Value added tax

5.30   The transfer from the partnership to the LLP will normally be of a going concern, and so no VAT consequences in practice will arise. It is possible for the VAT number to continue as before.

One possible exception is if land or buildings are included in the transfer, either because the transferor has made an option to tax in relation to the property or because they are new or incomplete buildings which are standard-rated anyway. In those circumstances, for them to be treated on the going concern basis, the transferee LLP will also need to make an option to tax.

See 9.28 for further consideration of the VAT position.

Intellectual property

5.31   All partnerships will have some intellectual property matters to consider on transfer, even if only in respect of the use of the partnership's name with the suffix chosen for the LLP. Nearly all will also be not only the owners, but also licensees, of some intellectual property, eg the copyright in respect of computer software used by them. Some will also be the owners of intellectual property which is licensed by them to others, eg if they themselves are a computer software house, or if as architects they have retained copyright in designs which others are authorised to use.

All of these matters need to be dealt with in the transfer agreement. All intellectual property used by the business, whether as owners or as licensees, is likely to need transfer or assignment to the LLP. The matters noted in 5.14 above with regard to novation of agreements will need to be considered in respect of licences to or by the business. Some licences may not need novating, but simply require notification of transfer to be given to the licensor.

Goodwill

5.32   Many partnerships still have provision for goodwill, either by reason of its having been purchased previously and hence appearing as an asset in the balance sheet, or because the existing partnership agreement provides for an element of goodwill to be paid to future outgoing partners as an entitlement. The LLP, however, will be governed by accounting requirements which state that only the former type of goodwill, ie purchased goodwill, may be shown in the accounts. Accounting treatment will be according to Financial Reporting Standard 10, and this will involve determining a finite period over which the goodwill is to be written off.

The transfer agreement will need to deal with how the balances attributable to the former partnership are to be transferred to the LLP, if they relate to purchased goodwill, or how they are to be eradicated if not. The members' agreement will need to cover future entitlements.

Conclusion

5.33   There is no requirement, either in the *LLPA 2000*, or elsewhere in law, for agreement as to any of the matters covered by this chapter to be dealt with in writing (though the subsequent transfer of any freehold or leasehold property would of course have to be written). It would be quite possible for the transfer of the business to be effected without any documentation.

Nonetheless the chapter has drawn attention to a number of the matters which ought to be considered at transfer – and indeed the range of issues covered is by no means exhaustive. If they are not covered, then confusion can arise in future (quite possibly when the people involved are no longer the same as at transfer) and if they are not recorded in an agreement then there will always be scope for disagreement or simply lack of remembrance as to what was agreed. Best practice therefore dictates that an agreement should be drawn up, even if it is simple, and even if in relation to any particular issue it merely records that it had been considered and that no provision was believed to be needed. This chapter should serve as a guide to the topics which ought to be covered, and to cross-refer to other relevant provisions such as the tax consequences of transfer.

Chapter 6

Membership Concepts

6.1   This chapter looks at the concept of persons (natural or corporate) as members of an LLP. It compares the role of member with that of a partner in an ordinary partnership, and explores the central part played by the concept of agency. It also looks at the increasing use of corporate members and issues arising as a result.

The terminology of membership

6.2   Presumably, the term 'member' was chosen by the Parliamentary draftsman to differentiate those individuals concerned with an LLP's business from those concerned with any other form of business vehicle, eg partners, directors or shareholders. That aside, there does not seem to be any particular magic in the term, and indeed it may prove difficult for people to get used to using the term as opposed still to describing someone as a 'partner' in an LLP.

Indeed, experience is showing that many businesses which have converted to LLP status are continuing to refer to their principals as 'partners' in at least some of their materials, eg business cards, websites etc. Some are even using this on their letterhead. The safer course would not be to use the term 'partner' at all, but the alternative 'member' is not favoured by many. Care is needed when adopting this approach to ensure that any third party dealing with the LLP does not believe that he/she is dealing with unlimited liability.

This confusion has been compounded by the desire of some firms to continue to call their senior employees 'partners', even though they are not registered at Companies House as members, in order to perpetuate their previous status as salaried partners, and not appear to demote them. The SRA has issued guidance to solicitors' practices which says that if they wish to follow this course they must, to avoid confusing clients and others as to the real status of their personnel, make certain statements on the letterhead and all other publicity materials to clarify the position. (See SRA Ethics Guidance: Limited Liability Partnerships which, as at the date of writing, is currently awaiting update to take into account changes introduced by the SRA Handbook and Solicitors' Code of Conduct in October 2011.)

The other relevant term, of which more in Chapter 7, is that of 'designated member'. Unhelpfully, this is nowhere defined, and it is left for the members and their professional advisers whether or not to draw a real management role out of the various statutory obligations which are placed on the designated members to the exclusion of their non-designated fellows or to simply define the role by the duties imposed on them by statute.

Subscriber members

6.3 The *LLPA 2000* provides that there are two ways of becoming a member.

The first members are those who subscribed their names to the incorporation document (*LLPA 2000, s 4(1)*) with the exception of any such subscribers who have died or (in the case of incorporated members) been dissolved in the interval between signing the incorporation document and the certificate of incorporation being issued.

Joining as a member by agreement

6.4 The other permissible route of entry, in addition to being a subscriber member, is simply 'by and in accordance with' an agreement with the existing members (*LLPA 2000, s 4(2)*).

There is no requirement in the *LLPA 2000* itself for such an agreement to be express, let alone in writing. In practice, however, an express agreement is likely to be needed, since the position will be governed either (if there is no members' agreement covering the point) by the default provision in *reg 7(5)* of the *2001 Regulations*, which states that a new member may only be introduced with the unanimous consent of all existing members; or under a provision in a members' agreement which specifically provides a route to membership, whether in the same terms as *reg 7(5)* or otherwise.

Eligibility for membership

6.5 Any legal 'person' may be a member of an LLP. Thus individuals, limited companies, or other LLPs may become members. On the other hand ordinary partnerships (or indeed limited partnerships under the *LPA 1907*) cannot, of themselves, be registered as a member, since they have no legal personality separate from that of their members although it is possible that an individual partner could be registered as a member of an LLP and hold the benefit of such membership on trust for the partnership as a whole. The partnership agreement should provide for how these arrangements between the nominee partner and the partnership itself in these circumstances, should be regulated.

It is also worth noting that a person who is bankrupt or disqualified from acting as a member pursuant to the *CDDA 1986* cannot be a member of an LLP without leave of the court.

Members are not usually employees

6.6   The *LLPA 2000* makes it clear, in *s 4(4)*, that in normal circumstances, members of an LLP are not *per se* employees of that LLP. It does not, however, prohibit a member also having the dual status of an employee, but merely states that he/she will not unless he/she would be so regarded if the business vehicle were a partnership not an LLP. The test, therefore, having regard to *PA 1890, s 1(1)*, is whether an individual member would be regarded as a partner 'carrying on the business in common with a view to a profit' with his/her fellow partners.

Since *LLPA 2000* was implemented, commentators have suggested that this means there can never be an employee member, since on a true analysis of a partnership no partner can be an employee: it is only those who are falsely held out as partners who can in fact be employees. The situation has recently been clarified in the case of *Tiffin v Lester Aldridge* [2012] EWCA Civ 25 where Mr Tiffin, who was a 'fixed share' member of the LLP, sought to argue that he should be treated as an employee by virtue of *LLPA 2000, s 4(4)* and therefore be entitled to rely on employment legislation. Whilst the Court of Appeal agreed that *LLPA 2000, s 4(4)* raised problems because in law 'it is not possible for an individual to be an employee of himself/herself and his/her co-partners' it nonetheless accepted that on its proper construction, under *LPA 2000, s 4(4)*, it is possible that a person can be both a member and an employee of an LLP. To come to this conclusion, Lord Justice Rimmer concluded that *s 4(4)* must be interpreted in a way that 'avoids the absurdity inherent in a literal application of its chosen language so that it can be applied in a practical manner'. Unfortunately for Mr Tiffin, the court found that he was a member, and not an employee of the LLP, notwithstanding that he had only limited voting rights and entitlement to profit, as opposed to other classes of members (full equity members) who enjoyed more extensive voting rights and entitlement to profit. The court held that these arrangements were not a sham (coupled with other factors including Mr Tiffin having made a small contribution of capital, and being a signatory on the firm's client and office accounts) and that the parties' intentions pointed clearly towards creating a partnership. Ultimately, each case must be decided on its facts.

An oddity, however, is that HMRC has confirmed that its view is that all members, whatever their status, are to pay income tax and NIC as if they were self-employed (see 9.6 below). This seems to create a unique instance of employees being taxed as self-employed with Revenue blessing.

Members as 'workers' for statutory purposes

6.7   Whilst the lack of 'employee' status for most members means that the majority of the mainstream employment legislation (unfair dismissal, redundancy, etc) will not apply to members, since they do not fulfil the test for applicants of being an 'employee'; they may nonetheless be covered by some EU-inspired, secondary employment legislation, particularly that which masquerades as being health and safety legislation.

Examples of the above are the *WTR 1998* as amended and the *National Minimum Wage Act 1998* as amended, which both use the term 'worker' to define the class of people given rights in accordance with their provisions. The definition of 'worker' in each case is:

'… an individual who has entered into or works under …

> (a)   a contract of employment; or
>
> (b)   any other contract, whether express or implied and (if it is express) whether oral or in writing, whereby the individual undertakes to do or perform personally any work or services for another party to the contract …'

and those providing professional services to a client are not excluded from this definition. Thought may therefore, for instance, need to be given to whether hard-working members need to sign a contracting-out agreement under *WTR 1998, reg 5* or can claim the exemption afforded to those who have the power to determine their own working hours (*WTR 1998, reg 20(1)(a)*). Ultimately, this will depend on whether the working practices of an individual are such that they constitute a contract for service, looking at the tests set out in the case of *Ready-Mix Concrete (South East) Limited v The Minister of Pensions and National Insurance* [1968] 2 QB 497. Whilst arguably a full 'equity member' is likely to be able to claim the exemption, this may not be so clear for fixed profit share or salaried members (see 6.6 above).

6.8   In addition to these protections (see 6.7 above), members of an LLP are also protected from discrimination by virtue of the *EA 2010*, s *545 and 46*, on grounds relating to age, sexual orientation, race, sex, religion or belief and disability.

The *EA 2010* will apply to all acts of discrimination which took place after 1 October 2010 or continuing acts of discrimination occurring after 1 October 2010 which were commenced under the previous discrimination legislation (provided that such acts were unlawful under that legislation). A member of an LLP is also protected under the previous discrimination legislation (which was set out in specific legislation ie the *Race Relations Act 1976* as opposed to one composite piece of legislation which is now the case with the *EA 2010*) for acts of discrimination that took place prior to 1 October 2010.

It is worth noting that it is possible to directly discriminate on the grounds of age where the aims of such discrimination satisfy social policy objectives and where the means by which those aims are fulfilled are proportionate. The recent case of *Seldon v Clarkson, Wright and Jakes* (a partnership) [2012] UKSC 16 has ruled that the aims of the firm in that case, which included the need to retain younger members of staff, were in accordance with social policy objectives. However, firms intending to impose a compulsory retirement age should take great care in doing so as the case has not, as some commentators have suggested, given the green light to having a compulsory retirement age. The firm in that case has still to prove that the chosen age of 65, as opposed to say 68, can be justified as a proportionate means of achieving its stated aims and this matter has been referred back to the employment tribunal for consideration of this point, the result of which is eagerly awaited.

A more detailed analysis of discrimination law is beyond the scope of this book and readers should consult Bloomsbury Professional's *Discrimination Law*.

The corporate member

6.9   Whilst the introduction of LLPs may have been as a result of concerns over the unlimited personal liability of individuals in professional service firms, over time there has been an increasing use of limited companies as members of LLPs; either as a result of tax planning or as a result of the LLP being used as a joint venture vehicle through which limited companies have agreed to operate.

The introduction of a corporate member creates issues that will need to be considered by the members in light of the LLP and its operations, eg:

• Should any controls be imposed as to who the corporate member can appoint as its representative at meetings?

• Will a change of ownership of the corporate member affect that member's right to remain as a member of the LLP?

• The impact of that corporate member becoming insolvent will need to be considered – and whether that should lead to expulsion of that member?

• Individual members should be aware of the limitation of liability of that corporate member in light of their own potential personal liability (see 6.21 and 6.22 below).

Interestingly in the case of *F&C Alternative Investments (Holdings) Limited v Barthelemy & Another* [2011] EWHC 1731 (Ch), the High Court considered the position of a corporate member of an LLP and in that case found that the representatives of the appointing corporate member were held to owe fiduciary duties to the LLP due to the degree of control that they exercised over the affairs of the LLP. Consequently, those representatives could not also owe fiduciary duties to their appointing corporate member as its agent. It was concluded that if those representatives came to the view that it would be in the best interests of the LLP to pursue a particular course of action, then they could not then obey instructions from the appointing corporate member to vote against such actions.

It is also worth noting that in that case, the parent company of the corporate member was held liable for the unfairly prejudicial conduct of the corporate member's representatives. The court concluded in that case there was no real distinction between the two parties with a corporate member in practice being a 'cipher' of the parent company (see 12.65).

The basis of membership

6.10   Just as a partner in a partnership is an agent of the partnership (*PA 1890, s 5*), so is a member of an LLP an agent of that LLP (*LLPA 2000, s 6(1)*). It had been previously thought that members would, therefore, owe fiduciary duties to the LLP as its principal. Examples of such fiduciary duties owed by an agent to its principal are:

•   to act in the principal's best interests;

•   to exercise appropriate care and skill;

•   to behave honestly and not make secret profits;

•   to refrain from allowing conflicting interests; and

•   to act in good faith.

However, the case of *F&C Alternative Investments* (see 6.9) has challenged this belief by finding that a member will not always owe fiduciary duties to the LLP. Although Mr Justice Sales acknowledged that *LLPA 2000, s 6(1)* provides that every member of an LLP is its agent, he concluded that members do not owe fiduciary duties to an LLP in relation to all actions taken by them but rather only those actions taken in circumstances where the member was acting as the LLP's agent. Therefore, in order to determine whether a fiduciary duty exists between a member and the LLP, one would need to consider the action taken by a member in order to determine whether the member was acting as agent of the LLP in relation to that action and, consequently, whether fiduciary duties would then be imposed. In that case, a corporate member was deemed not to have a sufficient degree of control over the LLP's affairs so as to impose fiduciary duties on that member. Therefore, if the members wish such duties to be imposed (which one would expect would be the case), then they must very clearly provide for this in the members' agreement.

No duty of good faith between members

6.11   Whilst the *LLPA 2000* did not expressly provide for a duty of good faith to apply between the members, it is possible that such a duty may exist. That is because the members of an LLP are free to draw up an express duty of good faith as between members, and to insert it in their members' agreement. Also, the government deliberately did not rule out the possibility of such a duty being found by a court to exist by implication.

The case of *F&C Alternative Investments* (see 6.9) specifically considered this issue and perhaps unsurprisingly the Honourable Mr Justice Sales ruled:

- members of an LLP will not owe fiduciary duties, including a duty of good faith to each other, simply because of their membership of the LLP;

- members of an LLP have a great deal of flexibility as to how to arrange their governance structure and whether or not to include express obligations of fiduciary duties, including a duty of good faith and in the absence of an express obligation it will be necessary to refer back to basic equitable principles in order to determine whether fiduciary duties will arise in particular situations.

The court also rejected the view that the *2001 Regulations, reg 7(9)* and *(10)* (members not to compete with the LLP or benefit from use of the LLP's property/income etc) supported the view that a general fiduciary duty of good faith is owed by the members to the LLP and referred again to the fact that the legislation expressly did not include such a duty.

Providing for a duty of good faith

6.12   In light of the decision in *F & C Alternative Investments* (see 6.9, 6.11 above), it is essential, therefore, that those proposing to convert to an LLP are asked to consider whether they wish to provide for a duty of good faith between the members or to exclude it from applying.

For partners, it is likely to be the first time that they will have specifically considered the point, so intrinsically enshrined is it in the partnership ethos. Many partnerships are likely to want to retain the duty but, increasingly, in light of the corporate structure of the LLP and its increasing use as a joint venture vehicle for corporate entities, members are choosing to expressly exclude this duty from applying on the basis that the parties wish to operate in a way that means that they are not obliged to act fairly towards the other members.

More importantly, it is also now essential that if fiduciary duties, including a duty of good faith, are to apply between the members and the LLP, that they are expressly provided for in the members' agreement. Without this, a member could arguably be free to act in a way which is not in the LLP's best interests, which is a situation that members must surely want to avoid.

Should the members wish to include a duty of good faith in the members' agreement, the practical application of such duty was also considered in *F&C Alternative Investments* (see 6.9) where the court held that, in exercising a duty of good faith owed by a member to the LLP, it was appropriate for a member to take his/her own interests into account alongside those of the LLP and to strike a balance that was fair as between the two conflicting influences.

Limitations on a member's authority

6.13   There may of course, as with any agent, be limitations upon the authority of any particular member. An example would be a member in an accountancy LLP who was, for instance, a corporate finance specialist, and hence was not authorised to carry out audit work and sign an auditor's certificate.

The *LLPA 2000* provides for such limitations in *s 6(2)*, which states that an LLP is not bound by a member's actions if two conditions are fulfilled. (The provisions parallel those in *PA 1890, s 5* applicable to partners, although there is no equivalent of *PA 1890, s 8*, specifically stating that the firm will not be bound if there is an agreement between the partners to limit a partner's authority, where a third party expressly cannot rely upon an act outside that limitation if he/she knows of the agreement.)

Actual lack of authority

6.14   The first condition referred to in 6.13 above is that the member in fact has no authority to act for the LLP in doing the act in question (*LLPA 2000, s 6(2)(a)*). The default position is thus that a member has full authority unless otherwise provided.

Therefore, an LLP which seeks to limit a member's authority must do so clearly and in a way that could be shown in evidence, if required. This could be provided for in the members' agreement; or in a subsequent resolution of the members, duly minuted. If power to introduce such limitations is to be delegated, eg to designated members, or to some form of committee, it would be as well for the members' agreement and/or the resolution granting delegated powers to spell out the rights to restrict an individual's authority.

Third-party lack of knowledge

6.15   The second condition referred to in 6.13 above is that the person with whom the member is dealing must either know that the member has no authority; or alternatively must not either know or believe the individual with whom he/she is dealing to be a member of the LLP in the first place (*LLPA 2000, s 6(2)(b)*).

In either case the third party cannot rely on the member's actions to bind the LLP as *LLPA 2000, s 6(2)* provides that in such circumstances the LLP is not bound by the actions of such a member.

Requirement for actual knowledge

6.16   The first limb of the test requires actual knowledge on the third party of a lack of authority. In the light of the default position referred to in 6.14 above, it would seem that a third party would be entitled to rely upon a presumption, when dealing with a member of an LLP, that that member did have authority to bind the LLP, unless the lack of authority is brought to his/her attention.

There is no provision for any sort of register of such limitations. Thus the onus will be firmly on the LLP to protect itself, eg in the accountancy example in 6.13 above, by including a provision in its standard letter of engagement for new clients of the corporate finance member to the effect that he/she cannot sign audit certificates. There could be circumstances where clients might find such statements somewhat curious, and it will be a matter of judgement for the members as to how important they regard the promulgation of limitations as being.

Lack of knowledge of the LLP connection

6.17   The other possibility is where the third party neither knows, nor believes, the person to be a member of the LLP at all. Such circumstances would prevail if the third party considered him/herself to be dealing with the member as an individual, not knowing of his/her membership status.

The LLP is thus sufficiently fixed with liability if the third party effectively has any reason to believe the person with whom he/she is dealing is a member (assuming of course that that belief is in fact correct). He/she therefore does not have to test that belief, eg by checking the register at Companies House although see 6.20 below as to the importance of checking the register in relation to dealings with a former member.

Comparison with directors' authority

6.18   The test as to actual knowledge referred to in 6.16 above does offer a contrast with the provisions of the *CA 2006* in relation to internal limitations on the powers of directors (which can of course be delegated to an individual director).

In *CA 2006, s 40*, not only are the powers deemed to be free of such limitation in favour of a third party (who is under no obligation to enquire as to limitations) providing that third party is acting in good faith, but also it is specifically provided that mere knowledge of the existence of a limitation does not, of itself, mean that the third party is acting in bad faith. In other words, in the case of a company, knowledge of an act being *ultra vires* an individual will not necessarily be fatal to a third party's attempt to fix the company with liability, whereas with an LLP it will.

Third parties and former members

6.19   The position becomes more complex when the relationship between third parties and the LLP is considered in the context of the acts of former members. In those circumstances the starting point is that the person in question is still regarded fully as a member for third-party purposes, subject to 6.20 below.

It should be noted that these provisions only apply if the person in question has completely ceased to be a member, and not merely if his/her abilities are limited by any of the factors in *s 7* (see 6.28 below).

The effect of cessation of membership

6.20   By virtue of *s 6(3)* of the *LLPA 2000*, a third party dealing with an individual who has been, but has ceased to be, a member of an LLP is (subject presumably to the *LLPA 2000, s 6(2)* limitations referred to above at 6.14 and 6.15) still entitled to fix the LLP with liability *unless* the third party has had notice that the individual in question has ceased to be a member, or notice of the cessation of the individual's membership has been delivered to the Registrar. In effect, therefore, delivery to the Registrar of notice of cessation of membership becomes immediate implied notice of cessation to all the world.

This could cause practical problems for a third party who, if dealing with a member, might be well advised to carry out a search at Companies House to see if the person in question is still a member. Further, since there is no concept of a priority period which would apply to ensure that the results of a search held good for a set period, whatever intervening changes might occur, that search would seem to need to be contemporaneous with the transaction in question. Therefore external contracting parties, even though *s 43* of the *CA 2006*, as amended, provides that an individual may bind an LLP by contract, may wish to have important contracts signed off by more than one member.

The possibility of an individual member's liability

6.21   Notwithstanding the principle of the limitation of the liability of the members of an LLP to their investment in that body, and the existence of that LLP as a separate and incorporated entity, circumstances may still exist where an individual member is personally liable to a third party.

This will principally occur where there is an act or omission of a wrongful (eg fraudulent or negligent) nature which is either the direct act or omission of the member in question, or where he/she is so closely associated with or responsible for it that personal liability will attach to him/her. Members may well wish to seek to phrase the LLP's terms of engagement so as to limit this risk, by getting clients to agree to the exclusion of members' personal liability. Such exclusion clauses will however be liable to the same limitations as any other exclusion clause, namely that by the *Unfair Contract Terms Act 1977* any exclusion must broadly be 'reasonable' to be valid, and cannot in any event exclude liability for death or personal injury resulting from negligence; and that (if the customer or client is not a body corporate) any 'unfair' terms must be avoided which would transgress the provisions of the *Unfair Terms In Consumer Contracts Regulations 1999 (SI 1999/2083)*.

The Solicitors Regulation Authority has given its blessing to the notion that, subject to the legislation referred to above, there is nothing to prevent a solicitors' LLP from contracting with its clients on the basis that no member or employee of the LLP shall be liable for any tortious act or omission.

The scope of personal liability

6.22   The scope of this possibility for personal liability is uncertain (see 6.21 above), and the *LLPA 2000* does nothing to remove or limit that uncertainty.

One view is that an individual would only be liable personally for his/her own negligent act if he/she assumed personal liability for the advice, where the third party relied upon that assumption of liability, and where it was reasonable for them to rely upon it. This was applied by the House of Lords to the liability of a company director in *Williams v Natural Life Health Foods* [1998] 1 WLR 830; [1998] 2 All ER 577. In the later case of *Standard Chartered Bank v Pakistan National Shipping Corpn (No 2)* [2002] UKHL 43 [2003]1 All ER 173, it was held that a fraudulent director could not, however, rely upon any term stating that he/she did not accept personal liability.

It seems however that the *Williams* test would sit uncomfortably with the later decision in *Merrett v Babb* [2001] 3 WLR 1, that a mere employee can be found to have assumed a personal duty of care and found liable for negligence even where the negligent employee had no significant personal dealings with the affected third party. In that case the Court of Appeal, after an extensive review of case law, including *Williams,* rejected the view that the voluntary assumption of risk was always the appropriate test, and asserted that an alternative was a combination of proximity and foreseeability with it being fair, just and reasonable to impose a duty of care. There were however quite clear public policy issues in that case, as the employing company was uninsured, and the court was at pains to find a remedy for the claimant.

The answer may lie in the closeness of the relationship between the negligent individual and the client. The more personally the individual has been involved, even down to the question of whether a personal rather than a business signature appears on documents (one of the features in *Merrett*), and the greater the dependence on that individual's advice, the greater the risk.

One aspect which has not yet been brought into any case however, since all have applied to companies not LLPs, is the public policy issue. The government's own explanatory notes to the *LLPA 2000*, as set out in 1.10 above, included specific desires to limit the impact of negligence claims upon professionals. It would seem perverse if the courts could override that by applying the much looser *Merrett* test.

The co-extensive nature of personal liability

6.23   What the *LLPA 2000* does, however, provide, in *s 6(4)*, is that in the hopefully unusual circumstances where such personal liability does exist, the LLP is liable to the same extent as the individual, provided that the act or omission either was in the course of the LLP's business, or was done with its authority. (It is not that it needs to have authorised the wrongful nature of the act or omission, or that wrongful steps *per se* can be taken as in the course of an LLP's business; it is merely the general nature of the act or omission itself which needs so to qualify.)

Liability as between members

6.24   An exception to this however is where the individual's liability, for his/her wrongful act or omission, is to another member of the LLP. Here, the principle of co-extensive liability (see 6.23 above) is excluded by the *LLPA 2000, s 6(4)*.

Presumably this was introduced to avoid internal membership disputes resulting in liability falling upon the LLP, eg so that if one member does something to the detriment of another in his/her management or administration of the LLP, the LLP is not itself liable to make the harm good. The provision does, however, go further than this, in that it does not require that member A's liability must be to member B in his/her capacity as a member for the exemption to apply. Thus, if A were to be negligent when acting as a conveyancer for B, his/her litigation fellow-member in a solicitors' LLP, in the purchase of a property for the purely private use of B, the exemption would still appear to apply, and the statutory application of co-extensive liability would not come into effect. This would leave B to ordinary principles as to whether he/she could establish liability against both; and if he/she did succeed would leave A and the LLP to resolve the extent of their respective liabilities between themselves.

This would seem to be an undesirable, and possibly unintentional, result which might need correcting by future amendment.

Availability of a member's indemnity

6.25   The question therefore arises of whether a member, who is co-extensively liable with the LLP as far as an outsider is concerned, can nonetheless turn to the LLP to indemnify him/her against the personal liability.

In the case of a 'wipe-out' claim, that indemnity would presumably be worthless, but in the great majority of cases the LLP's assets (and insurance cover – see 6.27 below) will suffice to cover the personal element.

Statutory indemnity

6.26   An agent is generally entitled to an indemnity from his/her principal, and indeed an indemnity in general terms is provided by *reg 7(2)* of the *2001 Regulations*. There is however a subtle (and, again, possibly unintentional) difference in wording between the provisions. *Section 6(4)* of the *LLPA 2000*, defining when co-extensive liability will apply, simply refers to a wrongful act or omission 'in the course of the business' of the LLP. *Regulation 7(2)(a)* gives an indemnity for personal liabilities incurred by a member 'in the ordinary and proper conduct of the business' of the LLP.

Can, for instance, a negligent act or omission, be said to be 'ordinary and proper'? In drafting a members' agreement, it may thus be prudent to deal expressly with the question and to clarify, one way or another, whether such an indemnity is to be granted to cover all liabilities to which s 6(4) may apply, or merely some, or none. In addition, provision may be inserted to regulate the right of the LLP and/or its members to make a contribution claim against the individual as a joint tortfeasor, in accordance with *s 7(3)* of the *Civil Liability (Contribution) Act 1978*. Thus it would be possible for an individual member to be protected (by indemnity) where a third party claimed against him/her but not the LLP, and (by excluding contribution obligations) where the external claim is pursued only against the LLP and not the individual; and for the position between those two extremes also to be regulated by the members' agreement.

Availability of insurance for personal liability

6.27   Insurers do not appear to regard the change from partnership to LLP status as being of particular importance to them, since the risk they are insuring will not alter. Further, they will often regard the possible co-extensive liability of an individual as included within that risk, so that one policy will provide cover for both the LLP and the member. (The Solicitors Regulation Authority's Minimum Terms and Conditions, for the primary minimum layer of insurance which must be taken out by each solicitors' LLP (currently £3 million) requires this to be the case.)

However, it is a point which individuals will be keen to ensure is covered when making their insurance arrangements and when drafting the members' agreement. Also, they will need to consider this in detail when leaving the LLP and examining what run-off cover is to be provided for personal liabilities which may not emerge for some years after retirement.

Restrictions on management or administration

6.28   The *LLPA 2000* provides that in certain circumstances members may not 'interfere' in the management or administration of the business of the LLP. This applies, by *s 7(1)*, if a member has:

- ceased to be a member;
- died (though it is difficult to see how a member could die without ceasing to be a member!);
- become bankrupt or been wound up;
- granted a trust deed for the benefit of his/her creditors; or
- assigned all or part of his/her share in the LLP (whether absolutely or by way of charge or security).

No restriction due to voluntary arrangements etc

6.29   One notable omission from the list in 6.26 above is where a member (whether individual or corporate) enters into a voluntary arrangement under the *IA 1986*. Such a member thus retains full capacity to act in the running of the LLP's business.

In practice, this would often be essential if such an arrangement was to succeed, particularly as individual arrangements for members will often need to be combined with such an arrangement for the LLP itself. Other omissions are for corporate members, where some form of insolvency-related provisions apply, which stop short of a winding up, eg receivership, administration or administrative receivership. Again, full capacity to act as a member is retained, although the members are free to agree contrary provisions in the members' agreement if they so choose.

Application of the prohibition

6.30   The prohibition in 6.28 above applies not only to the member or former member him/herself, but to his/her appropriate representatives. Thus it applies to the personal representatives of a deceased member; to the trustee or liquidator of a bankrupt or wound up member; to the trustee under a trust deed; or to a member's assignee.

The last example appears wholly illogical in circumstances where the assignment is absolute (rather than by way of security) and consented to in such manner as the constitution of the LLP may require (unanimity being the default requirement under *reg 7(5)* of the *2001 Regulations*). In such circumstances it becomes necessary to write into the provision, for it to have a practical effect, a limitation that the prohibition upon an assignee ceases upon his/her becoming a member in his/her own right.

Sanctions for breach of the prohibition

6.31   Breach does not give rise to any criminal sanction. It would seem therefore to be a section usable only by the fellow members of the member under the disability to restrain his/her, or his/her representatives', activities. Thus it appears to be no more than another default governance provision, even if one which, at least ostensibly, is not capable of being excluded by agreement. Since, however, its enforcement would only arise if the other members wished positively to take action, it seems likely to amount to much the same thing in practice.

The right to continued payments

6.32   A final part of the prohibition provision, and a further weakening of any effect it may have, is that, by *s 7(3)* of the *LLPA 2000*, the section does not in any event limit the right to receive any monies from the LLP as a result of the ban imposed.

Chapter 7

Designated Members

7.1   The *LLPA 2000* contains a completely new concept of 'designated members', as an optional subset of members. This chapter examines the logic behind this concept, the way in which designated members are to be appointed and notified, the powers and duties applicable to designated members, and the ways in which a members' agreement can be framed to accommodate the different options which designated members can offer for structuring the governance of an LLP.

Reasons for the creation of 'designated members'

7.2   In the explanatory notes to (what was then) the Limited Liability Partnerships Bill, the government gave, as one of five reasons for introducing the legislation (see 1.11 above), its concern that the existing partnership law did not give a suitable base for the structural requirements of a business with very large numbers of partners.

With one exception, however, the legislation does not appear to address this problem at all. The limited default provisions it contains for the management structure of an LLP are based very closely on partnership law. Its main administrative requirements come from the *CA 2006* and although there is much about accounting requirements, disclosure etc, there is nothing to equate the management structure of an LLP to that of a company, eg by having a shareholder/director style divide between the members. The sole exception is the concept of designated members, which is totally optional in the sense that there is no need for an LLP to differentiate between ordinary and designated members, and indeed the default position is that there is no such difference.

What are designated members for?

7.3   The answer to this seemingly straightforward question is that it is almost entirely up to the LLP, if it does opt to differentiate at all between designated and ordinary members, to decide what they should be and should do. All that the *LLPA 2000* does is to impose certain administrative duties (and therefore penalties for breach of those duties) upon them.

Further, even those limited duties were considerably weakened during the last stages of progress of the legislation through Parliament. For instance, in earlier stages, it was to have been the duty of the designated members alone to prepare, pass and file the LLP's accounts. By the time of the final version of the legislation, the duty to prepare and pass accounts had reverted to the generality of the membership, and it merely remains the duty of the designated members to sign the accounts thus passed and file them at Companies House.

What is a designated member?

7.4   There is no useful definition within the *LLPA 2000* of what a designated member is. They can be individual or corporate members.

Section 8 of the *LLPA 2000* deals with how members are appointed as being designated, how that designation can be removed, what particulars of designation require filing at Companies House, etc; but rather unhelpfully says nothing at all about what designation means. The definition section, *LLPA 2000, s 18*, states merely that 'designated member' shall be construed in accordance with *s 8* – as neatly circular a definition as you are likely to find anywhere.

Duties of designated members

7.5   The answer to the question of what is a 'designated member' therefore seems to be that a designated member is defined, not by what he/she is, but by what he/she must do. Those obligations may be created in one of two ways. First, there are those which are imposed by the statute or the *Regulations* (see 1.15 above) and whether expressly or impliedly by virtue of the designated members being liable with the LLP should the LLP fail to comply with the relevant obligation. A table of the main requirements is set out at Table A below. The second possibility is that they can be created by the members' agreement which may also vary or disapply certain of the provisions below, where permitted by statute.

Table A
Statutory requirements of designated members

Statutory provision	Refer to paragraph	Nature of obligation
LLPA 2000, s 8(4) and *(5)*	7.10	Sign and deliver Form LL DE01 as notice to the Registrar that either all members are to be designated; or that only certain individuals are.
LLPA 2000, s 9(1) and *(3)*	4.5; 4.6	Sign and deliver Form LL AP01, LL AP02, LL CH01, LL CH02 or LL TM01, as appropriate, as notice to the Registrar of certain changes in membership details.

Statutory provision	Refer to paragraph	Nature of obligation
CA 2006, ss 67, 68 and 76	3.12; 3.13	Ensure compliance with any specified direction to change the LLP's name.
LLPA 2000, Sch, para 5 (2)(b)	4.1	Sign and deliver Form LL NM01 as notice to the Registrar of a change of the LLP's name.
CA 2006, s 88	3.14	Sign and deliver Form LL AD05 as notice to change the situation of an England and Wales LLP or a Welsh LLP.
CA 2006, s 87	3.14, 4.13	Sign and deliver Form LL AD01 as notice to the Registrar that the LLP's registered office address has changed.
CA 2006, s 414	10.14	Sign accounts once approved by membership.
CA 2006, s 441	10.23	Deliver signed accounts and ancillary documents to the Registrar.
CA 2006, s 854	4.9	Sign and deliver annual return in Form LL AR01 to the Registrar.
CA 2006, s 485	10.49	Appoint auditors.
CA 2006, s 492	10.56	Fix auditors' remuneration.
CA 2006, s 512	10.58	Sign and deliver Form LL AA02 as notice to the Registrar that the members of the LLP have removed the auditors from office in accordance with CA 2006, s 510.
CA 2006, s 517	10.60	File notice of auditors' resignation with Registrar.
CA 2006, s 518	10.61	If required by resigning auditors, convene members' meeting to consider resignation and circulate auditors' statement.
CA 2006, s 1009	17.40	Apply by way of Form LL DS02 for an application to strike an LLP off the Registrar to be withdrawn.
IA 1986, s 2(3)	13.7;13.8	Prepare terms of proposed voluntary arrangement and supporting statement of affairs.
IA 1986, s 84	15.3	Deliver to the Registrar copy of determination for voluntary winding up.
IA 1986, s 89	15.6	Make statutory declaration of solvency in support of proposed members' voluntary winding up.

Statutory provision	Refer to paragraph	Nature of obligation
IA 1986, s 99	15.12	Make sworn statement of affairs in connection with proposed creditors' voluntary winding up, and appoint one of them to attend at and preside over creditors' meeting.
Criminal Justice Act 1967, s 9	7.18	Accept service of statements of evidence in criminal proceedings.

Creation of designated powers by agreement

7.6   It can be seen from the above that statute does not really vest any management powers in the designated members, but merely requires them to perform certain largely administrative and regulatory duties, with the consequential penalties for breach of those duties. In that respect, designation would seem to be an unenviable status, and something of a poisoned chalice.

If LLPs wish to make no more of the status than that, it would seem that they may well choose to treat the burden equally, and to have all members as designated members. (It is not possible to have a limited number of designated members, and to offer them an indemnity from other members against any personal financial penalties suffered by them, since such penalties will be in the nature of fines in criminal proceedings, and such an indemnity would therefore be void as being against public policy.)

Using the opportunity of designation

7.7   What the government has done, however, by the introduction of the concept of designated members is at least to offer the option of a differentiation in the status of different groups of members, which can be positively built upon by a members' agreement, in order to create a more corporate style of management structure.

Thus there would be nothing to prevent an LLP, in its members' agreement, from approximating the status of designated members to that of directors, and delegating a large range of management powers to them, subject to such controls by the general membership as they might wish to retain. In practice many of the larger LLPs have taken advantage of these provisions, with the designated members becoming the members of the management committee and consequently being given additional rights and obligations becoming of such a role.

Designation of all members

7.8   There are two possibilities, at the stage of incorporation, as to how the issue of designation can be approached.

The incorporation document, Form LL IN01, in accordance with *s 8(3)* of the *LLPA 2000*, asks whether all the members for the time being are to be designated members. If the relevant box is ticked, then not only will all the originally subscribing members become designated members, but so will all subsequently joining members. (Each member, whether as subscriber or when later joining, has to indicate by Form LL IN01, or Form LL AP01 (for an individual member) or LL AP02 (for a corporate member), as the case may be, whether he/she consents to become a designated member. Presumably, if all are supposed to be designated, but the relevant box is not ticked in respect of any particular member, then the paperwork will be rejected by Companies House.)

Designation of particular members

7.9   If, however, Form LL IN01 indicates that not all are to be so treated, then only those particular members whose details show that they are to be designated will be so. There must be at least two of them, or the incorporation document will be rejected by Companies House.

Those members so specified remain designated until their status is changed, either by positive action being taken, or by reason of their ceasing to be a member at all. Others may join their ranks, by means either of an existing member becoming designated, or a new member joining and being designated from the start.

Changing the approach

7.10   The LLP is able, at any time, to change its general approach, by *LLPA 2000, s 8(4)*.

Thus, if it has initially said that all members are to be designated, it can subsequently change to specify only certain members as being designated. Alternatively, if it has initially named particular members, it can determine henceforth to treat all members for the time being as designated. Notice to either of the above effects must be delivered to the Registrar in Form LL DE01. If the change affects the status of any particular member, then Form LL CH01 (for an individual member) or LL CH02 (for a corporate member) will also need to be filed in respect of that member.

Changes where certain individuals are designated members

7.11   Where the provisions at any time in force require certain named members only to be designated members, then the choice of those named can still be changed at any time. Any member may become or cease to be a designated member by agreement with the other members. Form LL CH01 or LL CH02 must be filed.

It is notable, however, that, unlike cessation of actual membership where, by virtue of the *LLPA 2000, s 4(3)*, the default position is that a member may resign his/her membership upon reasonable notice, there is no equivalent right in the absence of agreement to resign the status of designation whilst retaining membership. Likewise, there is no right for the LLP to remove the status of designation from a member. If the ability for a member or the LLP (as the case may be) to do this is desired, it must therefore be expressly included in the partnership agreement.

Reduction in numbers of designated members

7.12   There is no requirement that the number of designated members must in any way be proportionate to the overall number of members. Thus, if there are 50 members, there is still no obligation to have more than two designated members.

It is however provided by the *LLPA 2000, s 8(2)* that, if the number of designated members falls to one or none, then automatically all members become designated members. This could happen because of eg death or resignation. There is no period of grace during which members can appoint to fill the vacancy, without the automatic provision coming into effect. It will therefore always be prudent, for all except the smallest of LLPs (where probably all members will be designated anyway) to have three or four designated members at least, to avoid this possibility.

Automatic cessation of designation

7.13   A member automatically ceases to be a designated member, if he/she ceases to be a member at all (*LLPA 2000, s 8(6)*). In other words the designation cannot exist independently of membership, so there is no equivalent of a non-executive director having no shares or other stake in the business.

Notice of appointment etc of designated member

7.14   Amongst the changes in membership details which need to be notified to the Registrar under *LLPA 2000, s 9(1)*, is the situation where a member either becomes a designated member, or ceases to be so designated. Form LL CH01 or LL CH02 then needs to be filed.

The exception is where all members for the time being are designated, when, by virtue of *LLPA 2000, s 9(2)*, the ordinary notice of accession to or cessation of membership will suffice without a separate notice dealing with designated status.

Stated obligations of designated members

7.15   There is no statement of principle, in either the *LLPA 2000* or the *2001 Regulations*, as to what duties may be owed by designated members to the LLP, or to their fellow members, over and above the obligations of an ordinary member.

The only additional responsibilities, therefore, are those set out in statutes (see 7.5) which are enforceable by means of the various criminal sanctions to which designated members are exposed, and which their undesignated brethren are free of.

Contrast with directors' responsibilities

7.16   Contrast the situation described in the previous paragraphs with the approach found in the *CA 2006*, which builds upon existing common law obligations of directors by establishing a legislative statement of directors' duties covering:

- acting in accordance with the company's constitution, and only exercising powers for the purpose for which they are conferred;

- acting in a way which he/she considers, in good faith, would most likely promote, for the benefit of the members as a whole, the success of the company and considering (*inter alia*):
    - likely long-term consequences,
    - employees' interests,
    - relationships with suppliers, customers etc,
    - community and environmental impact,
    - the company's reputation, and
    - the need to act fairly as between members of the company;

- exercising independent judgement;

- exercising reasonable care, skill and diligence;

- avoiding conflicts of interest;

- not accepting benefits from third parties; and

- declaring any interest in any proposed arrangement or transaction.

Underlying obligations

7.17   Some of the duties in 7.16 above are likely to apply to all members anyway, in the LLP context, eg by reason of the limited provisions contained in the *2001 Regulations, reg 7(9)* and *(10)*. Some may be considered inappropriate where there is not the degree of separation of interests and powers that can occur in a company's shareholder/ director structure as all designated members must, by definition, always be a member of the LLP (see 7.13).

If, however, the status of designation is to be used to create a class analogous to directors (and, if not, it is difficult to see how LLPs can in structural terms satisfy the government's concern referred to in 7.2 above), then, in the absence of either legislative provision or any specific common law guidance as to designated members' particular obligations to other members, and to other stakeholders in the LLP (staff, creditors etc), it is left for either the courts in application of general common law principles, or the draftsman of the partnership agreement, to fill the gap. An instance of the former might be for a court to rule that designated members have a duty to exercise reasonable care and skill. On the assumption that the partnership agreement effectively delegates the day-to-day operation of the LLP's business to the designated members, the case of *F&C Alternative Investments* (see 6.9 *et seq*) has confirmed that in such a case, they may owe fiduciary duties to the LLP including a duty of reasonable care in the conduct of the LLP's business. In the latter case, provision could be made either way, eg by imposing duties upon the designated members in the partnership agreement, or by specifically excluding the application of potential duties.

Criminal Justice Act statements

7.18   One miscellaneous duty of the designated members is that, if there are court proceedings involving the LLP where, under *s 9* of the *Criminal Justice Act 1967*, there are witness statements to be served on the LLP, it is the task of the designated members to receive them.

Chapter 8

Governance of the LLP

8.1   This chapter starts by examining the overall question of whether a members' agreement is needed for an LLP. It puts the default provisions provided by the *2001 Regulations* into context, looks at them in detail, and compares them with their predecessors under the *PA 1890*. The chapter suggests ways in which properly drafted terms can replace or improve upon the default provisions. Lastly, it draws attention to areas which are not touched upon at all, but which nonetheless should be provided for in a members' agreement for the LLP.

General

Introduction

8.2   The philosophy of the *LLPA 2000* is that it is for the members of an LLP to arrange their own affairs as they think fit. In many instances, during the passage of the legislation through Parliament, the government refused to adopt a prescriptive stance on matters where the only consequences were of an internal nature.

Partly in order to achieve this, and to avoid attempts to import partnership concepts and case law into the LLP arena, partnership law in any shape or form was expressly excluded from applying to LLPs, unless specifically applied by the *LLPA 2000* or any other statutory provision (*LLPA 2000, s 1(5)*). Eventually, they did include a minimal level of default provisions, in *2001 Regulations, regs 7* and *8* (see 1.12 above).

Part of the theory seems to have been that, unlike an ordinary partnership which can be created without any formality (or even without knowing that the effect of the steps being taken is to create the relationship of partnership), the creation of an LLP requires the conscious taking of a number of decisions and public steps, so that it is reasonable to expect members to go through the process of deciding how they wish to regulate matters between themselves. The experience of those professionals who have had much to do with either partnership or company disputes suggests that this is optimistic.

The concept of a partnership agreement

8.3   Unless therefore an LLP and its members are content to rely on the default provisions (which would not be recommended in anything but the most simple LLPs), they will wish to have their affairs regulated by agreement(s). Such an agreement is referred to by *2001 Regulations, reg 7* as a 'limited liability partnership agreement' although for the purposes of this book it is referred to by its more commonly used term 'members' agreement'.

Notably, there is no requirement for any such agreement to be express, let alone in writing. Thus, any agreement, even an implied or verbal one, may be sufficient to displace the majority of the default provisions, ie those in *2001 Regulations, reg 7*. The only exception is the provision of *2001 Regulations, reg 8* that an ability to expel a member can only be imported by express (but again not necessarily written) agreement. The possibilities for evidential arguments about the existence or otherwise of implied or verbal agreements can only be imagined, and this situation should be avoided wherever possible as the case of *Eaton v Caulfield* highlights (see 8.7 and 8.17).

The parties to appropriate agreement(s)

8.4   The statute clearly contemplates two classes of agreement:

• an agreement between the members; and

• an agreement between the LLP itself on the one hand and its members on the other,

since in *s 5(1)(a)* of the *LLPA 2000* there is reference to the existence of the one sort of agreement 'or' the other.

In practice, however, it is likely that one document will suffice for both purposes. It does, however, need a change of mindset, on the part of the draftsman of such a document, from the usual drafting of a traditional partnership agreement, as he/she has constantly to bear in mind whether the obligation or right he/she is creating is in fact that of individual members, or of the LLP as a corporate entity, acting through its members.

Pre-incorporation agreements

8.5   It is specifically provided that it is possible to formulate an agreement to govern the operation of an LLP before its formal existence commences. *Section 5(2)* of the *LLPA 2000* provides that an agreement made before incorporation, if made between the subscribers to the incorporation document, can impose obligations upon the intended LLP, so as to take effect 'at any time' after its actual incorporation.

It is seemingly possible therefore to make such an agreement effective immediately after incorporation. It may however be prudent, as the moment of incorporation will not be known until after the event, to make the commencement of the agreement relate to the transfer of a business to the LLP, or a specific date set sufficiently far in advance to allow for the comfortable completion of the incorporation process. (One provision which might thus need to be included, particularly for start-ups, is an indemnity for pre-incorporation liabilities incurred by subscribing members on behalf of the future LLP, as the default indemnity conferred by *2001 Regulations, reg 7(2)* only covers things done in the ordinary and proper course of the LLP's business, or to preserve its business or property, which could arguably not be applicable to pre-incorporation events.)

The default provisions

The default provisions generally

8.6   Many of the default provisions will appear familiar to any draftsman, having been largely lifted from the *PA 1890*. However, it should not be assumed that the default provisions are appropriate for an LLP setting, and they should not be automatically incorporated either by leaving any reference to their subject matter out of a members' agreement, and hence impliedly accepting them, or by repeating them in a members' agreement.

Further, it is worth remembering that partnership law has been expressly excluded by the *LLPA 2000, s 1(5)*, so the interpretation of familiar principles in partnership case law will be of little help in their interpretation.

The default provisions therefore need consideration on an individual basis, as set out at 8.7 to 8.17 below. In what follows, the default provision itself is set out in bold type, and the *PA 1890* counterpart then follows in italics, with the relevant regulation and section numbers given.

Equal division of capital and profits

8.7

> **'All the members of a limited liability partnership are entitled to share equally in the capital and profits of the limited liability partnership.'** (*2001 Regulations, reg 7(1)*.)
>
> *'All the partners are entitled to share equally in the capital and profits of the business, and must contribute equally towards the losses whether of capital or otherwise sustained by the firm.'* (*PA 1890, s 24(1)*.)

This first default provision seems simple, but is far from being so. It provides that all members of an LLP are entitled to share equally in its capital and profits. The first limb of that statement requires careful consideration. It implicitly assumes that the initial capital, whatever that may be, has been contributed equally. That may well be the case in a start-up situation, but is considerably less likely to be so if the scenario is that of the transfer of an existing partnership business into an LLP. If the transferred capital is unequal, it should be noted that this provision is not merely talking about the distribution of future capital profits but about the ownership of existing capital as well, since it talks about capital 'and' profits. Thus if, in a partnership, A owns £100,000 of capital, and B owns £50,000, and they decide to transfer the business into an LLP without any express agreement, this regulation on the face of it provides that they are entitled to share equally in the capital, ie £75,000 each. Member A may well argue that there is some form of implication to be inserted by reason of the prior differential, but it places the onus upon him/her to prove that in order to restore the status quo.

Further, it begs the question as to what constitutes 'capital'. In *Eaton v Caulfield & Others* [2011] All ER (D) 63 (Feb), this was given its literal interpretation, ie the capital contributions of all of the members. The court ruled that, in the absence of agreement to the contrary, default *reg 7(1)* would apply, notwithstanding that the members might not have contributed capital equally.

However, if capital is deemed to be the aggregate of the sums which, on the winding up of the LLP, would be payable to the members after realisation of all the assets and payment of all the debts (including debts due to members), then that effectively includes not only original or specifically introduced capital sums, but also retained and unallocated profits. Even if shares of profit entitlement are equal, the reality is that retained profit levels are extremely unlikely to be equal, unless all drawings and payments to be treated as drawings are also exactly equal. If (as will be the case for many businesses) prudence dictates that funds are retained within the LLP to pay individual members' (almost certainly differing) tax bills, notwithstanding that the actual legal liability is a purely personal one, that of itself will result in a differential between the amounts charged to each member's account with the LLP.

Even if, therefore, equal division of 'capital', in the sense of specifically introduced capital, is required, then a careful definition of it is needed. (This may also be relevant for the purpose of calculating available loss relief for trading (ie other than professional) LLPs.)

The second limb of the default provision refers to profits. Since it does not differentiate, this must be assumed to include profits of a capital nature. If there is specific provision for unequal ownership of capital, it may well therefore make sense for there to be a provision for correlative division of capital profits. Thus if, in the above example, the status of A and B has been preserved by a statement that the capital of the LLP at the outset belongs two-thirds to A and one-third to B, and a capital asset such as a building transferred from the partnership's beneficial ownership into the LLP's name is sold at a profit, A will presumably want two-thirds of that profit, not just a half, even if the operating profits of the LLP are being split equally as per the default provision.

In many cases, of course, equal division of profits will not, for operational reasons, be the desired split, and specific provision will need to be made.

Another point to make in regard to this provision is that (unlike its counterpart in the *PA 1890*) it does not refer anywhere to apportionment of losses. Although of course any loss will show as that in the accounts of the LLP, as a separate entity, nonetheless it may in practice impact upon the members' several interests in the LLP, if the LLP is unwise enough to allocate losses to individual members, and thus its potential effect needs to be apportioned in just the same way as profits. Again, consideration needs also to be given to whether there should be any differentiation between the ways in which operating losses and capital losses are to be borne. To extend the above example, if A is to take two-thirds of any profit on the sale of the building, he/she should equally expect to bear two-thirds of the burden of any losses on it, even if he/she is only suffering one half of the general operating losses.

As an overlay to all this, the accounting treatment of LLPs (as the LLP Statement of Recommended Practice (31 March 2010)) indicates (see 11.13) that it is not until the moment that profits and losses are actually allocated or divided (whatever sharing agreements have previously been reached) that they cease to be treated as reflecting on the level of 'other reserves' of the LLP and come to affect the level of debts owed to individual members, which are therefore provable in a winding up.

In short, it is extremely difficult to think of any scenario where this default provision is safe to cover the reality of the members' positions in regard to the absolutely central concepts of capital and profits, and it should always be the case that a properly worded express provision should apply. There is no particular surprise in this, since the similar provision in the *PA 1890* has in practice almost always been displaced by express provision in any partnership agreement. It is also worth noting that where an LLP consists of members comprising both full equity members and/or salaried members, it is not uncommon for the profit-sharing provisions to be only generally provided for in the members' agreement (of which all members will be a party) with the specific profit-sharing arrangements being incorporated into a stand-alone profit-sharing agreement (of which only the full equity members will be a party).

Indemnity to members

8.8   'The limited liability partnership must indemnify each member in respect of payments made and personal liabilities incurred by him –

(a)   **in the ordinary and proper conduct of the business of the limited liability partnership; or**

(b)   **in or about anything necessarily done for the preservation of the business or property of the limited liability partnership.'** (*2001 Regulations, reg 7(2)*.)

'The firm must indemnify every partner in respect of payments made and personal liabilities incurred by him –

   (a)   *in the ordinary and proper conduct of the business of the firm; or*

   (b)   *in or about anything necessarily done for the preservation of the business or property of the firm.'* (PA 1890, s 24(2).)

This provision is less problematic, though it may require some refinement. It provides an indemnity to an individual member, from the LLP, in two circumstances. It is worth bearing in mind one fundamental difference between the indemnity thus granted to a member, and that granted to a partner in a partnership by the *PA 1890*. In the latter case, the indemnity is a liability from all partners and can be called upon to the extent of their personal assets. In this instance, however, the indemnity will only bind the available assets of the LLP itself, which may be far less extensive. This is accordingly one area where the principle of limitation of liability may work against the interests of a particular member (though, of course, in favour of all others) and members should accordingly be careful of allowing themselves to get into a position where they are dependent on such an indemnity to any extent which is significant when viewed against the asset base of the LLP.

One case where the matter may well be out of their hands is that of negligence, where there is sufficient evidence of a direct link between the act or omission giving rise to the negligence claim and the individual member to render him/her personally liable (see 6.21 above). There, in addition to the question of whether the default wording of the indemnity is wide enough to cover the situation, the risk of an indemnity claim being beyond the asset base of the LLP (perhaps in the situation where the claim exceeds the business's cover level, or where insurers either disallow a claim or are themselves insolvent) may be a relevant concern.

Reference has been made elsewhere to the potential for exclusion in the members' agreement of the reverse of this indemnity (see 6.26 above, and the surrounding paragraphs), ie the right for the LLP to recover a contribution from an individual member in circumstances where a third party chooses to sue only the LLP for, eg negligence, even though that third party could have established co-extensive liability against the particular member if it had chosen to do so, because of his/her assumption of responsibility for the negligent act or omission. Should the LLP have the right to seek a contribution against the member as a joint tortfeasor under the *Civil Liability (Contribution) Act 1978*, or should that right be excluded, as allowed by s 7 of that legislation? If the philosophy of the members' agreement is that the LLP should bear all claims, and an indemnity is therefore granted to members for occasions when action may be taken against them by third parties, clearly it makes no sense to allow the situation where, merely because there is no direct claim, the LLP can recover from the member.

Further, the right to seek a contribution could well give rise to great internal strife, with the other members effectively trying to establish a contribution claim against their fellow member when this has not even been contended for by the third-party claimant. It is suggested that the course of action most consonant with the idea of seeking limited liability protection in the first place is to grant members an indemnity against negligence, and to bar contribution claims against them, relying on the remedy of expulsion if needed for future protection. The alternative, to say that the indemnity to members did not extend to third-party tortious claims against them, and that contributions could be sought from them, seems contrary to the corporate concept of an LLP.

As mentioned, the indemnity itself has two limbs. The first is where the member has made any payment, or incurred any liability, in the 'ordinary and proper course' of the LLP's business. The second is where such a payment or liability arises from anything 'necessarily done for the preservation of the business or property' of the LLP. Any members' agreement is likely to contain such an indemnity, but there are still areas of concern. For one thing, from the LLP's viewpoint, there is no provision that, in return for the indemnity, the member has promptly and fully to provide vouchers and evidence to support his/her claim and a properly drafted members' agreement should include provision for this.

Secondly, from the member's stance, there may be times when he/she acts, with the full knowledge and consent of other members, outside what could normally be considered to be the scope of the 'ordinary' course of the business, or takes steps which are considered desirable but may not be strictly 'necessary' for the preservation of the LLP's business. He/she would reasonably wish and expect the indemnity to extend to cover such circumstances, if they are nonetheless genuinely for the LLP's benefit, but it would not extend that far on the statutory wording. One option when drafting a members' agreement would be to provide for such extended circumstances to apply to the indemnity if the act in question was either approved in advance, or subsequently ratified, in such circumstances as the agreement provided, eg by the designated members, or a management board etc.

Participation in management

8.9

> **'Every member may take part in the management of the limited liability partnership.'** (*2001 Regulations, reg 7(3).*)

> *'Every partner may take part in the management of the partnership business.'* (*PA 1890, s 24(5).*)

This short provision says simply that every member may take part in the management of the LLP. All members thus start from an equal theoretical standing in this respect. In all but the smallest of LLPs, this is unlikely to be the case in practice. Even if all members have an equal say in major management issues (accepting new partners, opening new offices etc) they are likely either to have their own management roles, or to play no active part in routine management, rather than everyone participating in every management decision.

The members' agreement may provide for this differentiation, or it may be left to more informal and more flexible decision-taking, although it is recommended that if not recorded in the members' agreement itself, any delegation of decision making to an individual member or particular group of members should be noted in writing (perhaps as an annexure to the minutes of the meeting at which such delegation was approved) to avoid any potential misunderstandings. Bear in mind also that the member's rights under this provision, and any express counterpart in an agreement, are subject to the provisions of *s 7* of the *LLPA 2000*, preventing those who acquire the interests of a member in an LLP from interfering in the management or administration of the LLP. As a sideline, this provision is an illustration of the fact that the functions of the designated members, as laid down in the statutory provisions, are not considered to be managerial functions. During the consultation process which accompanied the drafting of the legislation, it was considered whether it should in fact be only designated members who managed, but this was eventually rejected, and this default provision was substituted.

It is also worth noting that a member who has been disqualified under the *CDDA 1986*, or who is automatically disqualified by virtue of *CDDA 1986, s 11* (undischarged bankrupts etc) may not be a member of an LLP or take part or be concerned, amongst other things, with the management of an LLP. (See Chapter 18.)

No entitlement to members' remuneration

8.10

> **'No member shall be entitled to remuneration for acting in the business or management of the limited liability partnership.'**
> (*2001 Regulations, reg 7(4)*.)
>
> *'No partner shall be entitled to remuneration for acting in the partnership business.'* (*PA 1890, s 24(6)*.)

In this provision 'remuneration' presumably equates in common parlance to salary, since, of course, it does not mean that members shall not receive any return for their membership, but merely that it shall come through the medium of a profit share. It applies to two potential aspects of a member's activities. First, it states that he/she will not be entitled to remuneration for 'acting in the business' of the LLP. Since there is now a distinction between the 'business' and the 'management', the former presumably means providing the goods or services which the LLP exists to sell, and is more likely to be applicable to a member of an LLP in the professional services field than a retail or manufacturing LLP, since in the former case the member himself/herself is likely to be responsible for the direct delivery of client services.

Secondly, it provides similarly for anything done in the management of the LLP. If, therefore, a professional services partnership wishes to reward a member for taking on a managerial role in addition to his/her client service role, it will need specifically to do so. In drafting terms, this really fits with the requirements referred to in the consideration of the default provision on profits in 8.7 above, so that any special arrangements for prior profit shares, etc should be taken care of in an express agreement.

If it is envisaged that there may at any stage be salaried members, this possibility, and the need for remuneration to be paid to them, will need to be spelled out (though figures may be incorporated into other documentation, ie contract of employment). The reason for this is that salaried members will be full members (unlike those who are merely held out as partners and need not be party to the members' agreement) in the sense that they will have completed just the same Companies House paperwork as their profit-sharing brethren, and be regarded as having equal rights and obligations. Any sense in which this is not the case thus needs specifying.

Unanimity for new members and assignments

8.11

> **'No person may be introduced as a member or voluntarily assign an interest in a limited liability partnership without the consent of all existing members.'** (*2001 Regulations, reg 7(5)*.)
>
> *'No person may be introduced as a partner without the consent of all existing partners.'* (*PA 1890, s 24(7)*.)

Two separate aspects are rolled into one in this provision. The first is that unanimous consent is required for the introduction of a new member. This may well still be desired in all but the largest LLPs, since this has often been regarded even in large partnerships as one of the fundamentals which do indeed require unanimity, so personal is the relationship between individuals practising as partners. This does however seem an anachronism in the corporate setting of an LLP, especially in the larger ones, and particularly in the light of the fact that members are not agents of each other and may well not owe each other fiduciary duties.

In any event, the provision as written is potentially undesirably restrictive, in that actual and positive consent of all members is needed. Thus any move to introduce a new member could effectively be defeated, even by a member who was not prepared openly to vote against the admission, by his/her absenting himself/herself from any meeting where the matter was to be considered. The requirement is not that all members present and voting at a duly convened meeting must be in favour, but that all members must be. Similarly, if a member is prevented from participating in a decision by absence or illness, that would debar admission. Even if, therefore, unanimity is desired, thought should be given to whether that should in practice mean a vote by all those present and voting (in person or, if proxy voting is to be permitted, by proxy) at a properly convened and quorate meeting of members, rather than relying on the default provision.

The second limb, to which all the same considerations apply as are mentioned in the last paragraph, is that unanimous consent is required for the assignment of any member's share in the LLP. Such assignments may perhaps be thought to be likely to be more frequent than assignments of partnership shares, as LLPs are after all corporate bodies, and the equivalent of a share sale in a limited company is more applicable. It is commonly accepted that a member's 'share' in an LLP will include that member's right to vote and receive profits of the LLP as may be provided for in a members' agreement, although if a member is to be entitled to assign his/her 'share' then the members' agreement should be drafted to very clearly provide for this.

The default provision still leaves the situation, however, where, in theory, consent could be given under this provision but, if the arrangements did not go so far as expressly admitting the assignee as a member in his/her own right, the assignee could not participate in the LLP's management or administration, as provided by *s 7(2)* of the *LLPA 2000*. (This broadly follows the idea in *s 31* of the *PA 1890* that an assignee's only right is to receive the appropriate share of profits, and not in any way to participate in the firm.) Draftsmen will therefore need to consider first whether unanimity is appropriate for assignment, or an unfair restriction on a member's right to realise their investment in the LLP; and whether consent to an assignment should also be automatically classed as consent to the assignee's admission as a member.

Majority decisions

8.12

> **'Any difference arising as to ordinary matters connected with the business of the limited liability partnership may be decided by a majority of the members, but no change may be made in the nature of the business of the limited liability partnership without the consent of all the members.'** (*2001 Regulations, reg 7(6)*.)

> *'Any difference arising as to ordinary matters connected with the partnership business may be decided by a majority of the partners, but no change may be made in the nature of the partnership business without the consent of all existing partners.'* (*PA 1890, s 24(8)*.)

Having provided that admission and assignment both require unanimity, the *2001 Regulations* go on to provide that with one exception, ie a change in the nature of the LLP's business, all other decisions can be reached by a simple majority of members. A curious term is however used in the regulation, following the *PA 1890*, namely that all decisions as to 'ordinary' matters connected with the LLP's business can be so decided by simple majority (other than as excepted). What then of decisions as to extraordinary matters, if the reason they are extraordinary is nothing to do with the specific exception? Must the provision be read so as to imply that all matters, other than the specific exceptions of admissions, assignments or changes in the nature of business, are *ipso facto* ordinary – or is there an unspecified class of matters for which the *LLPA 2000* does not specify what majority is appropriate for which, presumably, unanimous consent would be required? There is very little case law applying directly to the meaning of *PA 1890, s 24(8)*. One example is the case of *Highley v Walker* (1910) 26 TLR 685, which held that the admission of a partner's son to the business was 'ordinary'. Once again, a clearer express provision in the members' agreement would be desirable.

For the exception, of the change in a business's nature, the same provisions apply as in 8.11 above in regard to the requirement for consent of all members, not just those attending a properly convened and quorate meeting. The other difficulty with this provision is that there is no definition of what constitutes a change in the 'nature of the business' of the LLP. Must it be such a change as involves the abandonment of the former nature of business, or is an enhancement sufficient to call the exception into play? In other words, if an accountancy firm wishes to start a professional recruitment agency, it would undoubtedly be a change in the nature of the business if accountancy were to be abandoned in favour of recruitment; but what is the position if what is started is merely a small offshoot providing a new service to existing clients, not intended or likely to provide more than a small percentage of the overall operation's turnover? It is no doubt a 'change' in the nature of business, since there was previously no business of the nature of recruitment, but is it such an extraordinary change as logically to require a different decision-taking structure from, for instance, moving the firm's office, for which no exception is made?

It is unlikely that decisions to enter into an insolvency process could be 'an ordinary matter' concerned with the business of the LLP and, therefore, such decisions are likely to require unanimity unless the members' agreement provides otherwise (see 8.25, 8.28 and 15.3 below).

Access to books and records

8.13

'The books and records of the limited liability partnership are to be made available for inspection at the registered office of the limited liability partnership or at such other place as the members think fit and every member of the limited liability partnership may when he thinks fit have access to and inspect and copy any of them.' (*2001 Regulations, reg 7(7)*.)

'The partnership books are to be kept at the place of business of the partnership (or the principal place, if there is more than one), and every partner may, when he thinks fit, have access to and inspect and copy any of them.' (*PA 1890, s 24(9)*.)

Part of the debate which arose during the passage of the legislation through Parliament, concerning the respective rights of ordinary members and designated members, related to the ability of the former to have access to the books and records of the LLP. In the end, the compromise position was not to enshrine such a right in statutory terms, but to put it in the default provisions where it is of course capable of being excluded by agreement. (This is different from the right of all members to receive a copy of the accounts, which is enshrined in *CA 2006, s 423(1) as modified*.).)

The requirement is twofold. First, it requires that the books and records (which presumably, these days, must be interpreted as including computer records) must be kept either at the LLP's office, or at such other place (singular) as the members think fit. Where those books and records include the LLP's register of members, register of debenture holders, charges register and copies, and the members resolve that such books and records shall be stored at an address other than the LLP's registered office then the LLP must file Form LL AD02 notifying the Registrar of the location of its registers (*CA 2006, ss 162, 743, 877 and 892, as modified*). Secondly, it gives any member the unfettered right, when he/she thinks fit, to have access to, and to copy, the books and records.

The provision refers to the 'books and records' of the LLP, without in any way defining that term. There is no qualifying word such as 'financial' or 'accounting', and it must seemingly go beyond the financial records, since the modified *s 388* of the *CA 2006* gives a similar right to members in respect of the LLP's 'accounting records', and if that were all that *2001 Regulations, reg 7(7)* was supposed to apply to, it would largely be redundant (save for the express right to copy as well as inspect). It seems logical therefore to consider the provision as including source documents for the preparation of accounts.

Further, if a purposive approach to construction is used, ie that the idea underlying the provision is to enable all members, in order to protect themselves and to discharge their managerial responsibilities, to form an independent view as to the position of the LLP, then it presumably would need to include documents relevant to that, such as:

- deeds;

- leases;

- finance agreements etc.

It may well go so far as to include records such as personnel files, etc. It will thus need adapting for a multi-site LLP, since the regulation applies only to one 'place', and it would otherwise be impossible to devolve functions and record-keeping to different sites. This provision is likely to need modifying therefore in many cases, and may also need some limits put upon it for larger LLPs, where the management may prefer to avoid the administrative burden of permitting such access.

It is, however, possible to contend for the contrary view, namely that all that is meant is those source documents which are necessary for the understanding of the statutory accounts, which all members must approve. This view is often adopted by firms with salaried members, who come from the background where, as partnerships, they did not show much (if any) accounting information to their salaried partners. Such firms will aver that since, for instance, the schedules breaking down individual members' capital and current accounts do not form part of the statutory accounts, there is no obligation on them to disclose such information to salaried members. It would be prudent, however, to provide specifically for this in the members' agreement.

Obligation to disclose information

8.14

> **'Each member shall render true accounts and full information of all things affecting the limited liability partnership to any member or his legal representatives.'** (*2001 Regulations reg 7 (8)*.)

> *'Partners are bound to render true accounts and full information of all things affecting the partnership to any partner or his legal representatives.'* (*PA 1890, s 28*.)

This is one provision which sits uncomfortably with all the others. It requires all members to render true accounts and give full information of all things affecting the LLP. That in itself is not an unreasonable requirement of an agent, when defining its obligations to his/her principal. The requirement, however, is not that the member should give such disclosure to the LLP, which is the principal, but that he/she should give it 'to any member or his legal representatives'. Seemingly therefore other members, and only they – to the exclusion of the LLP – have the right to call for such disclosure or to take action if it is not forthcoming. There is also no corresponding obligation on any member who has been so informed to pass on such information to the other members of the LLP. Again, it would not be unreasonable to argue that, as agent, the informed member was under an obligation to inform the other members and thus, by implication the LLP itself.

This seemingly cuts across the whole idea that there is no duty of good faith in an LLP between members directly, as distinct from such a duty being owed to the LLP itself. Since the government refused time after time to create such a direct duty, and set its face against derivative actions (with the sole exception of allowing for actions under the modified *s 994* of the *CA 2006* and even they can under *s 994(3)* be excluded for LLPs by unanimous agreement), it seems strange that they have allowed this exception. It is also unhelpful that, following the *PA 1890*, 'legal representatives' is nowhere defined. Is it restricted in its effect to those who have the legal power to represent a member, eg a trustee in bankruptcy or a donee of a power of attorney; or would it be apt, in accordance with common parlance, to include a member's duly appointed solicitors? There is not even any case law on this point in respect of the *PA 1890* provision – even if that were to be regarded as persuasive – to offer guidance. It is suggested that a draftsman of a members' agreement should seek to retain a consistent regime by excluding this provision as it stands, and replacing it by a similar duty owed by members to the LLP itself.

Profits from competing business

8.15

> **'If a member, without the consent of the limited liability partnership, carries on any business of the same nature as and competing with the limited liability partnership, he must account for and pay over to the limited liability partnership all profits made by him in that business.'** (*2001 Regulations, reg 7(9)*.)

> *'If a partner, without the consent of the other partners, carries on any business of the same nature as and competing with that of the firm, he must account for and pay over to the firm all profits made by him in that business.'* (*PA 1890, s 30*.)

There are two provisions which limit the ability of a member to profit from other activities at the expense of the LLP and which, it had been suggested by some commentators, could arguably import an element of a duty of good faith into the relationship between the members. Indeed, together they are the closest that the *LLPA 2000* gets to expressing a duty of good faith as being owed by a member. The duty is, however, owed to the LLP itself and not to other members as individuals and the court in *F & C Alternative Investments* (see 6.9), was quick to reject the argument that these provisions imposed a general duty of good faith on the members.

This first limb has three elements, ie that in order for a member to be obliged to account for and pay over to the LLP all 'profits' made by him/her in a business other than the LLP:

- the business must be of the same nature as the LLP; and
- the business must be competing with the LLP; and
- the LLP must not have consented to his/her carrying on the business.

The provision is therefore fairly limited in its scope. It certainly does not extend as far as the limitation found in many partnership agreements, banning partners from carrying on any other business at all without consent. It is not even enough for the business to be of the same nature as that of the LLP but it must also be competing with the LLP. If therefore the business is of the same nature, but is targeting a completely different customer or client group, it is presumably not caught by the provision.

Drawing lines of interpretation as to whether a business is of the 'same nature' as, or is 'competing with' the LLP is an exercise which may be difficult. Calling for an account to be taken by the court, in order to determine the extent of the 'profit' which is to be repaid by the offending member to the LLP if the offence is proved, will also be a complex and potentially costly process. Again, therefore, any help which can be offered by the draftsman of a members' agreement to clarify the circumstances in which, and the extent to which, any such restriction will apply, will be useful.

It is also worth considering what would constitute the consent of the LLP in light of default provision *2001 Regulations, reg 7(6)* (see 8.12 above). Arguably such a decision would not be comprised as an 'ordinary' matter and would, therefore, be another exception to that provision and require the unanimous consent of all of the members.

Use of the LLP's name or connection etc

8.16

> **'Every member must account to the limited liability partnership for any benefit derived by him without the consent of the limited liability partnership from any transaction concerning the limited liability partnership, or from any use by him of the property of the limited liability partnership, name or business connection.'** (*2001 Regulations, reg 7(10).*)

> *'Every partner must account to the firm for any benefit derived by him without the consent of the other partners from any transaction concerning the partnership, or from any use by him of the partnership property name or business connexion.'* (*PA 1890, s 29(1).*)

The provision which is associated with that last mentioned is one which forbids unauthorised transactions concerning the LLP, or the improper use of the LLP's property, name or connection. Again, it is the LLP which is the party having the benefit of the right, and hence the ability to enforce it, rather than any particular member. The provision is wider in its scope than that in 8.15 above, since it refers to 'benefit' rather than 'profits' and is thus apt to cover benefits in kind etc. The activities which may trigger a claim are also very broadly stated, and so may appeal to draftsmen of members' agreements. (The wording of the final part of the provision is less clear than its 1890 predecessor, and it needs the words 'or its' to be read into it, before 'name or business connection' to make sense.)

A number of cases noted to *s 29(1)* of the *PA 1890* in *Halsbury's Statutes*, Vol 8 (4th edition, 2009 reissue) may (bearing in mind the caution against using *PA 1890* cases at all) be illustrative of the scope of this provision. Two instances where the offending partner was held to account were where there was a secret commission (notwithstanding that the commission was earned before the partnership came into existence) (*Fawcett v Whitehouse* (1829) 1 Russ & M 132, 8 LJOS Ch 50), and where a partner was selling his own goods to the firm (*Bentley v Craven* (1853) 18 Beav 75). The provision was not, however, breached where one partner bought the interest of another (*Cassels v Stewart* (1881) 6 App Cas 64, 29 WR 636, HL); where a partner formed an independent company (*Fuller v Duncan* (1891) 7 TLR 305); where a partner bought a reversionary share in a building from which both the partnership and his sole businesses were conducted (*Bevan v Webb* [1905] 1 Ch 620, 74 LJ Ch 300); and where two partners bought a property independent of the partnership (*Trimble v Goldberg* [1906] AC 494, 75 LJPC 92, PC).

The comments above in relation to what constitutes the consent of the LLP would apply equally here.

The right to expel members

8.17

> **'No majority of the members can expel any member unless a power to do so has been conferred by express agreement between the members.'** (*2001 Regulations, reg 8.*)
>
> *'No majority of the partners can expel any partner unless a power to do so has been conferred by express agreement between the partners.'* (*PA 1890, s 25.*)

The final default provision is of a slightly different nature from the others. Instead of being a provision to be included unless specifically excluded, it is one which forbids the inclusion of one term by implied agreement alone. It prohibits the expulsion of any member by any form of majority vote, unless the power to do so has been conferred by express agreement. It does not prescribe what majority should be needed, and it would accordingly be open to an LLP to opt for a simple majority. It does not require that the express agreement shall be written or even recorded in writing (eg membership meeting minutes).

Many LLPs may think that they would not wish to include a power of expulsion, since that would run contrary to the partnership ethos they wish to retain, but in fact many will do so without realising it, eg with regard to the ability to require a member who suffers long-term illness to retire. In cases under the similar provision in the *PA 1890* (or earlier provisions), it has been held that a power to expel, if conferred, must in any event be exercised with the utmost good faith (*Carmichael v Evans* [1904] 1 Ch 486; 73 LJ Ch 329); and for the benefit of the partnership as a whole (*Blisset v Daniel* (1853) 10 Hare 493 at 522, 1 Eq Rep 484).

In *Eaton v Caulfield* [2011] All ER (D) 63 (Feb) the respondents, in the absence of a written members' agreement, could not prove that a power to expel had been expressly agreed upon. Draftsmen should therefore ensure that the circumstances in which expulsion is possible, and the decision taking processes which are necessary for it, are defined carefully.

Additional provisions

The need for additional provisions

8.18   In effect, any members' agreement will have three overlapping elements. One is simply those provisions which will be familiar from any partnership agreement – governing administrative matters such as banking, holidays etc. These are not examined here. The second is those matters which are covered in the default provisions above, and which may either be adopted as they are or, preferably, improved upon by the draftsman.

The third is those provisions which may not always be appropriate to members' agreements, and not covered in the default provisions, but which it would be prudent to include in any well-drafted agreement, since they refer to matters which may arise in the running of the LLP for which there is no other provision made. This part of this chapter suggests some such provisions.

Ratification of pre-incorporation contracts

8.19   One aspect of the consideration of pre-incorporation contracts has already been considered in 8.5 above, namely the need for the indemnity to members to be extended to include cover for acts properly done on the LLP's behalf in the run-up to incorporation.

The correlative provision which it would be prudent to include in any members' agreement – especially if it does itself precede incorporation – is that the LLP should subsequently adopt and ratify any such pre-incorporation contracts.

Liability under personal guarantees

8.20   Personal guarantees are likely to be needed in a number of circumstances, for many LLPs. It may be that they will be required from all members, eg if the LLP trades on a substantial overdraft, when the bankers may require such guarantees.

On the other hand, it may well be that only some are called upon. For instance, if a ten-partner firm converts to an LLP, and wishes to transfer the lease of the premises from which it trades, from the names of the four most senior partners, in whom it has for years been vested, into the name of the LLP itself, then it would not be unusual for the landlord to require those four individuals personally to guarantee the obligations in the lease.

In either instance there are two aspects to be considered. First, it should be checked that the indemnity given to individual members by the LLP is apt to cover liability incurred under the guarantee. Secondly, the position needs to be considered where that indemnity may be insufficient to cover the liability, so that there is resultant personal liability on one or more particular members. In most cases, it would be inappropriate for that liability to remain solely with those giving the guarantee, but rather it should be shared amongst the members. The members' agreement should therefore provide for how that sharing should take effect.

Meetings and voting

8.21   There are many instances in the *LLPA 2000* where reference is made to decisions being taken by either the members or the designated members. There are also a number of instances where reference is made to meetings being held, eg *s 518* of the *CA 2006* as modified (meetings to consider auditors' resignation) and *s 89* of the *IA 1986* as modified (meetings to give declarations of solvency on voluntary winding up), which again may concern either all or merely the designated members. There is even provision in some cases where the right is given to apply to the court to determine the procedures to be adopted for calling meetings, eg *s 92(3)* of the *IA 1986* as modified, dealing with provisions for filling a vacancy in the office of liquidator.

What does not appear, however, and what should therefore be provided for in the members' agreement, is what the mechanics for meetings should be. The questions which need resolving (and the answers to which may differ between meetings of the general membership and the designated members, who may thus require different provisions) will include:

- Who has the right to call meetings?
- What notice of meetings must be given?
- Can notice be abridged?
- Who is to chair meetings?
- What is an appropriate quorum?
- What majority or majorities can determine what matters?
- Is proxy voting allowed?
- When and how can written resolutions take the place of meetings?

Designated members' roles

8.22   Part of the consideration which will be relevant to meetings will concern the division of roles between members and designated members (unless all members are to be designated) (see Chapter 7).

There are certain roles which statute reserves to the designated members, eg the appointment of auditors, but there may well be other matters which members wish to delegate, and which will need to be provided for.

Duty of good faith

8.23   As has been mentioned in various places above, the government on many occasions refused to spell out a duty of good faith between members. It accepted, however, that there might well be circumstances in which such a fiduciary duty might be implied, but said that they would leave it to the courts to find and define any such duties. See Chapter 6 above for analysis of the case of *F&C Alternative Investments* in which this issue was considered and, in particular, the ruling that not only did members not owe a duty of good faith to each other but that they will not necessarily always owe a duty of good faith to the LLP, which has raised much concern amongst practitioners.

Clearly such uncertainty is undesirable. As it is no longer safe to assume that a member will generally owe fiduciary duties to the LLP itself, and on the basis that arguably members will want such duties to apply, then they must be expressly provided for in the members' agreement.

Likewise, if the members wish to provide for a duty of good faith as between themselves then they must expressly provide for this in the member's agreement which should be clear as to their exact nature. Alternatively, if the members so choose, the members' agreement can expressly exclude such duties. It is clear from *F&C Alternative Investments* that a well drafted members' agreement is more important than ever in providing certainty for the members as to their duties and responsibilities.

Termination or suspension of membership and/or privileges

8.24   Some aspects of termination of membership are touched upon either in the default provisions (the right to expel by express agreement) or in the *LLPA 2000, s 4(3)* (the right to withdraw on reasonable notice). The purpose of mentioning the topic here is to draw attention to the fact that neither of those sources provides the comprehensive code to govern termination which any well organised LLP will need, especially bearing in mind that members may not just be individuals, but corporations (whether companies or other LLPs) which will have their own circumstances for termination, eg dissolution rather than death.

The provisions will need to cover carefully the circumstances in which termination will take place, and what the consequences are to be. Most important under this latter heading is the requirement for comprehensive provisions defining the amounts and methods of withdrawal applicable to members' interests in the LLP after termination. Here there are no default provisions at all (save for the undesirable – and excludable – remedy of action on the ground of unfair prejudice under the modified *s 994* of the *CA 2006*) and, therefore, there is no automatic right to a return of capital. It is interesting to note that in *Eaton v Caulfield & Others* [2011] EWCH 173, (Ch), [2011] All ER (D) 63 (Feb) it was held that an agreement as to the return of capital would, in the absence of a written agreement, need to be shown to have been expressly agreed in order to be enforceable as such a term should not be implied under the general principles of contract.

It is also increasingly common for members' agreements to provide for two sets of circumstances relating (possibly) to termination. First, there is the right to suspend a member whilst investigations are carried out into alleged breaches on his/her part. That would normally entail suspension on a full profit share, and would spell out what a member can and cannot do (eg attend the office, contact clients) during a period of suspension.

The analogous provision is one which permits (not necessarily requires) the LLP to impose 'garden leave' restrictions upon a member who is known to be leaving. In practice, this will again need to spell out a number of steps which the LLP can take if it feels any or all of them to be necessary for the protection of the business, and to provide that the member's profit share is not affected.

Insolvency provisions – voluntary arrangements

8.25 Insolvency for LLPs is covered at length elsewhere (see Chapters 13 to 18), but there are three aspects of it which are relevant to the drafting of a members' agreement.

The first relates to voluntary arrangements (VAs). If the LLP proposes a VA under *s 1* of the *IA 1986* (as modified), it may be that modifications are proposed to it by a creditor. The chairman of the creditors' meeting must then seek the approval of the LLP to those modifications, under *IA 1986, s 4(5A)*. In the absence of agreement before the close of that meeting the LLP is deemed not to have agreed, and hence the VA cannot proceed. To avoid the need for potentially damaging adjournment of the meeting, there thus needs to be someone present at the meeting who is authorised to give consent on behalf of the LLP. For all but the smallest LLPs it will not be practical for all members to be present, so the members' agreement should deal with who that should be.

Insolvency provisions – determination to wind up

8.26   The *IA 1986* refers in many instances to a 'determination' by the LLP to wind itself up, but nowhere does it provide what constitutes a determination, or how such a determination is to be reached (see 15.3).

The members' agreement should therefore provide carefully for the manner and timing of the making of any such determination and delegation of authority (usually to designated members) to take subsequent steps including the determination of solvency in a members' voluntary liquidation and convening a creditors' meeting in a creditors' voluntary liquidation.

Insolvency provisions – administration

8.27   The LLP or its members have the power to appoint an administrator out of court (see 14.11) or to apply to court for an administration order (14.8). In a company context, such powers can only be exercised in accordance with the company's articles of association (see *Minmar (929) Limited v Khalastchi* [2011] EWHC 1159, discussed at 14.11), complying with all the relevant formalities for a directors' board resolution or a shareholder resolution. In an LLP, such powers must be exercised in accordance with the members' agreement, or unanimously.

The members' agreement should therefore make clear provision for appointment of administrators. This should specify the procedure to be followed (including notice, form of meeting and any special majority) and specific delegation of authority to certain member(s) to swear the necessary declarations and file the relevant documents at court on behalf of the LLP and/or its members.

If no provision is made in the members' agreement, then a single dissenting member could prevent the appointment of administrators.

Insolvency provisions – members' voluntary contributions

8.28   Perhaps the most curious provision in the whole of the LLP legislation is that found in *s 74* of the *IA 1986* (as modified), which states that, in a liquidation, a member will only be liable personally to contribute if he/she has agreed to make such a contribution.

Since that would appear to negate the whole purpose of seeking the limited liability protection of an LLP, it would seem unlikely that this would frequently be the case, so that it would be wise (and, indeed is common practice) to include a provision confirming that no member has agreed to make any such contribution.

There may however be practical reasons for such an agreement to be entered into (see 17.3 to 17.6 below). Either way, the draftsman of the members' agreement should make the position very clear.

Chapter 9

Taxation of LLPs

This chapter looks at the various taxes which may affect an LLP, and members' interests in it, namely income tax, capital gains tax, inheritance tax, stamp duty, stamp duty land tax, national insurance and value added tax. It starts from the general theme that the intention is for tax transparency, ie that it is the members of the LLP who are the taxable parties, rather than the LLP; and examines the exceptions to that rule, and various tax-avoidance provisions. Steps which need to be taken in mitigation of potential tax liabilities, especially for stamp duty land tax, are indicated.

General

Introduction

9.1   The avowed intent of the government in legislating for the tax consequences of LLP formation has been to achieve transparency, ie to arrange matters so that the authorities look through the entity of the LLP to the underlying members' interests in it, so that the LLP itself is not a taxpaying party.

In broad terms, when considering the tax positions of various business vehicles, the above means that an LLP equates to a partnership rather than a company, and has the consequent advantages and disadvantages. Thus, like a partnership, tax is payable on profits earned, whether or not they are distributed to members or retained within the LLP for working capital, whereas with a company tax is payable at a lower rate when earned, but a second taxable event occurs when profits are distributed (whether by way of salary, directors' remuneration, or dividends). The allocation of profits to members of an LLP (as distinct from the sharing arrangements) will not constitute such an event (see 11.11 to 11.13 below).

Effect of conversion to LLP status

9.2   As a result of what was said at 9.1 above, in effect, when a partnership converts its business to that of an LLP, its members will not notice any real change in the tax provisions which apply to them. With the one exception of stamp duty land tax, where active steps need to be taken within a year of incorporation if duty is to be avoided on any transfers of land or interests in land from the partnership (or its nominees) to the LLP, the change should be seamless and automatic.

This follows on from the introduction of the self-assessment regime in the late 1990s, under the *Finance Act 1994* and later legislation, at which time a partnership as a whole ceased to be liable for the payment of the tax liabilities of the constituent partners.

Exceptions

9.3   That is not to say that HMRC has given in without a fight! It has been concerned to preserve the overall amount of the tax take, and therefore has taken steps to prevent the use of the vehicle of the LLP simply for tax-saving purposes.

In this respect, HMRC's approach differs from that of other jurisdictions, particularly with regard to investment and property LLPs, which may make the UK a less attractive place to set up this type of business than other jurisdictions.

Finding the provisions

9.4   Much of the relevant law is to be found in the *LLPA 2000* itself, although it mostly operates through inserting provisions into other statutes. In addition, however, much of the anti-avoidance legislation appeared as last-minute amendments to a raft of measures in the *Finance Act 2001*, passed just before the dissolution of Parliament prior to the General Election of that year. *Section 75* of that latter Act therefore replaced the provisions in the former with regard to income tax and capital gains tax.

The *ITTOIA 2005* codified much of the law relating to income tax, eg by removing references to the familiar Schs D and E, but did not make any substantive alteration to the special provisions applying to LLPs. Stamp duty has almost entirely been phased out, and stamp duty land tax phased in, and much amended, by the Finance Acts in each of the years from 2003 to 2006 inclusive.

HMRC's interpretation of the legislation is found in the December 2000 edition (Issue 50) of its publication *Tax Bulletin*, which can be found on its website. Also helpful on the VAT front is Business Briefing No 3 of 2001 (February 2001) from the former HM Customs and Excise.

Income tax

The main provisions

9.5   The provisions of the *LLPA 2000* referring to income tax are to be found in *s 10(1), (2)* which originally inserted four extra sections, and one phrase, into the *ICTA 1988* and which are now re-written into *ITTOIA 2005*.

General treatment of LLPs

9.6   The first, and easiest to comprehend (and, for the majority of partnerships seeking to convert to LLPs, the only one they are really likely to be interested in) is *ITTOIA 2005, s 683*.

This provision deals with the general treatment of LLPs, and provides that a trade, profession or business carried on by an LLP, with a view to profit, shall be treated as carried on in partnership by its members and not by the LLP as such. For any LLP passing that test, there will therefore be no difference between the tax treatment before and after conversion from a partnership, ie it will be the members who will be taxed according to the regime appropriate to them. So, for instance, if a partner enjoys tax relief on the interest he/she pays on a loan, which was taken out for the purpose of investing in a partnership, he/she will continue to enjoy that relief if the partnership transfers its business to an LLP. Similarly, it is provided that the LLP's property shall be treated as partnership property, so that for instance there is no balancing event for capital allowance purposes, thus preserving those allowances. The transfer of business from a partnership to an LLP part way through the tax year will not mean that two sets of returns need to be filed by partners/members (even if the accounting year changes). Such returns will need to be signed by a nominated member, and default penalties may fall on him/her if returns are not in on time, according to the normal rules (for which he/she may well want an indemnity from his/her fellow members.)

One peculiarity is that HMRC has indicated that even 'salaried' members will be treated as taxable as self-employed – since they are 'members' within the statutory definition – even if in a partnership context they would have been taxed as employees. HMRC's manual at BIM 72115 states:

> 'If a LLP carries on a trade then each registered partner is taxable on the income they derive from the LLP as self-employed trading profits notwithstanding the fact that the registered member may have been a salaried partner (an employee) in a predecessor general partnership.'

Non-trading etc LLPs

9.7   HMRC, however takes the view that this – to its mind, favourable – treatment only applies to LLPs actively engaged in a trade, profession or business. It does not class the holding of investments, or of property for investments, as falling within these categories. As such relief on interest payable by a member on a loan for capital introduced into an LLP will not be available if that LLP is an investment LLP (*ITA 2007, s 399*).

Non-profit-making LLPs

9.8   It is also possible for an organisation to be engaged in a trade, business or profession, but not to seek to make a profit. Classically, this would apply to charitable or philanthropic organisations. Such an organisation should probably not be an LLP at all, since *LLPA 2000, s 2(1) (a)* requires that the business to be incorporated as an LLP should have been formed 'with a view to profit', but to make doubly sure, this phrase is repeated in *ITTOIA 2005, s 683* (see 9.6 above).

Should a charity or philanthropic organisation therefore somehow succeed in getting registered as an LLP, it would nonetheless not have the advantages of transparency (see 9.13 below).

Continuation of availability of reliefs

9.9   A number of reliefs will continue to apply with no break. The most significant are as follows:

- Relief on interest payable on a loan for monies to be invested into the partnership business will continue once those monies are passed to the LLP.

- Overlap relief (ie the relief available to a partner leaving a partnership as compensation for the double taxation element applicable to him/her under the commencement rules when he/she joined the partnership) will continue to be available when he/she leaves the LLP, provided that the LLP takes over all of the partnership's business, or at least sufficient part for the change not to be considered a 'demerger' of the partnership.

- Tax rate relief for continuing annuity payments continues to be available (and will also be available for incoming LLP members who accept future liability in respect of such annuities). Even if such annuity liability is not transferred to the LLP, the former partners who keep up the payments will continue to obtain such relief until they leave the LLP, or the business carried on by the LLP ceases, whichever is the earlier.

- The provisions for the 'catching-up charge', payable when partnerships moved from eg the cash basis to the 'true and fair' basis for their accounts, will continue to be phased as if there had been no change.

- The same will apply to the phasing provisions incorporated in *Sch 15* of the *Finance Act 2006*, relating to the changes in the accounting rules for the recognition of revenue.

Loss relief

9.10   A distinction is drawn, when looking at loss relief available to members of an LLP, between those LLPs whose business involves the carrying on of a profession, and others (referred to in this paragraph as 'trading LLPs'). The difference arises not when looking at what losses can be claimed against future profits of the LLP itself, but in respect of the 'sideways loss' provisions, ie the ability of a member to set a loss in the LLP against other income he/she has.

Essentially, for trading LLPs the member can only set off such of his/her originally subscribed capital as has not been withdrawn, or already used in respect of previous years' losses. For this purpose the member's share of retained and unallocated profit does not, unless the members' agreement expressly provides otherwise, count as capital. A further restriction applies both to members of LLPs carrying on a trade and those carrying on a profession where the loss arose from tax-avoidance arrangements.

The detailed examination of losses is beyond the scope of this work so reference should be made to a specialist tax work for further details.

Capital gains tax

General position

9.11   The position in respect of capital gains tax (CGT) for LLPs is straightforward unless and until the LLP ceases to trade. The relevant provision is *TCGA 1992, s 59A*.

Treatment as a partnership

9.12   By virtue of *TCGA 1992, s 59A(1)* (see 9.11 above), in three respects, the position of an LLP is treated as if it were that of a partnership. Thus:

- assets held by the LLP are treated as if they were held by the members, as partners;

- dealings by the LLP are treated as if they were dealings by the members acting in partnership (and not by the LLP as such);

- CGT chargeable to the members of the LLP on the disposal of its assets is assessed and charged on the members separately.

Therefore, a transfer of assets into the LLP's name has no adverse effect on the members' entitlement to entrepreneurs' relief, for example. Further, HMRC has indicated that if annuity rights and obligations are transferred, on substantially the same terms as before, neither the business nor any annuitant will be regarded as making a chargeable disposal.

Cessation of transparency

9.13   It is however possible that the right of the members of the LLP to take advantage of this favourable regime may cease, eg if they cease to carry on their trade or business, or if it should be held that it is not being carried on for profit. In those circumstances, by virtue of *TCGA 1992, s 59A(2)*, the picture changes completely.

In such an event, the LLP becomes liable for the tax on the disposal of any of its assets, as if it were a company; and the members as individuals become liable for CGT on any disposal by them of their interests in the LLP itself.

Movement between the two regimes

9.14   It is quite feasible for an LLP to move between the two possible CGT regimes as detailed above, eg by stopping, and then restarting, its trade.

There is no logical reason why any such change would necessarily involve an actual disposal of assets. Lest there be any doubt, *TCGA 1992, s 59A(3)* provides that any temporary cessation of business (and consequent movement in and out of the realms of transparency) should not of itself lead to a deemed disposal of assets. It looks therefore as if it is simply a case, with any actual disposal, of asking whether, at the time of disposal, the LLP satisfies the *s 59A(1)* test – if it does, the tax will fall on the members, but if it does not it will fall on the LLP.

HMRC has indicated that if there is a disposal of assets from one trade in order to raise funds to start another business, then it will still regard the assets as being disposed of by the members, not the LLP.

Cessation of trade

9.15   Further complications arise where an LLP ceases to trade and any members hold assets, or interests in assets, in which the base cost has been reduced under *TCGA 1992, ss 152* or *154* by a rolled-over gain on assets disposed of by the member.

The effect of cessation on deferred gains

9.16   The problem is that, if there is a cessation, a charge to tax upon a member arises, without the need for any actual disposal, at the time of cessation, if he/she him/herself had acquired the asset for a consideration reduced under the *TCGA 1992, ss 152* or *153*, ie if there had been any 'rolled over' element of gain held in respect of the asset.

Imagine, for instance, a sole trader who sold his/her shop in order to go into partnership; invested the proceeds with his/her new partners in the joint purchase of a new, larger, building; claimed roll-over relief in respect of his/her sale; transferred the building to a new LLP as successor to the partnership; and then ceased to operate the trade of the LLP which goes into liquidation. Under *TCGA 1992, s 156A* he/she as an individual would be liable for tax on cessation on the rolled-over element of gain.

Revenue concession

9.17 There is however some light to throw over this otherwise gloomy position. HMRC has indicated that it will only seek to implement this provision in the case of insolvent liquidation, or if the LLP, having ceased its business, is not acting in a timely manner to brings its affairs to a close.

So long as the reason for the termination of business is not tax avoidance, and that the period of informal winding up is not over-protracted, then transparency can continue until completion of the process, or until a liquidator is formally appointed. In other words, it is only if it feels that it will lose out by allowing transparency to continue that HMRC will stand on its rights under this section.

The provision is however such that, if partnerships have large amounts of gains rolled up into their assets, they may be put off forming LLPs, since the idea of a tax bill in advance of an actual disposal of property, at a time when almost by definition finding the funds to meet the bill is likely to be difficult, will be highly unattractive.

Inheritance tax

General position

9.18 The position on inheritance tax is refreshingly straightforward. *Section 267A* of the *Inheritance Tax Act (IHTA) 1984* gives four instances in which, for the purposes of that and any related statutes, LLPs are to be treated as partnerships. Thus:

- property which an LLP owns, uses or occupies, is treated as if used, owned or occupied by the members, as partners;

- any business carried on by the LLP is treated as if carried on by the members, in partnership;

- any incorporation, change in membership or dissolution of an LLP is to be treated as if it were the formation, alteration or dissolution of a partnership;

- any transfer of value made by or to an LLP is treated as if made by or to its members in partnership, not by or to the LLP as such.

The effect therefore is that all reliefs etc which are available to partners will continue to be available to them as members of the LLP which takes over from the partnership. HMRC has confirmed that there will be no adverse effect even if the LLP might otherwise be regarded as a close company.

Stamp duty and stamp duty land tax

General position

9.19   The general idea with stamp duty and stamp duty land tax is that no *ad valorem* duty should be payable on the transfer of assets held by a partnership, or by trustees or nominees on its behalf, into the ownership of the LLP itself, provided that those involved are careful to bring themselves within the scope of the exemption which is made available.

The idea of such a transfer is attractive in many cases, as it will avoid the fictions often necessary for partnerships, where freehold or leasehold properties are held by up to four partners as trustees for the generality of the partnership, and will facilitate the transfer of beneficial ownership on changes in the constituent members of the firm.

Further, for leasehold properties, a transfer of the lease into the LLP's name will usually be necessary, eg to avoid breach of a non-alienation covenant.

Such a desirable transfer of assets is however potentially the most hazardous part of the tax arrangements which will be applicable to an ordinary partnership on the change to an LLP. There are both time traps, and technical qualifications to be cleared, if the benefit of the exemption is to be obtained.

The move to stamp duty land tax

9.20   The *Finance Act 2003* introduced stamp duty land tax as a successor to stamp duty. In some ways this was a welcome change, not least because the range of assets to which it applies is much smaller. Thus, whilst it used in the early years of LLPs to be important to ensure that the exemption was available, even if the land held was lower in value than the dutiable limit, because otherwise stamp duty could bite on the transfer of, eg book debts and work in progress, now stamp duty land tax only applies to land and interests in it.

Stamp duty itself has not been fully abolished, but the only assets to which it will in practice still be likely to apply are stocks, shares and marketable securities, in respect of which duty is payable (unless the exemption is available) at 0.5%.

The disadvantage is that stamp duty land tax has been a draftsman's disaster, and the original 2003 provisions have been very extensively amended in the following three *Finance Acts*. Further, it is potentially a much more costly tax than its predecessor. For firms converting to LLP status, the availability of the exemption is therefore very important, if the aggregate value of land to be transferred exceeds the tax threshold of (presently) £150,000. (Broadly speaking, for these purposes, the value will, for freeholds, be the open market value; and for leases it will be the notional premium value of the lease. Reference should, however, be made to the statute for detailed consideration of these concepts, if necessary.)

Time limit

9.21   The first problem is timing. By *s 12(1)* of the *LLPA 2000*, no stamp duty is chargeable upon an instrument by which property is transferred or conveyed by anyone to an LLP, in connection with the incorporation thereof, provided that two conditions are met, as below, and provided that the date of the instrument is within the period of one year beginning with the date of incorporation.

Similar provisions were then made in *s 65* of the *FA 2003* with regard to stamp duty land tax.

The catch is that it is the date of incorporation, not the date of the transfer of the business to the LLP, which is relevant. Shortly after the *LLPA 2000* came into effect on 6 April 2001, it became apparent that some firms had registered LLPs at a time when they had not taken the decision to transfer their businesses to those LLPs, simply to secure their first choice of name. Not only had they possibly committed an offence under *s 2* by inaccurately stating on the incorporation document that they had 'associated for carrying on a lawful business', but they had inadvertently started the clock running as to the time within which, if they did decide to go ahead with their new LLPs as trading vehicles, they had to get their property transfers complete if they wished to avoid stamp duty. This is a strict statutory time limit, and it does not appear that HMRC would have any discretion (let alone incentive) to extend the period.

Identity of the transferor

9.22   Assuming the time limit can be complied with, the first condition is as to the identity of the transferor of the property. Two categories of transferor fulfil the condition.

The first category is a person who is him/herself a partner in a partnership, where the partnership is comprised of all the persons who are, or are to be, members of the LLP, and no one else. A further category of acceptable transferor, if the property is held on behalf of such a partnership as is referred to above, is someone conveying as nominee or bare trustee for one or more of the partners in that partnership. Such a person will qualify as a 'bare trustee' for a partner if that partner has the sole right to direct how the property shall be dealt with. (Any apparent restriction on that right arising from any charge, lien or other right of the trustee to resort to the property for the payment of duty, taxes, costs or other outgoings is ignored for the purposes of this test.)

Who are the members to be?

9.23   It is mentioned above that the transferor partners must be those 'who are or are to be members of the limited liability partnership (and no-one else)'. In other words, it is not possible to get the exemption if either some partners decide not to become members of the LLP; or if additional members are introduced at or before the moment of transfer of the business. This is a practical limitation which experience shows is often a drawback; as conversion is a natural punctuation mark in the life of the business, and often it would be desired to make just such changes.

One peculiarity is that, because of the words 'or are to be', it is not necessary for all partners to join in the incorporation, provided they are added as members before transfer. Thus, if there are 20 partners, and it is administratively more convenient for two to incorporate the LLP, and then add the other 18 later, that would not lose the exemption if all were registered before the transfer.

Beneficial interests in the property

9.24   The second condition concerns the beneficial interests in the property transferred or conveyed. With one exception, the proportions of the property to which the members in the LLP are entitled, after the transfer, must be exactly the same as they were entitled to at 'the relevant time' (see 9.25 below).

The idea is that if ten partners were beneficially entitled in equal shares before the transfer, then those ten members must be so entitled, in the same shares, afterwards. There is one logical flaw in this requirement, which is that, after the transfer, no person has any share in the beneficial ownership of the property itself – it belongs to the LLP as a corporate entity and all that any individual has is an interest in the LLP. HMRC has however said that it proposes to ignore this, and look at the underlying interests in the LLP, when ascertaining what beneficial shares it considers members to have. The exception referred to is that changes in the underlying beneficial interests will be allowed, provided they do not result from any scheme or arrangement wholly or partly designed for the avoidance of liability to any duty or tax. Thus, for instance, any change due to the death of a partner will not upset the relief. It may be possible to persuade HMRC that the long-planned retirement of a partner at the date of transfer is merely a coincidence, and so does not lose the exemption, but it would be rash to try this without checking HMRC's view in the particular circumstances.

The 'relevant time'

9.25   Both conditions above need to be fulfilled at 'the relevant time'. Thus the identity of the transferor has to be satisfactorily established at the relevant time; and the beneficial interests after conveyance or transfer have to be the same as they previously were at the relevant time.

Normally, the relevant time will be immediately before incorporation. If however the property transferred was not acquired by the transferor until after incorporation (as where a partner acquires a property after incorporation of the LLP but in anticipation of the transfer of the partnership business to it) then the relevant time will be immediately after acquisition.

Revenue concession on changes

9.26   Taking these conditions and the definition of the relevant time together, it would appear that the relief would be lost if there were any change at all in the constituent partners/members. It would thus be impossible at the time of transfer itself for outgoing partners to retire, or new blood to be brought in as members, even though in operational terms that might be just the most desirable moment.

HMRC has indicated that it will be generous in its interpretation, and allow changes of partners/members the instant before or after incorporation, though it will in such circumstances wish to see all associated documentation, and may call for further supporting information. It still seems however that, if circumstances permit, it might still be prudent for outgoing partners to retire well in advance of incorporation, and for no new members to be appointed until the property transfer process is complete, to avoid having to argue the finer points of timing with HMRC.

National Insurance

9.27   *Section 15(3A)* of the *Social Security Contributions and Benefits Act 1992* states where income tax is or would be payable by a member of an LLP, in respect of profits or gains arising from the trade or business carried on by the LLP, then Class 4 contributions are payable as if the trade were being carried on by the members of the LLP in partnership. In other words, members who are individuals are potentially liable to pay such contributions; but corporate members (companies or LLPs) are not. HMRC has also pointed out that Class 2 and Class 3 contributions may also be payable, just as with a partnership.

Value added tax

General position

9.28   The *LLPA 2000* itself is silent on VAT. Business Brief 3/01, issued by the then HM Customs and Excise, is however helpful as to the position of LLPs in relation to VAT.

There are no surprises. The LLP itself is the legal entity for VAT purposes, rather than its members and potentially must register for VAT, subject to the normal rules.

The members are not regarded for VAT purposes as supplying services to the LLP, so do not themselves have to register. LLPs will, as bodies corporate, be able to join VAT groups if they fulfil the normal conditions requiring common control of the constituent bodies within a group.

If there is a transfer of a partnership's business to the LLP, the normal rules applying to the transfers of going concerns will apply and, if the partnership ceases to exist, it may be possible for the LLP to take over the partnership's VAT registration number. (One practical problem which may arise is if not all of the partnership's business is transferred to the LLP, in which case the going concern rules, which are beyond the scope of this work, will need examining carefully to see if a sufficiently major part of the business is being transferred for the rules to apply.)

Chapter 10

Accounts and Auditing

10.1   This chapter looks at the requirements of legislation and standards as regards the accounting and auditing aspects of LLPs. The chapter is in seven parts. It starts by setting the legislative scene for accounts, etc, and looking at the applicable legislation. The duties as to record-keeping and the preparation of accounts, which fall upon members, are then considered; before moving on to the designated members' responsibilities for the approval of accounts, and the reports which go with them. Then the requirements for the delivery and distribution of accounts, to the registrar on the one hand, and to members and debenture holders on the other, are reviewed. Provisions for voluntary, or compulsory, correction of defective accounts are discussed. The important topic of exemptions from the full stringency of these requirements, as made available to small and medium-sized LLPs, is fully covered. Lastly, the respective rights and duties of LLPs and their auditors are reviewed.

Introduction

The overall accounting picture

10.2   Much of what has gone before has indicated the similarities of LLPs to the partnerships from which they have derived. This has especially been so in the field of the taxation treatment of LLPs.

It may seem paradoxical, therefore, that at the point where one turns to look at the accounting treatment of LLPs, which might logically seem the opposite side of the coin from taxation, one moves completely across to the area where the legislation equates LLPs to companies, and not to partnerships. If one thinks of an LLP, for all accounting purposes, as fundamentally a sub-species of company, one will not go far wrong.

The structure of the legislation

10.3   The *LLPA 2000* itself, in its 19 sections, is completely silent as to accounting and auditing requirements. Rather, it works through the medium of incorporating, by means of the 2008 Regulations, large chunks of the *CA 2006*. The *2008 Regulations* copy the full text of the relevant sections of the *CA 2006* with amendments specific to LLPs, such as referring to 'LLP' instead of 'company' and including references to 'members' where appropriate. Supplementing the *2008 Regulations* are the *2008 Large LLP (Accounts) Regulations* and the *2008 Small LLP (Accounts) Regulations* which specify the form and content of the accounts and which apply various provisions of the *Small Companies and Groups (Accounts and Directors' Report) Regulations 2008 (SI 2008/409)* and the *Large and Medium-sized Companies and Groups (Accounts and Reports) Regulations 2008 (SI 2008/410)* to LLPs, with amendments.

The previous incorporation of the *CA 1985* was particularly difficult to interpret as there was no one source to refer to. Instead, one had to consider the accounting regulations as they were applied to LLPs and then superimpose onto those regulations the amendments that were set out in *Sch 1* to the *2001 Regulations*. Thankfully, the draftsmen must have listened to the numerous complaints about the difficulty of interpreting the *2001 Regulations* and now we have one composite reference site for all applicable regulations with appropriate amendments made.

Statement of Recommended Practice

10.4 Alongside the accounting legislation referred to throughout this work is the LLP Statement of Recommended Practice (or SORP) which is issued by the Accounting Standards Board with the stated aim of 'establishing and improving' standards of financial accounting and reporting.

The first LLP SORP was published, after consultation, in 2002. It was revised in March 2006 and again in March 2010. The 2010 revised version is referred to in this work, and included as Appendix 3.

Preparation of accounts

General record-keeping requirements

10.5 The accounts to be prepared by an LLP have a number of different stakeholders whose interests they must serve. First, there are the regulatory and taxation authorities. Secondly, there are those who are to conduct business with the LLP. Thirdly, there are the members themselves.

CA 2006, s 386, as modified (which imposes record-keeping duties) states that those records must be such as to disclose the LLP's financial position with reasonable accuracy at any time, and to enable members to ensure that the balance sheet and the profit and loss account of the LLP satisfy statutory requirements. A parent LLP has the responsibility for ensuring that any subsidiaries, which may not themselves need to fulfil these requirements, nonetheless keep such records as will enable the parent so to comply. A failure to comply is an offence on the part of all members of the LLP, unless an individual member can persuade a court that he/she acted honestly and that his/her default was, in all circumstances, excusable.

Records which need keeping

10.6   *Sections 386(3)* and *(4)* of the *CA 2006*, as modified, indicates with some particularity the nature of the records which must be kept. These include:

- day-to-day entries for all sums received and paid by the LLP;

- similar entries for the items to which those sums refer;

- a record of all assets and liabilities;

- for LLPs whose business involves dealing in goods:

  - year-end stock statements;

  - stocktaking statements from which the above derive;

  - statements of all goods sold and bought (otherwise than by way of normal retail trade).

It is worth noting that the use of the phrase 'at any time' connotes more than just that the LLP must be able to produce 'true and fair' accounts at the end of the year. The members must have such records as will enable them to produce a snapshot of the LLP's full financial position at any mid-term stage. Some form of computerised management accounting system will therefore, for all but the very smallest of LLPs, be essential to enable the members to fulfil their obligations under this section. By *DTC (CNC) Ltd v Gary Sargeant* [1996] 1 WLR 797, an accountant to whom records have been passed for the purposes of accounts production, cannot exercise a lien over them for unpaid fees if the effect of that would be to place the LLP in breach of its statutory obligations under this section.

Location of records

10.7   The above records may, by the modified *s 388* of the *CA 2006*, be kept either at the registered office of the LLP, or at any other place the members decide. Wherever they are, however, they must be open to inspection at all times by all members.

The suggestion, at earlier stages of the legislation, that only designated members should have full access to the records, was not followed. Consequently, as this is an unequivocal statutory requirement rather than a default provision for the LLP's governance in *reg 7* of the *Regulations*, this is not something which can be altered by the members' agreement. Members are therefore in a more fortunate position than company shareholders, since it is only company officers who have this right in a company context. It should be noted, however, that (as mentioned in 8.13 above) this right does not extend to documents which are not needed to fulfil the statutory duty, such as schedules of members' individual current accounts. A diligent member might, however, be able to construct such schedules from the records of payments made and received.

There are specific provisions at *s 388(2)* and *(3)* for what records have to be sent to the UK, if the place the members decide to keep the records generally is outside the jurisdiction. Again, unlike in the early draft legislation, all members, not just designated ones, are potentially liable for any breach of these requirements, although the same defence as in *s 387(2)* is available to any individual member if his/her conduct was honest and excusable.

Duration of record keeping

10.8   Records must be kept for at least three years, under the modified *CA 2006, s 388(4)*.

Other statutory requirements which may affect many of the same documents may however require a longer period of keeping, eg the six years for which all tax records must be kept, or even the 20 years for which the Revenue can go back in the case of alleged fraud or negligence under *s 36* of the *Taxes Management Act 1970* (as amended). Any member who has failed to take all reasonable steps to ensure compliance with the above, or who intentionally causes any default in meeting this obligation, is guilty of an offence.

Accounting reference dates

10.9   . Under *CA 2006, s 391* as modified, LLPs must have accounting reference dates in the same way as companies. The first such date will normally be the last day of the month in which the anniversary of its incorporation falls.

It may, however, by *CA 2006, s 392,* as modified, alter that date, and may even make such a change retrospective for one year provided that the date on which the accounts for such year (prior to change) has not yet arisen. Notice in form LL AA01, which any member may sign, needs to be filed. The effect of the change may be to shorten or lengthen the accounting period, ie from incorporation or the last accounting reference date, as the case may be, up to the newly chosen date. The period thus created, however, cannot be more than 18 months nor, in the case of the first accounting period, less than six. Any notice to lengthen an accounting reference period cannot normally be given within five years of a previous extension by like means.

Financial years, by *CA 2006, s 390*, as modified, basically follow accounting reference dates, though seven days' leeway is allowed. If an LLP has a subsidiary undertaking to which these concepts do not apply, it has to ensure that its financial year follows that of the parent LLP, unless there are good reasons to the contrary.

The duty to prepare accounts

10.10   The accounts which an LLP is obliged to produce, under the modified *s 394* of the *CA 2006*, as what are referred to as its individual accounts, are to be prepared in accordance with either *CA 2006, s 396* as modified, ('non-IAS individual accounts') or in accordance with international accounting standards (*CA 2006, s 395* (as modified)) ('IAS Accounts'). Non-IAS individual accounts must comprise a balance sheet and a profit and loss account for each financial year. These must be on the basis that they offer a 'true and fair' view of the LLP's affairs.

It is open for the LLP to determine what accounting framework it wishes to follow. If an LLP chooses to prepare its accounts in accordance with IAS then, unless its prevailing circumstances change, it must continue so doing. If the LLP is a parent LLP, then all of the members of the group must prepare individual accounts on a consistent basis unless there are good reasons, in the opinion of the members, for not doing so (*CA 2006, s 407*, as modified). This work focuses on the accounting regime relating to non-IAS individual accounts on the basis that this will be the accounting structure most likely to be adopted by those consulting this work although, where relevant, consideration will be given to certain IAS accounting standards in consideration of non-IAS individual accounting standards being considered.

The responsibility for the production of these accounts lies with all members, not merely (as had been previously proposed) with the designated members. Where the LLP is a parent LLP, then under CA 2006, *s 399*, as modified, it must (unless it is subject to the small LLPs regime), in addition to its individual accounts, prepare consolidated accounts for itself and all subsidiary undertakings, unless it is itself a subsidiary of another undertaking, and that undertaking is itself under an obligation to prepare consolidated accounts, and the conditions set out in CA 2006, *s 400* and/or *s 401* and/or *s 402* are complied with. (The detailed requirements as to consolidated accounts set out in CA 2006, *ss 400* to *410* (inclusive), as modified, are beyond the scope of this work, and specific reference to them should be made by any affected LLP or their advisers.)

The format of accounts

10.11   As already stated, and whether individual accounts or consolidated ones, all accounts must be on a 'true and fair' basis and, indeed, under the *CA 2006, s 393*, as modified, the members have a primary responsibility not to approve the accounts unless they do show a true and fair view. In order to achieve this, they must follow the requisite format as provided by *Sch 1* to either the *2008 Large LLP (Accounts) Regulations* or the *2008 Small LLP (Accounts) Regulations* (as the case may be).

If those schedules are not of themselves enough to include all information necessary to give a true and fair view, then that additional information must be given in the accounts or a note to them. Equally, if observance of the requirements of those regulations would in special circumstances (see CA 2006, s 396(4) and *(5, as modified,)*) prevent a true and fair view being given, they may be varied, but a note of the reasons for and effects of the departure from the norm must be given in a note to the accounts. (The detail of those provisions is such as to be beyond the scope of this work.)

Disclosure of members' interests etc

10.12   In Chapter 11 below, there are detailed provisions as to what disclosure of members' financial positions is required by the legislation. At this point, however, it is worth noting in passing that *CA 2006, s 412* does not generally apply. This applies to benefits which directors may gain from a company, eg not just straight emoluments, but also pensions, compensation for loss of office, loans, quasi-loans etc. Most of these do not apply, by virtue of this section, to members, who are only subject to the particular requirements examined in Chapter 11, albeit that some particular provisions of *Sch 5* to the *Large and Medium-sized Companies and Groups (Accounts and Reports) Regulations 2008* (as applied by *Sch 1* to the *2008 Large LLP (Accounts) Regulations* are, as set out in that chapter, applied by *para 66* of *Sch 4* (see 11.17 below). (Note also the provisions as to members' annuities etc as referred to in 5.11 above.)

Approval of accounts and report

Approval of accounts

10.13   The members as a body have, as above (see 10.10), the responsibility for producing the accounts. Similarly, they have the responsibility for approving them, under *CA 2006, s 414(1)* as modified.

No process is, however, offered for how that approval is to be given for, as already noted, there is no provision for an annual general meeting, or indeed any other form of meeting, for their approval, unless one is to be put into place by the members' agreement. The *CA 2006* has followed suit in this regard by removing the requirement for a private limited company to hold an annual general meeting unless the company is required to do so by its articles of association. If not a meeting, however, by what means are the members of an LLP to signify the approval of the accounts which is needed of them since, as will be seen, such approval is not to be shown by their signing the accounts themselves?

The agreement should provide for some form of process which is demonstrable and acceptable, and affords some protection to members against any suggestion that they have approved accounts which they have not, since by *s 414(4)* if the accounts do not comply with the statutory requirements, all members may be responsible if they either knew or were reckless as to compliance and if such members either failed to take reasonable steps to secure compliance with the statutory requirements or, if applicable, to prevent the accounts from being approved.

Signing of accounts

10.14   It is, however, left for a designated member, under the modified *CA 2006, s 414(1)* to take the step of signing them off, albeit that that is on behalf of the total membership. It is the balance sheet which has to be signed, and the name of the signatory must be stated on all copies of the balance sheet. The copy of the accounts delivered to the Registrar must be so signed.

If these requirements are not complied with, then any member (ie not just any designated member) who is in default pursuant to *s 414(4)* (see 10.13 above) commits an offence. Clearly, it is in the interests of all members to ensure that all copies are properly approved and signed.

Directors' report

10.15   There is no equivalent, for LLPs, of the requirements for a directors' report, as in *s 415 et seq* of the *CA 2006*. Such a report normally requires two things, namely a fair review of the company's development during the course of the year, and its position at the end of it; and the directors' recommendations as to dividends. Clearly the latter would be inappropriate for LLPs, but it seems surprising that the former is omitted.

Unless the company is entitled to the small companies exemption, the directors' report must contain a business review. This must contain a fair review of the company's business which, taking into account the size and complexity of the business, should be a balanced and comprehensive analysis of the company's performance during the financial year. It must also show the company's position as at the end of that year, together with a description of the principal risks and uncertainties facing the company.

Although an LLP is required to submit a members' report, this is relatively restricted in nature (see 11.22 below).

The omission of all this indicates the government's view that such information is not of interest to any outsiders, eg financiers, customers or suppliers of the LLP, which seems a surprising conclusion. It is of course, open to the LLP itself to seek to pass this sort of information onto the public, whether compelled to or not and many of the larger LLPs have decided to operate on a more 'corporate' basis in this regard and to disclose some or all of this information on a voluntary basis.

Submission of accounts to auditors

10.16   The next step in the progress of the normal LLP's accounts, in theory, is that they are to be submitted to the LLP's auditors, in accordance with s 475 of the *CA 2006*, as modified. (The question of whether a particular LLP will be large enough to require the appointment of auditors is dealt with at 10.32 *et seq* below.)

In practice, of course, the accounts will have been prepared by the auditors anyway. The auditors must state whether the accounts have been properly prepared in accordance with statute, and in particular whether they present the required true and fair view of the LLP's position. The auditors' report must confirm their identity, and it and every copy of the accounts delivered and filed must be signed by the auditor (if an individual) or, in the case where the auditor is a firm, the report is required to be signed by the senior statutory auditor in his/her own name, but for and on behalf of the auditor (*CA 2006, s 503*, as modified) subject to the circumstances contemplated by *CA 2006, s 506* as modified, where the auditor may be at serious risk of violence or intimidation, and subject to compliance with the requirement of that section. If those statements and signatures are omitted, the LLP and every designated member who is in default will be treated as having committed an offence, and not the auditors themselves. As before, all members thus have an interest in ensuring proper processes are in place to ensure compliance.

Duties of auditors

10.17   In preparing their report, the auditors must observe duties imposed on them by *CA 2006, s 498* as modified. They must take into account whether:

- proper accounting records have been kept;

- adequate returns have been made by branches they have not visited; and

- the individual accounts agree with original accounting records.

If not satisfied, or if they do not get sufficient information or explanation, they must state this in their report. The requirement for such an audit is going to be new for those LLPs which are subject to it, as even those professional businesses which, like solicitors, are used to an element of audit (ie in respect of their client accounts), will not have had to suffer it in respect of their own office accounts.

There is concern as to the associated costs and resource commitments, and this may be a major possible disincentive to conversion to LLP status. It is not only LLPs which will be affected. Increasingly, for self-defensive reasons, auditors have been seeking to obtain external confirmation of companies' positions, and this has led to some controversy, eg by requesting companies' solicitors to confirm, in extremely broad terms, the legal health and freedom from threat of the company. Such attempts will no doubt be made in respect of LLPs which are subject to audit.

Delivery and distribution of accounts

Distribution to members

10.18   Once signed, the accounts must be distributed in accordance with the modified *s 423* of the *CA 2006* to:

- every member of the LLP;
- every holder of the LLP's debentures.

It is worth remembering that for this purpose 'member' will include a salaried member, and it will not therefore be possible (as still happens with some salaried partners in partnerships) for accounts to be withheld from such members. This distribution must be within nine months of the end of the relevant accounting reference period, ie the last date on which such accounts can be delivered to the Registrar or, if earlier, the date on which such accounts are actually delivered to the Registrar. If copies are sent out over a period, they are only deemed to have been sent on the last day of that period. In the event of default, the LLP itself, and every member in default, will be guilty of an offence.

Electronic publication

10.19   Although previously an LLP was able to avail itself of the *Companies Act 1985 (Electronic Communications) Order 2000 (SI 2000/3373)*, an apparent oddity of the introduction of the *CA 2006* is that the electronic communication provisions of the *CA 2006* do not apply to LLPs. The reason for this is that the government fears that, as a result of the responses it received to its consultation on the application of the *CA 2006* to LLPs, such provisions were not required. It was generally felt it should be left to the members of an LLP to decide how they would wish to communicate between themselves.

The draftsmen of the members' agreement should, therefore, ensure that it adequately provides for such methods of communication, if required by the members.

Demands for additional copies

10.20   In addition to the distribution obligations above, the LLP is obliged to provide a member or debenture holder with an extra copy of the accounts and auditors' report on demand, free of charge under the modified *s 431* of the *CA 2006*.

The additional copy must be sent within seven days of the demand. The LLP, and any member in default, will be guilty of an offence if this is not done. If, in such proceedings, the defence is raised that the demanding member has already been sent an additional copy, the burden of proof that that is so rests on the defendant.

Ancillary publication requirements

10.21   There are, in the modified ss 434 and 435 of the *CA 2006*, a number of ancillary requirements with regard to the publication of accounts by LLPs.

First, there are two restrictions with regard to the statutory accounts, each being designed to ensure that any reader of the accounts gets the full picture. On the one hand, therefore, the accounts cannot be published without the auditors' report (if applicable). On the other, if the LLP is part of a group, the individual LLP's accounts cannot be published without the accompanying statutory group accounts.

Beyond that, an LLP may wish to publish accounts (ie a profit and loss account and/or a balance sheet) which go beyond, or are differently presented from, the statutory accounts. If so, those non-statutory accounts must state that they are not the statutory accounts, and whether the relevant year's statutory accounts have been filed with the registrar. They must also exclude the auditors' report, but state whether such a report was prepared for the relevant year and, if so, whether it contained any qualification, or statement as to inadequate records etc.

'Publication', for the purpose of invoking the requirements of those sections (and s 433), is widely defined to include any form of publishing, issuing or circulating the document in a way which is available to the public and in a manner calculated to invite the public (or a class of the public) to read it. Although in this case there is no specific reference to electronic publishing, this would presumably be broad enough to include publication on a website. LLPs should therefore be careful, if publishing any form of accounting data on their websites (eg a summary profit and loss account to show how well they are doing, or the equivalent of a company's preliminary announcement or interim report), to observe the provisions of this section. Any LLP contravening the section, and any member in default, will be guilty of an offence.

Going public with the accounts

10.22   A key difference between partnerships and LLPs is the obligation to go public with the enterprise's accounts, by delivery of a copy of the accounts and, if appropriate, the auditors' report, to the Registrar, under the modified s 441 of the *CA 2006*.

There are two main areas of concern. One is the disclosure of the members' own positions, which is looked at in Chapter 11 below, dealing with specific disclosure requirements. The other is the mere fact of how the business is doing, where the fears are of the reactions of those associated with the business, eg customers or staff.

Whilst many of the larger professional practices had begun to publish their results as a matter of practice (whether or not they were legally obliged to do so) this has not been the case for the smaller to medium-sized practices, many of which have resisted and continue to resist conversion to LLP in order to protect their privacy.

Ultimately, it will, of course, be for each business to decide for itself whether the publication of accounts is too high a price to pay for the obvious advantages of LLP status.

The process of delivery of accounts

10.23 The obligation to deliver to the Registrar the LLP's signed accounts, and auditors' report if appropriate, is that of the designated members only. Accounts delivered in a language other than English must be properly translated.

(There is provision in the modified *s 1104* of the *CA 2006*, in relation to LLPs whose registered office is in Wales permitting annual accounts and auditor reports, to be delivered in Welsh, with the obligation for the production of a translation then being upon the Registrar rather than the LLP.)

The consequences of default for designated members

10.24 Potentially, all designated members who were designated members immediately before the expiry of the period during which the accounts should have been filed (not the LLP itself) are guilty of an offence if the accounts etc are not delivered within the specified period, currently nine months from the close of the financial year in most cases (*CA 2006, s 442,* as modified).

In that event, not only are designated members liable to a fine, but they also face a daily default fine for continued contravention. Further, it is possible for any member, any creditor, or the Registrar, to serve notice upon designated members in default requiring compliance, and, if that notice is not complied with, to apply to the court for an order that the designated members, or such of them as the court specifies, shall comply within such period as the court specifies. The court has, in these circumstances, power to award costs against the members of the LLP (*CA 2006, s 452(2),* modified).

There are two specific provisions as to potential defences to prosecutions for offences under this section. It is a defence for the accused to show that he/she took all reasonable steps for ensuring timely compliance. However, it is unsurprisingly not a defence to show that the requisite documents had not been prepared in the first place.

The consequences of default for the LLP

10.25   As mentioned above, there is no criminal sanction against the LLP itself for failure to deliver its accounts in time. There is, however, a civil sanction under the *Companies (Late Filing Penalties) and Limited Liability Partnerships (Filing Periods and Late Filing Penalties) Regulations 2008 SI 2008/497*, which is in addition to, not in substitution for, any liability of the designated members. This penalty is claimed by the Registrar. Again, it is no defence to say that the documents had not been prepared.

The penalty is calculated on a time basis, by reference to the gap between the time when the accounts should have been delivered, and the day when they actually are. The potential penalties are as follows:

Length of period of delay	*Amount of penalty*
Not more than one month	£150
More than one month but not more than three months	£375
More than three months but not more than six months	£750
More than six months	£1,500

It should also be noted that where the LLP had also failed to comply with the filing requirements in relation to the previous financial year *and* that previous financial year had begun on or after 6 April 2008, the penalty will be double that shown in the table.

Accounts in Euros

10.26   It is possible for accounts to be delivered and published which show the LLP's results in Euros. Members who consider that it is necessary to draw up the LLP's accounts in Euros in order to give a true and fair view of the LLP's affairs may do so without requiring the consent of any third party, ie HMRC – HMRC publishes a useful guide to assist those considering this option at www.hmrc.gov.uk/euro/faqs.

Time for delivery of accounts

10.27   As mentioned above, the normal period within which the accounts need to be delivered to the Registrar is nine months from the end of the relevant accounting reference period, under the modified *s 442* of the *CA 2006*.

If, however, the accounting reference period in question is the LLP's first, and is itself longer than a year, then the last date for delivery is the later of:

- nine months from the first anniversary of the LLP's incorporation; or

- three months from the end of the accounting reference period.

Variations of time for delivery

10.28 There are two possible variations on the above theme permissible under the modified *s 442* of the *CA 2006*.

First, if the LLP has served notice in Form LL AA01 to shorten the accounting reference period, then the period for delivery of the accounts is the later of:

- the normal (ie nine-month) period from the end of that shortened period; or

- three months from the date of Form LL AA01.

Secondly, there is provision that application may be made to the Secretary of State under *CA 2006, s 442(5)*, as modified, for an extension to the period for delivery. He/she may grant or refuse at his/her discretion, and, if he/she grants the request, shall notify the LLP of the period for such extension. There are no guidelines offered in relation to the circumstances in which such discretion is likely to be exercised in the LLP's favour.

Correction of defective accounts

Voluntary corrections

10.29 With the best will in the world, it is possible for accounts to be defective, and the legislation recognises this by allowing a number of ways for the correction of defects.

The first, in the modified *s 454* of the *CA 2006*, is an opportunity for voluntary correction, if the members (not just, it should be noted, the designated members) believe that the delivered accounts did not comply with the statutory requirements. They may then prepare and deliver revised accounts, provided that the revisions shall be confined to correcting the non-compliances and making any necessary consequential alterations.

CA 2006, s 454 as modified, provides that the *Companies (Revision of Defective Accounts and Reports) Regulations 2008 (SI 2008/373)* apply to

LLPs, as modified. These provide for the details of how the revised accounts are to be dealt with, either by way of substitution of complete accounts, or a supplemental note to the original versions. They also provide for the same penalties in respect of default as apply to the original delivery obligations.

Requirement of explanation by the Secretary of State

10.30   It may be that the Secretary of State is not satisfied that an LLP's delivered accounts (whether revised or not) comply with the statutory requirements. If so, he/she can, under the modified *s 455* of the *CA 2006*, serve notice upon the members (not the LLP itself, as the accounts are the members' responsibility) indicating the areas of his/her concern, and requiring an explanation within a specified period of not less than a month.

The Secretary of State can extend that period later if he/she thinks fit. If by the end of the period he/she is not satisfied with the explanation given (or indeed if none has been given) and if there has been no voluntary revision of the accounts, then he/she may make application to the court.

Application to court regarding defective accounts

10.31   An application, under the modified *s 456* of the *CA 2006*, may be made by the Secretary of State him/herself, or the Financial Reporting Review Panel. This application is twofold. First, it is for a declaration that the accounts do not comply with statutory requirements. Secondly, it is for an order requiring the members to prepare revised accounts.

A notice of the application, with a background statement, must be given by the applicant to the Registrar. If the court orders the preparation of revised accounts, it may give directions with regard to:

- the auditing of the accounts as revised;
- how members shall bring the revisions to the attention of third parties who may have relied upon the originals;
- such other matters as it thinks fit.

The court may also order that the costs of the application, and the extra costs incurred by the LLP itself in putting matters right, shall be borne by such of the members as were party to the original approval of the defective accounts, ie every member other than any who took all reasonable steps to prevent approval. The court's discretion in making such an order for costs and expenses is wide, and it may differentiate even amongst those members who were party to the approval. It must consider whether particular members knew, or should have known, that the accounts were defective. It may order different members to pay different amounts, and may exclude particular members from such obligations entirely, even if they were technically party to the original approval. Once proceedings are concluded, the applicant must notify the Registrar of the outcome including, where granted, a copy of the court order.

Exemptions for small and medium-sized LLPs etc

General

10.32 There are a number of exemptions from the full requirements of the *CA 2006*, in relation to accounting and auditing, which benefit 'small' and 'medium-sized' LLPs.

Broadly, these affect the requirement for audit to occur at all, the format of the LLP's accounts and the extent of disclosure of members' finances. Since the latter is one of the most contentious issues surrounding LLPs, these provisions are important to understand, as the determination of precisely which set of provisions is likely to apply if a partnership converts to an LLP could be a major factor in deciding whether to convert or not. The criteria which determine whether any particular LLP comes within these exemptions relate to turnover, the balance sheet total, and the number of employees.

Qualifying conditions

10.33 Small LLPs

Under *CA 2006, s 382* as modified, in relation to small LLPs, the qualifying conditions for any financial year will be met by an LLP if, in that year, it fulfils at least two of the three relevant criteria below unless that LLP is excluded from the small LLP regime by virtue of the *CA 2006, s 384* as modified, namely that it is an LLP whose securities are admitted to trading on a regulated market in an EEA state, a member of a group in which one of the members is a public company during that financial year, or is an authorised insurance company, a banking LLP, an e-money issuer, a MiFID investment or a UCITS management company, carries on insurance market activity or is a member of an ineligible group (see also 10.38):

Small LLP	
Turnover	Not more than £6.5 million
Balance sheet total	Not more than £3.26 million
No of employees	Not more than 50

Medium-sized LLPs

Under the modified s 465 of the *CA 2006*, the qualifying conditions for any financial year will be met by an LLP if, in that year, it fulfils two of the three criteria below:

Medium-sized LLP	
Turnover	Not more than £25.9 million
Balance sheet total	Not more than £12.9 million
No of employees	Not more than 250

If the accounting period is not one of 12 months, the maximum turnover figures are proportionately adjusted. The balance sheet total refers to total assets, not net assets. The staff numbers refer to the average number of staff employed during the year, calculated on a monthly basis (remembering that, by virtue of *LLPA 2000, s 4(4)* the members will not generally be regarded as employees for this purpose (see 6.6 above)).

When qualifying conditions need to be met

10.34 Normally, under the modified *ss 382* and *465* of the *CA 2006* (respectively), an LLP will, in order to qualify as a small or medium-sized LLP, need to meet the above criteria not only in respect of the year for which it seeks the exemption, but also the immediately preceding year. This does not apply in the LLP's first accounting year, however, ie there is no attempt to look at what the accounting position of any predecessor partnership may have been.

Exemptions for small LLPs

10.35 Generally speaking, the accounts of LLPs need to be drawn up in accordance with the very detailed provisions of *Sch 1* to the *2008 Large LLP (Accounts) Regulations*. For small LLPs, however, the less stringent requirements of *Sch 1* to the *2008 Small LLP (Accounts) Regulations* will apply, and the accounts delivered to members and debenture holders need only comply with that schedule. Further, if the members so determine, the copy accounts delivered to the Registrar need not include a profit and loss account at all although if it does this, and the accounts are not abbreviated accounts, it must state on the balance sheet that the accounts have been submitted in accordance with the small LLPs regime (*CA 2006, s 444(5)*).

Thus, the amount of information as to the LLP's affairs disclosable to the public will be very limited, though members will get more. Usual signing requirements and time limits apply to the shortened accounts, and they must also contain a statement that they have been prepared under the small LLPs exemption provisions.

Exemptions for medium-sized LLPs

10.36   As might be expected, the extent of the exemptions for medium-sized LLPs are less generous.

Such an LLP's accounts need to be produced under the general requirements of the *2008 Large LLP (Accounts) Regulations, Sch 1,* but do not need to give a statement as to whether they have been prepared in accordance with applicable accounting standards, or whether there have been any material departures from such standards. This applies to the accounts whether sent to members etc, or delivered to the Registrar. In relation to the latter there are also other relaxations, namely that most sources of income can be presented as one item, rather than being particularised. Any accounts which take advantage of this exemption must bear a statement to that effect.

Authorised persons under the Financial Services and Markets Act 2000

10.37   Despite the exemptions in the previous paragraphs, there are however certain types of business where it is judged to be against the public interest to allow anything less than full public disclosure of the LLP's financial position. The ambit of the above exemptions is accordingly limited by *CA 2006, s 384* (as modified) in relation to the small LLPs regime and *CA 2006, s 467* (as modified) in relation to medium-sized LLPs.

The first, and potentially most important of those restrictions, under *s 467(1)(b)(i)* is where the LLP had, at any time during the financial year in question, permission to carry on a 'regulated activity' under the *Financial Services and Markets Act 2000*. That removes the benefit of the medium-sized exemptions from those solicitors' and accountants' LLPs which are directly regulated by the Financial Services Authority. Note that those firms whose investment business is purely ancillary to their normal work, and who are simply registered with the Financial Services Authority, are not affected and can still claim the benefit of the exemption.

Other businesses which cannot take advantage of the above exemptions

10.38   Section 10.33 has already highlighted those other businesses which are excluded from the small LLPs regime. In relation to medium-sized LLPs, the other relevant restrictive provisions are *s 467(1)(a)* (as modified) excluding LLPs whose securities are admitted to trading on a regulated market in an EEA state and *s 467(1)(b)(ii)* excluding LLPs which carry on an insurance market activity. *Section 467(2)* (as modified) further provides that a group is ineligible for the exemptions for the reasons set out in that section including, if any of its members is:

- a public company;

- a body corporate (other than a company) able to offer shares or debentures to the public;

- a person who carries on an insurance market activity;

- permitted under the *Financial Services and Markets Act 2000* to carry on a regulated activity.

Sections 383(1) and *466(1)* of the *CA 2006* state that a parent LLP will not qualify unless the whole of its group complies as a small or medium-sized group (as the case may be), as set out below.

Small and medium-sized groups

10.39 *Sections 383* and *466* of the *CA 2006*, as modified, introduce the concept that not only may an individual LLP be considered as small or medium-sized (as the case may be), but so may a group.

The requirements for qualification as a small group are set out at *CA 2006, s 383)*, as modified, and for a medium-sized group at *s 466*, as modified. The principles and amounts are similar to those for individual LLPs, but the idea is introduced of being able to consider either gross or net figures. 'Net' in this context means after making the set-offs and other adjustments provided for in *Pt 1* of *Sch 4* to the *2008 Small LLP (Accounts) Regulations* or *Sch 3* to the *2008 Large LLP (Accounts) Regulations* (as the case may be). The LLP can use whichever of the gross or net figures is more favourable to it. Figures are aggregated across the whole group. To qualify in any year, the group must be able to satisfy two or more of the qualifying conditions. The qualifying conditions are:

Small group	
Aggregate turnover	Not more than £6.5 million net, or £7.8 million gross.
Aggregate balance-sheet total	Not more than £3.26 million net, or £3.9 million gross
Aggregate number of employees	Not more than 50
Medium-sized group	
Aggregate turnover	Not more than £25.9 million net, or £31.1 million gross
Aggregate balance sheet total	Not more than £12.9 million net, or £15.5 million gross
Aggregate number of employees	Not more than 250

The provisions for the years in which the group needs to qualify are the same as for individual LLPs, save that the reference to the first financial year is to that of the parent LLP. The accounts for the subsidiaries, which fall to be aggregated, are those for the financial years being either coincident with the parent's financial year, or ending last before the end of the parent's financial year, save that if those figures cannot be obtained without disproportionate expense or undue delay, the last available figures shall be taken.

Exemptions for small groups

10.40   Under *CA 2006, s 398* as modified, an LLP which is subject to the small LLPs regime and which is also a parent LLP may opt to prepare group accounts in addition to its own individual accounts but it is not obliged to do so. The previous exemption in *CA 1985, s 248* from preparation of group accounts by a parent company which heads up a medium-sized group was removed in the *CA 2006*, following on from the 2004 increase in financial thresholds for those groups.

Exemptions from audit requirements

10.41   Sitting alongside the above exemptions from certain requirements as to the contents of the accounts are some exemptions as to the requirements for the auditing of those accounts.

These exemptions use, but build upon, the above definition of a small LLP for their applicability. Thus, under the modified *s 477* of the *CA 2006*, in respect of any financial year, an LLP will be deemed to be totally exempt from the requirement for any form of audit if, using the same principles of calculation as are referred to in 10.33 above, it not only qualifies as a small LLP, but also has a turnover of not more than £6.5 million and a balance sheet total of not more than £3.26 million.

If exempt under these provisions (or the provisions referred to in 10.44 below), the accounts themselves need not (under *s 444(2)* of the *CA 2006*, as modified in relation to small LLPs and *s 445(2)* of the *CA 2006*, as modified, in relation to medium-sized LLPs) refer to an auditors' report in the copies for members and debenture holders, or include such a report in the copy delivered to the Registrar.

Cases where the audit exemption does not apply

10.42   There are a number of types of LLP to which the above exemption (see 10.41) cannot, however, apply. Under *s 478* of the *CA 2006*, as modified, these are:

- an LLP whose securities are admitted to trading on a regulated market in an EEA state;

- an LLP which has carried on an 'insurance market activity';

- an LLP which is an authorised insurance company, a banking LLP or an e-money issuer, a MiFID investment firm, or a UCITS management company;

- an employers' association as defined in s 122 of the *Trade Union and Labour Relations (Consolidation) Act 1992*

in each case, at any time during the financial year in question.

Further provisions relating to members of a group

10.43 *Section 479* of the *CA 2006*, as modified, qualifies *s 477* in two sets of circumstances. Thus an LLP which is a subsidiary undertaking will not lose its audit exemption for a year if it was dormant during that year.

Further, an LLP which is either a parent LLP or a subsidiary undertaking will not lose its audit exemption if it was a member of a group meeting certain additional qualifications. Those qualifications are:

- that the group qualifies as a small group (see 10.40 above);

- that it is not an ineligible group (see 10.39 above);

- that its aggregate turnover in the year is not more than £6.5 million net or £7.8 million gross;

- that its aggregate balance sheet total is not more than £3.26 million net or £3.9 million gross.

In short, therefore, for an LLP which is a member of a group to qualify for the audit exemption, the whole group must qualify.

Exemptions for dormant LLPs

10.44 *Section 480* of the *CA 2006*, as modified, introduces the concept of a dormant LLP, and includes the possibility of an LLP which has been dormant since its foundation.

This latter concept in particular seems not to sit well with the requirements of *LLPA 2000, s 2(1)* that the incorporation document must contain a declaration that two or more members have 'associated for carrying on a lawful business with a view to profit'. Nonetheless, this provision in *CA 2006* allows an exemption from the audit requirements of that Act if the LLP has thus been dormant since incorporation, or has been dormant since the end of the previous year, provided that it both qualifies as a small LLP (see 10.33 above) or would be so entitled but for the fact that it is a member of an ineligible group and does not have to prepare group accounts for the year in question. This exemption does not however apply to all LLPs and those LLPs ineligible to take advantage are listed at *CA 2006, s 481*, as modified.

For an LLP to be considered 'dormant' it must not during the year in question have had any 'significant' accounting transaction, ie one which needs recording under the general accounting duties under *CA 2006, s 386*, as modified (see 10.6 above) other than payment of fees to the Registrar for a change of name or for the filing of an annual return, or a penalty for late delivery of accounts.

Statements by LLPs exempt from audit requirements

10.45 If an LLP is entitled to take advantage of any of the above audit exemptions, then by *s 475(2), (3)* and *(4)* of the *CA 2006*, as modified, the balance sheet prepared must contain a statement by the members as to the exemption which is being taken advantage of, and confirming that the members acknowledge their responsibility for proper keeping of accounting records, and preparing accounts in accordance with the statute which give a true and fair view of the LLP's position.

This statement must appear in the balance sheet above the signature to the accounts (see 10.14 above).

Auditors

Introduction

10.46 The provisions of the *CA 2006* applying to auditors can be found in the remaining chapters of *CA 2006, Pt 16* as applied to LLPs by the *2008 Regulations*.

Not all of the provisions in relation to auditors are applied to LLPs. Amongst those so included are *ss 485* to *488, 492* and *494*, as modified, which deal with the role of auditors in the LLP context. Much is written in all the standard texts on company law as to the position, rights and especially obligations and duties of auditors. This topic is beyond the scope of this work, as an auditor's duty to an LLP client will not differ from his/her duty to a company.

Duty to appoint auditors

10.47 By *s 485* of the *CA 2006*, as modified, each LLP must appoint an auditor or auditors, unless the designated members determined, acting reasonably that it is unlikely that the accounts will need to be audited by virtue of the available exemptions (see 10.41 above).

Eligibility for appointment

10.48 It is beyond the scope of this work to go into detail as to auditors' qualifications, but suffice it to say that any auditor as defined by *CA*

2006, s 1210(1) (as modified) will be able to audit an LLP's accounts. This qualification may well pose a practical problem for many partnerships considering conversion, particularly for those which are at the smaller end of the market but do not actually rate as 'small' within the statutory provision, and for their advisers. Such firms may well, for many years, have been very satisfied with the services provided by their accountants, who may not themselves be registered auditors. It would be natural for them to turn to those advisers for input as to the merits or otherwise of conversion. This must create a conflict of interest for such advisers since, if they recommend conversion, they are in practice likely to lose the client. This conflict may be unavoidable, but is something of which both sides should be aware.

Appointment of auditors by designated members

10.49   For a financial year of the LLP for which such an appointment is needed (not necessarily, of course, the first year of the LLP's existence if exemptions are initially available to it), the appointment must be made at least 28 days before the earlier of the end of the time allowed for sending the LLP's accounts and auditor's report for the previous financial year and the date on which such accounts are actually sent out (see 10.18).

The appointment of the first auditor is reserved by *CA 2006, s 485*, as modified, to the designated members. Thereafter, the members are authorised to appoint the auditor (*CA 2006, s 485(4)*, as modified).

Appointment of auditors by members

10.50   The situation could however arise where the designated members fail to comply with their statutory duty (see 10.49 above). Such failure does not of itself render the designated members liable to prosecution.

Section 485(4) allows the members in this situation to step in and appoint an auditor if the designated members have failed to do so. An apparent problem with this right, however, is that there is no period of grace. Presumably, therefore, it cannot be said that the designated members have failed to exercise their powers until the very last day upon which it would be legitimate for them to do so.

Appointment by Secretary of State if designated members default

10.51   The difficulty mentioned in 10.50 above is compounded by the fact that the members are not the only ones who can act to fill the gap. So can the Secretary of State, under *CA 2006, s 486* as modified. Further, it is incumbent on the LLP, if appointment has not been made by the due date, to serve notice of that fact upon the Secretary of State within seven days of the last day for appointment, and failure to give such notice renders the LLP itself, and every designated member who is in default, liable to prosecution and, in addition to normal remedies, to a daily default fine.

If, therefore, the members of an LLP have given the designated members until the last day for appointment and then, on the designated members' default, have served a notice convening a meeting 21 days later, and have served the statutorily required notice upon the Secretary of State, it would appear at least theoretically possible for the members and the Secretary of State each to make a valid appointment of auditors. This may all sound far-fetched, but it does reinforce the need for the membership generally to ensure that they have the right, under the members' agreement, to know what is happening in this regard, and the ability to act promptly to remedy any default on the part of the designated members.

Filling casual vacancies

10.52   If a casual vacancy occurs in the office of auditor, this may be filled by the designated members. If there was initially a joint appointment, any surviving or continuing auditor may continue to act, which may be a point commending joint appointments where possible.

The relevant provisions here are found at *CA 2006, ss 485(3)(c) and 526,* as modified.

Appointment where exemptions expire

10.53   If it becomes apparent that an LLP, which was previously exempt as 'small' or 'dormant' from the requirement to appoint auditors, has ceased to be exempt, then *CA 2006, s 485(3)(b)*, as modified, provides for the appointment of auditors by the designated members.

The obligation on the designated members is to make such appointment 'at any time' before the LLP's next period for appointing auditors. The provisions of the modified *CA 2006, s 485(4)* gives the membership generally the power to appoint in the event of default by the designated members. There is, however, the same difficulty as is mentioned at 10.50 above as to not being able to point to any particular moment when default occurs.

Auditors' rights to information

10.54   Once appointed, auditors acquire wide-ranging powers of enquiry under *s 499* and *500* of the *CA 2006*, as modified. They have a right of access, at all times, to all the LLP's financial documentation, and are entitled to require all members and employees of the LLP to supply such information and explanation of any matter as they think fit. Any member who, knowingly or recklessly, gives any such information or explanation which is misleading, false, or deceptive, commits an offence (*CA 2006, s 501* as modified).

Similarly, any subsidiary undertaking and its auditor may be required to give information or explanation and, if it fails to do so, it is guilty of an offence, as is any auditor who fails to comply without reasonable excuse.

Auditors' rights to attend meetings

10.55   An LLP's auditors are entitled (but not obliged), under *CA 2006, s 502* as modified, to attend meetings of the LLP in certain circumstances.

This sounds unexceptionable, but the difficulty once again is that the Act and the legislation incorporated into it make virtually no provision for meetings of the LLP. The rights apply to any meetings where any part of the business to be conducted concerns the auditors in their statutory functions. They are entitled to receive notices of and communications concerning the meeting as if a member, and to attend and be heard at the meeting in respect of the relevant part(s) of it. If the chosen auditor is itself a body corporate or a partnership, it needs to nominate, in writing, an individual to attend such a meeting on its behalf.

Remuneration for audit work

10.56   The remuneration of the auditors for their work in their capacity as auditors shall normally be fixed by the LLP, as provided by *CA 2006, s 492* as modified.

The statute provides that the decision shall be taken by the designated members, or in such manner as the members of the LLP may determine. It would thus be open to the LLP, in its members' agreement, to leave the decision to the designated members or, at opposite ends of the spectrum, to delegate the decision to a particular member (eg the equivalent of a finance director), or to reserve it to the membership generally.

If the auditor is appointed by the Secretary of State (see 10.51 above) he/she determines the remuneration. The LLP's accounts must state the amount paid to the auditors as remuneration for their audit work, which for these purposes includes expenses and any benefits in kind (which must be stated and valued).

Disclosure of auditors' remuneration

10.57   *Section 494 of CA 2006*, as modified, applies to LLPs so that the *Companies (Disclosure of Auditor Remuneration and Liability Limitation Agreements) Regulations 2008 (SI 2008/489)* (as amended) will require an

LLP to disclose in its accounts the fees paid to auditors for audit and non-audit services. These regulations were recently amended in 2011 (by *SI 2011/2198*) for the purpose of re-classifying certain audit and non-audit services to large LLPs and groups. This came as a result of concerns raised about the fees paid to auditors for non-audit services in the run-up to the financial crisis. The revised classification of non-audit services has been introduced to identify possible threats to auditors' independence in line with auditors' own ethical standards.

Removal of auditors

10.58   There could be many, perfectly proper, reasons for getting rid of a particular firm of auditors. The problem is that there could also be one very improper reason, namely that they are doing too good a job, and asking questions which those being audited are neither willing to have asked, nor to answer.

For the protection of others associated with the business, and its creditors, there need accordingly to be special safeguards built into the process of removal of auditors. Whilst, *CA 2006, s 510* as modified, therefore, gives the members the right at any time to remove an auditor from office (subject, of course, to any contractual consequences which may flow from that removal), the LLP is also required to give notice of that removal to the Registrar within 14 days on form LL AA02, failing which the LLP and every designated member of it who is in default will be guilty of an offence. Note that under the previous correspondence provisions of the *CA 1985 (s 391)* it was the designated members who were given the authority to remove the auditors. This power has now been passed to all of the members.

Rights of removed auditors

10.59   The members who seek to remove an auditor from office, during his/her term of office are required to give the auditor at least seven days' notice (*CA 2006, s 511*, as modified).

Under *CA 2006, s 513* as modified, the auditor in question still has the theoretical right to attend any meeting of the LLP at which his/her term of office would otherwise have expired, or at which his/her replacement is to be proposed. Unlike a company where such a resolution can only be passed at a general meeting of that company, there is no such requirement on an LLP (it being free to regulate its affairs as its members see fit). Therefore, the members could deal with such removal by way of written resolution, thus avoiding the requirement for a meeting at all, rendering this protection relatively useless.

More useful is that the auditor being so removed, or not being re-appointed, may make representations of reasonable length to the LLP, and request that they be distributed to all members. That request must be complied with by the LLP upon receipt. There is, however, a protective ability for the LLP, or any other aggrieved person (not even necessarily a member) to apply to the court for relief against the obligation thus to circulate the auditors' representations, on the grounds that the auditors' rights are being abused to secure 'needless publicity for defamatory matter'. On considering such an application, the court has discretion to award the LLP's costs (whether or not it is actually a party to the application) wholly or partly against the auditor.

Resignation of auditors

10.60 Similarly, whilst an auditor's resignation may be for any one of a number of perfectly normal reasons, it might be because of his/her concern at wrongdoing within the LLP, and therefore protection again needs to be built in. By ss 516 and 519 of the CA 2006, both as modified, an auditor can resign at any time by depositing at the LLP's registered office:

- notice of resignation; and

- a statement of any circumstances, connected with his/her resignation, which he/she considers should be brought to the attention of the LLP's members or creditors (or, if all is well, that there are no such circumstances).

The notice of resignation is not effective unless accompanied by the statement. An effective notice may take effect either on the date it is deposited, or on such later date as it specifies. The LLP must then send a copy to the registrar within 14 days, or it, and every designated member in default, will be guilty of an offence.

Rights of resigning auditors

10.61 If, in the statement referred to above, a resigning auditor has indicated that he/she believes there are circumstances which should be brought to the attention of the LLP's members or creditors, then he/she may at the same time, under s 518 of the CA 2006, as modified, deposit with the LLP a notice requiring the designated members to convene a meeting of all members.

The purpose of the meeting is for him/her to give such explanation of the circumstances surrounding his/her resignation as he/she thinks fit. The designated members must act to call the meeting within 21 days of the notice from the auditor requiring them so to do, and the meeting must be not later than 28 days from the date of the notice calling it. If this does not happen, every designated member who did not take all reasonable steps to ensure that a properly convened meeting was called will be guilty of an offence.

Auditors' statement to members

10.62   The auditor may also, then or later, request the LLP to circulate to all members a statement of reasonable length of the relevant circumstances, in advance of the meeting. If this is not delivered too late for circulation to be practical, the LLP must then state in any notice of the meeting that such a statement has been made and circulate copies.

If it is not so circulated, either because the designated members fail to comply with their obligations, or because it was delivered too late, the auditor may require it to be read at the meeting. He/she is in any event entitled to attend the meeting. Similar rights to those referred to in 10.61 above, for the LLP or any aggrieved person to apply to the court in respect of an allegedly defamatory statement, apply.

Deposit of statement of circumstances

10.63   Reference has been made in 10.62 above to the deposit of a statement by a resigning auditor. That obligation not only applies, however, to the act of resignation, but also to a decision by the auditor simply not to seek re-appointment, or to removal by the designated members or their failure to reappoint.

If the auditor does not seek re-appointment, the statement must be deposited not less than 14 days before the designated members' time for appointing his/her successor runs out; and if there is any other cause, it must be deposited not later than 14 days after his/her term of office expires. If an outgoing auditor fails to comply with this obligation, he/she is guilty of an offence, unless he/she can show that he/she took all reasonable steps and exercised all reasonable diligence (*CA 2006, s 519, as modified*).

Distribution of statement

10.64   If the statement is to the effect that there are circumstances which the auditor believes should be brought to the attention of members or creditors, then the LLP has 14 days from the date of the statement's deposit to make a choice. It can either distribute the statement to all members, and all holders of debentures from the LLP; or it may apply to the court, and notify the auditor of that application (*CA 2006, s 520(2) (3), as modified*). If it fails to do either then every designated member in default, will be guilty of an offence (*CA 2006, s 520(6), as modified*).

To complete the loop, the auditor must, unless within 21 days of deposit of the statement he/she is notified by the LLP of an application to the court, send a copy of his/her statement to the Registrar within a further seven days (*CA 2006, s 521, as modified*).

The court's powers on application

10.65   The court's powers on an application under the modified *CA 2006, s 520(2)* (see 10.64 above) are similar to those referred to in 10.59 above. There are basically two possible outcomes, depending on whether the court is satisfied that the auditor is using the statement to secure needless publicity for defamatory matter.

If it is so satisfied, it shall direct that copies of the statement shall not be sent out; and it may order the auditor (even though not a party to the application) to pay the LLP's costs in whole or in part. In that event the LLP must, within 14 days of the court's order, send to all members and debenture holders a statement setting out its effect. If, however, the court does not believe the allegation of a defamatory reason, the LLP must within 14 days of the court's decision to that effect send copies of the auditor's statement to all members and debenture holders, and notify the auditor of the court's decision. Again, in those circumstances, it is for the auditor to complete the loop by sending the notification of the court's decision to the registrar within seven days of receipt.

Power of court to grant relief from auditor's liability

10.66   The final provision of the legislation relating to auditors is found in *s 1157* of the *CA 2006* (as modified). It deals with the situation where an auditor seeks relief from what would otherwise be a finding of fault against him/her.

The section can apply to any proceedings against the auditor (whoever the claimant may be) for negligence, default, breach of duty or breach of trust. If the court holds the view that the auditor is, or may be, liable for such an act or omission, it may nonetheless relieve him/her, either wholly or partly, from that liability, either absolutely, or on such conditions as it thinks fit. To do so, it must be satisfied that the auditor has acted honestly and reasonably, and that, in all the circumstances, he/she ought so to be excused.

There is also a power for the auditor, if he/she is fearful that such proceedings may be brought against him/her, to apply in advance for such relief, and the court has the same powers in respect of such a pre-emptive application as it would have on a substantive one.

Supplementary matters

Accounting standards

10.67   Statutory force is given to the concept of the establishment of accounting standards, set by various accountancy bodies, by *CA 2006,* *s 464*, as modified. The section applies the *Accounting Standards (Prescribed Body) Regulations 2008 (SI 2008/651)* to LLPs. In an LLP's case, the standards will be such as are relevant to its particular circumstances and accounts. In practice, the LLP will be governed by a range of Financial Reporting Standards and, importantly, by the Statement of Recommended Practice which, as mentioned elsewhere in this work, has been published by the Consultative Committee of Accountancy Bodies – see Appendix 3.

Such standards may be expected to play an even greater role in future, as the government believes that they should increasingly supplement formal Parliamentary regulation, since they are considered more flexible and more reflective of best professional practice.

Parent and subsidiary undertakings

10.68   *Sections 1161* and *1162* of the *CA 2006*, as modified, deal with the relevant definitions in respect of those LLPs which are linked to each other, or to other organisations, as a 'parent' or an 'undertaking', as referred to in various places, such as accounting groups.

The basic concept is that of an 'undertaking' which can be either:

- a body corporate, whether:
  - a limited company, or
  - an LLP;
- an unincorporated association carrying on a trade or business, whether for profit or not.

In other words it will encompass just about every sort of business other than a sole trader or practitioner.

An undertaking, A, is the parent of a subsidiary undertaking, B, if:

- A holds a majority of the voting rights in B; or
- A is a member of B and has the right to appoint or remove a majority of its board of directors;
- A has the right to exercise a dominant influence over B, either:
  - by virtue of provisions in B's memorandum or articles or the members' agreement; or
  - by virtue of a contract giving it such control;
- A is a member in B and controls alone, pursuant to an agreement with other shareholders or members, a majority of the voting rights in B;
- A actually exercises or has the power to exercise a dominant influence over B; or
- A and B are managed on a unified basis.

For these purposes, there is no specific indication that a majority of the members of an LLP would be regarded as equivalent to the board of directors of a company, but on the other hand there is the general provision in *reg 5(2)(b)* of the *2001 Regulations* (albeit in relation to the *IA 1986*) that references to directors include references to members of an LLP, so this would seem to bring LLPs within this limb of the definition. Similarly, *reg 5(2)(e)* equates a members' agreement to a company's articles of association. An undertaking can be regarded as a member of another even if its membership is indirect, ie through the medium either of another subsidiary undertaking, or by a nominee holding shares in the ultimate subsidiary.

Reference to the holding of shares, in the case of an LLP, ie an undertaking which does not have share capital, but does have capital, will be to rights to share in the capital of the LLP.

Chapter 11

Members' Financial Interests

11.1 This chapter looks in detail at one of the most controversial aspects of the LLP legislation, namely the accounting treatment of members' personal financial interests in the LLP, and the requirements for public disclosure of those interests. The former throws up some unexpected differences from the treatment of partnership accounts, which may require readers of an LLP's accounts to be educated in their true meaning. The impact of this disclosure varies considerably according to the size of the LLP, and those variances are considered fully. Overall, the examination in the chapter suggests that the burden is not as heavy as many may fear, and should not in many cases prove a disincentive to the conversion of existing businesses into LLP format.

Introduction

11.2 In many ways, it would have been logical for the contents of this chapter to have been considered in Chapter 10, along with the rest of the requirements for the format of an LLP's accounts.

However, frequently, businessmen and professionals considering converting to or trading as an LLP have been concerned above all with the question of their personal financial positions in relation to the LLP, and the extent of their obligation publicly to disclose those positions, so it was decided to give the topic particular prominence by allotting a chapter to it. Some 12 years on since the introduction of the *LLPA 2000*, concern over the requirement to disclose such information is still given as one of the key reasons as to why partners in traditional partnerships have still not converted to LLP status.

The underlying principles

11.3 From the outset, having determined to take the LLP legislation down the route of a body corporate, rather than a sub-species of partnership remaining an unincorporated undertaking, the government was clear that the price to be paid for the protection which limited liability status would afford members of an LLP was to be the obligation to make some disclosure.

The government's intention in doing so was not that those examining the accounts should know everything about members' finances; but rather that they should be able, by examining the accounts, to consider the overall financial health of the LLP, and how that was matched by the members' own willingness to invest their funds in it. In other words, this is intended to give reassurance to those dealing with the LLP that, notwithstanding its limitation of liability, their chances of having their contracts honoured are reasonable.

The degree of disclosure

11.4   In light of the government's intention, the legislation is not particularly concerned with information as to the position regarding any individual member, but rather with the members' aggregate position.

After all, the situation with an LLP, where the two constituencies are the members and outside contracting parties, is markedly different from that relating to a company, where there are three interested groups, ie the directors, the shareholders and outside parties. In that scenario, it is the need for protection of the shareholders from exploitation by the directors for their own benefit that gives rise to many of the detailed disclosure requirements (though how effective those are in the real world is a matter of some debate).

Comparison with other jurisdictions

11.5   Mention was made earlier in the book of the development of the LLP idea from the model of the US version of the concept, both initially by individual states, and later, by means of the application of the revised *Uniform Partnership Act*. An LLP in the US is not, unlike the UK, a newly created and separately incorporated body. It is simply a development of the existing partnership which determines to avail itself of limited liability protection. As such, it is not necessary for it to make any public declarations of its finances, any more than it is for a partnership (save that some states have minimum capital and/or insurance requirements).

Therefore there were some pleas to the effect that, if UK LLPs' members had to make personal disclosures which their overseas rivals did not, that would put them at a commercial disadvantage. Such pleas fell on deaf governmental ears.

Requirements for non-exempt LLPs – the balance sheet

11.6   As mentioned in Chapter 10, the requirements of LLPs vary according to the business's size. To start with, therefore, the position is that applying where there are no exemptions available to the LLP. That being so, its accounts will fall to be prepared under *Pts 15* and *16* of the *CA 2006* (as modified) and *Sch 1* to the *2008 Large LLP (Accounts) Regulations*.

The *2008 Large LLP (Accounts) Regulations* offer two options for the format to be adopted for the layout of the balance sheet. For these purposes, it makes no difference which is chosen. In each format, two main headings relevant to the disclosure of members' interests are given, namely 'Loans and other debts due to members', and 'Members' other interests'. Each of those headings is then split, either by note (10) in the first main heading, or in the balance sheet itself in the second main heading, into three sub-headings which have to be shown separately, as follows:

- Loans and other debts due to members:

  o the aggregate amount of money advanced to the LLP by the members by way of loan;

  o the aggregate amount of money owed to members by the LLP in respect of profits;

  o any other amounts.

- Members' other interests:

  o members' capital;

  o revaluation reserve;

  o other reserves.

Loans etc

11.7 The provisions clearly draw a distinction between capital on the one hand, and other amounts owed to members on the other. The first grouping is of the amount which the members would be entitled, on the face of it, to require to be repaid to them. There is no requirement to state whether there are any provisions restricting their right to take these monies out, eg by limiting the circumstances in which loans can be repaid, or requiring members to leave undrawn profits in the business. The presumption in the outsider's mind must therefore be that these monies would rank equally with any debt owed to him/her by the LLP (since, unlike in a partnership scenario, the LLP and the members will be separate legal entities, and the members will have the same rights as any other creditor, depending on whether or not they have taken any security, as they would be entitled to do (subject to the usual requirements as to registration of charges etc)).

Amongst the 'other debts' which may be owed to members, and which will therefore be covered by this section, according to the SORP (see Appendix 3 and 10.4 above), are:

- any unpaid element of 'members' remuneration charged as an expense', ie where the members' agreement provides for automatic allocation and division of profits, but not all has been drawn;

- any profits which have been the subject of a discretionary allocation during the year, but have not been paid;

- such of the members' 'capital' as is classed as a liability (see 11.9 below).

The SORP specifies that the layout of the information required under this heading should show the amounts brought forward from the previous year, the changes during the year, and the closing position.

Members' other interests

11.8   The heading 'Members' other interests' (see 11.6 above), and the three items in it, seem oriented more to what may be considered long-term investment in the business, and, by means of the inclusion of reserves, of the true, rather than nominal values of that investment.

The amounts to be shown in these headings will however only be such elements as are classed as equity, not liability (see 11.9 below).

One aspect to be aware of is that, according to the SORP, profits earned by the LLP but not yet allocated or divided will belong to the LLP until it is so allocated or divided and will, consequently, be regarded as included in 'other reserves' and thus an equivalent to capital. In some ways, in terms of third-party protection, the distinction is artificial, since capital can be withdrawn just as loans can (but either would be subject to the special provisions requiring repayment of withdrawals found in *s 214A* of the *IA 1986*, discussed at length in Chapter 17).

Members' rights – liability or equity?

11.9   A major difference between the original SORP and the current version is the approach to analysing the rights of members in the monies within the LLP. In the original version, as with a partnership, the monies which the members invested in the LLP, if not otherwise classified, were regarded as capital, and hence shown as an asset of the business. Now, it is necessary to separate monies out into those which are regarded as truly the unfettered property of the LLP; and those which it will at some time have to repay to the members, eg on retirement, resignation or death. The former remain classified as equity; but the latter are regarded now as a liability of the LLP, and will be shown as such. Where, therefore, the members' agreement is to the effect that all members are entitled to be repaid their 'capital account' at some time, there will be no equity capital at all. This apparently extraordinary conclusion may take some explaining to readers of an LLP's balance sheet.

Indeed, the point goes further. It has been accepted from the outset that it is technically possible for an LLP to grant to its members a debenture in respect of loans made by them to it, thus preferring them over the unsecured creditors in the event of a winding up. On the other hand, it was thought that members' capital, not being a debt due to them, was incapable of such treatment, and indeed would rank after creditors' claims. If, however, the 'capital' is to be classed as a debt due from the LLP to the members, what is the conceptual objection to this being secured by like means? The point is open to argument, at the very least.

Note that there is no default rule allowing a member to withdraw his/her contribution on leaving the LLP (see 8.24 above) and, therefore, where the LLP is operating in circumstances where the default rules apply and/or where they have not agreed anything to the contrary with regard to the withdrawal of their contribution, then these contributions will be classed as equity.

Members' post-retirement benefits

11.10   A large proportion of the revised SORP is devoted to the treatment of post-retirement benefits payable to members. In general terms, all these provisions operate to make an LLP's books look worse than would otherwise be the case. For some businesses thinking of converting from partnership to LLP status, this sole factor may be enough for them to have to rethink either the provision of such benefits, or the idea of conversion. In short, the balance sheet will have to show the capitalised value of any such rights as have accrued, as a liability of the business. Since no countervailing asset exists, the effect may be to depress the asset base of the business markedly. Since, under the new rules requiring much or all of what was previously thought to be an asset, in terms of members' capital, as a liability, such further reduction might in many cases tip an LLP's accounts into capital deficit.

If an entitlement in reality creates an obligation to pay what would commonly be termed an annuity (whatever it may be dressed up as) then it will need to be provided for, whether its term and amount are pre-determined or unknown. Under the revised SORP, this provision needs to be made not only for annuities which are already payable, eg because a former member has died or retired, but also for those which will become payable in future. Where a member earns his/her annuity rights over a period, the eventual costs to the business which will result from that gradual accretion need to be recognised every year. Amongst the drawbacks of this approach is that it is likely that the amount of the provision will need to be calculated by actuaries every year, and there will of course be direct costs of that exercise.

The amount thus recognised in respect of current and past members will not just be relevant for the balance sheet, but also for the profit and loss account (see 11.11 below). For the former, the annual amount will be included under the heading 'Members' remuneration charged as an expense', and for the latter it will be with other expenses.

Similarly, in the balance sheet, the liability in respect of current members will be shown under 'Loans and other debts due to members'; whereas that in respect of former members will be included in general creditors, as 'Post-retirement payments to former members'.

Profit and loss accounts

11.11   In *Sch 1* to the *2008 Large LLP (Accounts) Regulations*, there are again two possible formats for profit and loss accounts which are available for LLPs, but again there is no difference between them in this respect.

Allocation of profits under the initial SORP

11.12   In the original SORP, the concept was introduced of the 'allocation' of profits. Essentially, any profits earned by the corporate LLP belong to it, until a positive act is taken to change that position. What was perhaps surprising initially was that, even where:

- there was an agreement as to the proportions in which paid profits would be divided, and

- there were payments out of monies to the members according to that ratio,

there was nonetheless no 'allocation' of profits, in the absence of a separate decision to allocate. Indeed, the legal opinion of Robin Potts QC given in June 2001 in relation to the original SORP confirmed that the legislation supported this view and that *reg 7(1)* of the *2001 Regulations* (see 8.7 above) only provided for how the capital and profits of the LLP would be shared and did not constitute a default rule as to the actual division of profits as between the members.

In that scenario, therefore, the accounting treatment was that the entirety of the profits earned by the LLP were shown as an asset of it, represented as to part by the monies it held in respect of the undistributed portion of the profits, and the debt owed by the members to the LLP in respect of those monies which they had taken (as drawings). In other words, those who had been used to the partnership concept of 'drawings' had to get used to the idea that they were in effect borrowing from the LLP, on account of profits to be allocated to them at some future date and, in practice, such monies constituted a debt due to the LLP until such allocation had taken place.

There were, however, two ways in which that could be alleviated. At the other extreme of the spectrum, the members' agreement could provide that, at any time when payments were made to the members, there was a deemed automatic interim allocation of the whole thereof. Alternatively, as a half-way step, there could be periodic interim allocations of profit determined by the LLP as it went through the year (eg in relation to the level of drawings taken). Many firms have adopted the approach of only allocating profits in relation to a particular year upon approval of the annual accounts for that year, which is likely to occur many months after the financial year end. The risk of this approach if that until such allocation, the profits belong to the LLP and if there is an intervening period that prevents such allocation, eg insolvency, then it may be that such profits are never allocated, leaving the members with large overdrawn loan accounts that they are likely to be asked to repay.

No particular formality is required for an allocation, and in most cases this will be something like a minute of a members' meeting, accompanied by the consequent book-keeping entry to show the change in the nature of funds. But care is needed to ensure that the members' agreement (if indeed there is one) supports this practice. If not, and for example, the members' agreement provisions allow for automatic allocation only when the annual accounts have been approved, then this practice would constitute a variation to the members' agreement and the relevant provisions as to the procedure for varying the members' agreement would need to be complied with.

The practical effect of this was that the year-end figures for any LLP would depend very much on the policy as to allocations decided upon by it. This can be illustrated by thinking of an LLP with five members which, during the course of the year, makes a profit of £120,000; and which allows its members each to take £2,000 per month from the business. There are three possibilities:

- If it made no allocations until after the year end, eg until after it had seen the draft accounts, then at the end of the year its balance sheet would show an asset of £120,000, consisting of monies owed to it by the members. This would be so even if such monies had subsequently been distributed to the members prior to approval of the annual accounts.

- If it made quarterly allocations of £20,000, its balance sheet would show an asset of just £40,000, ie the £120,000 paid to members, less the £80,000 allocated (which would be treated as an expense within the profit and loss account (see 11.13 below)).

- If it automatically made interim allocation in respect of every payment, then it would have no asset at all at the end of the year in respect of profits.

Allocation of profits – treatment under SORP

11.13   The legislation requires that what is stated is the 'profit or loss for the financial year before members' remuneration and profit shares'. It had initially been thought that 'members' remuneration' in this context, being clearly differentiated from 'profits' would in effect only mean any salary or equivalent payment which might be made to members, which would not apply to many LLPs at all. However this is not the case as was introduced by the previous SORP and reaffirmed in the current version by defining what has to be regarded as 'members' remuneration charged as an expense'.

Therefore, this is defined as extending to three types of remuneration, one or more of which may be applicable to any LLP's particular agreement. The first is salary or equivalent. The second is an entitlement such as interest on capital. The third, and most controversial, is any non-discretionary division of profits. The only element which, it would seem, will therefore be treated as 'profits' in the commonly understood sense of the term is any element of profits over which the LLP has absolute discretion as to whether it will be distributed or not. The current SORP (31 March 2010) rather helpfully sets out different examples of the allocation of members' profit share and provides a very helpful analysis of the accounting treatment applicable in each case and which is well worth reading for those involved in either operating as, or those advising them.

In drafting terms, therefore, in addition to the question of whether interim allocations may be made, there is a choice with regard to the position once profits have finally (and inevitably after the year end) been ascertained. If the LLP is then obliged to divide those monies between the members, according to the agreed profit-sharing ratio, then all the profits earned will be shown as remuneration charged as an expense. If, on the other hand, the LLP has complete discretion, and can say that it will not divide the monies at all, then such monies will be regarded as profit retained for future discretionary division.

In many instances, the latter will not be the case. Members will not be happy with the idea that the LLP could decide not to divide profits from year 1 until, say, year 4, as the profit sharing ratios, and even the identity of the members, may be very different in the latter year. In the more common case where there is no such discretion, the absolute bottom line in the profit and loss account, ie 'retained profit' will be nil. This will take some explaining to readers of the accounts.

Allocation of losses

11.14   The concept of allocation can cause enough problems with respect to profits. It gets even more difficult, however, with losses. The scenario can readily be envisaged where available profits are not enough to cover over-optimistic 'drawings' which have been taken by members. The excess is a debt then due from the members to the LLP, and it is for the members' agreement, or an ad hoc decision, to say whether that debt shall be repaid once quantified, or shall be offset against future hoped-for profit entitlement.

What, though, if there are actual losses? If a loss is allocated to an individual, that becomes a debt due from him/her to the LLP. This clearly defeats the object of seeking limited liability in the first place. The likelihood is therefore that, unless the agreement requires otherwise, losses will not be allocated at all, but will be held in a reserve. (The concept of a negative reserve is one which some readers may find difficult to grasp.) Whether that reserve is later diminished by credits from subsequent years' profits, or simply remains outstanding, will depend on individual circumstances. The members are not, however, then personally liable to make it good.

Notes to the balance sheet

11.15 The notes to the balance sheet have to give supplemental information by virtue of *paras 47* to *61* of *Sch 1* of the *2008 Large LLP (Accounts) Regulations* which is required to enable an accurate assessment to be taken of the LLP's affairs – either by introducing new information or supplementing information already given.

Areas covered are:

* aggregate amounts of loans and other debts due to members during and at the end of the financial year and loans to members falling due after one year;

* aggregate amount of contributions made by members;

* aggregate amount of withdrawals made by members during the year;

* aggregate amount of monies transferred to or from profit and loss account during the year.

Once again, the intention is simply that the overall pattern of the movement of funds between the LLP and its members shall be visible, so that a third party can see whether the overall flow of funds is into or out of the business, or whether it is in equilibrium.

Notes to the profit and loss account

Average number of members

11.16 The third and final batch of information which needs to be given, and perhaps the most contentious, takes the form of a note to the profit and loss account, under *para 66* of *Sch 1* to the *2008 Large LLP (Accounts) Regulations*.

This deals with members' remuneration etc, and, for most people previously trading as a partnership will, for the first time, make some individual details available. It starts by requiring the note to give the average number of members for the year in question, with the average being worked out on a monthly basis to allow for variations over the year. Once that figure is given, it will not require any reader of the accounts to be Einstein to work out the average profit per member. That is hardly going to be radical news, however, once the overall profit is public, for it would not be difficult for anyone to find out by other means, eg an LLP's letterhead, or the statement of ownership to be kept at its registered office, or simply a search of the Companies House records, what the number of members at any given point in time happens to be. This requirement of itself therefore adds little to the burden of disclosure.

Highest earning member

11.17   There is, however, a second layer of information which needs to be given under *para 66(3)* of *Sch 1 to the 2008 Large LLP (Accounts) Regulations*, if (but only if) profit for the LLP for the year in question exceeds an aggregate £200,000. (Note that this is the profit before members' remuneration and profits, so the question of whether profit is an expense or not is irrelevant.) If so, then the amount payable to the member receiving the highest share of profit needs to be stated.

Two principles have to be applied in making all calculations for the purposes of this section (ie does profit exceed the threshold, who is the highest earner, and how much has that member received). The first is that 'profit' includes all remuneration and all specified classes of 'emoluments', whether they are received from the LLP itself, any subsidiary undertakings (whether incorporated or not, and therefore including partnerships) or indeed 'any other person'.

The second principle is that those 'emoluments' (which are defined by a cross-reference to *para 1(1)(a)(c)* or *(d) Sch 5* to the *Large and Medium-sized Companies and Groups (Accounts and Reports) Regulations 2008*) comprise all:

*   emoluments paid to or receivable by members for qualifying services (ie services to the LLP or associated undertakings);

*   money (or the value of assets – other than share option schemes) paid to or received or receivable by members under long-term incentive schemes in respect of qualifying services;

*   pension contributions for members' qualifying services in relation to money purchase schemes.

Information not needing disclosure

11.18   It may also be worth considering, before getting too hot under the collar as to the burden of disclosure (see 11.2 and 11.3 above), some areas where the *CA 2006* requires individual disclosure by company directors, but not members of LLPs.

Those additional areas would include details of:

- pension scheme benefits;
- compensation for loss of office;
- sums paid to third parties in respect of directors' services;
- loans, quasi-loans etc;
- guarantees.

Exemption for small LLPs

11.19 Although there are no different provisions for medium-sized LLPs in relation to the disclosure of members' interests, there are exemptions from some of the above disclosure requirements available for those LLPs which fit within the 'small' category (see 10.33 above as to the criteria) and which do not fall foul of the exclusion from the small LLP benefits which applies to ineligible businesses (see 10.37 and 10.38 above).

Such LLPs are referred to in the following paragraphs as 'qualifying small LLPs'. They need only prepare the simpler accounts required by the modified *Pts 15* and *16* of the *CA 2006* and *reg 3* of the *2008 Small LLP (Accounts) Regulations*. There is no change as to the information required for the balance sheet, or the way the profit and loss account is structured, or the additional information needed (see 11.15 above). However, there is no equivalent to the requirements as set out at 11.16 and 11.17 above in relation to members' profit entitlements.

Exemption for qualifying small LLPs with abbreviated balance sheets

11.20 Finally, there is a further exemption for those qualifying small LLPs which opt under *s 444* of the *CA 2006* (as modified) to deliver only an abbreviated balance sheet to the Registrar, in compliance with *Sch 3* to the *2008 Small LLP (Accounts) Regulations*. That balance sheet will have the same information as to members' debts and capital, but there is of course no profit and loss account, and there is no requirement for either the information as to the movement of funds (see 11.15 above), or information as to profit entitlements (see 11.16 and 11.17 above).

Note, however, that this only applies to the information deliverable to the Registrar, and thus to become public; it does not apply to the accounts to be distributed to members and debenture holders.

Summary of disclosure requirements

11.21   To sum up, the disclosure requirements look like this:

Statutory requirement	Application
Balance sheet information as to members' debts and capital	All LLPs
Profit and loss account excluding members' remuneration	All LLPs, save for the registrar's copy where a qualifying small LLP has opted to deliver only an abbreviated balance sheet
Paragraph 46 information on the movement of funds	Ditto
Paragraph 66(1) information on average member numbers	All LLPs other than qualifying small LLPs
Paragraph 66(3) information on highest earning member's remuneration	All LLPs except qualifying small LLPs, or those LLPs with profit before members' remuneration etc less than £200,000

Annual accounting documentation requirements

11.22   As noted above (10.15), LLPs do not have such onerous annual reporting requirements as companies in respect of annual business reviews, environmental reviews etc. Nonetheless, there are some matters which must be included in the annual report of an LLP which does not have the 'small' or 'medium'-sized exemptions (see 10.38 *et seq* above). This should include:

- the principal activities of the LLP and any subsidiary undertakings, indicating any significant changes during the year;

- whether there are any non-UK branches;

- a list of all who have been designated members at any time during the year;

- the policy regarding members' drawings (including what happens when the cash demands of members and the LLP may conflict);

- the policy regarding the amount and nature of monies to be paid into the business by members, and how they are to be repaid.

Chapter 12

Miscellaneous Provisions

12.1   This chapter considers the miscellany of items, other than in respect of accounts and auditing requirements (covered in Chapters 10 and 11), which are applied to LLPs by the *2009 Regulations*, importing provisions from the *CA 2006*. The consequences for an LLP whose membership falls below two are considered. The requirements for the making of contracts by an LLP, and entry by it into deeds, are then reviewed. Next come the interlinked topics of the creation and registration of debentures; and the registration of charges created by an LLP. The powers of the Secretary of State to appoint inspectors, and conduct investigations, into an LLP's affairs are set out. The law concerning the possibility of LLPs entering into arrangements and reconstructions is covered, and finally the potentially thorny problems of petitions alleging unfair prejudice, under the modified *s 994* of the *CA 2006*, are examined.

Introduction

12.2   Previously, the *2001 Regulations* operated, via *Sch 1* and *Sch 2*, to apply provisions of the *CA 1985* to LLPs. With the introduction of the *CA 2006*, this has now changed so that, for example, various Regulations have been introduced to apply different accounting principles to the LLP, depending on its size etc (see Chapter 10). In addition, the *2009 Regulations* apply certain (non-accounting) provisions of the *CA 2006* to LLPs.

The *CA 2006* and, where relevant the *CA 1985*, are, as before, referred to 'as modified' to reflect that that section has been specifically modified by the various Regulations to apply to LLPs.

Minimum membership

12.3   *Section 2* of the *LLPA 2000* requires that, on incorporation, an LLP must have at least two members (see 2.7). *Section 4A* of the *LLPA 2000* (added by the *2009 Regulations, Sch 3(1), para (3)*) deals with what happens if the number of members falls below this minimum threshold during the lifetime of the LLP.

The position is then as interesting for what does not happen, as what does. The first point is that, for six months after the situation has arisen where there is only one member, nothing at all happens. The LLP can continue to trade under that member's direction, and he/she incurs no penalty or added potential liability. After that six months, if it is still continuing with just one member, the LLP still continues to exist, and can still continue to trade. However that member (providing he/she knows that the LLP is carrying on business with just him/her as a member) becomes jointly and severally liable for such of the debts of the LLP as are incurred after the end of that six-month period.

It is not therefore until someone takes some active steps to remedy the situation, eg by petitioning for the winding up of the LLP, that it, as a legal entity with unlimited capacity, ceases to exist.

It is also worth bearing in mind that if the number of members falls below two at any time, the grounds for winding up an LLP under the *IA 1986, s 122(c)*, as applied to LLPs by the *2001 Regulations*, will apply (see 16.4).

Contractual requirements

Formalities for entering into contracts

12.4   There are two basic requirements for a contract to which an LLP is a party. Under *s 43* of the *CA 2006* (as modified), either the contract, if 'by' the LLP, may be made in writing under the common seal of the LLP (assuming it has opted to have such a seal) or, if it is 'on behalf of' the LLP, may be made by any party acting under its express or implied authority.

Further, if the general law applies any overlay of requirements as to formality (eg that a contract for the sale of land must be in writing), then that will apply to an LLP's contracts as well as to any others.

Execution of documents

12.5   Reference was made in 12.4 above to the fact that an LLP may choose whether to have a common seal or not. *Section 45(1)* of the *CA 2006*, as modified, specifies that. If it does opt for a seal, an LLP may execute a document by affixing the seal to it; if not, then any document must be signed by two members or by a member in the presence of a witness who attests his/her signature and expressed in some way to be executed by the LLP has exactly the same effect as if executed under seal (*CA 2006, s 44(2)*, as modified). This reflects the changes introduced by the *CA 2006* to private limited companies, removing the requirement for a company secretary and, thus, allow a company to operate where there is only one director. This does not, of course, mirror the situation in relation to an LLP where there would usually be a minimum of two members (although see 12.3 above). It is hard therefore to see the advantage of opting to have a seal, unless potential overseas use makes this desirable (see 12.8 below).

Such a document as above, whichever method of execution is chosen, will be regarded as a deed if it is clear on the face of it that it is intended to be. It will have effect on delivery, and will be presumed to be delivered upon execution unless a contrary intention is proved, eg by a statement that it is delivered in escrow. In favour of a purchaser acting in good faith and for valuable consideration (including a lessee, mortgagee or other person taking an interest in property), there are presumptions:

- of due execution, if the document purports to be signed by two members; and

- of delivery upon execution, if it purports to be a deed.

Pre-incorporation contracts

12.6   Pre-incorporation contracts are a danger for the person making them on behalf of the prospective LLP. The reason is that, by the modified *s 51* of the *CA 2006*, any such contract takes effect not as a contract between the third party and the LLP, but between the third party and the person purporting to act on behalf of or as agent for the LLP, and that person becomes personally liable. This applies to deeds just as it does to contracts.

It is however capable of being displaced by agreement, so if the third party can be persuaded to accept the liability of the as yet unformed LLP, all well and good. More likely, however, is that the third party will wish to adhere to his/her statutory rights, and that it will be incumbent on the person dealing on the LLP's behalf to ensure that he/she takes advantage of *s 5(2)* of the *LLPA 2000*, and puts in place a pre-incorporation agreement between the members and the LLP, which binds the LLP to ratify and accept liability for such pre-incorporation agreements, so that even though he/she may be primarily liable to the third party, he/she has the benefit of an indemnity from the LLP.

Bills of exchange etc

12.7   By *s 52* of the *CA 2006*, as modified, a bill of exchange or a promissory note, is deemed to have been made, accepted or endorsed on behalf of an LLP if this is done in its name, or by or on behalf or on account of the LLP, by someone acting under its authority.

Bear in mind also that, by *s 82* of the *CA 2006*, as modified, (applying the *Companies (Trading Disclosures) Regulations 2008 (SI 2008/495)* to LLPs, the LLP's name must be stated on all such documents, such as on cheques, and that, in the absence of reasonable excuse, if it is not, it, and every designated member, is guilty of an offence and is liable to a fine.

Sundry other documentary provisions

12.8   An LLP may, by way of a deed, authorise someone to execute deeds on its behalf both in the UK and outside the UK, and a deed or other document executed by such an attorney has the same effect as if executed by the LLP under the LLP's seal (*CA 2000, s 47*, as modified). The authority can be general or in respect of a specified matter only.

Further, if the LLP has a common seal, it may create facsimiles for use in specified overseas countries etc, and authorise someone to affix the same, which authority a third party may rely on (*CA 2006, s 49*, as modified) unless it appears from the face of the authority that it was for a limited and expired period, or unless the third party has notice of revocation or determination.

Events affecting an LLP's status

12.9   There may be certain events in an LLP's lifetime which it wishes to be able to rely on as having happened, and as binding a third party which it is dealing with. It may, however, be unable to do so if notice of that event has not been properly dealt with. This can apply to:

- the making of a winding up order for the LLP;
- the appointment of a liquidator in the voluntary winding up of the LLP;
- any change in the LLP's registered office (in connection with the service of any document upon it).

It will be unable, in accordance with *CA 2006, s 1079*, as modified, to rely upon such an event having happened, unless that event has been officially notified by it to the Registrar at the material time, or can be shown by the LLP to have been known at that time to the person concerned. Even if the official notification has been given, it cannot rely upon this if the material time is on or before the 15th day after official notification (or, if that 15th day is not a business day, the next business day after that) if the third party can be shown to have been unavoidably prevented from knowing of it.

In other words, if the LLP seeks to rely on such an event, it will, regardless of official notification, be in its interests specifically to draw the third party's attention to it at the material time, and it will not really be safe to rely upon official notification alone until the 15-day period has passed.

Debentures

Creation of debentures

12.10   One major potential advantage of the corporate status of LLPs is their ability, unlike partnerships, to create and issue debentures. Prospective providers of finance to LLPs will, for the first time, have the ability thus to take floating charges on the assets – and in particular on the book debts – of the business.

This may seem a one-sided benefit, but it may in practice work very much in members' favour, if such security can be offered in place of any personal guarantees, or security over the members' private properties, which banks and others may well otherwise require. It may even offer the only form of security which an LLP can find for its borrowing.

Certain professional LLPs may have to check their profession's rules, to see whether this may be thought to cause any problem with the consequent possibility of finance providers being entitled to receive fees direct from clients. This can raise issues of confidentiality and, if the LLP is a solicitors' business, legal professional privilege. Essentially, the debenture itself has to bind the lender so that, in the event that it ever has to appoint (out of court) a receiver or administrator, it must do so in such a fashion that:

- the receiver/administrator (or one of them if there are joint appointees) is a solicitor, or if not they must appoint a solicitor as special manager;

- only that solicitor can see any data relating to matters which might be confidential or privileged, such as invoices; and

- such solicitor owes the borrowing LLP's clients the same duties he/she would if part of the business.

This does not appear to be causing any concerns amongst the banking community, and mainstream banks are gradually adapting their standard forms accordingly.

The problem does not arise if an administrator or liquidator is appointed by the court, since their duties are then statutory and this overcomes the difficulty.

The members of an LLP may wish to get the LLP to grant them a debenture or similar security, to secure monies owed by it to them. This might, for instance, be loans made by them. Since the revised accountancy Statement of Recommended Practice (see Appendix 3), however, which classifies members' capital investment in most circumstances as debt rather than true equity, the possibility arises that it may be feasible for such security to extend to capital. This appears totally contrary to the idea of capital being for the benefit of the creditors, but nonetheless seems logical. It remains to be seen whether this device would be held effective.

The development of floating charges

12.11   There is no statutory provision saying that an LLP can create floating charges – nor is there for companies.

The concept of a charge which does not attach to specific assets until a defined event causes it to crystallise is a creation of Victorian ingenuity and common law, having been first accepted as a principle in *Re Panama, New Zealand & Australia Royal Mail Co* (1870) 5 Ch App 318. The development of the floating charge, and its interplay with other forms of security, is likewise largely a matter of case law. In more recent times, the relationship between floating charges and various insolvency provisions, such as administration orders, has been the subject of legislative development.

Areas of legislative provision

12.12   Although the floating charge, and hence the debenture, may be largely creatures of common law, there is much statutory provision for their administration, and this will apply as much to LLPs as to companies.

The right of debenture holders to receive copies of the LLP's accounts has already been examined in Chapter 10 above. *Part 25 of the CA 2006*, as modified, provides for the registration of charges by LLPs, which will apply to both fixed and floating charges created by LLPs, and this is dealt with from 12.22 below. There is also a group of miscellaneous provisions found in *Pt 21, Ch 1* of the *CA 2006* relating to debentures, and these are examined below.

Transfer and registration

12.13   Debentures are, ordinarily, assignable securities. By *CA 2006, s 770* as modified, any transfer must be by means of a proper written transfer, to be delivered to the LLP, in order for the transfer to be registered by the LLP (unless the transfer is by operation of law). The CREST system does not apply to transfers of debentures.

If for any reason the LLP declines to register the transfer, it must give notice of such refusal as soon as possible and by no later than two months after the date on which the transfer is lodged with it. If requested, the LLP must provide further evidence as to the reasons for the refusal as the transferee may reasonably request (although it does not have to provide copies of minutes of any members' meetings) (*CA 2006, s 771*, as modified). If it does not then it, and every member in default, will be guilty of an offence.

Certification of transfer

12.14   An LLP may certify the transfer of a debenture by marking the transfer with 'copy lodged' or something similar. If it does, it is taken to have certified not that the transferor has actual title to the debenture, but that there have been produced to it documents which on the face of it show a prima facie title (*CA 2006, s 775*, as modified).

The LLP must be careful in the exercise of this function, since third parties may rely upon the faith of the certification and, if the certification is negligently wrong, the LLP becomes as liable to that third party as if the wrong certification had been fraudulent. There are detailed provisions in *s 775(4)* as to the process for certification and signing of the certificate.

Issue of certificates

12.15   It is the task of the LLP to issue debenture certificates. It has a period of two months to do so from the time of an event which triggers that obligation. That event may, by *CA 2006, ss 769* and *776* as modified, be either the allotment of any debentures, or the lodgement of any (properly stamped) transfer, other than one which is refused. If it fails to issue the necessary certificates, every member in default is guilty of an offence, and daily default fines can be levied.

Further, if a third party who is entitled to receive a certificate serves notice on the LLP requiring it to fulfil its obligations, and it does not do so within ten days, then that person can apply to the court for an order directing the LLP and any member in default to perform its obligations, and to pay the application's costs (*CA 2006, s 782,* as modified). There is an exception for dealings through a 'recognised clearing house' etc (*CA 2006, s 778,* as modified).

Register of debenture holders

12.16   *Section 743* of the *CA 2006,* as modified, provides for the keeping of a register of debenture holders. (The provisions also apply to any duplicate, kept in the UK, of any such register the original of which is kept overseas.)

The register may be kept at the LLP's registered office, or such other place as may be specified in accordance with regulations introduced pursuant to the modified *CA 2006, s 743,* namely *The Companies (Company Records) Regulations 2008 (SI 2008/3006)* in Form LLAD02 (although, curiously, there does not seem to be the usual criminal sanction for failure to file this notice).

Inspection of register

12.17   The register is a public document. It may be inspected by anyone, under *CA 2006, s 744* as modified. Further, anyone may require a copy. Similarly, if there is a trust deed relating to an issue of debentures, a copy of that deed may be requested by any holder of a debenture within that issue, and the LLP must send him/her a copy. All of the above are dependent on payment of a prescribed fee (except for a registered debenture holder who need not pay to inspect the register).

If the LLP does not comply with any of these provisions, any member in default is guilty of an offence, and a daily default fine may be levied (*CA 2006, s 746*, as modified). Further, the court may by order compel immediate compliance. These provisions do not apply, however, if the register is closed, in accordance with the original debenture documentation, and such closure lasts for not more than an aggregate 30 days in any year. There is a specific provision that the LLP shall not be liable for any error in the register more than ten years after the error occurred in relation to causes of action arising on or after 6 April 2008. Prior to that, a period of 20 years is applicable to such claims.

Liability of debenture trustees

12.18 It is not uncommon for there to be a trust deed for an issue of debentures, with trustees appointed to secure the interests of the debenture holders.

By *s 750* of the *CA 2006*, as modified, any provision in the trust deed which purports to grant a trustee an exemption from, or an indemnity against, his/her potential liability for breach of trust where he/she fails to show the degree of care and diligence which is required of him/her as a trustee, is void. That does not, however, prevent a specific retrospective release being given to a trustee for anything done or omitted by him/her. Nor does it preclude a provision allowing a retrospective release to be given, if supported by not less than 75% of the debenture holders, which has effect:

- in relation to specific acts or omissions; or
- if the trustee dies; or
- if the trustee ceases to act.

If such a provision is to be incorporated, it will need to have detailed provisions for the calling of a meeting of the debenture holders, and for proxy voting if this is desired.

Redemption of debentures

12.19 It is usual for debentures to be redeemable under specific circumstances, ie for the monies originally advanced by the debenture holder to the LLP to be repayable on a specific date, or on the happening of a specific event. This is not, however, necessary, and *CA 2006, s 739*, as modified, specifically allows for debentures either to be irredeemable, or redeemable upon a contingency or a date, however remote those events may be.

Further, by *CA 2006, s 752* as modified, if debentures are redeemed, there is nothing to stop the LLP from reissuing them or replacing them, unless there is any contractual bar to this or the LLP has somehow determined to cancel them. If the debentures are reissued, the position is the same as if the redemption had never taken place, as far as the holder's rights are concerned, but the reissue is treated as a new issue for stamp duty purposes.

Finally, if a debenture is for the purpose of securing a current account, there is no deemed redemption merely because that account, for a time, goes into credit. This would, for instance, be relevant if the members of an LLP brought about the situation where their current account credit balances, being monies owed by the LLP to the members, are secured by debenture and thus preferred above the ordinary creditors.

Specific performance of contract to issue debentures

12.20 *Section 740* of the *CA 2006*, as modified, states, very simply, that if the LLP has entered into a contract with a third party to issue debentures, that third party can enforce the contract by means of an action for specific performance.

Floating charges and preferential debts

12.21 Almost invariably, debentures will be secured by a floating charge. For any such debenture, the modified *CA 2006, s 754* lays down the rules which apply as between the debenture holders, and those entitled to the payment of 'preferential debts', in the event that the debenture holders go into possession of assets subject to the floating charge, at a time when the LLP is not in the course of being wound up. Preferential debts are defined by *Sch 6* to the *IA 1986*, as heavily amended by the *Enterprise Act 2002*, and are now in effect merely some monies payable to staff in respect of pension contributions and recently due remuneration.

The *IA 1986* provides that the preferential debts are payable, by the person taking possession, in priority to any monies due under the debenture. The debenture holders must rely on a claim as an ordinary creditor for any shortfall which consequently arises.

Registration of charges

Registration generally

12.22 Following on from looking at the provisions for debentures created by LLPs, it seems logical to move on to look at the provisions of the *CA 2006* which deal generally with the registration of charges created by LLPs, which are to be found in *Ch I of Pt 25* of that Act, ie *ss 860 to 877* as modified.

These provisions have, over the years, caused many problems to the companies who have had to operate them, and there seems no reason to believe that they will not cause just as many difficulties for LLPs. The difficulties are on two levels. First, there is the question of what is or is not a 'charge' caught by the statutory provisions. An example is the line of cases which ran through the 1980s which concerned retention of title clauses in conditions for the sale of goods, and the often raised question of whether the various draftsmen's attempts to retain security over unpaid-for goods created a registrable charge (eg *Re Bond Worth Ltd* [1980] Ch 228, or *Clough Mill Ltd v Martin* [1984] 3 All ER 982).

The second difficulty is the draconian consequences of failing correctly to recognise a charge or, having recognised it, failing punctually to register it, namely that it is rendered void against creditors etc, as below. The professions abound with apocryphal stories of massive negligence claims due to failure to register a charge within time. Detailed consideration of what may or may not constitute a charge is beyond the scope of this work, and readers are referred to standard company texts, such as *Tolley's Company Law*. What this part of the current chapter will do is to look at the procedural requirements as to charges created by LLPs.

The consequences of failure to register

12.23   If an LLP creates a charge to which *ss 860* and *861* of the *CA 2006*, as modified, apply then it must, within 21 days after the date of the charge's creation (*CA 2006, s 870*, as modified), deliver to the Registrar for registration the required particulars of the charge in Form LL MG01, together with the original instrument (if any) by which the charge is evidenced or created.

If the LLP does not, then any security conferred by the charge is wholly void as against any liquidator, administrator or creditor of the LLP. It is not that the contract between the chargor LLP and the chargee creditor is invalidated, merely that the security is adversely affected. Indeed, it is specifically provided that, when a charge becomes void by reason of the provision, the money due under the contract which created the charge becomes immediately due and payable.

Charges which have to be registered

12.24   The following are in relation to LLPs the categories of charge (for which 'mortgage' is expressly stated to be synonymous) which, under *CA 2006, s 860*, as modified, have to be registered, namely:

- a charge for the purpose of securing any issue of debentures;

- a charge created or evidenced by an instrument which, if executed by an individual, would require registration as a bill of sale;

- a charge on land (wherever situated) or any interest in it (other than for rent or other periodical sum issuing out of land);
- a charge on the LLP's book debts;
- a floating charge on the LLP's undertaking or property;
- a charge on a ship (or any share in one) or an aircraft;
- a charge on goodwill, or on any intellectual property.

Supplemental provisions

12.25   *Section 861* of the *CA 2006*, as modified also contains a number of supplemental provisions which amplify the above categories. These are:

- If an LLP gives a negotiable instrument to secure the payment of book debts, depositing that instrument in order to secure an advance to the LLP is not to be regarded as a charge on the book debts.
- The holding of debentures, which entitle the holder to a charge on land, is not itself deemed to be an interest in land.
- 'Intellectual property' is defined to include any patent, trademark, registered design, copyright or design right; or any licence under or in respect of any such right.

Registration of debentures

12.26   There are specific provisions which apply to the registration of a series of debentures, ie where the benefits of the debentures apply to a number of debenture holders ranking *pari passu*. Here, it is sufficient if, within the same 21-day period as is referred to in 12.23 above, the Registrar is given, in Form LL MG07, the following particulars:

- the total amount secured by the series;
- the dates of:
    - the LLP's determination(s) to issue the series; and
    - the covering deed (if any) by which the security is created or defined;
- a general description of the property charged;
- the names of the trustees (if any) for the debenture holders.

In addition, the LLP needs to send the Registrar the deed which created the series. If it did not have such a deed, then a sample one of the series of debentures must be produced. If the issue of the debentures in the series is staggered, then each time there is an issue particulars of the date and amount of each issue must be sent to the registrar in Form LLMG08 (though if this is not done it does not invalidate the debentures).

Notification of discount etc

12.27 Either Form LL MG07 or Form LL MG08, as the case may be (see 12.26 above), also needs to give a further set of details, under *CA 2006, s 864* as modified.

These relate to any discount, allowance or commission which may have been paid or made (directly or indirectly) by the LLP to anyone, in relation to his/her taking or procuring anyone else to take such debentures. The form in question must disclose the amount or rate of any such payment etc. It does not count as a discount if the LLP deposits any of the debentures with anyone to secure its debt. If the details of discount etc are not given, it does not invalidate the debentures.

Overseas charges

12.28 A charge needs to be registered even if it is created abroad, and is secured on property situated abroad. In that situation, however, it is sufficient if a verified copy, rather than the original, is delivered to the Registrar (*CA 2006, s 866(1)*, as modified).

The time for compliance in such a case is also extended to 21 days after the copy could, in due course of post and if sent promptly, have been received in the UK. If however the charge is taken over property situated overseas, but it is actually created in the UK, the original is still needed by the Registrar, even though there may be further steps, to be taken abroad, to validate the charge.

Finally, if the property charged is in Scotland or Northern Ireland, and further action is needed in the appropriate one of those jurisdictions to validate it, it will be sufficient to produce to the Registrar in place of the original charge document:

- a verified copy of the charge; and
- a certificate in Form LL MG09 to the effect that the charge has been presented for registration in the appropriate jurisdiction.

The duty to register charges

12.29 The primary duty to register charges created by an LLP is that of the LLP itself, under *CA 2006, s 860,* as modified.

However, such registration can be effected on the application of any person interested in it. In other words if the chargee does not trust the LLP to register the charge, and hence to protect his/her security, he/she can do it him/herself. In practice, that is common, and banks etc will almost always insist on dealing with the registration formalities themselves. Anyone so registering a charge is entitled to recover from the LLP the fee they have paid to the Registrar.

If the LLP fails to register a charge, and no-one else steps into the breach and does it for them, then the LLP, and every member in default, is guilty of an offence, and a daily default fine can be levied.

Charges existing on property acquired

12.30   An LLP may, of course, acquire property which is already subject to a charge (*CA 2006, s 862*, as modified). This might, for instance, arise on the transfer of a partnership's business to an LLP, where the LLP could take over premises already subject to a mortgage. In such circumstances, the LLP has 21 days from the completion of the acquisition to send to the Registrar a certified copy of the charge, and the necessary particulars, in Form LL MG06.

If, however, that property is outside the UK, and the charge was created outside the UK, then the compliance period is extended to 21 days after a promptly posted copy of the charge should have arrived in the UK. The penalties for failure to comply with these requirements are the same as for failure to register a new charge, as above (see 12.29 above).

The register of charges

12.31   The Registrar's duty is to keep the register of charges, under the modified *CA 2006, s 869* for each LLP. The register thus created is public, and open to inspection by anyone. This will therefore show:

- details of any series of debentures (see 12.26 above);
- the date of:
  - ○ creation of the charge by the LLP; or
  - ○ acquisition of any already charged property;
- the amount secured by the charge;
- short particulars of the property charged;
- who is entitled to the charge.

Upon registration of any charge, the Registrar shall give a certificate of registration, stating the amount secured, which shall be conclusive evidence of the satisfaction of the requirements as to registration. It is common practice to attach such a certificate to the original charge document and indeed, by *CA 2006, s 865* as modified, it is obligatory to endorse a copy of the appropriate certificate of registration upon any debenture, or certificate of debenture stock, which is secured by the charge, and which was issued on or after the creation of the charge.

Entries of satisfaction and release

12.32   A feature of the system of registration of company and hence LLP charges, which always seems odd to those who are used to the procedures for dealing with individuals' mortgages, is that it is the borrower, not the lender, who is entitled to say that a charge has been paid off, and to inform the Registrar accordingly, without verification from the lender.

Section 872 of the *CA 2006* (as modified) requires that a statement (and not a statutory declaration as was the case under the former *CA 1985*) shall be made in support of such information, to the effect that either the debt for which the charge was given has been paid or satisfied wholly or partly (in which case Form LL MG02 is appropriate), or that part or the whole of the property charged has either ceased to be charged, or ceased to belong to the LLP (for which Form LL MG04 is used).

Rectification of register

12.33   Mention was made above of the strict time limits which apply to the registration of charges, and the potentially dire consequences of failure to comply (see 12.23). There is, however, power under *CA 2006, s 873* as modified, for the court to act to alleviate the consequences of this.

Under the above provision the court must be satisfied that the omission to register, or correctly to provide a required particular, was accidental or for other reasonable cause, or did not prejudice creditors, or that it is otherwise just and equitable to grant relief. In those circumstances, either the LLP or a person interested (eg the chargee) may apply for an order that the time for registration be extended, or that any omission or misstatement be rectified. It may impose such terms and conditions as it believes are just and expedient. The court's discretion is wide, but it is unlikely to be exercised in the LLP's favour if it has already gone into administration, and only exceptionally (eg if there has been fraud) will it be exercised if the LLP is in liquidation.

Further, any order for relief is likely to contain a provision that it shall not prejudice the position of any creditor in respect of the interim period, between the time when registration should have been effected and the date of order, so that the position of, for instance, a subsequent and properly registered charge would not be adversely affected (*In Re Ashpurton Estates Ltd* [1983] Ch 110).

Appointments of receivers or managers

12.34   If any chargee appoints a receiver or manager of an LLP's property, he/she must under *CA 2006, s 871* as modified, notify the Registrar within seven days of appointment, in Form LL LQ01.

Further, the receiver or manager so appointed must notify the Registrar in Form LL LQ02, when he/she ceases to act. Anyone not complying with these obligations is guilty of an offence, and a daily default fine may be levied.

The LLP's own charges records

12.35 In addition to the Registrar's records, an LLP has its own obligations under *CA 2006, ss 875* and *876*, both as modified. It must keep a copy of every registrable charge which it creates and in the case of a series of uniform debentures, a copy will suffice.

It must also keep a register of charges, on which it must enter all fixed or floating charges, giving a short description of the property charged, the amount secured, and the name(s) of the chargee. Accidental failure to comply is not punishable, but any member knowingly and wilfully authorising or permitting an omission from the register will be guilty of an offence.

These registers should be located at its registered office or at its SAIL address (see 4.10).

These records are public and, under *s 877(4)* of the *CA 2006* (as modified), they must be kept open for inspection by any member or creditor (free) or by any member of the public (who can be made to pay a fee, but not more than the princely sum of £3.50 for each part of a whole hour during which the inspection takes place). If inspection is refused, every member in default is guilty of an offence, and the court may order immediate inspection.

Investigations of an LLP's affairs

The concept of investigations

12.36 One area of the LLP legislation which will be totally new to those who have come from a partnership background is the ability of the Secretary of State to conduct far-reaching investigations into an LLP's affairs.

The privacy of partnership, which could only be disturbed by possible criminal investigation, or on application by a partner to a court, does not protect LLPs. They are subject to the same potentially stringent regime of inspection as any company. The vast majority of LLPs, like the majority of companies, will never encounter anything to do with these provisions, but if things are going wrong for the business the members need to be aware of these powers. Indeed, they themselves may wish to invoke them, if they believe the affairs of the LLP are being wrongly administered, against the law and against their interests.

Application for investigation by the LLP or its members

12.37   It is for the above reason (see last sentence of 12.36 above) that the first power of application for an investigation is given, by the modified *s 431* of the *CA 1985* (note that these provisions remain mainly intact and have not been repealed by the *CA 2006* and that application and consequent modification of the *CA 1985* to LLPs is by virtue of the *2001 Regulations*), to the LLP itself, or to not less than one-fifth of those notified to the Registrar as members. There is no minimum number, so that in a five-member LLP it would be open to one member to make such application. In a proper case, this is therefore a powerful weapon in an aggrieved member's hands.

The application to the Secretary of State must be supported by such evidence as he/she requests, to show that there is good reason for investigation, and by a deposit of not more than (currently) £5,000, for the costs of the investigation. If he/she is sufficiently persuaded, he/she may appoint one or more inspectors to report to him/her, by such means as he/she thinks fit. Note that the report is to the Secretary of State, not the applicant. How he/she deals with it is a matter for him/her, as shown in 12.40 below.

Other causes of commencement of investigation

12.38   There are two other routes, under the modified *s 432* of the *CA 1985* (as modified), to the commencement of an investigation. One is if a court orders the Secretary of State to undertake the task.

The other route is if he/she him/herself is satisfied that he/she should, on the basis that:

- the LLP's affairs are being, or have been, conducted:
  - fraudulently; or
  - in a manner unfairly prejudicial to some members or their successors in title;
- any particular act or omission is or would be so prejudicial;
- the LLP was formed for a fraudulent or unlawful purpose;
- those who formed or are managing it have been guilty of fraud, misfeasance or misconduct towards the LLP or its members;

the members have not been given all reasonably expected information.

Inspectors' powers

12.39   The powers given to the appointed inspectors are wide, in accordance with *ss 433* and *434* of the *CA 1985* (as modified).

They may themselves determine to widen the scope of their investigations to any other body corporate (whether LLP or company) in the same group as the LLP. They can require assistance from anyone, and such assistance can include a requirement to attend before them, and/or to produce any documentation of or relating to the LLP or to their investigations. For this purpose 'documentation' will include any form of records, eg computer data and records. They may decide to take evidence on oath from any person. Those whose help they may seek specifically include the LLP's past and present members and agents; and its bankers, solicitors and auditors.

Any answers given by anyone may be used against them in civil proceedings, but generally not in criminal proceedings (save in certain specified circumstances in a perjury prosecution). If anyone fails to comply with any requirement of the inspectors, or to reply to their questions, the inspectors may certify that to the court, with a view to the court's investigating the non-compliance and, if appropriate, holding the person in question liable for contempt of court (*CA 1985, s 436*, as modified).

Inspectors' reports

12.40   Under the modified *s 437* of the *CA 1985*, the inspectors report to the Secretary of State. They may submit interim reports, or bring particular matters to his/her attention, or be required to do so.

If, during the investigation, it appears that criminal offences may have been committed, and the relevant prosecuting authorities have been informed, the Secretary of State may call a halt to the investigation or a defined part of it, in which case the inspectors shall only be required to make a report if their original appointment was by the court, or if the Secretary of State directs them to do so.

The inspectors' reports are, under the modified *s 441* of the *CA 1985*, admissible in any proceedings as evidence of their opinion and, in proceedings under the *CDDA 1986*, as evidence of fact. If their appointment was initially by the court, a copy of their report must be given to that court. Otherwise, the Secretary of State normally has a discretion as to how (if at all) he/she wishes to make the report known to anyone, unless the original appointment was directed by him/her of his/her own volition, and on terms that the report was not for publication. He/she may decide to:

- forward a copy to the LLP's registered office; or

- publish the report; or

- provide copies, on request and on payment, to:

    ○   any member;

- o   anyone whose conduct is referred to in the report;

- o   the auditors;

- o   the original applicants for the investigation;

- o   anyone else whose financial interests appear affected, whether as a creditor or otherwise.

(*CA 1985, s 437(3)*, as modified).

Power to sue on the LLP's behalf

12.41   If, as a result of any investigations as above, the Secretary of State concludes that it is in the public interest for any civil proceedings to be brought by him/her on the LLP's behalf, he/she may under *s 438* of the *CA 1985*, as modified, take such proceedings in the LLP's name.

He must however indemnify the LLP against any costs and expenses related to the litigation.

Costs of investigations

12.42   Although the Secretary of State is initially liable for all of an investigation's costs, he/she can in certain circumstances seek under *s 439* of the *CA 1985*, as modified, to recover those costs, which will include general staff costs and overheads, and the costs of such civil proceedings as above.

Recovery may be effected against anyone convicted in proceedings brought as a result of the investigation, or against whom an order for costs is made in any such civil proceedings as above. Further, if such civil proceedings result in a payment to or a recovery of property by the LLP, then the costs of the investigation are a first charge on the sums payable or money recovered.

The LLP itself may have to pay the expenses (though the Secretary of State may grant relief against this) if the original application was made neither by it, nor by the Secretary of State. If the original application was by the LLP or its members, the emphasis is slightly different, in that the applicants are liable, to such extent as the Secretary of State directs. (In the exercise of this discretion, the Secretary of State may be guided by any comments made by the inspectors.)

Power to require production of documents

12.43   There is also a lesser power available to the Secretary of State, if he/she is concerned about an LLP's affairs, but does not want to launch a full-scale investigation. He/she may, instead, exercise the power given to him/her under *s 447* of the *CA 1985*, as modified (as substituted by the *C (A, I & C E) Act 2004*) to require the LLP to produce such documents as he/she may specify to him/her or an appointed officer. ('Documents' has the same wide interpretation as in 12.39 above.) He/she does not have to justify such demand.

The power extends to anyone in possession of the appropriate documents (but without prejudice to any lien on them). The power includes the right to copy documents as produced, and to require an explanation for them. If the documents are not produced, the Secretary of State or his/her duly appointed officer has the right to require a person to provide general or specific information (whether as to the whereabouts of such documentation or otherwise) as he/she thinks fit. A person on whom the request is served is under an obligation to comply with such request. Any statement made may be used in proceedings, as in 12.39 above (but with the same restrictions on their use in criminal proceedings as are mentioned there).

Entry and search of premises

12.44   All the powers discussed above are of course subject to efforts to circumvent them, and as a back-up it is necessary for there to be powers to enter and search premises. Those powers, under *s 448* of the *CA 1985*, as modified, are however exercisable only on obtaining a warrant from a justice of the peace, who is satisfied by evidence on oath given by or on behalf of the Secretary of State or his/her appointees, as to the relevant circumstances. A warrant is effective for a month.

There are two distinct possibilities. One is where there has already been a demand for the production of documents, which has not been complied with. The other is a pre-emptive strike, where it can be shown to the JP that:

- there are reasonable grounds for believing that a serious offence has been committed;

- there are documents relevant to that offence upon the premises;

- there is power to demand the production of the documents;

- there are reasonable grounds for belief that, if the warrant is not granted, the documents would be removed, hidden, tampered with or destroyed.

The offence in question must be one which is punishable, on indictment, by at least two years' imprisonment.

Undertaking the search

12.45   The warrant (see 12.44 above) grants authorisation to the police and to any other named person, such as the investigating inspector. Such persons may use reasonable force to enter the premises in question. They may search for, take possession of, and copy any of the appropriate documents, which again are widely defined and could include computer data.

They may also ask any person named in the warrant for an explanation of the documents or, if they are not found, to state where they are. Any documents found can be kept for three months or, if consequent criminal proceedings are taken, until the end of those proceedings. Note this extended period does not apply in the event that the proceedings commenced are civil proceedings (as per 12.41 above). Anyone intentionally obstructing the exercise of these rights, or failing without reasonable excuse to give a requested explanation, is guilty of an offence.

Handling information received

12.46   Naturally, information obtained under these procedures may be extremely sensitive. Unless therefore it is required for official purposes, it must not be published or disclosed without the LLP's prior written consent, and anyone who does disclose or publish such information is guilty of an offence under *s 449* of the *CA 1985*, as modified (as substituted by the *C (A, I & CE) Act 2004*).

For this purpose there are however a wide range of possible official purposes, which can range from a conventional prosecution to professional disciplinary proceedings. In the legislation 20 instances are stipulated, and 16 possible prosecutors are listed. This applies not only to information obtained under the *s 447* procedure, but also, by *s 451A* of the *CA 1985*, as modified, to information obtained during an investigation.

Destruction etc of an LLP's documents

12.47   It may of course be that even a pre-emptive strike is too late, and that the relevant documents (again including computer records) have been got at before the authorities get to them. It is therefore an offence, under *s 450* of the *CA 1985*, as modified, for any person to destroy, mutilate, falsify or make a false entry in any document affecting or relating to the LLP's property or affairs, or to be privy to any such act. It is, however, a defence to be able to prove that the defendant had no intention to conceal the state of affairs or to defeat the law.

Similarly, it is an offence fraudulently to part with, alter, or create an omission in any such document, or to be privy thereto. The statutory defence mentioned above is not available here due to the fraudulent nature of the charge.

Giving false information

12.48   Another natural risk is that any statement made, or explanation given, will be false. Accordingly, it is an offence under *s 451* of the *CA 1985*, as modified (as substituted by the *C (A, I & CE) Act 2004*) knowingly or recklessly to make or give a statement or explanation which is false in a material particular.

Privileged information

12.49   There are, under the modified *s 452* of the *CA 1985*, two specific exceptions to the obligation to co-operate in an investigation, or to produce documents demanded or an explanation of them.

The first exception applies if the information of which disclosure is sought would, in High Court proceedings, be subject to legal professional privilege. (One exception is that a lawyer must, if asked, disclose the name and address of his/her client.)

The other exception is if the information is held by bankers who owe, in respect of it, an obligation of confidence to the LLP (or other body corporate) under investigation. In that instance bankers are only obliged to disclose if either the person to whom the duty of confidence is owed consents, or the Secretary of State specifically so directs. In the case of the production of documents, bankers must produce the document only if the demand for its production relates to an investigation into the customer's affairs, or the customer is someone of whom a demand under *s 447* has been made (see 12.43 above).

Order for production and inspection of books

12.50   The last provision with regard to the investigation of an LLP's affairs, is now incorporated into the *CA 2006* and is tucked away right at the end, in the modified *s 1132*. There, it is provided that a court has power to make an order for the production and inspection of an LLP's books.

Application must be made to the High Court, by the Director of Public Prosecutions, the Secretary of State or a chief officer of police. He/she must show to the court that there is reasonable cause to believe that someone has, whilst a member of an LLP, committed an offence in connection with the management of the LLP's affairs, and that evidence thereof is to be found in any books or papers of the LLP. If so satisfied, the court may authorise any person named in its order to inspect the books and papers in question for the purpose of investigating the alleged offence. It may also require any named member of the LLP to produce the books and papers to a named person at a named place.

Such an order can also be made in respect of any bankers' books and papers so far as they relate to the LLP's affairs, save that no order can be made for the production of the documents, as distinct from requiring inspection of them.

Financial Services and Markets Act 2000 investigations

12.51 Investigations may of course also be conducted into an LLP's affairs under other, more specific, statutes. One is the *IA 1986*, and reference is made in the chapter on insolvency to these (see Chapter 16).

Chief amongst the other statutes is the *FSMA 2000*. There are a number of sets of provisions in the *FSMA 2000, Pt XI*, some of which link in with the *CA 1985* investigation procedure examined in the previous paragraphs above.

Facing an investigation

12.52 In a number of cases above, reference has been made to the forms of investigation etc, and to the position facing the individual of whom questions may be raised. Has that person, such as a member in an LLP, any way out?

One option is to challenge, by way of judicial review, the decision to launch the investigation in the first place. Such a challenge is, however, unlikely to succeed, in the light of the decision in *Norwest Holst Ltd v Secretary of State for Trade* [1978] Ch 201, to the effect that the decision to start an investigation is a purely administrative one to which the rules of natural justice do not apply. Further, the Secretary of State may not be obliged even to disclose his/her source, or his/her reasons. (In passing, any LLP suspicious that the source of information leading to any investigation may be a member of staff will need to bear in mind the effect of the 'Whistleblowers Act', ie the *Public Interest Disclosure Act 1998*, which may well give protection to the staff member in question.)

Another possibility, especially if proceedings have already been commenced against the individual of whom questions are being posed, is attempting to justify refusal on the grounds of self-incrimination. This may or may not help in any given circumstance, but at least it should go to the 'reasonableness' of any refusal to co-operate where that is necessary.

Arrangements and reconstructions

Available remedies

12.53 The various subsequent chapters on insolvency (see Chapters 13 to 17) deal with the more formal ways of an LLP dealing with difficult financial situations, including voluntary arrangements under the *IA 1986*.

However, there is also power under the modified *Pt 26* of the *CA 2006* for an LLP to effect a compromise with either its creditors, or its members; and power to carry out a reconstruction or amalgamation. These provisions are contained in *ss 895* to *900* of the *CA 2006* (as modified). Compromises and arrangements are widely construed, and are much wider than reconstructions and amalgamations. The LLP must, however, be a party to any such new terms, and in an 'arrangement' there must be some real degree of give and take between the interested parties. There is a major body of case law in respect of these provisions, consideration of which is beyond the scope of this work, and reference should be made to any of the standard company law texts, such as *Tolley's Company Law,* for detailed guidance as to the parameters of the provisions and the method of their implementation. This text will simply give an overview.

Summoning meetings to consider compromises

12.54   A compromise can be between the LLP and either its creditors, or its members (or, in either case, any class of them). If a compromise is proposed, an application can be made to the court by anyone prospectively affected, ie the LLP itself, or any creditor or member.

Further, if the LLP is in the course of being wound up, or if an administration order has been made, the liquidator or administrator also has power to apply. The court may direct a meeting of the creditors, or the members, or the affected class of either. The court directs the manner of summoning the meeting (which, in the light of the voting provisions below, presumably needs to include provision for proxy voting).

Proceedings at meetings to consider compromises

12.55   To be effective, a compromise or arrangement needs approval from two sources. First, it needs the sanction of the court. Broadly, that sanction is likely to be based on the objective test approved in *Re Dorman Long & Co Ltd* [1934] 1 Ch 635, to the effect that the court will grant sanction if the proposals are something that an 'intelligent and honest' person considering their interest 'might reasonably approve'.

Secondly, it needs the approval of at least 75% of those voting either in person or by proxy at the meeting (ie as the case may be, the creditors, or the members, or the appropriate class of them). (Confusingly, the statute refers to 'a majority in number representing 75% in value of the creditors … or members …'. The expression 'in value' is easy enough to understand in the case of creditors, but it is difficult in the case of members. Presumably, if it is intended to apply to members, it has to refer to their investment in the LLP, but there is no guidance as to whether that might only be initially invested capital, or would for instance include retained profit. However, it does seem to rule out a one-member-one-vote arrangement in this scenario.)

If thus dually sanctioned, the compromise is binding on all those for whom the meeting was called, ie creditors or members etc. It is also binding on the LLP itself, and, if the LLP is being wound up, on the liquidators and contributories. The order only takes effect upon an office copy thereof being delivered to the Registrar.

Information as to the compromise

12.56 When any such meeting as is referred to in the three previous paragraphs is called, each creditor or member entitled to attend has to be sent notice of the meeting. That must be accompanied by a statement explaining what the effect of the compromise would be, and in particular whether it would have any distinct effect on members because of their material interests.

If the meeting is to be advertised, there needs to be either a statement as above published with it, or an indication of where and how creditors or members could access without charge a copy of such a statement. Additionally, if the rights of debenture holders would be affected, relevant information must be given.

If the LLP defaults in any of these procedural conditions, an offence is committed by it and by any member (which for this purpose includes any liquidator and any debenture trustee) in default. It is, however, a defence for any person to show that the default was due to the refusal of a member or debenture holder to supply to him/her the necessary details of that person's material interest in the compromise. Such persons in turn are under a duty to supply those details, and commit an offence if they do not.

Reconstructions and amalgamations

12.57 Amongst the circumstances in which such compromises or arrangements may be proposed is where the idea is for either a reconstruction of any LLP(s), or the amalgamation of any two or more LLPs.

There is guidance in the body of case law which has developed in the company context as to what may fall within the terms 'reconstruction' or 'amalgamation'. Essentially, the former will normally require some degree of restructuring, and involves the passing of most of business A's undertaking to business B, where both businesses are controlled by substantially the same group of people – *Re South African Supply and Cold Storage Co* [1904] 2 Ch 268. It may apply to a partition of a business, or a demerger. It may be important to establish whether any proposals do fall within the definition, as it may have tax and duty implications. Amalgamations are simpler to consider, and can include the absorption of one business within another, rather than needing the creation of a wholly new entity.

Detailed orders

12.58   If, in any such scenario, all or any part of the undertaking or property of an LLP (the 'transferor') is to be transferred to another LLP ('the transferee'), then there are certain specific matters which the court may rule upon, either when giving the sanction for proposals, or at any subsequent time. These are:

- the transfer of all or any part of the undertaking, property and liabilities of the transferor;

- the appropriation to any person of any shares, debentures, policies or the like of the transfer;

- the continuation by or against the transferee of any pending litigation;

- the dissolution (without winding up) of the transferor;

- provisions for what is to happen in regard to dissenters;

- incidental and supplemental matters needed to effect the changes.

The order itself effects the vesting of any property or liabilities ordered to be transferred, and it can, if the arrangements so provide, free the property of any charge. An office copy of any such order made, whether in relation to the sanction and meeting, or the detailed provisions, must be deposited by the LLP with the Registrar within seven days of its making. If this is not done, the LLP, and every member in default, is guilty of an offence and a daily default fine may be levied.

The use of the compromise provisions

12.59   To an extent, these provisions may have had their day, except for reconstructions or amalgamations of solvent LLPs. The relevant provisions in the *IA 2000* for voluntary arrangements for companies and LLPs may be more attractive for some insolvent LLPs, as they introduced for eligible businesses a moratorium such as that which had always been available for individual voluntary arrangements (or IVAs). There are however snags – see 13.9 to 13.12.

There may, therefore, still be advantages in an insolvency context in following the arrangement and reconstruction route, such as the fact that there is no requirement for a nominee/supervisor, so that the operational costs of a compromise may be less. Otherwise, the likely area for their use will be where LLPs can seek to overcome unreasonable minority dissent to sensible and financially viable restructuring.

Protection from unfair prejudice

The remedy in CA 2006, s 994

12.60 Having dealt with the position where an uncooperative minority may be overcome (see 12.53 onwards), it is perhaps appropriate to turn to the opposite side of the coin, ie where there is unfair action being taken against the minority by the majority.

During the progress of the LLP legislation through Parliament, one much-debated topic was whether it was appropriate for there to be any protection for a minority or whether, since the basic philosophy of the legislation was to leave members to sort out their own arrangements by their members' agreement, this would be inappropriate. This was chiefly considered in the context of an individual member seeking to get his/her investment out of the LLP. The government eventually took the stance that it would not legislate at all for the removal of capital etc, but that it would permit the same degree of protection for a member as for a shareholder, under the now *s 994* of the *CA 2006*, as modified.

Excluding the section

12.61 One important proviso, however, was that the LLP's members were to be able to exclude the section. Hence, by the modified *s 994(3)* of the *CA 2006*, it is provided that the members of an LLP may, by unanimous agreement, exclude the rights in the section, for such period as they may agree – either indefinitely or for an agreed fixed period.

The section provides not that the unanimous agreement must be in writing but that it must be recorded in writing, so presumably properly written-up minutes of a members' meeting would suffice although this could still leave matters open to ambiguity if a member, for example, claims never to have seen the minutes and disputes the existence of unanimous agreement. There is nothing to say that this cannot be dealt with in the initial members' agreement. Indeed, it is recommended that it should be, as that is the time the members and the agreement's draftsman will be considering not only the issue of future capital withdrawal but all matters relating to the operation of the LLP, and hence this would be the sensible time for this issue to be aired and determined. There is no halfway house – either the section applies in its totality, or it does not.

The nature of the right

12.62   The essential right is for a member of an LLP to petition the court, on the grounds that the LLP's affairs are being, or have been, conducted in a manner which is unfairly prejudicial. The prejudice can be either to all members, or some part of the membership, including the petitioner at least.

The petition may also apply to any specific act or omission, whether actual or proposed. The procedure for any petition is laid down in the *Companies (Unfair Prejudice Applications) Proceedings Rules 2009 (SI 2009/2469)* and the *Insolvency Rules 1986 (SI 1986/1925)* (as amended).

An alternative route to the court, however, is that the Secretary of State may, under *s 995* of the *CA 2006* (as modified), apply to the court if he/she believes there is or has been any such prejudicial conduct, or that any actual or proposed act or omission would be so prejudicial, if he/she is drawn to that conclusion by any investigations etc which he/she has conducted, or any inspector's report which has been presented to him/her. Such an application may be in addition to, or in place of, a petition by the Secretary of State for the winding up of the LLP.

Available remedies

12.63   The court's available remedies are very wide, in that under *s 996* of the *CA* as modified), it may, if it is satisfied that the petition is well founded, 'make such order as it thinks fit for giving relief in respect of the matters complained of'.

Without prejudice to the breadth of the above power, there are certain specific provisions which may be included in the list of remedies, namely orders to:

- regulate the future conduct of the LLP's affairs;

- stop the LLP from doing or continuing an act complained of;

- require the LLP to do an act it has omitted to do;

- authorise civil proceedings to be brought in the LLP's name, and on its behalf, on such terms as the court may direct;

- provide for any member's interest in the LLP to be bought out by other members, or by the LLP itself;

- restrain the LLP from generally or specifically altering the members' agreement without leave.

Judicial application of s 994

12.64   There is a large body of case law concerning the predecessor of *s 994*, namely *s 459* of the *CA 1985* in general, and the derivative remedy (ie the taking of action in the LLP's name) in particular. Readers are referred to the standard company law texts, such as *Tolley's Company Law*.

It has been very difficult to draw principles out of this body of law, as courts have often indicated that their judgments are related only to the facts before them. There is, however, one case which is of considerable importance to an understanding of the position. This is *O'Neill v Phillips* [1999] 2 All ER 961, where the House of Lords attempted to strike a balance between the apparent breadth of discretion given to the courts by the section, and the desirability of legal certainty. Their view was that 'fairness' had to be judged in the context of the commercial structure within which people had chosen to work. In the company context, that related to the memorandum and articles of association, and any shareholders' agreement. In the LLP context, it would presumably relate to the members' agreement and such of the default provisions as are applicable. Nonetheless, 'unfairness' did not have to relate to a breach of the duties imposed by those agreements, but could consist of 'using the rules in a manner which equity would regard as contrary to good faith'.

Practical application to LLPs

12.65 Members could be said to have more opportunity than company shareholders to choose the rules by which they will conduct their business. That being so, the instances where, in the absence of a breach of those rules, equity will permit the courts to step in would apparently seemingly be limited. There have been two recently decided cases involving LLPs in which a remedy pursuant to *CA 2006, s 994*, as modified, has been sought and which support this view. The decisions of the court in both of those cases found that unfairly prejudicial conduct had arisen as a result of actions taken in breach of the agreed commercial arrangements which governed the LLP.

In the first case of *Eaton v Caulfield & Others* [2011] EWHC 173 (Ch), an application was made to the court under *CA 2006, s 994* and *IA 1986, s 122* (all sections as modified). In that case, a majority member attempted to expel another member. There was no members' agreement and the respondent was unable to persuade the court that express agreement had been reached between all of the members so as to disapply the *2001 Regulations, Reg 8* (no majority can expel a member without express agreement – see 8.17). Proudman J ruled that the expulsion was unlawful and that such action was 'a clear example of unfairly prejudicial conduct' which consequently entitled the applicant to wind up the LLP.

The second case is that of *F&C Alternative Investments* which is considered in detail elsewhere (see 6.9). However, a further matter considered by the High Court was a claim made by the defendants in that case under *CA 2006, s 994*, as modified. A members' agreement had been entered into although it had not excluded the application of *CA 2006, s 994* to that LLP (see 12.61). Representatives of the corporate member attempted to move decision making away from the agreed process as set out in the members' agreement so as to enable their appointing corporate member to have an increased influence over decision making. In addition, the representatives took action on behalf of the LLP in situations where the other members should have been consulted. The court held that the corporate member was liable under *CA 2006, ss 994* to *996* for the unfairly prejudicial conduct of its representatives. The court further held that the parent company of the corporate member was also liable under these sections as it had actively intervened and therefore the corporate member had simply been a 'cipher' for its actions.

In both of these cases, the actions taken and which led to the finding of unfair prejudice, were seen as being in contravention of the agreed commercial structure in which the parties operated (either under the *2001 Regulations*, or the members' agreement) and so seemingly follow the guidance given by the House of Lords in *O'Neill v Phillips*.

Orders under s 994

12.66   There were, however, also some guidelines in *O'Neill v Phillips* (see 12.64 above) as to the nature of an order which might be made, in the typical situation where a minority shareholder was trying to compel the purchase of his/her shareholding, where the 'unfairness' underlying his/her claim was his/her exclusion from the affairs of the business without a fair offer being made for his/her shares.

The principles which applied to a reasonable offer, which presumably would apply to a member of an LLP with little adjustment, were:

* The offer should be without any minority shareholding discount.

* If not agreed, the value should be determined by an expert.

* The offeror should agree to such expert determination.

* Both parties should have equal access to the expert and equal opportunity to pass information to him/her about the company.

* The offeror should not automatically have to pay costs, if not given a reasonable time to make an offer before the petition was issued.

Unilateral withdrawal

12.67   The legislation provides that a member may unilaterally withdraw from membership by notice. There is, however, no statutory provision for his/her right to withdraw his/her capital. There may of course be a mechanism in an express agreement for him/her to do so, either because it gives other members the right to acquire his/her share, and they choose so to do, or because they are required by the agreement to do so.

What then of the situation where either there is no agreement, or where the remaining members choose not to exercise an option to buy out the retiring member? He/she has, of course, the possibility of applying for the winding up of the LLP, on the grounds that it would be just and equitable (see 16.6 and 16.7 below), but this will not necessarily be readily granted. Will he/she, just because he/she has decided to go, have the right to a remedy under the modified *s 994* of the *CA 2006*? *O'Neill v Phillips* suggests not. It was there stated that it was not the case that 'a member who has not been dismissed or excluded can demand that his/her shares be purchased simply because he/she feels that he/she has lost trust and confidence in the others'.

There seems no reason to think that the above would not be applied to LLPs, and any member considering unilateral withdrawal should therefore consider very carefully, before giving his/her notice, what rights the members' agreement gives him/her.

The Registrar

12.68   The Registrar of Companies is referred to throughout this work as 'the Registrar' (or occasionally and colloquially as 'Companies House'). His/her position, establishment and powers in relation to LLPs are set out in *Pt 35* of the *CA 2006* (as modified). They are effectively exactly the same as for companies, and so are not examined in detail here.

Miscellaneous and supplementary provisions

12.69   In similar fashion to provisions about the Registrar (see 12.68 above), the miscellaneous and supplementary provisions contained in *Pt 37* of the *CA 2006* are applied to LLPs, without any substantive variations.

Chapter 13

Voluntary Arrangements

13.1   This chapter looks at the first set of provisions under the *Insolvency Act 1986 (IA 1986)*, as applied to LLPs, namely voluntary arrangements. These are provisions designed to allow an LLP which is in financial difficulty to put forward a proposal to its creditors in settlement of its existing debts in order (usually) to ensure the LLP's survival. The chapter looks at the ways of creating such arrangements and how they operate in practice.

Applying the 1986 Act

13.2   The *IA 1986* is applied to LLPs by virtue of the *2001 Regulations* (see 1.15 above). This applies six of the first seven Parts of the First Group of Parts of the *IA 1986* (*Pt V* being the exception) and the Third Group of Parts. Further, *reg 10* of and *Sch 6* to the *2001 Regulations* apply the *Insolvency Rules 1986* (and various other ancillary insolvency-related statutory instruments) so that references in this chapter and in Chapters 14 to 17 to 'Rules' are to the *Insolvency Rules 1986*. In effect the legislation equates LLPs to companies in the insolvency context. It applies the provisions with some standard modifications, eg that references to a director or officer of a company are to be taken to include reference to a member of an LLP, and that references to a 'shadow director' shall include references to a 'shadow member'. It also equates an LLP's members' agreement to the memorandum and articles of association of a company. Certain more detailed adaptations are, however, needed, and it therefore goes on to set these out in the *2001 Regulations, Sch 3*. All references in this chapter and in Chapters 14 to 17 which also deal with insolvency issues, are to the *IA 1986* as so applied.

The *Enterprise Act 2002*, which amended the *IA 1986* in very many particulars, is a constant overlay to the above provisions. References to the earlier statute are to its form as amended by the later legislation, and the latter is specifically referred to when major changes of note are made. The same conventions will apply to all subsequent chapters of this book which deal with insolvency matters.

The concept of voluntary arrangements

13.3   The underlying basis of an arrangement is that a deal is struck between an LLP and its then creditors as to a partial and/or delayed payment of its debts in full and final satisfaction of their claims, which becomes binding on the creditors. The non-contractual overlay is that it only needs 75% (by value) of the creditors to approve the arrangement for it to become binding upon all, ie it is an agreement to which a creditor may become bound despite never having approved it.

The idea is not normally that, as in a receivership, the insolvency practitioner appointed over the voluntary arrangement ('the Supervisor') actually takes over the running of the LLP's business but rather that the LLP is allowed to continue to run its own affairs, provided that it hands over to the Supervisor any assets specified in the proposals as being for the benefit of the arrangement creditors, whether those be tangible assets for sale, lump sums, or periodical payments from the LLP's revenue.

Once in the hands of the Supervisor, these sums become subject to a trust in favour of the arrangement's creditors, which may be implicit, but is spelt out in the better drafted sets of proposals, for the avoidance of doubt.

The role of the Nominee/Supervisor

13.4 Another difference from the straightforward concept of an agreement is that a third party is introduced into the equation. An independent professional is called upon to act first as the Nominee, in the framing of the proposals for the arrangement, and then, if they are approved, as Supervisor of the arrangement, with his/her fees being provided for in the arrangement. The Nominee/Supervisor owes duties to the creditors and the court, as well as to the LLP. This can lead to some difficult situations, and the members of an LLP who fail to fulfil their obligations under an arrangement may find that the friendly Supervisor who helped them out of their problems in the first place ends up petitioning for the winding up of the LLP, in order to fulfil the duties placed upon him/her.

Framing the proposals

13.5 The *IA 1986* is quite deliberately silent as to what needs to go into proposals. Since arrangements became a possibility, certain principles surrounding the framing of proposals have become evident.

The key elements to a successful proposal are:

- It should contain an offer which is likely to be attractive to the creditors or at least attractive to the key creditors – in this regard it is essential that the proposal offers a better outcome to creditors than the outcome in any other insolvency process.

- The proposal should be realistic – a significant number of 'trading-on' arrangements fail because the LLP is unable to produce the level of profits necessary to be able to pay an agreed sum into the arrangement.

- It must (as far as possible) be fair and even handed as between the creditors.

- It must be persuasive with regard to the reasons why the proposal (and the business) will succeed.

- It should be comprehensively drafted to cater for all reasonably foreseeable contingencies.

Practical difficulty of LLP arrangements

13.6   There is a practical difficulty which may afflict those seeking to put proposals together for an arrangement for an LLP. This is one which LLPs will share with partnerships, namely that in many cases where the LLP hits difficulties, its members as individuals will also be having difficulties, which will include failure to pay their income tax. Such tax is now, under the self-assessment regime, a personal debt, and not a debt of the LLP, and so it will not be affected by the LLP's arrangement. If the members are not to end up being bankrupted personally, and thus unable to fulfil the roles needed of them in order for the LLP's arrangement to work, then there will need to be interlocking personal voluntary arrangements, which adds to the cost and complexity of the operation.

Proposing the arrangement

13.7   There are two ways in which an arrangement for an LLP may be proposed. First, if the LLP is not already the subject of insolvency proceedings, it may itself propose the arrangement to its creditors (*IA 1986, s 1(1)*, as modified).

The other way is that, if the LLP already has an administrator or a liquidator in charge of its affairs, that person may also propose such an arrangement (often as a means of closure to the formal insolvency proceedings). In the latter case the proposal is not only to the creditors, but to the LLP as well (*IA 1986, s 1(3)*, as modified).

In either case, whether by making the proposal, or by considering an administrator's or liquidator's proposal, the LLP has to make a decision of fundamental importance. The members' agreement should therefore contain provision for how this is to be considered, eg is a meeting necessary and, if so, what rules apply to it.

The LLP's proposal

13.8 Where the proposal is that of the LLP itself, it is for the designated members to submit to the Nominee the proposals for the arrangement, followed within seven days by a statement of affairs (though in practice these will both be drafted by the Nominee with the aid of information given to him/her) (*IA 1986, s 2(3)*, as modified). (*Rules 1.3* and *1.5* respectively govern the minimum contents of the proposals and the statement of affairs.)

The Nominee then first has to endorse a copy of the notice with his/her willingness to act, and return the endorsed copy to the LLP (*r 1.4*). Next, he/she submits a report to the court (within 28 days, or such longer period as the court may allow, after he/she is given notice of the proposal) stating whether in his/her opinion, a meeting of creditors should be called to consider the proposals and, if so, where and when (*IA 1986, s 2(2)*, as modified). He/she then summons that meeting by notifying all creditors of whom he/she is aware (*IA 1986, s 3*, as modified).

The date of the meeting must be not less than 14, nor more than 28 days from the date of the filing of his/her report, and notice must be given as above not less than 14 days before the meeting, accompanied by copies of the proposal, the statement of affairs, a note of the Nominee's comments, and information as to the court in which the proposals were lodged (*r 1.9*). Notice of the creditors' meeting should be given not only to all members, but also to all those who have been members in the immediately preceding two years, if the convenor thinks their presence needed (*r 1.16*). The convenor may, however, exclude any such member or former member from the meeting (whether or not previously notified) – this provision being inserted to prevent disruption of the meeting by a dissatisfied member. The proposals may or may not include proposals for a moratorium.

Proposing a moratorium

13.9 One major problem with voluntary arrangements for LLPs was that, since they are treated under the *IA 1986* as companies, not individuals, there was no provision for a moratorium on court proceedings against the LLP between the submission of the proposals and the meetings at which they are hopefully to be approved. This situation was, however, altered when the relevant provisions of the *IA 2000* (*s 1* and *Sch 1*, introducing a new *Sch A1* to the *IA 1986*) were brought into force in 2003.

However, the moratorium scheme under a proposed voluntary arrangement is so complex, and the duties of the Nominee during a moratorium are so onerous, that the use of a moratorium in a corporate voluntary arrangement is extremely rare. Where a voluntary arrangement is the best option but the LLP requires urgent protection against creditor action, the advising insolvency practitioner is likely to suggest a voluntary arrangement under the protection of an administration.

Obtaining a moratorium

13.10   The moratorium scheme is too complex to go into fully in this work. Briefly, however, the provisions allow most small LLPs (using the same definitions as for the 'small' accounting exemptions set out in 10.39 *et seq.* above) which are not already the subject of insolvency proceedings, and which have not recently taken advantage of these provisions, to seek a moratorium. To do so, it needs to file at court, with the proposals for the arrangement, a statement by the Nominee that the arrangement has a reasonable chance of approval, and that the LLP has sufficient funds to trade through the period of the moratorium. The moratorium will last from the date upon which the papers are filed, to the sooner of the expiry of 28 days or the date of the meeting(s) of the creditors (and the LLP if appropriate) which are to consider approval of the arrangement. The Nominee must, at both the start and end of the moratorium, advertise the fact, and notify the LLP and any creditor he/she knows of (save that at the start only creditors who have actually petitioned for the LLP's winding up need specifically be notified).

The effect of a moratorium

13.11   During the period of the moratorium, none of the following steps may be taken (except, in some cases, with the leave of the court):

* any petition for winding up or administration of the LLP;
* any appointment of an administrative receiver;
* any meeting of the LLP or its members;
* any forfeiture by a landlord;
* any enforcement of security or the taking of possession of goods on hire purchase;
* any commencement or continuation of any proceedings or execution;
* any crystallisation of a floating charge.

The Nominee's responsibilities

13.12   In practice it is likely to be very difficult to find a Nominee willing to act in arrangements where there is a moratorium, at least if the arrangements proposed are of a non-interventionist nature.

The reason for this is that the Nominee's responsibilities are considerably increased in these circumstances. He/she is expected continually to monitor the progress of the LLP during the moratorium, to check the likely acceptability of approval of the proposals, and the likely ability of the LLP to fund its operations through the moratorium period. He/she (or a moratorium committee if appointed) is required to approve any disposal or payment by the LLP as being for the LLP's benefit. Anyone claiming that any act or omission of the Nominee has led to loss to the LLP has the ability, if the LLP itself does not act against the Nominee to recover such loss, to seek the sanction of the court to do so. Any Nominee will therefore have to take a much more interventionist role in the running of the LLP during the moratorium than otherwise, with no doubt a consequent effect upon fee levels.

The creditors' meeting

13.13   The purpose of the meeting referred to in 13.8 above, which is governed by *s 4* of the *IA 1986,* is to consider whether to approve the proposals, with or without modifications, amongst which may be the substitution of another suitably qualified practitioner for the initially proposed Supervisor.

Modifications are often proposed by Crown and other major creditors, eg banks, and they inevitably tighten the conditions of the proposals, eg by introducing tougher criteria for defining the failure of the proposals. Often they are only put forward at the last minute. Care needs to be taken that they are not contradictory to or inconsistent with other provisions in the proposals, which are not directly affected by the modifications, or there can be later difficulties in interpretation of the amended proposals. Certain proposals or modifications may not be accepted without the approval of anyone adversely affected, ie:

• those which affect the rights of a secured creditor to enforce his/her security;

• those whereby any preferential debt is not to be given its proper priority over other debts;

• those whereby there is any difference between the proportional dividends payable to creditors in respect of different preferential debts.

Conduct of the meeting

13.14   When notice of meetings is sent out, a form of proxy must be enclosed (*r 1.13*). Whoever convenes the meeting must act as chairman or, if he/she cannot be present, must nominate someone from within his/her firm who is either a licensed insolvency practitioner in his/her own right, or an employee of the convenor's firm experienced in insolvency matters (*r 1.14*).

In practice, the senior manager who has the day-to-day conduct of the file in the Nominee's office will often be so appointed. Frequently, the chairman will hold proxy votes, but must not use such proxies to increase his/her firm's remuneration unless specifically so directed (*r 1.15*).

Voting at creditors' meetings

13.15   Any notified creditor is entitled to vote at the creditors' meeting, in person or by proxy. His/her vote is governed by the size of his/her debt as at the date of the meeting (or, if the LLP is already in administration or being wound up, as at the date of commencement of the relevant proceedings).

If the debt is unascertained or unliquidated, the only way it can be admitted to vote is if the chairman puts a minimum agreed figure on it. Decisions on how much debt is to be admitted, or whether a claim is to be rejected, are left to the chairman of the meeting, though an aggrieved creditor can appeal to the court. If a chairman is in doubt about whether to admit a contested claim, he/she should allow it to be voted, but mark it as objected to, on the basis that a successful objector can then seek to have that creditor's vote declared invalid (*r 1.17A (4)*).

A dissatisfied creditor can apply to court on the grounds of 'unfair prejudice' or 'material irregularity' in relation to the process. Any application to the court must be commenced within 28 days of the chairman's report to the court of the outcome of the meeting, and the court has no discretion to extend that period – *Re Bournemouth & Boscombe AFC Co Ltd* [1998] BPIR 183. If a court considers that there has been material irregularity or unfair prejudice it may reverse or vary the chairman's decision approving the proposal, or summon another meeting, or make such order as it thinks fit.

All the above procedures are laid down in *rr 1.17* and *1.17A*.

Voting at members' meetings

13.16   What is less clear is what the procedures are to be for voting at members' meetings, if requisite, ie if the proposals are made by an administrator or liquidator (see 13.26 below).

Rule 1.18, in the company context, gives members of a company votes equivalent to the voting rights represented by their shares. No such concept is of course applicable to members of an LLP. The rule goes on to say that references to a member's shares include 'any other interest which he/she may have as a member of the company'. It might be suggested therefore that members of an LLP should have votes equivalent to their proportionate interests in the capital of the LLP. The problem is defining what such capital might be, eg should it be considered to include a member's share of retained and undrawn or unallocated profits.

This is an area where the draftsman of an LLP members' agreement should attempt to lay down some clear principles, in the hope that these would be followed by the court, even though the rule itself is not adapted for the LLP scenario and therefore makes no reference to such agreements (even by reference to articles).

Majorities at creditors' meetings

13.17 The requisite majorities at a creditors' meeting are calculated under *r 1.19* by reference to the aggregate value of the creditors voting for or against any resolution, either in person or by proxy. In the case of a resolution to approve any proposal or modification, a majority in excess of 75% is needed (ie exactly 75% is not sufficient). For any other resolution a majority in excess of 50% will do. Claims shall be omitted (wholly or partly as appropriate) if they are un-notified; or wholly or partly secured; or wholly or partly derived from a bill of exchange or promissory note (though there are exceptions to the latter).

There is a further hurdle that any resolution (including a resolution to approve the proposal) which is rejected by more than 50% of unconnected creditors is also invalid (*r 1.19(4)*). Under the modified *IA 1986, s 249* 'connected' persons include members or shadow members of the LLP and 'associates' – a term broadly defined to include relatives, partners, employees and trustees as well as companies over which a connected person has control (*IA 1986, s 455* (as modified)). See *Kapoor v National Westminster Bank Plc* (2011) EWCA (Civ) 1083 for consideration of parallel provisions in an IVA context.

Majorities at members' meetings

13.18 By contrast (see 13.17 above), at members' meetings called by a proposing administrator or liquidator (see 13.26 below), a majority in excess of 50% will by *r 1.20* suffice for any resolution.

In this instance, however, this is expressed to be subject to any contrary provision in the members' agreement.

Adjournments of meetings

13.19 The chairman has a fairly broad discretion to deal with necessary adjournments, under *r 1.21*.

He/she can, for instance, adjourn until later on in the originally designated day, and may even decide to combine the members' and creditors' meetings (if the former is needed – see 13.26 below). Alternatively, he/she may adjourn for up to 14 days. Notice of adjournment shall be given to the court.

Acceptance of modifications by the LLP

13.20   One specific addition to the modified provisions of *s 4* of the *IA 1986* is a new subsection (*s 4(5A)*) requiring the chairman of the meeting to ascertain from the LLP, before the end of the meeting, whether it approves of any modifications. If the LLP is silent, it is presumed not to agree to them.

In practice, this means that there have to be some representatives of the LLP present at the meeting who are authorised by the LLP to give its consent to modifications, of which the LLP as a body may have had no prior notice. If it is not in a position to do this, then unless the chairman adjourns the meeting its dissent is presumed, creditors who would approve amended proposals may vote against the original version, and the proposals may fail. The members' agreement should therefore clearly provide for who is to be so authorised, and how.

Passing of property

13.21   As soon as an arrangement is approved, ie without needing any court sanction, any assets which are due to go to the Supervisor on the basis that they form assets in the voluntary arrangement should be passed to him/her under *r 1.23* by the LLP (or the administrator or liquidator thereof if the proposals were made by him/her – see 13.26 below).

In the latter case the appropriate practitioner's fees (including any monies due to the Official Receiver) need to be discharged, or an undertaking given to discharge them out of the first tranche of monies received by the Supervisor, since there is a charge over the assets to that effect.

Reporting the meeting

13.22   After the meeting, it is the task of the chairman of the meeting, under the modified *s 4(6)* of the *IA 1986* and *r 1.24*, to report the outcome, including any modifications, to the court within four days and to the LLP and all those originally entitled to notice of the meeting(s).

If the proposals are accepted, the Supervisor must also send a copy of the chairman's report to Companies House.

The effect of approval

13.23   If the proposals are approved, either with or without modifications, they take effect, under *s 5* of the *IA 1986* (as modified), as from the date of the creditors' meeting. The deal thus approved binds every creditor who was entitled to vote at the meeting, whether or not they were present at the meeting in person or by proxy and whether or not they had notice of the meeting.

Thus a creditor who was either silent, or who was in an unsuccessful minority of opposers, may nonetheless be bound to the arrangement. He/she (or, more improbably, a member of the LLP) may, however, apply to the court under *s 6* of the *IA 1986* (as modified), within 28 days of the chairman's report, if he/she considers that an arrangement unfairly prejudices his/her interests, or that there was some material irregularity at or in connection with the meeting.

The Court of Appeal has confirmed (in the context of an individual voluntary arrangement) that such an irregularity may include 'secret deals' to secure approval of the arrangement, and that creditors and the debtor owe a wider duty to be open and transparent in their dealings (*Cadbury Schweppes v Somji* [2000] EWCA Civ 340). Irregularity may also arise from a disputed valuation of a creditor's claim (*re Newlands (Seaford) Educational Trust* [2007] BCC 195 and *re Gatnom Capital and Finance Ltd* [2010] EWHC 3353 (Ch)).

Unfair prejudice as a ground to challenge a CVA is a question of fact, judged on the overall effect of the CVA. The fact that some unsecured creditors are treated in different ways to others may be prejudicial, but will only be fatal to the CVA if such prejudice cannot be justified in the context of the CVA as a whole.

A CVA was successfully challenged for unfair prejudice, in *Prudential Assurance Co Ltd v Powerhouse PRG Ltd* [2007] EWHC 1002 (Ch) where the CVA had the effect of releasing parent company guarantees without any compensation.

In such circumstances, the court may revoke or suspend the approval of the arrangements, or give directions for further meetings to be summoned (failure to comply with which can in turn lead to a later order for suspension or revocation). It can also give such supplemental directions as may be necessary, related in particular to events which may have taken place between the meeting and its order. Irregularities which do not lead to such an application do not invalidate the meeting.

Subsequent court intervention

13.24   The court may also have a role to play during the course of the implementation of the arrangement, and various powers are given to it by *s 7* of the *IA 1986* (as modified).

Anyone, creditor or not, may apply to the court for relief if he/she is dissatisfied with any act or omission of the Supervisor. If the Supervisor has been acting within the framework of the proposals, the court is unlikely to interfere. If it intervenes, the court has power to confirm, reverse or modify any act or decision of the Supervisor; or to give directions to him/her; or to make any other order it thinks fit.

Equally, if the Supervisor is him/herself unsure of what action he/she should take, he/she may apply to the court for directions. He/she is specifically included amongst the list of those who may apply, in suitable circumstances (eg failure of the arrangement according to its own designated criteria) for the winding up or administration of the LLP.

Appointment of a Supervisor by the court

13.25 It may be that the court is itself called upon to appoint a Supervisor. It may do so under *s 7(5)* of the *IA 1986*, if it is satisfied that it is expedient for it to do so and that in practice it is not feasible for the appointment to be otherwise made.

Such an appointment, of a suitably qualified practitioner, may be either to replace an original appointee, or to fill a vacancy. This can apply to multiple appointments as well, ie the court could appoint a second or subsequent Supervisor, or replace one of joint appointees.

Proposals by administrator or liquidator

13.26 As mentioned above (see 13.7), it is possible for the proposals to be made by an administrator or liquidator of an LLP, rather than by the members. Differently modified versions of *ss 2* and *3* of the *IA 1986* cover this eventuality.

Within that possibility, there is then a further split of ways forward, in that the proposer may put forward a third party as the Supervisor of the arrangement, or may suggest him/herself. In the former instance, the Nominee's statement to the court must provide for the necessity of and arrangements for a meeting of the members of the LLP as well as, but separate from, a meeting of its creditors, to consider the arrangement. The details necessary for the statement of affairs etc must be given to the Nominee by the proposer. It is the duty of the Nominee to summon the two meetings.

In the latter instance, ie if the administrator or liquidator is proposing him/herself as Supervisor, then, presumably since his/her appointment already has court sanction, he/she may proceed to the summoning of the two meetings without the interim step of reporting on their advisability to the court.

Whoever is the proposed nominee, if the LLP is already in liquidation, notice of the proposals and the identity of the nominee must also be given to the Official Receiver (*rr 1.10* and *1.12*).

Revocation or suspension of the arrangement

13.27 As mentioned above (see 13.23 above), the court has the power, in certain circumstances, to revoke or suspend the arrangement. *Rule 1.25* deals with the consequences.

The person who obtained the revocation etc order must serve it upon the Supervisor, and the proposer of the arrangement, and Companies House. If further meetings need to be called, whoever is responsible for that must also be notified. It is then the job of the proposers (ie the members of the LLP, or its administrator or liquidator) first to notify anyone who was originally notified of the initial meeting(s) or who they think may be affected by the order; and second to notify the court within seven days if it intends either to submit revised proposals, or to re-submit the original ones.

The Supervisor's duties

13.28 The Supervisor must of course keep full accounting records and, at least annually, send an account, together with a report on how the arrangement is progressing to, amongst others, the court, Companies House, the creditors and the LLP.

He must also provide such information and documents to the Secretary of State as the latter may request. *Rules 1.26* and *1.27* relate to these obligations. His/her fees for the performance of his/her duties are, by *r 1.28*, generally sanctioned by the terms of the arrangement.

Completion of the arrangement

13.29 All concerned hope that the arrangement will proceed successfully to completion.

At that stage, the Supervisor must, under *r 1.29*, send all the arrangement's creditors and all members, a notice of conclusion, and a final report and summary account, together with an explanation of any difference in the result from that envisaged in the initial proposals. He/she then has to send copies to the court and to Companies House as well.

Failure of an arrangement

13.30 It may, however, be that an arrangement may fail. What constitutes 'failure' should, as discussed above (see 13.5), normally be clearly designated in the original proposals or, if things start to go wrong, there can be great confusion.

The most common cause of failure is a simple lack of the promised payments due to the Supervisor, so that he/she cannot discharge the arrangement creditors' debts as planned.

Normally, the proposals will have provided that, in that event, he/she may petition the court for the winding up of the LLP, and that, to cover that eventuality, he/she should at all times retain sufficient funds in hand to allow him/her to do this.

The Court of Appeal has held (in re *N T Gallagher & Sons Ltd* [2002] EWCA Civ 404) that when a CVA is terminated by the company entering liquidation, the terms of the CVA itself will determine what happens to any monies held in trust for creditors by the Supervisor of the CVA. If the CVA does not so provide, then the trust over the CVA monies continues unaffected by the liquidation and may be paid out to CVA creditors. CVA creditors are also entitled to prove in the liquidation for the balance of their debt (after giving credit for dividends received from the CVA).

Voluntary arrangements affecting solicitors' and other professional LLPs

13.31 Particular considerations apply to voluntary arrangements relating to professional practices incorporated as LLPs. There is likely to be a duty to notify professional regulators on any insolvency event (eg the duty to inform the Solicitors Regulation Authority of any insolvency event including a voluntary arrangement affecting a solicitors' practice).

In addition, there may be specific regulatory requirements to protect client confidentiality or client moneys.

Where an LLP is FSA authorised, then the FSA has specific powers to receive notice and information about (and to intervene in) voluntary arrangements and other insolvency procedures (see FSA Enforcement Guide Chapter 13).

Chapter 14

Administration

14.1   The second option for an LLP which is insolvent is administration. This procedure gives more effective protection against creditor action than a voluntary arrangement, and administration together with voluntary arrangement may be used in some cases to provide this additional protection. Administration is only an option, however, if it is likely that one of three objectives is likely to be achieved. These are set out in greater detail below.

The procedures for administration, and the effects of it, will be considered. A prime task of the administrator is to formulate and implement proposals for the administration and this area is also examined. The administrator's powers and duties are described. The rights of creditors of the LLP and other parties to object to or seek redress for the administrator's actions are looked at. The procedures applying to the termination of the administration are set out. Lastly, brief mention is made of the position regarding receivers and administrative receivers.

Introduction

14.2   The purpose of an administration is to fill the gap between the relatively relaxed regime of a voluntary arrangement, and the finality of a liquidation. An administration can sometimes be used to provide an opportunity for the LLP to continue to trade under the control of a licensed insolvency practitioner with protection against action in the hope that the LLP's fortunes can be turned round. The outcome will depend on the success of the revival attempt, and may vary from a return to members' control to the dissolution of the LLP. The usual objective of an administration though is to increase the return to the LLP's creditors by facilitating a sale of the business and assets of the LLP as a going concern to a new entity, and the subsequent winding up of the LLP.

The 'pre-pack' administration (where the business is sold immediately after the LLP is placed into administration) has been subject to criticism. However, the courts have upheld the validity of pre-pack sales (see *DKLL Solicitors v HMRC* [2007] EWHC 2067 (Ch) and *re Halliwells LLP & Others* [2010] EWHC 2036 (Ch)), provided that the administrator has complied with the requirements of the best practice guidelines for insolvency practitioners as set out in Statement of Insolvency Practice 16 (SIP 16) (*re Kayley Vending Limited* [2009] EWHC 904 (Ch)).

Under SIP 16, administrators must demonstrate how the pre-pack was in the best interests of the company's creditors as a whole and disclose information about the sale to the creditors including the identity of the purchaser, any connection with the directors or shareholders, valuations of the assets and consideration paid. The SIP 16 disclosure, however, does not need to be sent to the creditors until after the pre-pack sale has completed.

The effect of administration is that whilst the regime is in force the affairs, business and property of the LLP are managed by the administrator. This is therefore a much more forceful and involved role than that of a supervisor of a voluntary arrangement, as described in Chapter 13.

The provisions which govern administration are to be found in *Schedule B1* to the *IA 1986 (Sch B1)*, which sets out the full administration provisions. References in this Chapter to paragraph numbers are to the paragraphs of that Schedule. The regime under *Sch B1* was applied to LLPs by *The Limited Liability Partnerships (Amendment) Regulations 2005 (SI 2005/1989)* with effect from 1 October 2005.

Under *Sch B1*, creditors of the LLP or the members can apply to court for an administration order. Alternatively, the members or the holder of a qualifying floating charge (see 14.10 below), can appoint an administrator by simply filing certain forms with the court ('out-of-court procedure').

The objectives of administration

14.3   There are three objectives for which administration may be appropriate, which are specified in *para 3*, and which reflect the above range of possible outcomes. Following the spectrum of optimism, they are as detailed below:

- To allow the survival of the LLP, and the whole or any part of its undertaking, as a going concern. In other words it is hoped that the administrator will, at some stage, be able to hand all or part of the enterprise back to the members, without any other intervening process.

- To bring about a more advantageous realisation of an LLP's assets than would be the result of a winding up. This is intended to give the freer range of an administrator to an insolvency practitioner than the restricted duties of a liquidator, even if, once the assets have been so realised and distributed, a winding up needs to be commenced to administer the last rites. (For such a purpose, the administrator is both a potential petitioner and a potential liquidator.)

- To realise property in order to make a distribution to one or more secured or preferential creditors. (It is worth remembering that it is quite feasible for members of the LLP to be its secured creditors, so this aim could be for their benefit.)

The administrator must try for the highest of those aims, and can only progress down the scale if he/she thinks it is not reasonably practical to aim higher, and that other creditors will not be unreasonably harmed.

The status of an administrator

14.4   Anyone to be appointed as an administrator must be qualified to act as an insolvency practitioner for the LLP (*para 6*). Once appointed, he/she will be an officer of the court, whether or not he/she is actually appointed by the court (*para 5*).

The choice of administrator is likely to be made by the members and any qualifying floating charge holder.

Applying for an administration order

14.5   The applicant for an administration order will need first to satisfy the court that it has the jurisdiction to make an order under *para 11*, namely that the LLP is insolvent, ie unable to pay its debts within the meaning of *IA 1986, s 123*.

Next, it has to persuade the court that making an order would achieve one of the statutory objectives set out above (at 14.3).

Presentation of the application

14.6   The application may be presented under *para 12* by any one, or more, of the following:

• the LLP itself or its members;

• any actual or contingent creditor(s);

• a justices' chief executive enforcing fines on behalf of a magistrates' court;

• the Financial Services Authority, in respect of an LLP under its jurisdiction (*FSMA 2000, s 359*) (see 14.2 above).

Once the application is presented, it cannot be withdrawn without the leave of the court (*para 12(3)*). In the ordinary course, an administration application is generally only made when the out-of-court procedure (see 14.10 to 14.11 below) is not available.

Notification of application

14.7   Notice of the application must be given to certain people as soon as is reasonably practicable. Those to whom notice must be given are:

• anyone entitled to appoint an administrator or administrative receiver;

- anyone who has already been appointed as an administrative receiver or supervisor of a voluntary arrangement;

- anyone who has issued a winding up petition or distrained against the LLP or its property;

- any enforcement officer instructed to take action against the LLP's property.

The LLP as petitioner

14.8   In the light of the fact of the LLP's ability to act as applicant, the members' agreement should provide the mechanism for the LLP to reach a determination to apply. The agreement should also provide for a mechanism to authorise the LLP or its members to appoint an administrator under *para 22* (see 14.11 below).

If it is the members of the LLP who apply (as distinct from the LLP itself), they should take care to avoid an order that the costs may fall upon them personally if the application is unsuccessful, as in *Re WF Fearman Ltd (No 2)* (1988) 4 BCC 141.

Orders to be made

14.9   The court, on hearing an application, has a range of options open to it. It may of course grant or dismiss the application. It may also adjourn the hearing either conditionally or unconditionally.

It may make an interim order or any other order it thinks fit and, if it makes an interim order, it may restrict the powers of either the members of the LLP or the LLP itself. A final option is that it may decide to treat the application as a winding up petition, and deal with it accordingly.

Out-of-court appointment by a 'qualifying floating charge holder'

14.10   The holder of a floating charge, which is of a qualifying type, may appoint an administrator using the out of court procedure (*para 14*). Qualifying types of floating charge are ones which (i) are immediately enforceable; (ii) relate to the whole or substantially the whole of the LLP's property; and (iii) which:

- state that *para 14(2)* applies to the charge; or

- state that the holder of the charge can make such an appointment; or

- state that the holder of the charge can appoint an administrative receiver.

191

In practice, a debenture over an LLP's business and assets is likely to contain a qualifying floating charge if the LLP is in default under the debenture.

Such an appointment may not be made if there is a provisional liquidator, a liquidator, or an administrative receiver already in office.

If there are any prior floating charges to the appointor's charge, the appointor must either obtain the prior charge holder's consent, or serve two working days' notice on him/her in form 2.5B.

Appointment by the LLP or its members

14.11 Either the LLP itself, or its members, may appoint an administrator using the out-of-court procedure, except in certain defined circumstances. The most common circumstance which prevents an out-of-court appointment by the members of the LLP is the existence of a winding up petition (*para 22*).

If it is proposed to make an out-of-court appointment, then not less than five working days' notice has to be given to anyone entitled to appoint an administrative receiver/administrator. It must specify who the proposed administrator is to be. The notice must then be filed at court, with a statutory declaration from the applicant that the LLP is or is likely to become unable to pay its debts, but is not in liquidation.

Notice must also be given to the LLP itself (by service at its registered office) and to the supervisor of any LLP voluntary arrangement or any person who has distrained against or is charged with execution over the LLP's property (*r 2.20*).

Once any necessary notice has been given, the administration takes effect when another notice is filed at court (in form 2.9B, Notice of Appointment). Certain documents need to be filed at court with the notice including a written confirmation from the proposed administrators stating that they are prepared to act and that they believe that the purpose of the administration is reasonably likely to be achieved.

The validity of out-of-court appointments has been challenged in a number of cases where the relevant rules and procedures have not been followed. For example in a company case, an appointment was held invalid because a meeting of directors was not called in accordance with the company's articles of association, and because notice had not been served on the company as required by r 2.20 (*Minmar (929) Limited v Khalastchi* [2011] EWHC 1159). In other cases, invalidity was caused by use of the wrong form (*re G Tech Construction* [2007] BPIR 1275 and *Pillar Securitisation SARL v Spicer* [2010] EWHC 836 (Ch)) and by failure to serve notice on a charge holder (*re Law for All Limited* [2011] EWHC 2672) or on the supervisor of a voluntary arrangement (*National Westminster Bank Plc v Msaada Group (a firm)* [2011] EWHC 3423 (Ch)).

The courts have also held that an appointment which is invalid cannot be cured, however technical the defect may be. Where an out-of-court appointment has not been validly made, there are no insolvency proceedings and the court has no jurisdiction to correct any errors. In some cases the court has instead made retrospective administration orders under *para 13(2)* (*re Derfshaw Limited & Others* [2011] EWHC 1565 (Ch)), but in other cases the court has declined to do so (*Pillar Securitisation* above). There are conflicting first instance decisions in this area and clarification is awaited from the Court of Appeal.

Therefore members (and/or the LLP) appointing an administrator should take legal advice to ensure they comply fully with the *Insolvency Rules* (in relation to notice and forms) and with the provisions of their LLP members' agreement (in relation to formalities for meetings and authority of those members making the administrator's appointment).

Interaction with an administrative receiver

14.12   No out-of-court administrator's appointment can be made when an administrative receiver is in office. If an application for an administration order is issued at a time when an administrative receiver has already been appointed, then the court will ordinarily dismiss the petition.

The effect of entering into administration

14.13   The commencement of an administration occurs when an order is made, or, if the appointment is made out-of-court, when notice of that appointment is filed at court. Thereafter:

- No determination may be made by the LLP that it should be voluntarily wound up.

- No order may be made that the LLP shall be compulsorily wound up (*para 42*).

Further, without the consent of the administrator or the court (which may attach conditions to any such consent):

- No landlord may forfeit a lease of an LLP's premises by peaceful re-entry for breach of the lease.

- No steps may be taken to enforce any security over the LLP's property.

- No steps may be taken to repossess any goods in the LLP's possession under a hire purchase agreement etc.

- No proceedings, execution or other legal process may be commenced or continued against the LLP or its property.

- No distress may be levied against the LLP or its property (*para 43*).

Interim moratorium before the administration

14.14   The restrictions set out in 14.13 above will also apply during any 'interim period' (*para 44*) prior to the administration of the LLP. If the chosen route to administration is through court application it runs from the time the application is filed in court to the time of its final disposal in a court hearing. If a floating charge holder is seeking to appoint using the out-of-court method, it runs from the time notice of intention to appoint is filed at court, for a period of five working days. Similarly, if the LLP or its members are seeking to appoint out of court, the interim period runs from the time of filing the notice of intention to appoint at court, but in this case it lasts for ten working days. In either of the out-of-court methods, the moratorium lapses if no appointment is made, or becomes permanent when the administrator's appointment is filed at court.

Moratorium and creditor leave

14.15   Guidance was given in *Re Atlantic Computer Systems Plc* [1992] 1 All ER 476 as to the circumstances in which leave is likely to be given to a creditor to take action notwithstanding the moratorium.

The court will balance the interests of the claimant against the interests of the creditors (including the financial loss suffered) to assess if it is inequitable for the court to prevent proceedings being commenced or continued. (See also *Innovate Logistics Limited v Sunberry Properties Limited* [2008] EWCA Civ 1261.)

Note that these provisions do not (save in relation to forfeiture) prevent a party from exercising a right to treat a contract as terminated by breach, so that, eg a third party may, if the contract so allows, treat the commencement of the administration as an act justifying its withdrawal from a contract otherwise requiring future performance on its part.

Notification of the order

14.16   After the appointment of an administrator, and for so long as it lasts, all relevant documents issued by or on behalf of the LLP or the administrator must give the administrator's name, and state that the affairs, business and property of the LLP are being managed by him/her. This applies to invoices, orders for goods, or letters. If this is not done, the LLP itself is liable to a fine, as also may be the administrator and/or any member of the LLP who, without reasonable excuse, has authorised or permitted the default (*para 45*).

Further provisions are also found in *para 46*, which requires the administrator forthwith to notify the LLP of the order, and publish it in the prescribed manner.

The administrator must also send notice of his/her appointment to the Registrar within seven days. He/she must notify all known creditors. If he/she fails without reasonable excuse to carry out these functions, he/she is liable not only to a fine, but also to a daily default fine.

Submission of a statement of affairs

14.17 One of the first jobs of an administrator is to require the submission to him/her of a statement of affairs, by one or more of those qualified to give such a statement. Those concerned may be:

- present or past members of the LLP;

- anyone participating in the formation of the LLP, if it was within the year before the making of the order;

- present employees of the LLP, or those who were employees within the last year, if the administrator thinks they can help;

- present members or employees of an LLP, or those who were in either of those categories during the previous year, where that LLP in turn is, or was within that year, a member of the subject LLP.

'Employee' in these circumstances is sufficiently widely defined to include someone acting under a contract for services, such as the LLP's accountants or solicitors.

Anyone so required to give a statement must do so within 11 days of being notified of the requirement to do so, unless the administrator releases them from the obligation, or agrees to extend the time limit. If an administrator is asked so to release a person, or to grant an extension of time, and refuses, the person concerned may apply to the court for a release or extension, which is within the discretion of the court.

If the person subject to the requirement fails without reasonable excuse to comply with it he/she will be liable to both a fine and a daily default fine for continued non-compliance.

Contents of the statement of affairs

14.18 The statement, which must be verified by a statement of truth, needs to deal with the LLP's assets and liabilities, and to give details of its creditors and their respective securities. *Rules 2.11* and *2.12* apply to the requirements for the statement.

The administrator's proposals

14.19 It is the intention of the legislation that administrations should not be long-winded affairs. Thus the administrator has, under *para 49*, to present proposals within eight weeks of appointment (though the court can extend this period), as to how (if at all) he/she is to achieve the purpose(s) specified in the original order. The proposals may include proposals for a voluntary arrangement; or a compromise or arrangement to be sanctioned under *CA 2006, s 899*.

He/she then has to deal with those proposals by:

- sending a copy to the Registrar;
- sending a copy to all creditors;
- laying a copy before a meeting of creditors convened by him/her for the purpose, within 10 weeks of the commencement of the administration, on not less than 14 days' notice;
- sending a copy to all the LLP's members, or publishing a notice telling members where they can write to get a copy of the statement.

If the administrator fails to comply with any of these requirements, he/she will be liable to a fine and, potentially, to a daily default fine.

When creditors' meeting may be unnecessary

14.20 There are, however, three sets of circumstances in which the administrator may not normally need to summon a creditors' meeting. These are:

- if he/she believes the LLP has enough assets to pay all creditors in full;
- if (by complete contrast) he/she believes that there are insufficient assets for anything at all to be distributed to unsecured creditors (other than that fraction of monies, which would otherwise be available for floating charge holders, which are reserved for unsecured creditors by the modified *IA 1986, s 176A(2)(a)*); or
- if he/she believes that he/she cannot either rescue the LLP as a going concern or secure a better outcome through administration than through winding up.

Even in such circumstances, however, a meeting must be summoned by the administrator if at least 10% of the creditors (by value) properly request him/her to do so.

Consideration of proposals by creditors

14.21 It is the task of the creditors, at the meeting called as above, to decide whether to approve the administrator's proposals.

The creditors can suggest modifications, but can only incorporate these if the administrator approves. If they approve the proposals, they may also decide to appoint some willing creditors as a creditors' committee, which may then require the administrator to give it such information as it may reasonably ask for, and to attend its meetings.

Creditors may also call for subsequent meetings if at least 10% (by value) of them properly request this; and such additional meetings may also be ordered by the court.

Notifying the outcome of the meeting

14.22 The result of the initial creditors' meeting must be notified by the administrator to the court, to the Registrar, and all known creditors (*para 54(6)*).

If that report is to the effect that the meeting had rejected the proposals (with or without modifications) the court has a number of options open to it. It may discharge the appointment of the administrator from such time as it thinks fit, and make any consequential orders it thinks fit. Alternatively, it may adjourn the hearing either conditionally or unconditionally, or make an interim order, or make any other order it thinks fit.

Revision of proposals

14.23 If, after proposals have been approved, the administrator seeks their revision, he/she must go back to the creditors.

Thus, he/she must send to all the creditors notice of the intended revisions, and convene another creditors' meeting for their consideration. He/she must also send a copy of the intended revisions to all members of the LLP, or publish a notice telling them where they can get copies. Consideration of the suggested revisions follows the same pattern as the original proposals, ie the creditors may reject them, or accept them with or without modifications, but they may be modified only on the basis that the administrator consents.

The administrator must notify the outcome of the meeting to the Registrar, the court, and all creditors. In exceptional cases, if revisions are commercially necessary, and simply cannot wait until the 14 days necessary for calling a creditors' meeting have elapsed, then the court has jurisdiction to fill in the gap by using its power to give directions effectively to grant consent to revisions, as in *Re Smallman Construction Ltd* (1988) 4 BCC 784.

General duties and powers of the administrator

14.24 The immediate task of the administrator, under *para 67*, is to take over custody and control of all the property and assets of the LLP. It is then up to him/her to manage the affairs, business and property of the LLP. He/she is given wide powers under *paras 59* and *60*, to do all the things he/she needs to in order to carry out that latter task.

A list of specific powers is contained in *Sch 1* to the *IA 1986*, but they are merely examples of the general power. (Not only does he/she have power to manage, but he/she also has the power to stop anyone else (eg a member of the LLP) from doing so. Any powers vested in the LLP or its members, whatever their source, capable of interfering with the administrator's role, can only be so exercised with his/her general or specific consent.)

The administrator can appoint a manager to carry out these tasks on his/her behalf. If he/she considers a meeting of the members of the LLP, or of its creditors, is needed, he/she may summon such a meeting. Relevant procedures are imported from the modified *s 92* of the *IA 1986*, so that the holding of the meeting shall be as per the procedure set out in the LLP's members' agreement, with a quorum as provided therein (or a default quorum of two if the agreement is silent). If no provisions are made, then the administrator may apply to the court for directions. That, in fact, is merely an example of the administrator's broader power to apply to the court for directions in respect of any matter arising in connection with his/her duties.

As far as third parties are concerned, the administrator is acting as agent on behalf of the LLP (and, as such, he/she does of course owe to the LLP the same duties as any agent owes to his/her principal). If the third party is acting in good faith, and for value, he/she is not concerned to enquire whether the administrator is acting within his/her powers.

One power which is conspicuous by its absence is the ability to act like a liquidator in disclaiming a lease or other onerous contract. Administrators are liable to pay (as an expense of the administration) the full passing rent which falls due under the lease (where the LLP is a tenant pursuant to the lease) during the administration if they 'use' any part of the property for the purpose of the administration (*Goldacre (Offices) Limited v Nortel Networks UK Ltd (in Administration)* [2009] EWHC 3389 (Ch)). However, an administrator may avoid lease costs if he/she ceases 'using' the property immediately from the start of the administration. Liability for rent due prior to the administration usually ranks as an unsecured claim in the administration.

Power to deal with property subject to floating charge

14.25 Specific provisions as to the administrator's powers to deal with property which is subject to some form of charge are contained in *para 70*. He/she may without needing any consent dispose of or deal with any such property, if it is subject to what was – at the date of its creation – a floating charge, as if it were not subject to such security.

The holder of the security then acquires, however, such priority over any property which comes into the LLP's hands to replace the disposed of asset as he/she previously had over that asset. In other words, if it is prudent for a property subject to a floating charge to be sold, eg because it has high running costs, the original security holder takes substitute security over the proceeds of sale.

Power to deal with property subject to fixed charge

14.26   *Paragraph 71* deals with the situation where the property in question is subject to a fixed charge, or to a hire purchase or similar agreement, or to a retention of title clause.

In such a case, if the administrator can show that the property's disposal would be likely to aid the purpose(s) of the administration, he/she may apply to the court for permission to make the disposal free from the security. If the court orders a disposal, the net proceeds must be paid to the secured creditor. If permission is sought to make a disposal at less than market value, the administrator must make up the difference to the secured creditor. If such an order is obtained by the administrator, he/she has to notify the Registrar within 14 days, or face a fine and daily default fine in the absence of reasonable excuse for his/her default.

Challenges to the administrator

14.27   Not all administrations can be expected to run smoothly. Often, this will not be the administrator's fault, but there are provisions in *para 74* designed to protect aggrieved creditors or members, in certain circumstances.

If any such person believes that the way in which the administrator is managing or has managed the affairs, business and property of the LLP has caused him/her unfair harm, or that any actual or proposed act or omission of the administrator would do so, then he/she can apply to the court for aid. The alleged harm may be to creditors or members generally, or to any particular section which includes the petitioner. Further, such an application may be made on the ground that the administrator is simply not performing his/her duties as quickly or · efficiently as is reasonably practicable.

In exercising its powers under this paragraph, the court is unwilling to interfere with the discretion of professional administrators and particularly to give detailed directions in the conduct of the administration, unless there is evidence that the administrator is acting improperly (*re Lehman Brothers International (Europe) (in Administration)* [2008] EWHC 2869

(Ch)). If there is a particular issue in the administration with which a creditor disagrees, the Court of Appeal has suggested that this is best addressed by the creditor applying to the court to give directions to the administrators (under *para 68*) rather than a challenge under *para 74* (*Finnerty v Clark* [2011] EWCA Civ 858).

The court's powers on such an application are broad, as below, but unless the application is made within 28 days of the passing of any proposals or any revisions thereto, no such order may prejudice or prevent the implementation of those proposals or revisions. Nor, in any event, may such an order prejudice or prevent the implementation of any voluntary arrangement which creditors have approved or any compromise or arrangement sanctioned by the court.

Potential orders on an application

14.28   In general terms, the court has its usual range of options on an application as described at 14.27. It may of course decline the application. It may adjourn the hearing conditionally or unconditionally. It may make an interim or any other order it thinks fit.

If it finds the alleged prejudice to have occurred, it may make such order for relief as it thinks fit and, in particular, may:

- regulate the administrator's future management of the LLP;

- require the administrator to do or cease to do something;

- require the administrator to remedy an omission;

- require the administrator to summon a creditors' meeting, to consider any point the court directs;

- provide for the administrator's appointment to cease, and make such consequential orders as it thinks fit.

The courts are reluctant to use their power to remove administrators under *paras 74* or *88* (*Finnerty* above), though they are likely to do so where there is evidence of potential impropriety or where the administrator no longer has the support of the majority of creditors (*Clydesdale Financial Services Ltd v Smailes* [2009] EWHC 1745 (Ch)).

Misfeasance

14.29   The court has power to investigate the conduct of anyone who is or has been (or purports or has purported to be) the administrator of an LLP, where there are allegations that such a person has used the LLP's money or property wrongly, or has become accountable for such money, or has in some other way been guilty of breach of a fiduciary or other duty or of misfeasance. It can commence such investigations only on an application by one of the following:

- the Official Receiver;

- the administrator (presumably if someone else is falsely purporting to be the administrator);

- the liquidator of the LLP;

- a creditor of the LLP; or

- a contributory of the LLP.

The court has power to order the repayment or restoration of money or property, or that such be accounted for. It can also award interest, and order compensation for breach of duty or misfeasance.

Ending administrations

Effluxion of time

14.30 Just as there are now more ways of starting an administration than was the case before the *EA 2002*, so there are now many more ways of ending it.

The first possibility is that it may simply expire by effluxion of time, one year after it was begun (*para 76*). That time period may, however, be extended either:

- by the court, on application by the administrator, for one or more specified periods; or

- by consent, once, for a specified period of not more than six months, where there has been no previous court-related extension, and that consent has come from all secured creditors and over half (by value) of the unsecured creditors (unless the original proposals indicated that the unsecured creditors would get nothing, in which case consent from preferential creditors replaces that of the unsecured creditors).

Another time-linked possibility is that the court, when appointing an administrator in the first place, may itself set a fixed time for his/her appointment, after which it shall cease automatically.

Application by the administrator

14.31 The administrator him/herself may apply for the ending of the administration, if he/she believes that the original purpose has been achieved; or has proved incapable of achievement, or even that the administration should not have been entered into in the first place. Alternatively, he/she may be directed to do so by a meeting of the creditors.

The court has the usual panoply of powers, ie it can grant or refuse, it can adjourn conditionally or unconditionally, or it can make an interim or any other order.

Achievement of the objectives

14.32 Where an administrator has been appointed, either by the holder of a floating charge, or by the LLP or its members, he/she may come to the conclusion that the objective of the administration has been sufficiently achieved for the administration to be ended. He/she can then notify the court and the Registrar, and the administration is then over. He/she must also notify all known creditors (by publication in the latter instance if he/she so wishes).

Application by a creditor

14.33 If a creditor believes that the very appointment of the administrator is tainted by improper motive, on the part of the original applicant for the administration order, or (as the case may be) the appointor of the administrator, then he/she may make application to the court for the ending of the administration. As usual, the court may grant or refuse the application, it can adjourn conditionally or unconditionally, or it can make an interim or any other order.

Linkage with winding up

14.34 The general thrust of the *EA 2002* is to encourage administrations rather than liquidations, where feasible. Nonetheless there are some circumstances where an existing administration may be overridden by a liquidation, with consequent effects upon the administration.

The first is where a winding -up order is made (or a provisional liquidator is appointed) as a consequence of a petition based on a public interest, or one which is brought by the Financial Services Authority. In such circumstances, the court shall order whether the administration shall continue or not and, if it is to do so, what powers are thenceforth to be exercisable by the administrator.

Secondly, an administrator may reach the position where all secured creditors have been provided for, and a dividend is due to unsecured creditors, and the only way that such a dividend can be paid is by moving from administration to voluntary winding-up. In such a case he/she may file a notice with the Registrar (with copies to the court and all known creditors) and if he/she does so then his/her appointment as an administrator ceases, and the LLP will move into voluntary liquidation, with the administrator taking the role of liquidator (unless the creditors nominate someone else).

A third possibility is that the administrator may conclude that the LLP has nothing to distribute to creditors and that, in effect, there is nothing more he/she can do. In such circumstances, he/she can again notify the Registrar (copying the notice as above). His/her appointment will then cease. The LLP will then be dissolved three months later, unless a court is asked to intervene and extends or suspends the period, or indeed countermands dissolution.

Discharge of administration order

14.35   A final method of terminating an administration is that, where it was created by an administration order, and the court for any reason makes an order terminating the appointment of an administrator, it shall thereupon discharge the administration order.

Replacing an administrator

14.36   An administrator may only tender his/her resignation, (except with the leave of the court) on the grounds that the administrator is ill, intends to resign his/her insolvency practitioner's licence, has a conflict of interest, or has had a change in personal circumstances. Such resignation should be effected by notice to the court (for an administration order), or to his/her appointor (in any other case). Similar notice should be given if for any reason the administrator ceases to be qualified to act as an insolvency practitioner.

The court may at any time remove an administrator from office, but is generally unwilling to do so in the absence of evidence of potential bias or misfeasance (*Finnerty v Clark* (2011) EWCA Civ 858, see 14.27 above).

Naturally, the holding of the office also ceases upon death.

Filling a vacancy

14.37   Where an administrator ceases to hold office for any of the reasons mentioned in 14.36 above, there is power for a substitute to be appointed.

If the administration was commenced by administration order, then an application may be made to the court for such a substitute appointment by a creditors' committee, or any surviving joint appointee.

If there is no creditors' committee, such an application for a substitute appointment may also be made by:

- one or more creditors;
- the LLP; or
- the members of the LLP.

Where the original administrator was appointed by a floating charge holder, or by the LLP, or by its members, then the original appointor may make a substitute appointment, save that where that is the LLP or its members this can only be done (unless the court orders otherwise) with the consent of all the holders of qualifying floating charges over the LLP's property.

Where the committee or person with the power to make an application to the court or a direct substitute appointment fails to do so, then again application for a substitute appointment may be made by:

- one or more creditors;

- the LLP; or

- the members of the LLP.

There are also provisions covering clashes between would-be appointors who are floating charge holders, to sort out the priority as between their charges and consequent appointment rights; and the position where a creditors' meeting wishes to override the wishes of an LLP or its members wishing to make a substitute appointment.

Release of the administrator

14.38 In principle, an administrator's release from his/her responsibilities occurs when he/she ceases for any reason whatever to be the administrator. The time at which that takes effect may, however, vary, as follows:

- for a deceased administrator, it is the time when notice of his/her death is filed at court;

- for an administrator appointed by a floating charge holder, or by an LLP or its members, it is the time when the creditors (acting through a creditors' meeting if appropriate) so resolve; or

- in any case, it may be such time as the court orders.

From the appropriate time onwards, the administrator is discharged from any liability for his/her acts and omissions whilst in office, and also in any other way relating to his/her conduct as an administrator. The only exception is that the court's powers relating to misfeasance (see 14.29 above) are preserved.

Administrator's remuneration and expenses

14.39 On any cessation, the administrator's remuneration and expenses are a charge upon any assets in his/her custody or control at the time of cessation. That charge ranks ahead of any third-party security under a floating charge, but behind a charge which attaches to those assets in respect of expenses of the administration.

The categories of administration expenses accorded priority under *para 99* (ahead of the administrators' remuneration and floating charge holders) have been expanded by decisions of the courts in recent years. They now include:

- 'qualifying liabilities' under contracts of employment incurred during the administration, where the contract is 'adopted' (*para 99(5)* see below);

- rent falling due under leases of property used for the purposes of the administration (*Goldacre v Nortel* see 14.24 above); and

- other statutory liabilities falling due during the administration, including business rates (*Exeter CC v Bairstow* [2007] EWHC 400 (Ch)) and a contribution notice from the Pension Regulator (*re Nortel Gmbh (in administration)* [2011] EWCA Civ 1124).

The 'super-priority' accorded to such expenses seems out of line with the rescue culture of the new administration regime, and these decisions may in future be reversed by appeal to the Supreme Court or legislative amendments.

A liability under a contract of employment is a 'qualifying liability' if it is in respect of services rendered wholly or partly after the adoption of the contract and relates to wages, salary, holiday/sickness payments and occupational pension scheme contributions. The administrator has a 14-day window from his/her appointment to decide which employees the business needs and can afford, but after 14 days the administrator is automatically deemed to adopt the contracts of all remaining employees (*re Paramount Airways No 3* [1995] 2 AC 394).

Any liabilities relating to services rendered before adoption of the contract are excluded and rank as unsecured liabilities in the administration. The same applies to:

- statutory redundancy payments and payments for unfair dismissal (*re Allders Department Stores Ltd (in Administration)* [2005] EWHC 172 (Ch));

- payments in lieu of notice and protective awards (*Krasner v McMath* [2005] EWCA Civ 1072); and

- damages for wrongful dismissal (*re Leeds United AFC Ltd* [2007] EWHC 1761 (Ch)).

However, employees may be entitled to claim from the National Insurance Fund (via the Redundancy Payments Office) for statutory redundancy payments, notice pay and unpaid wages or salary (subject to a statutory cap on a week's pay).

Joint and concurrent administrators

14.40   It is possible for appointments to provide for more than one person to be appointed, so that there are either joint, or concurrent, administrators. In any such case the appointment must make it clear what each individual can do separately (if anything) and what they must do together for it to be effective. Such joint or concurrent appointments may not only be made at the time of the original appointment, but they may be added later, and there are detailed provisions in *para 100 et seq* governing this. A statement under *para 100(3)* is filed at court by the appointor (or included in the administration order) to give joint and several authority to each of the joint administrators on their appointment).

Receivers and administrative receivers

14.41   At this point, mention should be made very briefly of the position regarding the appointment etc of receivers or administrative receivers in the LLP context.

Quite simply, the provisions of *IA 1986, Pt III*, which deal with this subject, apply to LLPs as they do to companies, with no modifications other than the general ones needed to make them referable to LLPs. Since this book does not set out to be one on insolvency, readers are simply referred to the standard texts on this subject, and can apply them easily to LLPs.

Administration and receivership affecting professional practice LLPs and FSA-authorised LLPs

14.42   Particular considerations apply to the insolvency of solicitors and other professional practice LLPs. In most cases there is a duty to notify the regulator of the insolvency event, and related powers for the regulator to apply to court or intervene to protect client confidentiality or client moneys.

In the case of solicitors, the Solicitors Regulation Authority (SRA) will sometimes require that only a solicitor has access to confidential or privileged data (by appointment of a solicitor as special manager, receiver, administrative receiver or administrator). The SRA also has the power to intervene in a practice in the event of insolvency, and is likely to use this intervention power where there is any risk to client moneys.

Where an LLP is FSA authorised, the Financial Services Authority also has significant powers in an insolvency, including:

- to receive notice of and appear in any application to court for an administration order;

- to apply to court on public interest grounds for an administration order;

- prior approval of any administration appointment by the LLP or its members;

- to receive information circulated to creditors and to attend creditors' meetings; and

- to apply to court if it believes that the conduct of the administration unfairly prejudices the interests of some or all creditors.

The FSA has further powers in voluntary arrangements (see 13.31) and liquidations (see 15.25 and 16.9). For further details see FSA Enforcement Guide Chapter 13.

Chapter 15

Voluntary Winding Up

15.1   In this chapter, the first of the two overall methods of winding up an LLP – a voluntary winding up – is considered. This encompasses both a members' voluntary winding up, where the LLP remains solvent; and a creditors' voluntary winding up where the LLP is insolvent. In neither case is the court necessarily involved, though it may make occasional interventions on procedural matters if called upon. The differences between the two methods, with the ability of the members to give a declaration of solvency being a key issue, and the possibility of converting from a members' to a creditors' winding up, are examined. The appointment and role of the creditors' liquidation committee is described. Procedures for the appointment and removal of liquidators are explored, as are their powers and duties, particularly with regard to the possibility of transactions for consideration other than cash, and the distribution of the LLP's property.

General

Introduction

15.2   It is made clear in *s 73* of the *IA 1986* (as modified) that an LLP may be wound up either voluntarily, under *Chs II* to *V* inclusive of *Pt IV* of the *IA 1986*; or compulsorily by the court, under *Ch VI* of that Part. Some provisions, ie *Ch I* and *Chs VII* to *X* relate to all types of winding up.

Compulsory winding up, and those general provisions, are dealt with in Chapters 16 and 17 of this work. Many of those provisions are unchanged from the original *IA 1986*, save for the incorporation of references to LLPs instead of companies etc. A detailed treatment of the law relating to liquidations is of course beyond the scope of this work, and the intention is therefore not to cover ground which is treated in the main works on that subject, but rather to give an overall picture of the position, and to concentrate on those aspects which are peculiar to LLPs. References to the *Insolvency Rules* (see 13.2 above) are kept to a minimum.

A determination to wind up

15.3   The terminology used for a decision by an LLP to enter into a voluntary winding up, of either sort, is referred to as a 'determination' that it should be so wound up.

Before the LLP can determine that it is to be wound up voluntarily, it must give at least five business days' notice in writing to the holder of any qualifying floating charge (or obtain their consent in writing) (*IA 1986, s 82A,* as modified).

The exact time at which such a determination occurs is important, as it represents the formal commencement of the winding up (*IA 1986, s 86,* as modified), and various time periods within which actions need to be taken start with that determination. Thus, within 15 days, it must deliver a copy of the determination to the Registrar, or it and every designated member in default is liable to a fine (*IA 1986, s 84,* as modified). Similarly, within 14 days, it shall give notice of the determination in the *London Gazette,* or it and the liquidator and every member in default (not, this time, the designated members only) is liable to a fine (*IA 1986, s 85,* as modified). It must cease to carry on its business, except so far as it is needed for the purposes of the winding up, from the moment of commencement (*IA 1986, s 87(1)* as modified).

The problem is that there is no indication whatever of what constitutes a determination, or by what means it must be reached. The default provisions in *reg 7* are silent (for discussion of the *Regulations,* see 1.15 and Chapter 8 above). It is however unlikely that a determination would be an 'ordinary matter' for the LLP, and hence (if the default provisions apply) would probably be a 'change in the nature of the business' requiring unanimity under *2001 Regulations, reg 7(6).*

This is, therefore, an area which the draftsman of the members' agreement needs to provide for carefully, in order that there can be no confusion as to eg whether a formal members' meeting is needed, and what voting requirements there shall be.

There is no bar on a determination for a voluntary winding up being made because there is already a voluntary arrangement in force, but the subsequent winding up may not have the effect of terminating the trusts applicable to property in the hands of the arrangements supervisor (see 13.30 above).

Continuation of the corporate entity

15.4   One of the reasons for bringing LLPs into the corporate arena for winding up is that there should continue to be an accountable entity throughout the carrying out of the liquidation process, so that it only terminates once those procedures are completed and the LLP is thereafter dissolved.

Section 87(2) of the *IA 1986,* as modified accordingly provides that the corporate state and corporate powers of the LLP continue, whatever the members' agreement may say, until the eventual dissolution. The interests of the members within that entity cannot change during that period, and the modified s 88 of the *IA 1986* accordingly provides that any transfer of a member's interest, and any alteration of the member's status (eg presumably, changing from designated member to non-designated) is void unless sanctioned by the liquidator.

Declaration of solvency

15.5   A voluntary winding up can either be a members' voluntary liquidation (MVL) or a creditors' voluntary liquidation (CVL). An MVL is a solvent winding up and a CVL is an insolvent winding up.

The distinguishing feature which determines whether a voluntary winding up is to be an MVL or CVL (as recognised by s 90 of the *IA 1986* (as modified)) is whether a declaration of solvency has been made by the members, in accordance with the modified s 89 of the *IA 1986*. Where a declaration of solvency has been made, the winding up will be an MVL. Where the LLP is insolvent and consequently the members are unable to make a declaration of solvency, the voluntary winding up will be a CVL.

To be effective, such a declaration must have been made within the five weeks immediately preceding the determination to wind up. Making it on the day of the determination is acceptable, provided it precedes the determination.

The declaration must contain a statement of the LLP's affairs as at the last practical date before the declaration. Once made, it must be delivered to the Registrar within 15 days of the determination to wind up, and if this is not done the LLP, and every member in default, is liable both to a fine and a daily default fine.

Responsibility for the declaration

15.6   It is the designated members' job to deal with the declaration (referred to in 15.5 above), and indeed it is one of the rare occasions when the legislation specifically provides for there to be a meeting of the designated members (though it lays down no mechanism for this). If there are more than two designated members, a majority of them may make the declaration.

The declaration is to the effect that, having made a full enquiry into the LLP's affairs, the declarants have formed the opinion that the LLP will be able to pay all its debts (together with interest) within such period from the determination as they may specify, not exceeding a year.

The responsibility for this is high, and the declarants would be foolish indeed if they did not ensure that they had evidence of proper accountancy support for this opinion, since if a declarant does not have reasonable grounds for the opinion in question he/she is liable not only to a potential fine but also imprisonment. Further, there is a presumption that he/she did not have reasonable grounds if, in the events which subsequently happen, it becomes apparent that the LLP did not in fact have enough to pay such debts and interest within the chosen period.

Members' voluntary winding up

Appointment of the liquidator

15.7   In a members' voluntary winding up, the members pick their own liquidator(s). Upon that appointment their own normal powers cease, unless their continuance is sanctioned either by the liquidator, or by a specially convened members' meeting. Similarly, a members' meeting may fill any subsequent vacancy in the office of liquidator.

These meetings are to be held in the manner provided for in the *IA 1986* (which in practice is silent) or by the members' agreement, or as the court may determine. That agreement should also spell out what constitutes a quorum, but if it does not the quorum will simply be two. *Sections 91* and *92* of the *IA 1986* (as modified) apply.

Meetings and reports to creditors during the winding up

15.8   In England and Wales, a liquidator has a duty to report to creditors (*IA 1986, s 92A* as modified) at the end of each year, but there is no requirement to hold interim meetings (unless demanded by more than 10% by value of creditor or contributions under *IA 1986, s 168(2)* as modified). Where the liquidator needs a resolution of contributions or creditors, he/she can either call a meeting (under *IA 1986, s 168*, as modified) or circulate a resolution by correspondence (under *r 4.63A*).

Once the winding up is concluded, the liquidator shall make up a final account showing how the winding up has gone and how the LLP's property has been disposed of, and shall lay that before a members' meeting (*IA 1986, s 94*, as modified).

In the case of the final meeting, there is an additional requirement to advertise the meeting at least a month beforehand in the *London Gazette*, and to send a copy of the final account and a report of the meeting to the registrar within a week after the meeting. A liquidator is liable to a fine for any failure to report or hold meetings as required.

Effect of the LLP's insolvency

15.9   It may be that, during the course of the winding up, the liquidator forms the opinion that, contrary to the statutory declaration made by the designated members (see 15.4 and 15.5 above), the LLP will not in fact be able to pay its debts and interest thereon within the specified period.

If the above is the case, the liquidator has to take a number of steps. First, he/she has to organise a meeting of the creditors with a view to the creditors resolving to convert the MVL to a CVL (*IA 1986, s 95(2A)*, as modified).

15.10   The liquidator calls a meeting of creditors within 28 days of forming the opinion that the LLP is insolvent. The creditors are given at least seven days' notice of the meeting, which is also advertised. The liquidator presides over the meeting and puts a statement of affairs (detailing the assets and liabilities of the LLP) before the creditors, who then vote on whether the LLP should be placed in CVL.

Once the creditors resolve to place the LLP into CVL, from that time the LLP is treated as being in CVL (in respect of which see below).

Creditors' voluntary winding up

The creditors' meeting

15.11   As mentioned above (see 15.10 above), it is possible for what starts off as a members' voluntary winding up to be converted into a creditors' one. The much more common route, however, is where the declaration of solvency is absent, and so it is intended from the start that it will be a creditors' winding up.

In those circumstances (where there is no declaration of solvency), the LLP has, under the modified *s 98* of the *IA 1986*, to call a creditors' meeting at the outset, ie not more than 14 days after reaching its determination to wind itself up. It must give the creditors at least seven days' notice of the meeting by post and advertise in the *London Gazette*. It may also advertise it elsewhere as the members think fit.

The notice of the meeting must give two pieces of information. The first is the name of a licensed insolvency practitioner (in practice, the LLP's own nominee for liquidator) who will in the run-up to the meeting give creditors such information as to the LLP's affairs as they may reasonably require, without charge. The second is a local address at which, in the last two days of that interim period, a list of the LLP's creditors' names and addresses can be freely inspected. Failure to comply with these requirements renders the LLP (but not, on this occasion, any individual members) liable to a fine.

Statement of affairs

15.12   It is however the role of the designated members to take charge of the arrangements for the creditors' meeting itself, and to appoint one of their number to preside over the meeting.

They must also make out a statement of affairs, covering similar information to that referred to 15.10 above, and lay that before the meeting. Failure to do any of this renders the designated members liable to a fine.

Appointment of liquidator

15.13   A liquidator may, under *s 100* of the *IA 1986* (as modified), be nominated by the LLP itself, or by the creditors at their meeting, or by both.

The creditors will occasionally nominate their own candidate, if they feel uncomfortable with the idea of the LLP choosing its own. Their nominee will prevail in those circumstances. There is, however, power in those circumstances for any member or creditor, within seven days, to apply to the court for an order that the members' nominee be appointed, either instead of or jointly with the creditors' nominee; or that a new third choice be appointed instead of the creditors' nominee. In practice such a court application, though, is very rare.

Once the liquidator is appointed, all powers of the members cease under the modified *s 103* of the *IA 1986*, save to the extent that the liquidation committee described at 15.14 below (or, if no such committee is appointed, the creditors generally) consent to their continuance. If there is a subsequent vacancy in the office, the creditors may under the modified *s 104* of the *IA 1986* make the necessary appointment to fill that vacancy, unless the original appointment was by the court.

Note that if a liquidator is purportedly appointed by the members at their meeting, with the creditors' meeting being some time later, there are restrictions under the modified *s 166* of the *IA 1986* as to what steps the possibly temporary appointee may take in that interim period, so that essentially only protective action can be taken.

Liquidation committee

15.14   The creditors also have the option, at their meeting, to appoint, from amongst their own number, up to five people to serve on a liquidation committee, as provided in *s 101* of the *IA 1986* (as modified).

If the creditors' meeting does so, then the LLP in turn can at any time appoint up to five members from its own ranks. The LLP's nominees may however be objected to by the creditors and, if so, they are debarred from membership of the committee (unless the court otherwise directs). An application may also be made to the court for substitutes to be appointed in place of those so removed.

Liquidator's reports and meetings

15.15 In the context of a creditors' voluntary winding up, there are obligations on the liquidator similar to those referred to in 15.8 above, to produce annual progress reports and closing accounts, and to hold a final meeting (*IA 1986, ss 104A* and *106,* as modified).

In this instance, however, the final meeting must be of both the creditors and the members of the LLP.

Creditors and contributories holding more that 10% by value may require the liquidator to hold meetings (under *IA 1986, s 168* as modified). The liquidator requiring a resolution of members or creditors may also circulate a resolution by correspondence (under *r 4.63A*) instead of holding a meeting.

Provisions applying to all types of voluntary winding up

Appointment or removal of liquidator by the court

15.16 The continuity of the office of liquidator is clearly vital to the success of any liquidation. *Section 108* of the *IA 1986* (as modified) thus gives the court the power to appoint a replacement liquidator if, for any reason, there is no liquidator acting, and no limit on who may ask it to exercise this power.

Similarly, the court has power, under the same section, to remove a liquidator and appoint another, and again no limitation is put upon the identity of potential applicants. There must naturally be good cause shown for this to be done. The court may also use its discretion to transfer appointments en bloc to another liquidator on death, retirement or illness.

Notice by the liquidator of his/her appointment

15.17 Any liquidator under a voluntary winding up must, on his/her appointment, give notice of his/her appointment, in the prescribed form.

This notice must be sent to the Registrar, and also be advertised in the *London Gazette*. Failure to do so will render the liquidator liable to a fine and a daily default fine. *Section 109* of the *IA 1986* (as modified) applies.

Acts possible prior to appointment

15.18   In the unlikely event that the members take steps to put the LLP into liquidation but fail to appoint or nominate a liquidator, the legislation provides, in order to protect the creditors, that the members' powers in relation to the business cease except to the extent necessary to protect the LLP's assets, to dispose of perishable goods or to complete the steps to liquidation.

Distribution of the LLP's property

15.19   Having collected in the LLP's property, the liquidator's duty is naturally to distribute it, and the modified *s 107* of the *IA 1986* so provides. He/she first distributes realisations from charged assets to holders of fixed charges, then to preferential creditors (now restricted to certain employee claims) and then to floating charge holders. Any surplus realisations (and any realisations not subject to charge) are then distributed *pari passu* among unsecured creditors.

Lastly, if there are still funds left after all creditors have been paid in full, he/she is to distribute the assets amongst the LLP's members, according to their interests in the LLP (unless the LLP members' agreement directs a different method of distribution amongst members).

In an MVL, It may be desirable (particularly from a tax perspective) to distribute the assets of the LLP amongst the members *in specie* (ie distributing the assets in the form they are in, rather than realising those assets and distributing the cash realisations). In a situation where the members' agreement does not provide for a distribution *in specie*, it may be prudent to resolve, at the same time as appointing the liquidator, upon a mechanism for him/her to achieve this, eg by valuing the assets etc, and by giving him/her such indemnity as may be needed. Note, however, that all proper expenses of the winding up, including the liquidator's own remuneration, are to be paid in priority to all of the above distributions, in accordance with *s 115* of the *IA 1986*, as modified.

Taking shares in consideration of sale of the LLP's property

15.20   It may be the case that the liquidator wants to dispose not just of the LLP's assets, but of a substantial part of the LLP's business or property, in circumstances where the consideration being offered by the potential buyer is not cash, but a part of the ownership of its own business.

The simple example of the above is shares in the buyer if it is a limited company, but it could be other forms of interest in such a company; or it could be the equivalent interests in an LLP acting as buyer (though this would presumably be more complex in view of the more personal involvement expected of a member of an LLP as distinct from a shareholder). In such circumstances, *s 110* of the *IA 1986* (as modified) provides that a broad range of such transactions, including those where the right to participate in the transferee's profits is or is part of the consideration, can in principle be entered into by the liquidator, but only with the 'requisite consent'. The tax treatment of such a disposal may be advantageous in some circumstances, particularly where the LLP business is to be split between two different buyers.

Obtaining the requisite consent to a *s 110* arrangement

15.21   In the case of a creditors' voluntary winding up, the 'requisite consent' referred to in 15.20 must come from the liquidation committee, if there is one, or from the court if not (ie there is no provision for a meeting of creditors generally, if there is no committee).

In the case of a members' voluntary winding up, however, the liquidator must summon a meeting of the members to determine whether they are prepared either to give the liquidator general authority to enter into transactions of this nature on their behalf, or to authorise a specific transaction. A suitably authorised transaction, once entered into, is binding on the members. The LLP can, if such a situation is anticipated, give such authority before, or at the time of, its initial determination to wind up.

The final subsection of the modified *s 110* of the *IA 1986* (see also 15.20 above) does indicate, however, that if the LLP is subject to a court winding-up order within a year of such a determination, the LLP's authority is not valid unless sanctioned by the court. Presumably this is intended to relate only to any lasting effect of such a consent, ie to any still-pending transaction, rather than requiring retrospective consent to an already-implemented deal, but the section is not specific on this.

Dissent from such arrangements

15.22   There may be members of the LLP who are not content with the decision reached at the members' meeting. A right of dissent is thus given by the modified *s 111* of the *IA 1986* to any member who did not vote in favour of the transaction at the members' meeting (ie not only any member who voted against, but also any one who abstained or was absent).

Such a dissenter has the right to notify the liquidator in writing, within a week of the relevant meeting, of his/her objection. The liquidator then has a choice. He/she may simply refrain from entering into the transaction, since the result of the meeting is merely to authorise him/her to enter into the transaction, not to oblige him/her to do so. Alternatively, he/she may decide to go ahead, in which case he/she must purchase the dissenter's interest in the LLP at a price to be determined by agreement or arbitration. The price for this must be paid prior to the LLP's dissolution. The method of raising the necessary cash is to be determined by the LLP.

Guidance by the court

15.23   The *IA 1986* recognises that a number of questions may arise during the course of a winding up which will require the guidance of the court, and the modified *s 112* therefore gives the right to seek such guidance to the liquidator, or to any contributory, or to any creditor.

Surprisingly, although these provisions apply to a members' voluntary winding up as much as to a creditors', no such right is given to a member of the LLP, if not a contributory or creditor. The court may not only be invited to determine any question referred, but also to exercise any power which it would have if the winding up was a compulsory one.

The court is given very wide powers to decide how to deal with any such application, provided only that it is satisfied that it would be 'just and beneficial' for it to intervene. It can essentially make what order it thinks fit. If the order is to the effect that the winding up be stayed, then the LLP must forthwith notify the Registrar.

Subsequent compulsory winding up

15.24   The fact that an LLP is being wound up voluntarily does not bar the right of a creditor subsequently to apply to the court to have it compulsorily wound up. Nor does it bar the similar right of a contributory, but in the latter case the contributory must be able to satisfy the court that the interests of contributories generally will be prejudiced by allowing the winding up to continue on a voluntary basis. However the court has discretion to refuse a winding-up order (under *IA 1986, s 125*, as modified) and so it would be unusual for a winding-up order to be granted unless there were real concerns about the progress of the voluntary liquidation which were supported by a majority of creditors.

Section 116 of the *IA 1986* (as modified), which reserves the above rights, makes no mention of the rights of the members, if not contributories or creditors, and it may be that the inference is accordingly that their right to petition for a compulsory winding up is lost once a voluntary winding up commences.

Financial services

15.25   Under *FSMA, s 365* where an LLP is FSA authorised, the FSA is entitled to be heard at any court hearing, or at meetings of creditors or any creditors' committee during the winding up. The FSA must also receive all invoices and documents sent to creditors. Voluntary winding up does not preclude the FSA's right to petition for compulsory winding up (see 16.9).

Chapter 16

Winding Up by the Court

16.1 This chapter deals with the processes peculiar to the winding up of LLPs by the court. It looks first at the grounds upon which a petition may be brought, and who may bring it. The position between the presentation of the petition and any eventual order on it is considered. The process by which the LLP's affairs are then investigated is covered. A key issue is who the liquidator is to be, and so the methods by which he/she may be appointed, as well as his/her general duties and his/her role in the conclusion of the winding up, are reviewed.

Introduction

16.2 A winding up by the court is the second of the two overall methods of winding up an LLP (the other method, voluntary winding up, is dealt with in Chapter 15).

This may either be the first exposure of the LLP to any of the range of insolvency measures, or may follow other attempted remedies, such as a failed voluntary arrangement, or the discharge of an administration.

Choice of court

16.3 There is concurrent jurisdiction for the High Court, and the county court, in relation to compulsory winding up matters, under s 117 of the IA 1986 (as modified). The county court in question will be that having insolvency jurisdiction for the area in which the LLP has its registered office. If the county court is chosen, it has the same powers as the High Court for winding up purposes.

If the wrong court is inadvertently chosen, anything done before the mistake is discovered remains valid in accordance with s 118 of the IA 1986 (as modified), and indeed it may be decided to retain the proceedings in that incorrect court, eg if a judge already has experience of the matter and it is deemed sensible to keep the case there for case management reasons.

Further, if a matter is proceeding in the county court, but the opinion of the High Court is desired on a particular aspect, this can be sought by way of a case stated, if so desired either by all the parties, or by one party with the approval of the county court judge, and the proceedings are then temporarily transferred to the High Court. *Section 119* of the *IA 1986* (as modified) refers.

Circumstances leading to compulsory winding up

16.4   There are, under *s 122* of the *IA 1986* (as modified), five sets of circumstances in which an LLP can be compulsorily wound up. These are as follows:

- If the LLP determines it should be wound up by the court. In other words, if an LLP's members decide that the end of the line has been reached for their business and the LLP is insolvent, they have the choice of determining to wind up via the voluntary route, or by means of the court's intervention.

- If the LLP does not start its business for a year from incorporation, or suspends its business for a whole year. This shows that the LLP is not intended to be allowed to be a dormant vehicle, as can quite legitimately be the case with a company for many years. (Some professional firms, which registered LLPs when the legislation came into force on 6 April 2001, simply in order to protect their names from being registered by rivals but without any fixed intention to start to practise as active LLPs, discovered this to their potential cost.)

- If the number of members of the LLP is reduced below two. Thus, though the incorporated body of the LLP does not automatically cease to exist if membership falls below two (as made clear in other provisions, such as *LLPA 2000, s 4A*) (making a sole member jointly and severally liable with the LLP for debts incurred after six months' trading without another member), it is nonetheless a reason for an active application for winding up.

- If the LLP is unable to pay its debts (as defined in 16.5 below).

- If the court is of the opinion that it is just and equitable that the LLP should be wound up. This is likely to be the least certain area, and is looked at in more detail in 16.7 *et seq.* below.

Inability to pay debts

16.5   There are in effect four sets of circumstances in which an LLP may be deemed to be unable to pay its debts.

If any one of these prevails, this is sufficient to ground a successful petition, even if the LLP can show that its finances amply pass the tests posed by the other possibilities. The example of the application of these principles to companies has shown on many occasions that failure by a company to observe the requirements of the first of these possibilities, ie a statutory demand, has led to a valid petition against an otherwise solvent company and, even if not to an eventual order, then at least to some sudden and intensive negotiation and high cost to the company in order to wriggle out of its predicament.

The possibilities, in accordance with s 123 of the *IA 1986* (as modified), are as follows:

- if a creditor serves a statutory demand (see 16.6 below) which is not satisfied within three weeks;

- if execution or other court enforcement process is returned wholly or partly unsatisfied;

- if the LLP is unable to pay its debts as they fall due (the 'cash-flow test'); and

- if the value of the LLP's assets are less than the amount of its liabilities (including those of a contingent and prospective nature) (the 'balance sheet test').

The last two of these tests require an exercise in judgment and financial analysis by the court, but effectively mean that if the court is satisfied of the LLP's insolvency on either a cash-flow approach or a balance sheet approach, that will enable it to grant a winding-up order.

The clearest example of cash-flow insolvency is a statutory demand which has not been fulfilled, but other evidence showing a failure to pay a debt which is due and not disputed may suffice (*re Taylor's Industrial Flooring* [1990] BCC 44). The balance sheet test is less commonly used and is harder to prove. The Court of Appeal decision in the *Eurosail* [2011] EWCA Civ 227 case has confirmed that the balance sheet test is not a mechanical assessment of the latest balance sheet, but instead a judgment as to whether the LLP has 'reached the point of no return due to an incurable deficiency in its assets'.

Statutory demands

16.6   The first of the reasons described at 16.5 above relates to the 'statutory demand', as it has come to be known, i.e. a demand, framed in the prescribed form, that the LLP should pay a sum due. That sum must be at least £750, or such other amount as may be set by the Secretary of State. In practice, it has been £750 since the inception of the *IA 1986*, and so with the effects of inflation has encompassed progressively more and more debts. The demand must be served on the LLP by leaving it at the LLP's registered office.

The LLP then has three weeks to pay up, or to secure or compound for the sum in question. It may, if it disputes the debt, challenge the demand itself in the court. Where many companies have erred is in not taking such demands sufficiently seriously, either by ignoring them or, even if the debt is genuinely disputed, by choosing to carry on that dispute in correspondence rather than with the court's protection, thus handing to the creditor on a plate the negotiating advantage of being able to petition for winding up.

The area of the statutory demand has been a fertile ground for case law, as a result of which the following principles have emerged:

- Service by registered post is acceptable (*Re a Company (No 008790 of 1990)* [1992] BCC 11), but receipt must be proved or admitted and proof of posting alone is insufficient.

- The fact that a demand may overstate the debt does not invalidate it (*Re a Debtor (No 490 SD 1991), ex parte the Debtor v Printline (Offset) Ltd* [1992] 2 All ER 664) so that the recipient should pay the undisputed part.

- The court does have jurisdiction to set aside a demand (despite the lack of a defined procedure to parallel similar applications in the context of individual insolvency) but only if there is a genuine dispute as to the claimed debt, and the setting aside application is not merely tactical (*Re Janeash Ltd* [1990] BCC 250).

- Thus a serious cross-claim for an amount exceeding the original debt will normally be enough for a setting aside (*Re Bayoil SA* [1999] 1 BCLC 62).

- A petition against a solvent company or LLP based on a disputed debt is an abuse of process, which the court will restrain by injunction and penalise in costs (*re a Company (12209 of 1991)* [1992] 1 WLR 351).

Just and equitable

16.7   The ability of the court to wind up an LLP on the ground that it is 'just and equitable' to do so gives it an avowedly broad discretion, and it has been held that it should not fetter that discretion by deciding only to follow the lead of other previously accepted instances of unjust and inequitable behaviour (*Ebrahimi v Westbourne Galleries Ltd* [1973] AC 360).

Some examples may be fairly straightforward, eg fraud on the part of a controlling member. Total deadlock in the management of the LLP may also be sufficient. More difficult, however, is where there is an exclusion of one or more members from the running of the business, and a breakdown of trust and confidence. In practice, the court is unlikely to wind up an LLP under this head save in exceptional circumstances.

Potential petitioners

16.8   A range of people may have the status necessary to present a winding-up petition. This may, by *s 124* of the *IA 1986*, include:

- the LLP itself;
- the members;

- any creditor(s) (even if only contingent or prospective);
- any contributory(ies);
- a magistrates' clerk seeking to enforce fines;
- the Secretary of State (see 16.9 below);
- the Official Receiver (where a voluntary winding up is already in progress).

One point to note is that the reference to 'the members' as potential petitioners is plural, whereas in the case of creditors or contributories the alternative of the singular is also offered. Thus, the inference is that only the membership acting together by a duly passed resolution may petition; but this seems at odds with the idea of a 'just and equitable' petition being available to remedy wrongdoing on the part of one or more members, and in such circumstances individuals may need to rely on other capacities than mere membership (ie their status as creditors and/or contributories).

Petition by the Secretary of State

16.9   The powers of the Secretary of State are to be used, under *s 124A* of the *IA 1986*, where it appears to him/her to be expedient to do so in the public interest, and where the court consequently considers it just and equitable to agree the winding up.

This may follow (*inter alia*) an investigation undertaken by the Secretary of State acting by the Insolvency Service under his/her powers under the *CA 1985* (see the discussion in 12.36 *et seq*). It may also include grounds based on information or reports obtained under *Financial Services and Markets Act 2000*. The Financial Services Authority also has parallel powers under that Act (*ss 367 and 371*) to petition for winding up or to be heard and to participate in any existing winding-up proceedings.

Commencement of a winding up

16.10   It is not just the making of a winding-up order which may potentially affect an LLP. There are various provisions which apply in the period from commencement of the winding up to the time when the petition is finally ruled upon by the court.

Commencement, in this context, means (under *s 129* of the *IA 1986*, as modified) either the time of a determination by the LLP for voluntary winding up; or in other cases the presentation of the petition. (Note therefore that if the determination is for the compulsory winding up of the LLP, so that the LLP is to be the petitioner, it is the petition not the determination which is the trigger for commencement.)

Dispositions between commencement and order

16.11 A provision which has tripped up many a company, and has the potential to do so for LLPs, is *s 127* of the *IA 1986*. As modified, this provision states that, after commencement of a winding up, any disposition of an LLP's property is void (without a court order to the contrary) if the LLP is later wound up pursuant to the winding-up proceedings.

In the company context it has often been the case that the first the company has known of this is when its bank, having read in the *London Gazette* of the presentation of a winding-up petition, freezes the bank accounts, and the company then realises that the petitioning creditor (whose statutory demand they have ignored, and whose petition they have regarded as just another debt collecting tactic) has actually achieved the closure of their business before the matter has ever reached the court. A frantic application then follows for what is known as a validation order, ie permission to carry on trading if the court can be persuaded that there is not an insolvent situation. Another possibility is an application to restrain the advertising or publicising of the petition, if the danger is spotted in time and the petition is alleged to be groundless or vexatious.

Protection between commencement and order

16.12 The other side of the coin (from what is discussed at 16.12 above) is that, under *s 128* of the *IA 1986* (as modified), commencement will afford the LLP's property some protection, in that any subsequent process of execution against its property is also void where the LLP is later wound up on that petition.

Further, under *s 126* of the *IA 1986* (as modified), if other proceedings are in train against the LLP, it can apply for those to be stayed. That application may be to the court in which those proceedings are going on, if that is the High Court or the Court of Appeal; or to the winding up court in other instances. The court hearing the application has discretion as to whether to grant the stay and, if so, upon what terms.

The court's powers

16.13 The court has wide powers on hearing a winding-up petition, under *s 125(1)* of the *IA 1986* (as modified). It may of course simply grant or refuse the application. It may adjourn either conditionally or unconditionally. It may make an interim order, or any other order it thinks fit. However: (i) if the petition in question is a creditor petition; (ii) the court is satisfied that the debt is valid; (iii) the LLP is unable to persuade the court that it is likely to be able to pay the debt if a short adjournment is granted, the court is likely to make a winding-up order.

One restriction on its powers is that it must not make a winding-up order simply because the LLP has no assets, or because any assets it has have been mortgaged to an amount equal to or in excess of their value and provided the LLP is not insolvent. Another is that referred to in 16.8 above (alternative remedy available – *IA 1986, s 125(2)*, as modified).

If a winding-up order is made, then the LLP (or anyone else so directed by the court) must send a copy to the Registrar (*IA 1986, s 130(1)*, as modified).

The court may also, under *s 147* of the *IA 1986* (as modified), make an order to stay the winding up (either altogether or for a limited time) upon such terms and conditions as it thinks fit. Application for this may be made by the Official Receiver, the liquidator, or any creditor or contributory. Copies of any order so made must be sent to both the LLP itself and the Registrar.

Further, there is a power for the court to order a rescission of the winding-up order (eg if the LLP is able to pay the debt or if there is irregularity in the winding-up process), but application for this must be made within five business days, and the power will be sparingly used. (Both an inherent power and a statutory one under *r 7.47* apply.)

The LLP's statement of affairs

16.14   Once a winding-up order is made, there is a broad duty placed upon the Official Receiver to investigate, under *s 132* of the *IA 1986* (as modified), the promotion, formation, business, dealings and affairs of the LLP and, if it has failed, the causes of that failure. If he/she thinks fit, he/she may report his/her findings to the court, and that report becomes *prima facie* evidence of the facts stated in it.

The first routine step in that investigation is to require one or more people to give a statement of affairs as to the LLP. This is to give the same information as referred to in 15.10, and any other information the Official Receiver requires. The categories of people who may be required to make the statement include past and present members of the LLP; anyone who took part in the formation of the LLP within the last year; any employee within that year; or anyone who is or has during that year been a member or employee in an LLP which in turn is a member of the subject LLP. (In this context, 'employee' includes anyone acting under a contract for services, and is likely to include the LLP's accountants and solicitors, as well as other self-employed contractors.)

Once notice of the requirement is given to any such person, they have 21 days to produce the statement, unless the Official Receiver later releases the obligation or extends the period. There is, however, a power for anyone subject to such a requirement, if they have requested a release or an extension of time which has been refused, to apply to the court for relief. (These requirements for the production of statements of affairs also apply if a winding-up order has not yet been made, but a provisional liquidator has been appointed.) Any person subject to a valid requirement who does not comply with it is subject to a fine and a daily default fine.

Public examination of members

16.15   Another weapon in the locker of the Official Receiver (or any subsequently appointed liquidator) is the power to apply to the court for a public examination under *s 133* of the *IA 1986* (as modified). This is within the discretion of the liquidator, save that (unless the court orders otherwise) he/she may be required to make such an application by creditors representing at least one half of the overall creditors by value, or by contributories representing at least three-quarters of the contributories by value.

Those potentially subject to such an order are:

* any past or present member;

* any previous receiver or manager, liquidator or administrator;

* anyone who has been involved in the promotion, formation or management of the LLP.

The court will, if it grants the application, make procedural orders for the holding of the examination, which may range over any aspect of the LLP's affairs, or the conduct or dealings of the examinee. Questions may be posed not only by the Official Receiver or liquidator, but also by any special manager, any proving creditor, or any contributory.

This is a potentially fearsome procedure, and its seriousness is underlined by the fact that not only is failure to comply punishable as a contempt of court, but a court may, if it fears the prospective examinee might abscond, order his/her arrest and the seizure of any books, papers, records, money or goods in his/her possession (*IA 1986, s 134*, as modified).

Provisional liquidators

16.16   The court may, at any time before a winding-up order is made, appoint a provisional liquidator of an LLP, to carry out such tasks as the court may give him/her usually to ensure that the LLP's assets are preserved until the petition hearing, and subject to such limitations as the order appointing him/her may contain.

Section 135 of the *IA 1986* (as modified) applies here.

Appointment of a liquidator – the Official Receiver's role

16.17 The starting point is that, under *s 136* of the *IA 1986* (as modified), the Official Receiver is (subject to 16.20 below) the liquidator as from the making of a winding-up order, and continues as such until another is appointed. He/she may also revert to the role in the event of a subsequent vacancy.

In his/her first 12 weeks of office, he/she must consider whether he/she believes it appropriate to invite the creditors and contributories to appoint a liquidator. If he/she decides it is not, he/she must notify the court, the creditors and the contributories accordingly. If he/she thinks it is appropriate, he/she has to summon separate meetings of the creditors and the contributories. In any event, he/she can be required to summon such meetings by not less than a quarter of the LLP's creditors by value.

If the above process is not to be used, the Official Receiver may ask the Secretary of State, in accordance with *s 137* of the *IA 1986* (as modified), to appoint a liquidator (and in any event he/she must consider whether to do so if meetings of creditors and contributories are held but do not result in an appointment). The Secretary of State may make such an appointment (though he/she is not obliged to) and any liquidator so appointed must notify his/her appointment to all creditors (or, if the court permits, simply advertise it) and in the notice or advertisement, deal with the question of whether he/she intends to summon a creditors' meeting to consider appointing a liquidation committee.

Appointment of a liquidator by creditors and contributories

16.18 Each of the creditors and the contributories may, at their separate meetings, nominate a liquidator. Not surprisingly, if they make different choices, the creditors' nominee will prevail (*s 139* of the *IA 1986*, as modified).

That does not mean the making of a choice by the contributories is a waste of time, as if the creditors do not make a choice at all then their candidate will get the job. If there is a real dispute after different nominations, any creditor or contributor can apply to the court to ask it either to appoint the contributories' choice instead of, or jointly with, the creditors' nominee; or to appoint a third candidate not previously chosen by either side.

Appointment of a liquidator after voluntary arrangement or administration

16.19 A final variation on the theme of appointment of a liquidator is that the Official Receiver may never be involved at all.

If the LLP has previously been the subject of a voluntary arrangement, or an administration, then if a winding-up order is made during the arrangement, or immediately upon the discharge of the administration, the insolvency practitioner previously acting as supervisor or administrator may, with their consent, be appointed by the court as liquidator, under *s 140* of the *IA 1986* (as modified).

Liquidation committees

16.20   If the possible meetings of creditors and contributories referred to above have been called (see 16.18), then at those meetings they may appoint a liquidation committee (*s 141* of the *IA 1986*, as modified). Alternatively any liquidator (other than the Official Receiver) may if he/she thinks fit summon such meetings specifically for the purpose of enabling consideration of whether such a committee should be appointed, and, if so, who should be on it; and indeed he/she must do so if requested by not less than one tenth of the LLP's creditors by value.

Rules 4.151 to 4.178 apply to the establishment process. The committee has certain functions designated for it by the legislation. If, however, there is no such committee, or if the liquidator at the time is the Official Receiver, those powers are normally vested in the Secretary of State. In the latter case, therefore, the committee's actual involvement is held in suspense until another liquidator is appointed.

The position regarding contributories

16.21   Under *s 148* of the *IA 1986* (as modified), it is the task of the court, as soon as possible after a winding-up order is made, to make a list of all contributories, unless it appears to the court that it will not be necessary either to call on contributories to make any payment, or to adjust the rights of the contributories *inter se*.

The court may then call upon any contributory so listed to pay to the liquidator either any monies generally due to the LLP (*IA 1986, s 149*, as modified), or any monies due as calls (bearing in mind that members can only be liable insofar as they have chosen to be). If it needs to distinguish between contributories, it can be practical and consider the likelihood of actual payment being received when adjusting the contributions called for.

The court may also adjust the rights of contributories *inter se*, and in particular rule upon the distribution of any surplus assets (see 16.24 below). If a contributory is seen as likely to abscond, or to remove or conceal property in order to avoid payment of calls, then the court may order his/her arrest, and the seizure of his/her books, papers, and movable personal property, under *s 158* of the *IA 1986* (as modified).

The liquidator's general duties

16.22   It is not the place of this work to look in detail at the role of liquidators, for that generally will be the same in the LLP context as it is in the company context, but it is worth pausing to look at those provisions which may impact upon an LLP, and the anticipation of which may help in the drawing up of the members' agreement.

The liquidator's general duties are stated in the modified *s 143* of the *IA 1986*, namely to get in, and realise the LLP's assets. By *ss 144* and *145* of the *IA 1986* he/she is to take over all the LLP's property (including intangibles) and may apply to the court for an order vesting any property held by the LLP (or any trustees for it) in his/her name. He/she may bring or defend any proceedings which are necessary in relation to the LLP's property, or generally to effectuate the winding up. At the end of the process, he/she is to distribute the LLP's property.

Distribution of surplus

16.23   The distribution is of course normally to the secured, preferential and unsecured creditors, but in the (admittedly rare) instance where there is a surplus after all expenses and creditors have been paid, there may be a need to distribute that surplus.

The statute simply refers to the distribution being to 'the persons entitled to it'. In the company context, ascertaining who those people are is a comparatively straightforward exercise, as their shareholdings will determine the position. In an LLP context, however, the position is more difficult. Admittedly, the distribution will be to the members, but in what proportions? The most obvious would be the proportions which capital accounts bear to each other, but this may not always represent the wishes of the membership. There seems no reason (other than that it may seem unduly pessimistic to consider such matters when setting up the LLP) why the members' agreement should not attempt to determine the question, especially if any form of distribution *in specie* is considered both possible and desirable.

Final meeting

16.24   At the end of the process, when all has been collected in, the liquidator's task under *s 146* of the *IA 1986* (as modified) is to summon a final creditors' meeting to consider whether to accept his/her final report and grant him/her his/her release, and he/she must keep sufficient funds in hand to enable him/her to do this.

That may be simultaneous with the final payments out but, if before that, must be adjourned until those payments are made.

Chapter 17

General Winding Up Provisions

17.1 This chapter looks at those provisions which are common to all types of winding up as regards an LLP. It starts by considering the role of contributories in a winding up, and the potential application of that role to members of the LLP. It reviews briefly the powers of a liquidator, and who needs to sanction some of those powers, before moving on to potential removal of a liquidator. A range of matters regarding malpractice in relation to winding up is then covered, including various offences of fraud etc, the summary remedies available to the court for breach of duty, wrongful trading, and the potential clawback of 'withdrawals' taken by members (a provision unique to LLPs). Sanctions for the improper use of 'phoenix' trading names for LLPs are explained. Following the malpractice theme, the provisions guarding against transactions at an undervalue, and preferences, are examined, together with the convoluted definitions applicable to the concept of being an 'associate' in relation to those provisions.

Introduction

17.2 A substantial number of provisions apply to all sorts of winding up of LLPs, whether the liquidation in question is a members' voluntary, a creditors' voluntary or a compulsory one. These are found in the provisions of the *IA 1986* set out in the table below.

Part of the Act	Sections	Nature
IV (Ch I)	73–82	Members as contributories*
IV (Chs VII to X)	163–219	Liquidators and malpractice*
VI	230–246	Miscellaneous (including transfers at undervalue and preferences*)
VII	247–251	Interpretation
XII	386–387	Preferential debts
XIII	388–398	Insolvency practitioners and qualifications
XIV	399–410	Public administration
XV	411–419	Subordinate legislation
XVI	423–425	Debt avoidance
XVII	426–434	Miscellaneous and general
XVIII	435–436	Interpretation (including 'associate'*)
XIX	438–444	Final provisions

Limits of presentation

17.3   The point needs making again that this is a book on LLPs, not a treatise on insolvency. For that reason, a large number of the provisions listed above are not touched on at all, since they are not substantively varied by the LLP legislation from their company equivalents, and readers should refer to the standard insolvency texts for detailed discussions of them.

This chapter tries simply to pick out those provisions which either can be predicted as likely to impact in some instances on LLPs, or which are different for, or unique to, LLPs. Those areas are indicated by an asterisk in the above table.

Members as contributories

Agreement to contribute

17.4   It is possible for members of an LLP to agree between themselves, or with the LLP itself, that in the event of the liquidation of the LLP they will contribute to its assets, in order to help meet the debts and liabilities of the LLP and the expenses of the winding up.

This agreement may relate to liquidation generally, or in specific circumstances. It may be to whatever extent of contribution is agreed. The agreement may provide for adjustment of the rights of the contributories between themselves. Even past members may be included within the agreement, if it made clear that their liability is to survive their ceasing to be members. All this is provided for in *IA 1986, s 74* (as modified).

Reasons for agreeing to contribute

17.5   What *s 74* of the *IA 1986* (see 17.4 above) does not make clear, however, is why on earth the members would wish to enter into such an agreement in the first place. Since the whole point of seeking the status of a limited liability partnership would seem to be to avail the members of that limitation, what motive could there be for voluntarily assuming even a restricted degree of personal liability?

It is suggested that, for the avoidance of doubt, and subject to the point made in 17.6 below, it may well be prudent for the members' agreement specifically to state that no such agreement exists, since the section does not specify what form the contribution agreement might take, and it would be as well to avoid any possibility of a later contention that there was some form of implied agreement to that effect.

There seem to be only two possible reasons for agreeing to contribute. One is dealt with in 17.6 below. The other is if such an agreement is necessary to persuade third parties that the LLP is sufficiently financially sound for them to deal with it. Even in such circumstances the agreement to contribute should be limited and precisely defined, or the whole LLP formation will be pointless, since such an agreement will be analogous to giving a personal guarantee for the benefit of unsecured creditors generally.

Status as contributories

17.6 In the event of there being any such contribution agreement (see 17.5 above), those present and past members of the LLP who have agreed to contribute are referred to as 'contributories', under *IA 1986, s 79* (as modified).

The term also includes anyone alleged to be a contributory. It does not, however, include anyone whose liability to contribute is the compulsory result of proceedings being taken against him/her for fraudulent or wrongful trading, or by way of the provisions referred to later in this chapter relating to the 'clawback' of withdrawals (see 17.24 below). The attainment of this status appears to be the only other possible reason for agreeing to make a contribution on a winding up. Thus, if an agreement provided that, in the event of liquidation, each member should contribute, say, five pounds (rather like a member of a company limited by guarantee) this would give all members the position of contributories in a winding up, with consequent rights to eg present a petition, or vote in a compulsory winding up for the appointment of a liquidator, or have a say in the appointment of a liquidation committee. If members feel that such a status, in the event of a winding up, would benefit them, then they should include provision for this in the members' agreement. It seems unlikely, however, that this will be at all common, especially as in most cases members will also be creditors of the LLP, and will as such have rights as good as, if not better than, contributories.

Contribution as a debt

17.7 The contributory's liability creates a civil debt payable when called upon.

The debt binds a deceased contributory's estate, and his/her personal representatives in turn are brought into the definition of contributories, and if they default, the court may order the administration of the estate to be taken over in order to enforce the payment (*IA 1986, s 81*, as modified).

Similarly, if the contributory becomes bankrupt then, under *s 82* of the *IA 1986* (as modified), his/her trustee represents him/her and becomes a contributory, with the debt being provable in the bankruptcy, not only for calls already made, but also in an estimated amount for future calls.

Liquidators

General

17.8   A number of provisions relating to the appointment of liquidators have already been dealt with in the previous chapters (see Chapters 15 and 16) relating to both voluntary and compulsory winding up.

Sections 163 to *174* of the *IA 1986* (as modified) deal more generally with the liquidator's position, once appointed.

A liquidator's powers

17.9   The powers attaching to a liquidator are set out in *IA 1986, Sch 4* (as modified). Most of those are vested in him/her automatically.

Some, however, only vest in him/her with the requisite consent. In the case of a members' voluntary winding up of an LLP, the consent which is requisite, under *IA 1986, s 165* (as modified), is that of the members of the LLP. The liquidator is accordingly given power to summon a meeting of the members to consider whether to give that consent, and provision is made for the procedures applying to such a summoning.

In relation to a creditors' voluntary winding up, if the LLP is dilatory in calling the necessary creditors' meeting, or if the designated members fail to provide the necessary statement of affairs (under *ss 98* and *99* respectively of the *IA 1986*), then the liquidator is given the responsibility of applying to the court for directions, under *IA 1986, s 166(5)* (as modified), if either is more than a week late.

Removal of a liquidator

17.10   In the case of removal of a liquidator, again a members' meeting may have a part to play. If a members' voluntary winding up is proceeding, a meeting of the members summoned specially for the purpose may determine to remove the liquidator from office (*IA 1986, s 171*, as modified). In the case of a creditors' voluntary winding up, the liquidator may be removed by a meeting of the creditors summoned specially for the purpose.

Malpractice before and during winding up

17.11   In the period before an insolvency process, where the members realise that the LLP is in financial difficulty, there is a temptation to remove assets of the business and put them out of reach of the creditors and/or to continue to trade even though there is no reasonable possibility of ultimately avoiding insolvency.

The administrator or liquidator has a duty to investigate the affairs of the business prior to the insolvency and they have a range of claims that they can bring against members personally, and others which have the effect of 'clawing back' assets into the LLP. This section deals with some of the more common clawback claims.

Detailed advice to members who become aware of financial distress in the LLP is beyond the scope of this book, but it is essential that the members take professional advice once they become aware of financial distress on the LLP.

Transactions at undervalue and preferences

General

17.12   The linked provisions governing transactions at an undervalue (see 17.13 below), and preferences (see 17.14 below), are found in *ss 238* to *241* of the *IA 1986* (as modified), and the modified *s 435* of the same statute which defines the relevant term of 'associate'.

These provisions apply both in the context of an administration and a liquidation (whether voluntary or compulsory) and so there are various references to the role of the 'office holder', meaning the liquidator or administrator. Both have the concept of whether events have occurred within a relevant time, and that expression is similarly defined for both sets of circumstances by *s 240* (as modified) (see 17.15 below). The orders which may be made, if the various circumstances are made out, are likewise similar, and governed by the modified *s 241* (see 17.16 below).

Transactions at an undervalue

17.13   Under *s 238* of the *IA 1986*, a transaction made at a relevant time at an undervalue may be the subject of an application by the office holder to the court for an order to restore the position to what it would have been if the LLP had not entered into the transaction.

A transaction at an undervalue between an LLP and a person is deemed to have occurred if:

- the LLP makes a gift to that person; or

- the LLP enters into a transaction with that person on terms which mean the LLP receives no consideration; or

- the LLP enters into a transaction with that person where the consideration received by the LLP is substantially less than the consideration given by it.

Consideration in this sense can be in money, or money's worth. Even if the transaction is thus at an undervalue, however, the court shall not make an order if it believes that the LLP entered into the transaction in good faith, for the purpose of carrying on its business, and in the reasonable belief that it was for its own benefit.

Preferences

17.14   A preference under *s 239* of the *IA 1986* (as modified) can be given at a relevant time by an LLP to two classes of people. The first is its creditors. The second is any surety or guarantor for its debts or liabilities. It is given if the LLP does anything (or allows anything to happen) which has the effect of putting that person in a better position than they would otherwise have been in, in the event that the LLP later goes into insolvent liquidation.

The fact that an event may thus be a preference is not, however, of itself, enough to justify an order being sought. It must also be shown that the LLP was influenced by a desire to produce the effect of thus benefiting the third party. That intention is, however, presumed in the case of a preference where the beneficiary is a person connected with the LLP (though merely being employed by the LLP is not enough to imply connection). The fact that the act alleged to constitute a preference was actually done in pursuance of a court order does not prevent its being attackable under the section.

Relevant time

17.15   The time periods which are indicated by the modified *s 240* of the *IA 1986* as relevant are calculated by reference to the 'onset of insolvency'. Where an LLP goes into administration, this date is either the date that notice of intention to appoint was filed at court, or the date on which an application for an administration order was filed. If the LLP enters liquidation without first going into administration, the relevant date is the presentation of the winding-up petition or the passing of a resolution for voluntary winding up.

For a time to be a 'relevant time', it has to be one at which the LLP was unable to pay its debts (on any of the tests set out in *IA 1986, s 123* as modified) or became unable to pay its debts as a result of the event in question. Such an inability is, however, to be presumed (unless proved otherwise) if the third party benefiting from the event is a connected person.

Subject to those tests, the relevant time limits, outside which the office holder cannot make application, are two years before the onset of insolvency if the event is either a transaction at an undervalue, or a preference given to a connected person; or six months before the onset if the preference is given to an unconnected person. (In either case, additional relevant periods are those between the presentation of an application for an administration order and the making of an order on that application; or the time of filing a notice of intention to appoint an administrator, and his/her appointment.)

Available orders

17.16   *Section 241(1)* of the *IA 1986* (as modified) lists a number of types of order which, without prejudice to the breadth of the court's powers, it can make on an application in relation to such events as above.

In broad terms, these orders are:

- to require the re-vesting in the LLP of any property transferred;

- to require the vesting in the LLP of the proceeds of sale of any property transferred;

- to release or discharge any security given by the LLP;

- to require any person to repay any benefits received;

- to provide for the restoration of any released or discharged surety or guarantee;

- to create and give appropriate priority to security required to ensure the performance of the order;

- to provide for the extent to which the person who is to be subjected to the order can prove in the winding up for debts and liabilities due to him/her.

The effect of orders on third parties

17.17   It is not always the case that the person against whom an order (see 17.16 above) is sought will be the same as the person who actually entered into the original transaction, or was given the original preference. Property may have passed into third-party hands. Such an order may not, however, under the modified s *241(2)* of the *IA 1986*, affect property or a benefit acquired by such a third party in good faith and for value.

However, a lack of good faith is presumed (unless otherwise proved) if that third party had notice of both the 'relevant surrounding circumstances' and the 'relevant proceedings'; or if the third party was connected to, or an associate of, the LLP, or the original beneficiary of the transaction or preference. For this purpose the 'relevant surrounding circumstances' are that the third party either knew that the transaction was at an undervalue; or knew of the circumstances which made the event a preference. The 'relevant proceedings' are, in short, the commencement of the particular form of insolvency proceedings which relate to the LLP.

Similar provisions for individuals

17.18   In passing, it should be noted that there are provisions in the modified *ss 423 to 425* of the *IA 1986* which are similar to those relating to transactions at an undervalue, but in the context of individuals' bankruptcy. These could thus apply to members as individuals.

They are mentioned here only because the concept of association referred to in 17.21 below includes specific extra definitions for members.

Meaning of 'associate' in relation to the LLP

17.19   Reference was made above to whether a person was an 'associate' of the LLP. This term is defined by the modified *s 435* of the *IA 1986*.

Being 'associated' is, incidentally, a two-way concept, so that if A is deemed associated with B they are associates of each other. In the context of an LLP, the idea of association needs to be considered first in relation to the LLP itself, and second (see 17.18 above) in relation to the members of an LLP as individuals (see also 17.21 below). In the former case, it is provided by *s 435(6)*, that an LLP is an associate of another LLP if:

- the same person has control of both; or

- a person has control of one, and the other is controlled by him/her and/or his/her associates;

- the same group of two or more people have control of both; or

- the groups having control of each could be regarded as consisting of the same persons if one or more members of either group were replaced by a person who is his/her associate.

Further, by *s 435(7)* of the *IA 1986* (as modified), an LLP is an associate of another person (ie not necessarily of another LLP) if he/she, or he/she and his/her associates, together have control of it. Control in this context means the ability to ensure that the LLP is accustomed to act in accordance with the controller's directions or instructions, or the ability to exercise (or control the exercise of) at least a third of the votes at any meeting of the LLP or its parent LLP.

Meaning of 'associate' in relation to members of the LLP

17.20   There is special provision in *s 435(3A)* of the *IA 1986* (as modified) in relation to those who are to be defined as a member's associates.

These are the LLP itself, every other member of it, and the spouse or relative of every other member of it.

Meaning of 'associate' in relation to individuals

17.21   All the above discussion of association includes, to some extent, consideration of when an individual is an associate of another. This is so if that other is his/her:

- spouse or civil partner; or
- relative; or
- relative's spouse or civil partner; or
- spouse's or civil partner's relative; or
- spouse's or civil partner's relative's spouse or civil partner; or
- partner in a partnership; or
- partner's spouse, civil partner or relative; or
- employee; or
- employer.

'Relative' is in turn defined to mean any brother, sister, uncle, aunt, nephew, niece, lineal ancestor or lineal descendant. Half-blood relationships are included, as are step-relationships or those deriving from adoption, and illegitimate relationships. A member of an LLP is treated as an employee of it for this purpose.

Wrongful trading

The concept of wrongful trading

17.22   In practice, the concept of wrongful trading will be much more frequently a concern than that of fraudulent trading. Most often, that concern will be in a genuine attempt to avoid the possibility of being accused of wrongful trading, and thus to manage the LLP's affairs, when insolvency threatens, in such a manner that the accusation cannot be levelled at members.

Wrongful trading, under *s 214* of the *IA 1986*, can apply to a member (or shadow member) who, before the LLP went into insolvent liquidation, knew or ought to have concluded that there was no reasonable prospect of the LLP avoiding insolvent liquidation. If a member has that awareness, it is incumbent upon him/her to take all steps necessary to minimise the potential loss to the LLP's creditors. The section also explicitly includes omissions and failure to act (*s 214(5)*). Usually, that will mean shutting the doors and ceasing to trade. However, the question becomes more difficult if the member, whilst aware that such liquidation is likely, genuinely believes that continuing to trade will improve the creditors' lot. It is essential for the LLP members to obtain appropriate insolvency advice in this situation (see 17.11 above).

Remedies for wrongful trading

17.23   The liquidator may, if the LLP has gone into insolvent liquidation (ie if its assets are insufficient to pay both its debts and other liabilities on the one hand and the expenses of the winding up on the other) and if he/she considers that there has been wrongful trading (see 17.22 above), apply to the court. (No-one else has the right to apply, eg the creditors cannot.)

If the court finds the necessary facts made out, it can order the offender to make such contribution to the LLP's assets in the winding up as it thinks fit. It may be necessary for the court to consider the state of mind of the member at the time of the alleged acts. It is entitled to consider the facts which the member knew or ought to have known, the conclusions which he/she ought to have reached, and the steps which he/she ought to have taken, from both an objective and subjective perspective.

The first perspective is based on the viewpoint of the general knowledge, skill and experience which may reasonably be expected of a person carrying out the same functions as are carried out by that particular member in relation to the LLP. Secondly, they may be considered from the actual general knowledge, skill and experience of that particular member. Thus, it will not be enough for a member to allege that he/she should be excused because his/her is purely an operational and not a financial role (eg a junior member in a large legal LLP who plays no part in the firm's day-to-day operational decisions), if he/she actually does know the position or ought to know it from generally available facts. Further, it does not absolve a member who was required to carry out functions to say that he/she has not in fact carried them out, eg it would be no use for a member given a financial management role to say that he/she had not actually bothered to look at the accounts recently.

The court will assess the liability of each member separately, and payment by one member does not discharge the liability of any other member (*re Continental Assurance 2001 BPIR 733*).

The clawback provision – general

17.24   The one provision in the modified version of the *IA 1986* which is exclusive to LLPs is the new *s 214A*, headed 'Adjustment of withdrawals', but popularly known as the 'clawback' provision.

This has led some observers to wonder whether the government has been sufficiently serious about the principle of excluding personal liability as to make the adoption of the LLP vehicle worthwhile, but the fact remains that there are at least limitations on the attacks upon members which can be launched under this section, whereas there are no such limits in an ordinary partnership.

There is no reported case law on *s 214A*, but it has been used by the liquidators of Halliwells LLP as a basis for demanding repayment of drawings by fixed share and equity partners in the firm.

The first point to note is that this is an overlay to the existing legislation, and not a substitute for it. It applies in the context of any form of winding up; but not in that of any other form of insolvency proceedings, eg a voluntary arrangement or an administration. It potentially affects any member, or shadow member.

The concept of 'withdrawals'

17.25   *Section 214A* of the *IA 1986* (see 17.24 above) can potentially be used by a liquidator to attack any 'withdrawal' made during the relevant period.

A 'withdrawal' is a very widely defined concept, and can be anything from salary to normal monthly drawings to loan repayments, and includes any form of withdrawal of property. It does not therefore need to be anything abnormal or outside the normal commercial practice. It would, for instance, seem apt to cover repayments of capital to a member. The relevant period is two years from the commencement of the winding up. Anyone who was a member during this period is vulnerable, whether or not he/she has continued to be a member up to the commencement of the winding up.

Tests applicable to clawback

17.26   The liquidator has to be able to prove to the court that, at the time of the particular withdrawal (see 17.25 above), the member either knew, or had reasonable ground for believing, one of two things. The first is fairly straightforward, namely that, when the withdrawal was taken, the LLP was unable to pay its debts within *IA 1986, s 123* (see 16.5 above). That can of course relate to the LLP's inability to pay its debts on a cash flow or balance sheet basis.

The second thing is markedly more vague. It refers to the possibility that the LLP, though not unable to pay its debts before the withdrawal, would become so after the withdrawal, by means of the depletion of assets caused by that act. In some instances, this might be simple (eg if there were to be such a major capital withdrawal as to change the picture entirely). Even the second limb of this aspect of the test does not cause too many problems, ie that not only the withdrawal by that particular member has to be taken into account, but so also do those taken by the other members. Thus if it is a month's drawings which tip the balance, it is the aggregate change in the LLP's fortunes which count.

The problems come with the last words of the relevant subsection, which say that it is enough for the liquidator to prove that the member knew, or had reasonable cause for believing, that the LLP would become unable to pay its debts as a result of all withdrawals 'in contemplation' at the time of the particular withdrawal which the liquidator seeks to recover. No guidance is offered on how this contemplation is to be approached, and no time limit is indicated. Would it, for instance, be sufficient to enable the liquidator to invoke the section if members were to continue their normal drawings pattern if they recognised that to continue to do so for two years, unless trading conditions altered, would be enough to make the LLP insolvent?

The court's discretion on clawback

17.27   Fortunately, the court's jurisdiction in regard to clawback is discretionary. If it finds the liquidator has proved his/her point, it 'may' make an order in relation to any particular person. It may therefore decline to do so, and it may differentiate between various members.

The order it can make is for the member to make such contribution to the LLP's assets as the court thinks proper. It cannot, however, make an order for the contribution of a sum which exceeds the aggregate of the withdrawals made by the individual in question during the relevant two-year period.

The member's state of mind on clawback

17.28   There is also a further test that the court has to pose in regard to clawback. It is confusingly worded, with a double negative (by contrast with the similar provision relating to wrongful trading under s 214 of the *IA 1986* discussed at 17.22 above), but what it seems to say is that the individual has to be considered to have posed to him/herself, each time he/she makes a withdrawal, the question whether, having taken that withdrawal, there remained a reasonable prospect that the LLP would be able to avoid insolvent liquidation. (As with s 214, insolvent liquidation means one where the LLP's assets are inadequate to pay not only its debts and liabilities, but also all the winding up expenses as well.)

Unless the individual knew that such a prospect did not exist, or unless he/she should have realised that, the court may not make an order against him/her. That is a relatively familiar concept, from experience of the operation of *s 214*. The problem, however, is that *IA 1986, s 214A* states that the court's ability to make an order is excluded only if the relevant belief is established at the time of 'each' withdrawal during the two-year period. It does not say that the court shall pose the test in respect of all particular withdrawals (though that may well be what it meant to say). It seems therefore that if there is *any* withdrawal during the two-year period, in respect of which the member cannot say that he/she neither knew nor ought to have known that insolvent liquidation loomed, that is sufficient to open the court's jurisdiction to attack *all* withdrawals during the period. It is to be hoped that the court will interpret this liberally, and in effect apply the test to each withdrawal separately.

Guidance on the member's state of mind

17.29   Whatever the way the test is to be applied (see 17.28 above), there is at least guidance (similar again to that under *s 214* of the *IA 1986*: see 17.24 above) on what aptitude is expected of any individual, when considering what he/she should have known as to the LLP's future prospects.

He/she is considered to have been under a duty to know or ascertain relevant facts, and to reach appropriate conclusions from them. That duty is to be applied on an individual basis, from an objective and subjective perspective (as in wrongful trading under the modified *s 214*, see 17.22 above).

Conclusions on the clawback provision

17.30   In practice, *s 214A* of the *IA 1986* may not be as easy for a liquidator to apply as it may seem. He/she has a number of points to prove, and the burden of that proof is firmly upon him/her. He/she needs to do that in respect of each and every member or shadow member, and the court will have to consider the position on an individual basis, so that the costs may potentially be substantial.

The work involved in trying to prove what the state of mind of someone ought to have been two years before the liquidation commenced – and hence inevitably several years before the matter reaches court – will be considerable. It may in practice be the case that it is only in fairly clear-cut cases that this weapon will be wielded. It is suggested therefore that – particularly going back to the point that no such right is needed in respect of partnerships because the partners' assets are all at risk anyway – the existence of this section should not be sufficient to put people off the idea of forming an LLP.

Misfeasance

17.31 By *s 212* of the *IA 1986* (as modified) a liquidator, creditor or contributor can bring a claim against a member, where the LLP has been wound up and the member has misapplied, retained or become accountable for any money or other property of the LLP or where the member is in breach of any fiduciary duty in relation to the LLP.

If the claim is successful then the court will order that the member either repays or restores or accounts for the money or property with interest or (in a breach of duty case) contributes to the LLP's assets by way of compensation.

A misfeasance claim is used relatively often by liquidators, because there is no requirement to show fraud on the part of the members.

An action undertaken by a member which prejudices the position of the creditors at a time when the LLP is financially distressed could well amount to 'misfeasance' or breach of fiduciary duty.

Fraud

17.32 There are a wide range of claims that can be brought by an office holder where a member has acted fraudulently prior to an insolvency process.

These claims include:

- fraudulent trading – where the business has been carried on to defraud creditors of the LLP and creditors of any other person (*s 213* of the *IA 1986*, as modified); and

- transactions defrauding creditors – where assets have been gifted or transferred out of the LLP at an undervalue where the purpose was to put the assets beyond the reach of a person who is making or may at some time make a claim against the LLP (*s 423* of the *IA 1986*, as modified).

Generally, office holders rarely bring fraud proceedings because (i) of the difficulty in providing the mental state of the defendant together with the other additional hurdles required in demonstrating fraud and (ii) most acts which might fall into the fraud category can be dealt with as transactions at an undervalue, preferences or as misfeasance.

However, fraud proceedings might be considered where the time frame within which the acts occurred mean that a transaction at an undervalue or preference claim is barred (ie the actions took place more than six months/two years ago (as appropriate)), or where it is difficult to demonstrate insolvency at the time in question.

Restrictions on re-use of LLP names

17.33 There are considerable restrictions, under *IA 1986, s 216* (as modified), upon the activities of any person (natural or corporate) who has been a member of an LLP which goes into insolvent liquidation (for which the test is the same as in preceding paragraphs) within the year before it went into liquidation. (Curiously, here, the relevant time is not the commencement of the winding up, but the day before the actual liquidation took effect.)

Any name by which the LLP has been known during that final year, and any name which is so similar to it as to suggest an association with the LLP, becomes a 'prohibited name'. This does not have to relate to the official name of the LLP only, but can also relate to any trading name used by it. For five years from the day the LLP goes into liquidation, such a person must not (without the leave of the court) be:

- a member of another LLP known by a prohibited name;

- involved at all in the promotion, formation or management of such an LLP;

- involved at all in any business carried on, under a prohibited name, by a vehicle other than an LLP.

Sanctions for wrongful use of prohibited names

17.34 There are two sanctions for breach of the provisions discussed at 17.33 above.

First, under *s 216* itself (as modified) (see also 17.33), there is a criminal offence of wrongful use of a prohibited name, punishable by imprisonment, a fine or both. Secondly, under *IA 1986, s 217* (as modified), the offender will be personally liable for the debts of any entity (whether an LLP, company or unincorporated business) carrying on business under a prohibited name if he/she is involved in its management.

Further, if anyone (whether a member of the former LLP or not) who is involved in the management of that new entity's business, acts or is willing to act upon the instructions of someone he/she knows to be contravening *s 216*, he/she acquires such personal liability as well. Anyone who is thus personally liable is jointly and severally liable not only with the entity itself, but also with any other person who picks up such personal liability under the section. This applies to all debts incurred whilst so involved in the entity's management. The provisions of *s 216* will not apply where the whole (or substantially the whole) business of the LLP is sold by a liquidator or administrator and members of the old LLP who are involved in the new business send a notice in prescribed form to all the creditors of the old LLP (under *r 4.228*). Alternatively, the member involved can apply to the court (*IA 1986, s 21(3)*). There is also an exception if the new entity has already been trading actively for the full 12 months leading up to the liquidation of the LLP (*r 4.230*).

The section is drafted broadly to encompass management of or taking part in the new business, and is not restricted to those formally appointed as members of an LLP or directors of a company.

Members' duties to the office holder

17.35   The members have wide-ranging duties to assist the office holder in progressing the insolvency. Under *s 235* of the *IA 1986*, they include the requirements to:

* give the office holder such information concerning the company and its promotion, formation, business, dealings, affairs or property as the office holder may reasonably require; and

* attend on the office holder at such times as the latter may reasonably require.

If the member fails to assist, then the office holder can require the member to attend court to be examined and if the member fails to attend or provide information to the court, he/she can be arrested.

Members should be aware, though, that their requirement to provide information is not absolute. There are certain limitations, particularly where the office holder is trying to obtain information in order to bring a claim against the member and a member should take legal advice if he/she is concerned that by providing the information they may be incriminating themselves.

Matters arising after winding up

Declaring an LLP's dissolution void

17.36   There may be circumstances where, even after an LLP has been wound up and consequently dissolved, it becomes necessary to revive it. In such circumstances, the court has the power to declare the dissolution to have been void (*CA 2006, ss 1029*, as modified). This would normally be in order to enable litigation against the LLP to proceed. Application may be made either by the LLP's liquidator, or by any other person the court believes to have an interest. Application cannot normally be made more than two years after dissolution, but this restriction does not generally apply if the prospective claim would be for personal injuries (including funeral expenses under the *Law Reform (Miscellaneous Provisions) Act 1934, s 1(2)(c)*), or for damages under the *Fatal Accidents Act 1976*. If the court grants an order, the successful applicant must deliver an office copy of the order to the registrar within seven days, or become liable to a fine. The court may also order that the period between dissolution and restoration shall not count towards any relevant limitation or similar period.

Striking off a defunct LLP by the registrar

17.37   Mention has already been made of the fact that, unlike a company, an LLP is not intended to be a dormant vehicle for long. The Registrar may accordingly (under *CA 2006, ss 1000 to 1002*, as modified), take steps to remove a defunct LLP from the register. His/her first move is to write to the LLP, if he/she believes that it is not carrying on business or operating, to enquire if that belief is correct. There is no minimum period for which that inactivity must have applied. If no reply is received within a month, he/she sends a reminder letter by registered post, warning that striking off may follow. If either there is still no answer within a month, or the LLP confirms that it is inactive, the registrar may issue a notice that, unless cause to the contrary is shown within three months, the LLP will be struck off the register and dissolved.

This notice must be given to the LLP, and published in the *London Gazette*. (Such a notice may alternatively be given in like manner if the LLP is being wound up anyway, and the registrar has reasonable cause to believe that no liquidator is acting, or that the LLP's affairs are fully wound up, or six consecutive months' liquidator's reports have not been received.)

Once such notice expires, unless reasonable cause to the contrary has been shown, the registrar may strike the LLP's name off the register, and publish notice of that fact in the *London Gazette*. Upon publication of that notice, the LLP is dissolved. That dissolution does not affect the potential personal liability of any member of the LLP, in circumstances where they would have been liable had the LLP continued to exist. Nor does it affect the ability of the court subsequently to order a winding up of the LLP.

Striking off a defunct LLP on application

17.38   Application may also be made, on behalf of the LLP, for a striking off. This application must be made with payment of a fee (currently £10), on Form LL DS01, by two or more designated members, under *CA 2006, ss 1003 to 1111*, as modified. On receipt of such an application, the registrar will publish a notice in the *London Gazette* stating that, after three months, he/she may exercise his/her powers to strike off, and inviting any person to show cause why he/she should not do so. If no such cause is shown, he/she can then decide to strike off, and publish a notice of that fact in the *Gazette*, upon publication of which the LLP is dissolved (though, as in 17.37 above, this does not affect any potential personal liability of a member, or the ability of the court to order a winding up).

Such an application may not, however, be made in certain circumstances, namely:

- if, in the last three months, the LLP has:

  ○ changed its name;

  ○ traded or otherwise carried on business (which will not be connoted simply by paying earlier trading debts);

  ○ sold property or rights which, when active, were part of its normal trade;

  ○ otherwise been active except (broadly) for concluding purposes;

- if an application is currently before the court in relation to a compromise or arrangement under *CA 2006, Pt 26*;

- if a voluntary arrangement, administration or winding up of any sort is still current;

- if a receiver or manager of the LLP's property is still acting.

When such an application is made, it must be served within seven days on all members, employees and creditors of the LLP, and on the manager or trustee of any employees' pension fund. Also, it may be required to be served on any type of person specified by the Secretary of State by regulation, but no such regulations have yet been made.

Members' duties on application

17.39   If, after an application is made for voluntary striking off, any person joins any of the categories of people upon whom the application originally had to be served, a designated member must serve a copy upon him/her within seven days. Further, a designated member must, under *CA 2006, s 1009*, as modified, serve notice in Form LL DS02 to withdraw the application for striking off if, before the application is finally dealt with, any of the circumstances which would have prevented the LLP from launching an application in the first place (see 17.38 above) arises. Thus, if the LLP should, eg resume its trade, or have any insolvency procedure commenced against it, the application must be withdrawn.

Supplemental provisions regarding striking off

17.40   The formalities of service of applications, eg with regard to the correct addresses etc, are dealt with in *CA 2006, s 1008*, as modified. Enforcement of the duties imposed by the provisions governing striking off applications is in turn dealt with by *CA 1985, s 652E*, as modified. Anyone breaching or failing to perform a duty imposed on them commits an offence and is liable normally to a fine, but if the breach in question relates to a deliberate failure to serve notice of the application with the intention of concealing it, then imprisonment may also follow. There are various specific defences offered, however, which vary according to the particular nature of the breach, but are all based around the concepts of either being unaware of the breach, or having taken all reasonable steps to perform the duty.

Objections to striking off and restoration to the Register

17.41 If an LLP has been struck off by the Registrar, acting on his/ her own initiative under the provisions summarised in 17.38, then the Registrar may, on the application of a member, order the LLP's name to be 'administratively restored' under *CA 2006, s 1024*, as modified. The director can only do so if the LLP was actually operative at the time of the striking off, and where application is made within six years from the striking off. Restoration can also be ordered by the court under *CA 2006, ss 1029 to 1032* if (i) the company was struck off by the Registrar when it was active, or (ii) the company was struck off by the voluntary strike-off procedure (and the requirements were not fully complied with), or (iii) the court considers it just. Restoration can generally only be ordered if application is made within six years of strike-off (with an exception in the case of proceedings against the LLP for personal injury).

The effect of any such restoration order is that the striking off is deemed never to have happened. The court may give any necessary directions for putting the clock back, as far as may be possible, to the original position.

Effect of dissolution on property

17.42 When an LLP is dissolved, all its property (except any it holds as trustee for a third party) becomes *bona vacantia*, ie vests automatically (by virtue of *CA 2006, s 1012*, as modified) in the Crown (or, depending on its location, in the Duchy of Lancaster or the Duke of Cornwall). The Crown may then dispose of the property. If, however, an order is made either for the dissolution to be declared void or for the restoration of the LLP to the register (see 17.36 above) then it does not affect any disposition which has been made by the Crown, but compensation for the value of the disposed of property must be paid by the Crown to the LLP. The Crown may, however, disclaim any such property (under *CA 2006, s 1013*, as modified), either within three years of becoming aware of the vesting, or within 12 months of a notice from any interested party requiring it to decide whether to disclaim or not. Upon disclaimer, the effect is that the property is deemed by *CA 2006, s 1014*, as modified, never to have vested in the Crown.

Chapter 18

Company Directors Disqualification

18.1   This chapter, finishing off the consideration of insolvency-related topics, looks at the way in which LLPs and their members have been fitted into the regime of the *Company Directors Disqualification Act 1986* (*CDDA 1986*). The interaction between disqualification procedures applying to companies and LLPs is examined. The ways in which, and the reasons for which, disqualification may be brought about are set out. In particular the criteria for making a member 'unfit' to manage are looked at. Lastly, the criminal and civil penalties for contravention of an order or undertaking are discussed.

Introduction

General application

18.2   The *CDDA 1986* is applied to LLPs in general terms by the *2001 Regulations, reg 4(2)* (see 1.15 above in regard to the *Regulations*). Certain general modifications are provided for in that regulation, so that:

- references to a company include references to an LLP;

- references to a director, or an officer, of a company include references to a member of an LLP;

- references to a shadow director include references to a shadow member.

There is also one specific modification found in *Pt II* of *Sch 2* to *2001 Regulations*, with the insertion of a new *para 8A* in *Pt II* of *Sch I* to the *CDDA 1986*. The *CDDA 1986* as set out is as amended also by the *IA 2000*, the relevant provisions of which were brought into effect on 2 April 2001; and by certain provisions of the *EA 2002*, with effect from 20 June 2003.

Disqualification under the Act is triggered either:

- by convictions under or breach of *CA 2006* or *IA 1986* (see 18.7 to 18.10); or

- (more generally) due to 'unfitness' (see 18.11 to 18.17) following the insolvency of an LLP or an investigation into its officers.

Given the potential for disqualification, members of an LLP should always take appropriate legal and accountancy advice if the business of the LLP is in financial difficulty.

Overall effect

18.3   The effect of the above is to bring LLPs fully into the *CDDA 1986* regime. LLPs are effectively treated as companies, so that orders under the *CDDA 1986*, as applied to LLPs, which are obtainable against members will not only disqualify them from acting as members of an LLP, but also as directors of a company.

Disqualification in the LLP context

18.4   Anyone subject to such a disqualification order as described above may therefore not be a member of an LLP or a director of a company; be a receiver of an LLP's or company's property; or in any way (directly or indirectly) be concerned or take part in the promotion, formation or management of an LLP or a company (*CDDA 1986, s 1(1)*).

The court can grant leave to override such restrictions under *CDDA 1986, s 17*. It is worth noting that disqualification proceedings are normally regarded as civil proceedings, not criminal ones, and this affects such issues as the burden of proof, and human rights issues such as the admissibility against an individual of evidence compulsorily required of him/her (*R v Secretary of State for Trade & Industry, ex parte McCormick* [1998] BCC 379).

Disqualification undertakings

18.5   Quite commonly, in practice, disqualification issues are dealt with by way of undertakings, ie the individual threatened with court proceedings to obtain a disqualification order offers or agrees an undertaking with the Secretary of State that he/she will be subject to such restrictions as are referred to above for an agreed period of time.

A disqualification undertaking is only available in the case of proceedings for unfitness under *s 6* (see 18.11) and *s 8* (see 18.13) of *CDDA 1986*.

Statutory force is now given to such arrangements by *CDDA 1986, s 1A*.

Register of disqualifications

18.6   In accordance with *s 18* of the *CDDA 1986*, the Secretary of State keeps a register of all disqualification orders and undertakings; of all variations to them or instances of leave being granted in connection with them; and of their termination. This register is open to public inspection.

Extracts from this list in the register can now be inspected on the Companies House website (www.companies-house.gov.uk), and the Insolvency Service has an Investigations Hotline for the reporting of conduct which might lead to disqualification. Instances of orders and undertakings are steadily increasing.

Becoming disqualified

Causes of disqualification – indictable offences

18.7   The cause of disqualification does not have to be criminal behaviour, but occasionally it will be. Under s 2 of the *CDDA 1986*, the court may therefore make a disqualification order against any person on conviction of an indictable offence, where that offence relates to:

- the promotion, formation or management of an LLP;
- the liquidation or striking off of an LLP;
- the receivership of an LLP's property;
- his role as administrative receiver of an LLP.

Where the court is one of summary jurisdiction, the maximum length of disqualification is five years; otherwise it is 15 years.

Causes of disqualification – persistent companies legislation breaches

18.8   The legislation is also targeted (in addition to the offences described above at 18.7), however, at those who are habitually in breach of the provisions of company legislation aimed at requiring the public availability of information, ie the filing with the Registrar of accounts, returns, notices etc.

Any court having winding up jurisdiction over the LLP may under the modified s 3 of the *CDDA 1986* make a disqualification order in such a case for up to five years. On an application under this section, such habitual breach may (*inter alia*) be proved by a person having been found guilty three or more times in the previous five years (whether in criminal proceedings or by means of default orders for failure to file accounts or other returns under the modified *CA 2006, ss 452, 456* or *1113* or *IA 1986, ss 41* or *170*).

Causes of disqualification – convictions

18.9   Tying into these last provisions (see 18.8 above) is the ability of a court of summary jurisdiction, acting under s 5 of the *CDDA 1986* (as modified), to impose a disqualification order, for up to five years, upon convicting any person of any offence relating to a failure to comply with any requirement to file with the Registrar any return, account, notice or other document.

That failure can include the situation where the default is that of the LLP, as well as that of the individual. Disqualification can, however, only be imposed if there have been findings of guilt (whether by conviction or default order as in 18.8 above) in respect of three relevant defaults (including the instant one) in the last five years.

Causes of disqualification – fraud in winding up

18.10 Another possible trigger to disqualification proceedings is conviction under *s 993* of the *CA 2006* for fraudulent trading (see 17.32 above), or conviction of a member (including shadow member), liquidator, receiver or administrative receiver of an LLP for fraud in relation to the LLP or breach of duty. *Section 4* of the *CDDA 1986* refers.

Again, jurisdiction is conferred on the same basis as a winding up. Similarly, if a court makes an order in respect of fraudulent or wrongful trading, under the modified *ss 213* and *214* of the *IA 1986*, that a person should make a contribution to the LLP's assets, it may make a disqualification order against that person of its own volition, under *CDDA 1986, s 10*. Note that this does not however apply in the case of an order for contribution following clawback of withdrawals under *s 214A* of the *IA 1986*, notwithstanding that responsibility for such withdrawals is a factor in considering whether an order, triggered by other events, should be made (see 17.24) In any such case the maximum term of the order is 15 years.

The court's duty to disqualify

18.11 The most frequent source of disqualification order is an application of the Secretary of State under *CDDA 1986, s 6* following the administration, liquidation or administrative receivership of the LLP. There is an overriding duty on the court under *CDDA 1986, s 6* to disqualify a person if, on application, it is satisfied that the conduct of a past or present member of an LLP (which has been placed into one of the above insolvency proceedings) makes him/her unfit to be concerned in the management of an LLP.

An application under *s 6* can result in a disqualification order of 2 to 15 years.

This may apply to his/her conduct whether viewed in respect of the one LLP alone, or collectively in respect of that LLP and other LLPs or companies. (If the latter is the case, there has to be sufficient connection with the collateral bodies to show the member's unfitness to manage the subject LLP, but the conduct is not required to be of a similar nature to that in relation to the subject LLP (*Secretary of State for Trade and Industry v Ivens* [1997] 2 BCLC 334).) For this purpose, an insolvent LLP is one whose assets are not enough to pay its debts and liabilities, and the expenses of a winding up; or one which has entered administration or had an administrative receiver of it appointed. Member includes shadow member.

Procedures on application

18.12 The decision as to whether or not an application should be made under *CDDA 1986, s 6* is that of the Secretary of State but in practice this power is devolved to a government body called the Insolvency Service, which falls under the Department of Business Innovation and Skills.

In order that the Insolvency Service can reach that decision, any relevant office holder (ie the Official Receiver, liquidator, administrator or administrative receiver, as appropriate) who thinks there may be circumstances to justify such an application must report the fact to the Insolvency Service, who may then require all necessary information and documentation etc.

The Secretary of State must consider not only that the person, against whom action is to be taken, is unfit to act, but also that it is expedient in the public interest for action to be taken. If it reaches those conclusions, it may either make an application itself or, if the application is against a member of an LLP which is being wound up, he/she may direct the Official Receiver to do so. Such an application may not be made, however, more than two years after the date upon which the relevant LLP became insolvent, unless the court gives leave otherwise.

An alternative to an application as above is that the Insolvency Service may accept a proffered disqualification undertaking, if it thinks it is expedient in the public interest to do so.

Application after investigation

18.13 As noted in various sections of this work, the Secretary of State has powers of investigation under a number of provisions, eg those under *s 437* of the *CA 1985* (see 12.40 above). If, as a result of any such investigation, he/she considers it expedient in the public interest to seek a disqualification order against any past or present member (or shadow member) of an LLP, he/she may apply to the High Court under *CDDA 1986, s 8* for such an order.

If the court considers that the conduct in question makes the person concerned unfit to be concerned in the management of an LLP, it may make the order, for up to 15 years. Again, however, the Secretary of State may as an alternative accept a disqualification undertaking, rather than taking proceedings, if he/she considers it expedient.

Variation of undertakings

18.14   Where a disqualification undertaking is given in place of an order under *CDDA 1986, s 6* or *8* (as modified) (see 18.5, 18.12 and 18.13) above), the person subject to such an undertaking is given the power, by *s 8A* of the *CDDA 1986*, to apply to the court for the undertaking to be reduced in time, or terminated.

The Insolvency Service on behalf of the Secretary of State is to appear on any such application to draw the court's attention to all relevant matters, and may give evidence or call witnesses.

Matters for determining unfitness

18.15   A number of the above provisions have referred to a member (or shadow member) being deemed 'unfit' (eg see 18.11 and 18.13). What then constitutes unfitness?

By *s 9* of the *CDDA 1986* (as modified), the court or the Secretary of State, as the case may be, when considering whether to make an order or accept an undertaking, shall have regard in any event to the provisions set out in *Pt I* of *Sch I* to the *CDDA 1986* and, if the LLP in question has become insolvent (see 18.10 above) to the matters in *Pt II* of that *Schedule*. (The Secretary of State may by order vary the terms of *Sch I*.)

The scheduled terms

18.16   In broad terms, *Sch I* to the *CDDA 1986* covers:

Part I:

- misfeasance or breach of fiduciary or other duty;
- misapplication or retention by the member of the LLP's funds or property;
- responsibility for any avoidable transactions of the LLP;
- responsibility for any failure of the LLP relating to certain specific record-keeping obligations;
- responsibility for members' failure to comply with accounting requirements

Part II:

- responsibility for the causes of the LLP becoming insolvent;
- responsibility for the LLP's failure to provide goods and services which have been paid for;

- responsibility for any transaction attackable (whether or not so proved) as:

  ○   a void disposition of the LLP's property after commencement of the winding up of the LLP, or

  ○   a transaction at an undervalue or preference;

- responsibility for any declaration requiring clawback of withdrawals (whether made in his/her favour or not);

- responsibility for failure to call a creditors' meeting in a voluntary winding up;

- failure to comply with various requirements of members as to cooperation during the course of sundry insolvency proceedings.

Other provisions regarding unfitness

18.17   It should be noted, however, that *Sch I* to the *CDDA 1986* (see 18.15 and 18.16 above) is indicative, not exhaustive, and that regard may be had to other factors considered relevant in any particular case, the primary aim being not to punish the individual, but to protect the public.

There are numerous reported cases on unfitness. In the leading Court of Appeal judgment (*re Sevenoaks Stationers (Retail) Limited* (1991) Ch164), the Court of Appeal held that the test of unfitness is 'framed in ordinary words which should be simple to apply in most cases' and that it is important to adhere to the statutory wording. The judge in any particular case has a wide discretion to decide, on the specific facts, whether the conduct 'varied accumulatively and taking into account any extenuating circumstances, has fallen below the standards of probity and competence appropriate for persons to be directors of companies' (Hoffmann LJ in *re Grayan Building Services Limited* (1995) Ch 241).

Each case is likely to turn on its own facts. Factors such as irresponsibility, dishonesty, deception and breach of trust are common themes. Incompetence alone must be 'of a high degree' to prove unfitness. Extenuating circumstances (which may influence a court not to make an order, or to reduce the period of disqualification) may include:

- acting on professional advice (or employing qualified personnel to advise);

- absence of dishonesty;

- events outside the member's control;

- youth and inexperience;

- the fact that a member is employed for his/her own specialist knowledge and is entitled to rely on the expertise and qualifications of other board members.

However, purely passive conduct may also lead to disqualification if the member does not take action when other more active directors are allowing the company to run up losses.

Automatic disqualification of undischarged bankrupts

18.18   One set of prohibitions which applies without the need for any specific order or undertaking relates to any undischarged bankrupt, or to someone who has had a bankruptcy restrictions order made against him/her. Such a person may not, whether directly or indirectly, take part or be concerned in the promotion, formation or management of an LLP. *Section 11* of the *CDDA 1986* (as modified) applies.

The only exception to the prohibition is if the leave of the court is given. Anyone seeking such leave has to serve notice of his/her application upon the Official Receiver, who may attend and oppose it if he/she thinks it in the public interest to do so.

Consequences of disqualification

Criminal penalties

18.19   In the case of both disqualification orders and undertakings, or in the case of automatic disqualification under *s 11* (as modified), it is an offence under *s 13* of the *CDDA 1986* (as modified) to act in contravention thereof. Such an offence may be tried either on indictment or summarily, and in either case is subject to imprisonment and/or fine, with different maxima applying in each case.

Further, under *s 14* (as modified), there may be additional prosecutions if the contravention is actually that of a body corporate, since in such cases not only may that body be liable, but so may any actual or purported member or other officer who consented to or connived at the breach, or facilitated it by his/her negligence.

Personal liability for debts

18.20   Personal liability for an LLP's debts can attach, under *s 15* of the *CDDA 1986*, to two groups. First, it can apply to anyone who, whilst themselves under a disqualification order or undertaking, is involved in the LLP's management. Secondly, it can apply to someone who, though not him/herself disqualified, acts, or is willing to act, upon the instructions of someone he/she knows to be a disqualified person.

Either person will be personally liable for all the debts of the LLP incurred whilst the relevant circumstances prevail. Such liability will be joint and several with the LLP and with any other person who, for any reason, is also so liable.

There is no procedure for any order under this section, so it will be for a claimant who believes that anyone is under such liability to satisfy the court hearing the main claim, on the normal balance of civil proof, that the circumstances contemplated by the section were prevailing at the time the debt was incurred.

A liquidator of the LLP has a right of action against all those liable under the modified *s 15* of *CDDA 1986* for a contribution arising out of their joint and several liability for the relevant debts of the LLP (*re Prestige Grindings Limited* (2006) BCC 421).

Chapter 19

Mergers, Acquisitions and Joint Ventures

19.1 This chapter looks briefly at the increased range of options which is offered by the existence of LLPs when it comes to the combining of two or more businesses in the professional services field and also increasingly in the wider arena of property acquisition and development, together with other areas such as social housing. Ways of combining businesses whereby the original constituent LLPs either remain in existence or are absorbed by the new venture are considered. The role of the LLP as a potential participant in either partnerships or companies is also reviewed. The impact of the differing styles of accounting which apply to mergers and acquisitions respectively is touched upon. Finally, the role of the LLP as a potential vehicle for joint ventures is examined.

Introduction

19.2 In the professional services industry, firms are increasingly looking to consolidate in what is a highly competitive market in order to ensure business succession. When putting two partnerships together, in what is normally referred to simply as a merger, the options are fairly limited. Essentially, one business is going to need to be absorbed into the other, with the structure of the latter prevailing.

With LLPs, because of their corporate nature, the possibilities are more varied. Whilst there is nothing to stop the same happening, ie one LLP effectively being taken over by another, with just the one entity emerging, it is quite possible for many variations to be played on the theme. Those managing the merger process will need to consider first what shape they want the eventual business(es) to be, and then choose the route that suits them best.

For legal services businesses in particular, these issues have a particular current pertinence, in the light of the *Legal Services Act 2007*, with the ability for such businesses to be funded by non-lawyer investors. Such investors are likely to prefer to look at businesses whose accounts are prepared under *Companies Act* format, thus simplifying their due diligence tasks, and so LLPs and, of course, limited companies will be more favoured in this respect than general partnerships.

Increasingly, LLPs are seen as the vehicle of choice for those entering into a joint venture, combining limited liability with the organisational flexibility of a partnership, allowing members to regulate more freely the operation of the LLP, movement of capital etc.

Memberships in common

19.3   One possibility in a merger of two LLPs would be to use the corporate status of the LLP so as to allow each of the two existing LLPs to continue its separate existence, but with each being a member of the other.

This continuation might, for instance, be of use where each of the two had separate niche businesses and distinct 'brand' value, so that it would be a pity to lose one of those values by killing off one of the names, but there would be synergy to be derived from combining resources. The strength, and rewards, of the respective memberships in each other would not necessarily have to be identical, although this option would be at risk of failing to deliver a 'unified' business with each of the respective partners and employees remaining within their own respective business. One would suggest that unless there was an overriding reason for this structure that could not be dealt with in any other way, then this option would be best avoided for one of the alternative solutions detailed below.

A central vehicle

19.4   Conversely, it may be that two businesses perceive that there would be added strength, in marketing terms, by representing themselves as being one dominant business. In reality, however, they do not want to give up their separate financial structures, so that they can remain separate profit centres contributing to central marketing, training and administrative functions. In such a case the existing two LLPs could become the members in a third LLP, which would be the publicly apparent vehicle, using an amalgamated name.

Thus Smith & Co LLP could ostensibly join with Jones & Williams LLP to form Smith Jones Williams LLP, but with the two original bodies in fact continuing to exist. This is of course quite possible (and indeed not uncommon) with a coming-together of partnerships, but it is a much more cumbersome process, as all individual partners are likely to be involved, whereas with LLPs it is simply the corporate entities, with the underlying memberships left undisturbed.

LLPs as partners

19.5   Yet another variation is that an LLP can be not only a member in another LLP, but also a partner in a conventional partnership.

Previously, if partnership AB as an entity wanted to become a partner in partnership CD, it had to do it through the medium of a nominee partner X. This raised issues as to the indemnities to be offered to X for his/her personal exposure to the legal liabilities of CD, and as to the tax position of X in respect of the income ostensibly derived by him/ her from his/her position as a partner in CD. With LLPs, however, that problem disappears, so that even if AB wishes for some reason to remain as a traditional partnership, its partners can form the entity of AB LLP which can then become a partner in CD.

LLP groups

19.6   Finally, it is also possible for LLP groups to be created, with the same form of hierarchical structures as company groups (and similar accounting requirements). Thus LLPs can be parents or subsidiaries.

LLPs cannot, however, be quite the same, in that they cannot be wholly-owned subsidiaries, since a subsidiary LLP will need at least two members in order to pass the test of *s 2(1)(a)* of the *LLPA 2000*, namely the requirement that an LLP must have 'two or more persons associated for carrying on a lawful business with a view to profit'. There are, however, no rules on how small or large the interests of each member have to be, so to all intents and purposes a group structure can be replicated. Equally, if 100% ownership of the subsidiary is deemed essential, it could be a company (see 19.7 below).

The interface with companies

19.7   A merger may also involve a coming-together of an LLP with a company.

Again, this is easier with an LLP than with a partnership. Depending on the circumstances, the LLP may acquire shares in a company (without the need for nominee arrangements which would apply to a partnership taking shares); or the company can become a member of the LLP.

Accounting on mergers and acquisitions

19.8   In many cases the term 'merger' will be used to refer to combinations of businesses. In accounting terms, however, mergers and other acquisitions are different animals, and subject to different treatments. This is dealt with in Financial Reporting Standard 6, whose avowed aim is to:

> '... ensure that merger accounting is used only for those business combinations that are not, in substance, the acquisition of one entity by another but the formation of a new reporting entity as a substantially equal partnership where no party is dominant; [and] to ensure the use of acquisition accounting for all other business combinations ...'

In other words, mergers will be the exception rather than the rule.

The five criteria for a merger are that:

- no one portrays either original party as either acquirer or acquired;

- all parties arrive at a selection of a management structure and team by consensus;

- no party dominates by reason of relative size;

- the consideration for the deal is largely equity in the new enterprise, not cash etc;

- no members retain a material interest in the future performance of part only of the new enterprise.

The differences involved

19.9   A detailed examination of the differences between the two types of accounting is well beyond the scope of this work. In broad terms, merger accounting will involve showing an amalgamation of both parties' accounts as though they had always been part of the same reporting entity. Acquisition accounting will show the results of the acquired business being brought into the group accounts only from the date of acquisition onwards.

The nature of the adjustments on the combining of the accounts will be different. The point to be made for present purposes is that these are factors which will shape the public accounting face of the new enterprise, and may well be relevant to the method which, on taking proper accountancy advice, is appropriate for the businesses' combination. In particular the values given to the constituent parts of the consideration, eg both tangible assets and intangibles such as goodwill, will need to be carefully examined.

Joint ventures

19.10   Although it has taken time for the concept to catch on, probably because those advisers and parties involved with such issues are more familiar with the working practices of a limited company, LLPs are increasingly being used as a vehicle for a specific and limited purpose (ie a joint venture).

In this situation, neither of the original parties will lose their identity, but the LLP will offer a demarcated and incorporated vehicle for the undertaking of a common purpose. LLPs have many advantages over limited companies in this regard. The transparency of the tax position may help, for one thing. (The government is, however, wary of the use of LLPs solely for tax-avoidance reasons. It has already removed the benefit of LLP tax status for certain specific ventures, eg in the property field.)

The informality and privacy of the relevant agreement may also be an advantage, as may the limited disclosure provisions applicable to LLPs. The ability to adjust the capital structure of the venture without needing to jump through all the procedural hoops relating to companies' share capital, and the general flexibility of the LLP model, may also be attractive. If, however, it is envisaged that the joint venture may eventually require a Stock Market flotation, then company status is still likely to be the preferred route.

Chapter 20

Risk Management and LLPs

20.1 This chapter deals with various elements of the risks which attach to LLPs and their members. It looks first at ways of minimising the residual elements of personal risk which attach to members, before it then turns to address particular risk issues which arise in the context of insolvency. Operational risk issues are then considered, in the context both of the quality assurance management techniques which are available, and the insurance implications for the LLP and its members alike.

LLPs as a risk-management tool

20.2 In many instances, an LLP will owe its selection as a business vehicle to a process – albeit perhaps an unconscious one – of risk management. In other words, the whole purpose of creating an LLP is to minimise personal exposure to the present and future risks of the business to be operated by the LLP. Logic dictates therefore that the advantages conferred by the LLP's existence need to be maximised.

To look at it in another way, the business needs to be run in such a way that the exceptions which bring back into play the possibility of personal liability need to be minimised. This chapter therefore brings together a number of strands which have appeared elsewhere in this work, and reviews the risks and the ways in which they can be controlled.

Personal liability

Pre-incorporation debts

20.3 Prospective members are potentially personally liable on pre-incorporation debts.

Such members should therefore ensure that use is made of s 5(2) of the *LLPA 2000*, which allows a partnership agreement to be made before incorporation, in such a way as to bind the LLP to grant an indemnity for such debts immediately upon incorporation.

Dropping below the two-member level

20.4 Members of particularly small LLPs need to be alive to the consequences of continuing to trade for more than the six-month period of grace allowed if the number of members drops below two.

This is because after that time they will acquire joint and several liability (with the LLP) for the debts accrued by the LLP, under *s 4A* of *LLPA 2000* (as inserted by *para 3, Pt 1, Sch 3* of the *2009 Regulations* (as amended).

Personal liability for negligence etc.

20.5   It is not possible to completely exclude the risk of personal liability attaching to an individual member for the tortious consequences of his/her actions within the context of the LLP's business (see 20.3 and 20.4 above), but it is possible to limit this potential exposure.

Carefully written letters of engagement, and a minimisation of moves whereby an individual can be said to have assumed personal responsibility to the client so that he/she personally owed a duty of care to the client to carry out the work with reasonable skill and care, should be effected. It is worth noting that in *Merrett v Babb* [2001] 3 WLR 1, one of the things which went against the hapless Mr Babb, an employed surveyor found negligent for a report written on behalf of his soon-to-be insolvent employer, was that he had signed the report in his own name.

Anything which helps to build the view that it is the incorporated entity of the LLP which is dealing with the customer or client will help to reduce personal risk. It is worth noting that the SRA (and formerly the Law Society) allowed solicitors' firms to limit their potential tortious liability by contract, provided they did not seek to reduce it to less than the then current minimum level of professional indemnity insurance cover, and have issued guidance clarifying that they have no objection to similar contractual moves being used to limit or even extinguish any potential personal liability of members, so long as the LLP's minimum liability remains. (Such attempts are of course always subject to the legislation on unfair contract terms, like any other exclusion clauses.)

In addition to minimising risk of potential personal liability to a third party, the members should consider whether they wish to limit their personal liability further in relation to a potential claim by the LLP as a contributory in a claim brought against the LLP (see Chapter 6).

Compliance with statutory obligations

20.6   Time and time again, throughout this work, reference has been made to instances where, in default of compliance with statutory procedures, members or designated members may be personally liable for fines or daily default fines. Many people becoming members in an LLP will be coming afresh to the world of such procedural requirements, especially if they have come from the relatively informal background of a partnership.

Members should ensure that they are aware of their responsibilities, and what systems are in place for ensuring that the necessary steps are taken. Systematic management of the compliance requirements – which are not particularly onerous if they are undertaken in due time – is essential.

Clarifying limits of authority

20.7 The LLP is essentially liable for its members' acts or omissions, in their capacity as its agents.

If there are to be restrictions placed upon the authority of any member, the means of communicating those limits to the relevant third parties need to be carefully considered, so that advantage can be taken of *s 6(2)* of the *LLPA 2000*, and the LLP can escape liability for any steps which go beyond those limits (see Chapter 6).

Insolvency-related risks

The onset of insolvency

20.8 One of the classic mistakes that many businesses make, when the financial tide starts to turn against them, is that they fail to take proper professional advice until the eleventh hour is long past. Their resistance to the idea of acknowledging even the possibility of failure makes them soldier on, in the hope that something will turn up.

Often, this course of action means that they miss out on the possibilities of recovery procedures which might help them, such as a voluntary arrangement. In the LLP context, however, the personal consequences of adopting the ostrich position can go beyond whether the business survives, or not.

Orders for personal contributions

20.9 Even if the traditional traps of the provisions governing wrongful trading, transactions at an undervalue and preferences (see 17.12 *et seq* above) do not catch the members, the wholly new clawback provisions may (see 17.24 *et seq* above). It is essential, if members are going to avoid the risks of clawback claims, that they effectively and continually monitor the financial health of the business.

The two key elements in avoiding the above risks are that the members must consider whether their withdrawals, or other withdrawals 'in contemplation' at the time, risk making the LLP insolvent; and they must be able to show whether it was reasonable for them to conclude that insolvent liquidation could be avoided. 'I didn't see it coming' is not a defence.

Mention has been made above of the ability of members to spread the risk of such contributions, and of the impact of any personal guarantees, by suitable provision in the partnership agreement.

Contributions to a winding up

20.10   In two ways, members can control in advance what their personal exposure in a winding up is to be.

The first way is that they can avoid any direct obligation to make any contribution, since they will only be liable to the extent that they have actively agreed to make a contribution. Even in the (perhaps comparatively rare) circumstances where they have agreed to make such a contribution, either because of a wish to have the status of contributory in a winding up, or because this has been necessary to persuade customers to trade with the LLP, it is possible to control and define the limits of this exposure.

Repayment of members' debts

20.11   The other way (see 20.10 above) is that it lies in the members' hands to control the nature of their funds within the LLP itself. In this context it should be borne in mind that debts to them owed by the LLP will rank *pari passu* with other creditors in the winding up (and can even, if there has been sufficient foresight, be secured so as to take priority over those unsecured creditors), subject to avoiding potential for challenge as transactions at an undervalue or preferences (see Chapter 17).

Post-insolvency trading

20.12   Two aspects of post-insolvency trading may also pose personal risks to anyone involved.

The first is if the trading is controlled by a person subject to a disqualification order or undertaking under the *CDDA 1986*, where both a disqualified individual and anyone acting under his/her instructions may be liable. (The *CDDA 1986* is considered in Chapter 18.)

The other aspect is if a new trading enterprise is started with a 'phoenix' name, ie one identical to or so similar to the name of the insolvent LLP as to be a prohibited name and to fix the individuals operating it with potential personal liability (see Chapter 17).

Operational risks

Risk management as an operational habit

20.13   Whatever the nature of an LLP's business, it will have many operational risks attached to it. Recognition of this, and of the need for LLP status to be available for businesses to limit the personal impact of potentially catastrophic claims (especially in the professional services sector) was after all one of the government's reasons for introducing the legislation.

Increasingly there is an awareness that it is for businesses to control those risks in a much more positive and proactive manner than has previously been the case. Essentially, the ability to do this lies in the development of systematic management procedures, designed with a recognition of where problem areas lie, and intended to limit risk exposure wherever possible.

Often, the main practical difficulty is getting acceptance of these procedures at operational level. Businesses converting to LLPs should use the opportunity of the conversion to demonstrate their commitment to risk management and so more easily embed the concept into their culture. They should also ensure that their management structure takes proper account of the risk-management imperative, eg by the establishment of a risk-management committee at suitably senior level, so that its thinking pervades all aspects of the business's operation.

Risk management and insurance

20.14   Insurance is a part of risk management, not something which is separate. It is in effect a recognition that, however good control procedures may be, claims may result and it is prudent to lay off some of that risk by buying insurance. It may also be necessary either to pacify clients, or to fulfil statutory obligations.

Increasingly, however, insurers themselves are focusing on the risk-control procedures of their insured. This has, as an illustration, been thrown into sharp relief by the experience of the legal profession. In September 2000, solicitors' professional indemnity insurance was available on the open market (having previously been effected via a mutual fund). Legal firms have found it increasingly difficult to obtain insurance and this has culminated in an increasing number of firms being placed in the SRA assigned risks pool (insurance cover for those firms unable to obtain or afford market insurance) for reasons not only including ongoing claims but also due to other risk factors, of which poor risk management must surely be one.

The link with quality management

20.15   There are strong links between the concepts of so-called 'quality management programmes' and risk management. These may be such generic systems as ISO 9001, or industry-specific programmes such as the Law Society's 'Lexcel' scheme. There is also the government's 'Investors in People' programme which, although differently targeted, has a number of risk control advantages.

These various programmes are often combined by firms. All of these have very positive implications for risk management. Some, like Lexcel, have indeed recognised this by specifically increasing the risk-management elements of their programmes. Insurers are taking account of these qualifications in their premium-setting exercises.

In October 2011, the SRA further recognised the importance of risk management by the introduction of its new Handbook moving from rules based on principles, to a 'risk-based approach' to regulation.

Insurance in the LLP context

20.16 Many LLPs will be in the professional services sphere, and as such will need to carry professional indemnity insurance. This will cover the LLP as an entity.

There remain, however, as mentioned earlier in this chapter (see 20.2, 20.3 and the following paragraphs), some personal risks, and members will therefore want to know that their personal exposure is also covered, eg if they themselves are vulnerable to claims for negligent acts or omissions by reason of being personally identified with them. Reassuringly, insurers are normally willing to cover this risk as well for no extra premium, since from their viewpoint there is only one risk.

Directors' and officers' insurance

20.17 In addition to the normal professional indemnity cover, however, members of LLPs may well wish to follow their brethren in the company field, and to cover the risks attached to them as managers by taking out the equivalent of directors' and officers' insurance cover.

This cover relates to wrongful acts or omissions in the course of an individual's duties as an officer of the business, and can cover duties which may be owed to a wide range of people, from creditors and the public generally, through staff, to fellow members and the LLP itself.

Run-off cover

20.18 One of the most difficult aspects of professional indemnity cover is the issue of run-off, ie the continuation of cover for individuals after they have ceased their association with the insured business.

This difficulty was thrown into sharp perspective by *Brocklesby v Armitage & Guest* [2001] 1 All ER 172. This case considerably increased the range of circumstances where a claimant could assert that there was 'deliberate concealment' of facts, so that the limitation clock would not start to run against him/her until discovery of those facts. It therefore greatly reduced the protection offered to individuals by the concept of statutory limitations of actions, and increased the possibility of claims crawling out of the woodwork long after an individual's retirement. However, the subsequent case of *Cave v Robinson Jarvis & Rolf (a firm)* [2002] UKHL18 overturned this ruling and re-established the position that a professional who has acted conscientiously and in good faith in attempting to perform an obligation should not be faced with the statutory time limit applicable to cases of deliberate concealment.

The mere fact of operating through the medium of an LLP will help to minimise the above risk, since it will be easier for a potential claimant to pursue the identifiable LLP than a long-gone member, and there will be no need for the claimant to establish who the members generally were at the operative time.

Individuals will, however, still want the reassurance of run-off cover. So long as the LLP continues, this should not be too much of a problem, and can be provided for in the partnership agreement (subject to possible problems if the uninsured excess escalates over the years in a manner which the retired member neither controls nor knows of, but which may impact upon him/her).

Care needs to be taken, however, with regard to run-off cover if the LLP ceases to trade, and there is no successor practice. The terms of the policy (eg for a policy within the SRA's Minimum Terms and Conditions) may require the insurer to offer run-off to potential claimants for, say, six years. The case of *Jones v St Paul International Insurance Co Ltd* [2004] EWHC 2209 (Ch) indicates that an insurer is entitled to recover run-off premiums in respect of an LLP from the members personally in the event of the LLP's insolvency, albeit that some doubts have been cast on the ability of an LLP to bind its members so as to be personally liable in such circumstances.

A further layer of insurance can be obtained by individuals to cover the circumstances where an LLP, having exhausted all its assets, and having also used up all its normal professional indemnity insurance cover (basic and top-up) has a remaining excess claim where liability can be established by the claimant against both the LLP and one or more such individual members. Such circumstances must, however, necessarily be very remote and many firms have found the premium for this cover too high to be worthwhile.

LLP Forms[1]

LL AA01	Change of accounting reference date of an LLP
LL AA02	Notice of removal of auditor from an LLP
LL AD01	Change of address of registered office of an LLP
LL AD02	Notification of the single alternative inspection location (SAIL) of an LLP
LL AD03	Change of location of the records to the SAIL address of an LLP
LL AD04	Change of location of the records to the registered office of an LLP
LL AD05	Notice to change the situation of an England and Wales LLP or a Welsh LLP
LL AP01	Appointment of a member to an LLP
LL APO2	Appointment of a corporate member to an LLP
LL AR01	Annual return of an LLP
LL CH01	Change of details of a member of an LLP
LL CH02	Change of details of a corporate member of an LLP
LL DE01	Notice of change of status of an LLP
LL DS01	Application for striking off an LLP
LL DS02	Withdrawal of application for striking off an LLP
LL IN01	Application for incorporation of an LLP
LL LQ01	Notice of appointment of administrative receiver, receiver or manager by an LLP
LL LQ02	Notice of ceasing to act as an administrative receiver, receiver or manager by an LLP
LL MG01	Particulars of a mortgage or charge created by an LLP
LL MG02	Statement in satisfaction in full or in part of mortgage or charge by an LLP
LL MG04	Statement that part [or the whole] of the property charged (a) has been released from the charge; (b) no longer forms part of the LLP's property

LL MG06	Particulars of charge subject to which property has been acquired by an LLP
LL MG07	Particulars for the registration of a charge to secure a series of debentures in respect of an LLP
LL MG08	Particulars of an issue of secured debentures in a series by an LLP
LL MG09	Certificate of registration of a charge comprising property situated in another UK jurisdiction by an LLP
LL NM01	Notice of change of name of an LLP
LL RP01	Replacement of document not meeting requirements for proper delivery for an LLP
LL RP02A	Application for rectification by the Registrar of Companies for an LLP
LL RP02B	Application for rectification of a registered office address by the Registrar of Companies for an LLP
LL RP03	Notice of an objection to a request for the Registrar of Companies to rectify the Register for an LLP
LL RP04	Second filing of a document previously delivered for an LLP
LL RT01	Application for administrative restoration of an LLP to the Registrar of Companies
LL TM01	Terminating the membership of a member of an LLP
LL VT01	Certified voluntary translation of an original document that is, or has been, delivered to the Registrar of Companies for an LLP
Scotland LLPs	
LL AP03	Appointment of judicial factor (Scotland) to an LLP
LL CH03	Change of service address for a judicial factor (Scotland) of an LLP
LL MG01s	Particulars of a charge created by an LLP registered in Scotland
LL MG02s	Statement of satisfaction in full or part of a fixed charge by an LLP registered in Scotland
LL MG03s	Statement of satisfaction in full or part of a floating charge by an LLP registered in Scotland
LL MG04s	Statement that part [or the whole] of the property charged (a) has been released from the fixed charge; (b) no longer forms part of the LLP's property, by an LLP registered in Scotland

LL MG05s	Statement that part [or the whole] of the property charged (a) has been released from the floating charge; (b) no longer forms part of the LLP's property, by an LLP registered in Scotland
LL MG06s	Particulars of a charge subject to which property has been acquired by an LLP registered in Scotland
LL MG07s	Particulars for the registration of a charge to secure a series of debentures by an LLP registered in Scotland
LL MG08s	Particulars of an issue of secured debentures in a series by an LLP registered in Scotland
LLP 466	Particulars of an instrument of alteration to a floating charge created by an LLP registered in Scotland
LL TM02	Termination of appointment of a judicial factor (Scotland) of an LLP

1 www.companieshouse.gov.uk/forms/formsOnline.shtml#LLP

LLP Fees

SI 2009/2101 – The Registrar of Companies (Fees) Companies, Overseas Companies and Limited Liability Partnerships Regulations 2009 (as amended by the Registrar of Companies (Fees) (Amendment) Regulations 2009 (SI 2009/2439) and the Registrar of Companies (Fees) (Companies, Overseas Companies and Limited Liability Partnerships) (Amendment) Regulations 2011 (SI 2011/309)

Limited Liability Partnerships Fees			
Matter in relation to which fee is payable	*Amount of fee*		
	Paper filing	*Software filing*	*Web filing*
Registration of a limited liability partnership on its incorporation under the *2000 Act* (excluding Welsh LLPs filing in Welsh):			
(a) other than same-day registration	£40.00	£14.00	
(b) same-day registration	£100.00	£30.00	
Registration of a limited liability partnership on its incorporation under the *2000 Act* with constitutional documents in Welsh	£20.00		
Delivery by a limited liability partnership of all relevant documents during a relevant period, payable at the end of that period on delivery by the limited liability partnership of its annual return under the modified *s 854* of the *2006 Act*	£40.00	£14.00	£14.00

Registration of a change of name of a limited liability partnership under *para 4* of the *Schedule* to the *2000 Act* (other than a change made in response to a direction of the Secretary of State under *para 4(2)* of that Schedule):			
(a) other than same-day registration	£10.00	£8.00	
(b) same-day registration	£50.00	£30.00	
Administrative restoration of a limited liability partnership	£100.00		
Registration of a charge by a limited liability partnership	£13.00		
Voluntary strike-off of a limited liability partnership	£10.00		
Application to make an address unavailable for public inspection by an individual member	£55.00 (per document suppressed)		
Application to make all addresses unavailable for public inspection by a person who registers a charge	£55.00 (per document suppressed)		

For a full list of Companies House fees or to obtain copy documents or copies of various registers (of members, charges etc) and certified copy documents see www.companieshouse.gov.uk/toolstohelp/ourprices

Appendix 3

The Consultative Committee of Accountancy Bodies

PO Box 433
Chartered Accountants' Hall
Moorgate Place, London EC2P 2BJ
Telephone: 020 7920 8100
Facsimile: 020 7628 1874
Email: admin@ccab.org.uk
Website: http://www.ccab.org.uk

The Institute of Chartered Accountants in England and Wales
The Institute of Chartered Accountants of Scotland
The Institute of Chartered Accountants in Ireland
The Association of Chartered Certified Accountants
The Chartered Institute of Management Accountants
The Chartered Institute of Public Finance and Accountancy

Statement of Recommended Practice

Accounting by Limited Liability Partnerships

Effective for periods commencing on or after 1 January 2010

31 March 2010

STATEMENT OF RECOMMENDED PRACTICE
ACCOUNTING BY LIMITED LIABILITY PARTNERSHIPS

CONTENTS

This Statement of Recommended Practice does not purport to deal with all possible questions and issues that may arise in any given situation. The Consultative Committee of Accountancy Bodies and the authors do not accept responsibility for loss caused to any person who acts or refrains from acting in reliance on the material in this publication, whether such loss is caused by negligence or otherwise.

PREFACE

Background to the SORP

This Statement of Recommended Practice (SORP) is issued by the Consultative Committee of Accountancy Bodies (CCAB), the members of which are:

The Institute of Chartered Accountants in England and Wales
The Institute of Chartered Accountants of Scotland
The Institute of Chartered Accountants in Ireland
The Association of Chartered Certified Accountants
The Chartered Institute of Management Accountants
The Chartered Institute of Public Finance and Accountancy

The Accounting Standards Board (ASB) has approved the CCAB for the purpose of issuing a recognised SORP for Limited Liability Partnerships (LLPs) incorporated in Great Britain under the Limited Liability Partnerships Act 2000 ('2000 Act'). As part of the process for obtaining this approval, the CCAB agrees to follow the ASB's Code of Practice for bodies recognised for issuing SORPs. The Code of Practice sets out procedures to be followed in the development of SORPs. These procedures do not include a comprehensive review of the proposed SORP by the ASB, but a limited review is performed.

SORPs issued by SORP-making bodies include a statement by the ASB that:

(i)   outlines the limited nature of the review that the ASB has undertaken; and

(ii)   confirms that the SORP does not appear to contain any fundamental points of principle that are unacceptable in the context of current accounting practice, or to conflict with an accounting standard or the ASB's plans for future standards.

The ASB Statement is included on page 5.

CCAB Steering Group and Working Party

The SORP for LLPs differs from a number of other SORPs in that it does not apply to a specific industry or sector, but to a legal entity.

The process of developing and reviewing the SORP is overseen by a Steering Group. Membership of the Steering Group is drawn both from trades and professions that have member firms that commonly have LLP status, including the accountancy and legal professions and the construction industry, and from amongst users of LLP accounts. The Steering Group deals with strategy and high-level issues, while the Working Party concentrates on technical detail.

Membership of these two groups at 31 March 2010 is set out below.

Steering Group

Andrew Vials (Chairman)	The Institute of Chartered Accountants in England and Wales
Jonathan Beckerlegge	The Association of Chartered Certified Accountants
David Berragan	Barclays plc
Matt Blake	HMRC
George Bull	Construction Industry Council
Ian Dinwiddie	Allen & Overy LLP
Steve Gale	The Institute of Chartered Accountants of Scotland
Peter Graham	The Law Society
Barry Lawson	British Venture Capital Association
Frances Paterson	Construction Industry Council
Peter Saunders	SORP Working Party
Richard Turnor	Association of Partnership Practitioners
David Tyrrall	Department for Business, Innovation and Skills

Working Party

Peter Saunders (Chairman)	Deloitte LLP
Phil Barden	Deloitte LLP
Kathryn Cearns	Herbert Smith LLP
Hannah King	PricewaterhouseCoopers LLP
Yvonne Lang	Smith & Williamson Limited
Janet Marton	KPMG LLP
David Snell	PricewaterhouseCoopers LLP

Review of the SORP

The ASB approved the CCAB for the purposes of issuing a SORP on 2 March 2000. The first edition of the SORP *Accounting by Limited Liability Partnerships* was published on 29 May 2002, and the second edition on 31 March 2006. In keeping with the ASB's Code of Practice, the CCAB reviews the SORP for changes in accounting practice and new developments, and accordingly published an Exposure Draft of a revised SORP for public comment on 29 July 2009. As well as requesting comments on all aspects of the Exposure Draft, certain issues on which the CCAB particularly sought views were also presented, as discussed in the Basis for Conclusions in Appendix 6.

All responses to these questions and regarding other matters were carefully considered during the development of the final version of the revised SORP. The ASB approved the SORP for publication on 18 March 2010 and the third edition of the SORP *Accounting by Limited Liability Partnerships* was published on 31 March 2010

Future editions of the SORP

In keeping with the ASB's Code of Practice, the CCAB will keep the SORP under review for changes in accounting practice and new developments.

Note on legal issues

The SORP discusses a number of legal issues relating to LLPs. Such discussion is included solely to explain the principles adopted in the SORP and should not be relied upon for any other purpose.

STATEMENT BY THE ACCOUNTING STANDARDS BOARD ON THE SORP 'STATEMENT OF RECOMMENDED PRACTICE: ACCOUNTING BY LIMITED LIABILITY PARTNERSHIPS'

The aims of the Accounting Standards Board (the ASB) are to establish and improve standards of financial accounting and reporting, for the benefit of users, preparers, and auditors of financial information. To this end, the ASB issues accounting standards that are primarily applicable to general purpose company financial statements. In particular industries or sectors, further guidance may be required in order to implement accounting standards effectively. This guidance is issued, in the form of Statements of Recommended Practice (SORPs), by bodies recognised for the purpose by the ASB.

The Consultative Committee of Accountancy Bodies (the CCAB) has confirmed that it shares the ASB's aim of advancing and maintaining standards of financial reporting in the public interest and has been recognised by the ASB for the purpose of issuing SORPs. As a condition of recognition, the CCAB has agreed to follow the ASB's code of practice for bodies recognised for issuing SORPs. The code of practice sets out procedures to be followed in the development of SORPs. These procedures do not include a comprehensive review of the proposed SORP by the ASB, but a review of limited scope is performed.

On the basis of its review, the ASB has concluded that the SORP has been developed in accordance with the ASB's code of practice and does not appear to contain any fundamental points of principle that are unacceptable in the context of current accounting practice or to conflict with an accounting standard or the ASB's present plans for future standards.

18 March 2010

STATEMENT OF RECOMMENDED PRACTICE
ACCOUNTING BY LIMITED LIABILITY PARTNERSHIPS

INTRODUCTION

Accounting requirements

1.   The detailed accounting requirements relating to Limited Liability Partnerships (LLPs) are currently set out in the following Statutory Instruments:

- The Limited Liability Partnerships (Accounts and Audit) (Application of Companies Act 2006) Regulations 2008 (SI 2008/1911);

- The Small Limited Liability Partnerships (Accounts) Regulations 2008 (SI 2008/1912); and

- The Large and Medium-sized Limited Liability Partnerships (Accounts) Regulations 2008 (SI 2008/1913).

These are collectively referred to in this SORP as the 'Regulations'. The Regulations apply to accounts for financial years commencing on or after 1 October 2008, replacing the accounting provisions previously contained in the Limited Liability Partnerships Regulations 2001 and the Limited Liability Partnerships Regulations (Northern Ireland) 2004. The Regulations apply, with modifications, the accounting and auditing provisions of the Companies Act 2006 to LLPs. The Regulations apply to the whole of the United Kingdom, reflecting the scope of the Companies Act 2006. Statements of Standard Accounting Practice (SSAPs), Financial Reporting Standards (FRSs), UITF Abstracts and other components of UK Generally Accepted Accounting Practice (GAAP) also apply to any financial statements of LLPs intended to give a true and fair view. They do not apply where the LLP adopts International Financial Reporting Standards (IFRS).

Scope and objectives

2.   This statement applies to LLPs incorporated in the United Kingdom under the Limited Liability Partnerships Act 2000, or which were incorporated prior to 1 October 2009 under the Limited Liability Partnerships Act (Northern Ireland) 2002, that report under UK GAAP. It does not seek to set out all of the reporting requirements that apply to LLPs reporting under UK GAAP and it is intended to complement, not replace, accounting standards, which comprise FRSs, SSAPs and UITF Abstracts. This statement should therefore be used in conjunction with the Regulations and accounting standards rather than on a stand-alone basis. In the event of conflict, the Regulations and accounting standards take precedence over this SORP.

3.   The recommendations of this SORP are applicable to all LLPs, as defined in paragraph 13, that do not adopt IFRS. (For LLPs that follow the Financial

Reporting Standard for Smaller Entities (FRSSE), see paragraphs 27 - 29 below). The ASB has no authority to frank guidance on IFRS, and interpretations of IFRS are not permitted. Application of the SORP is therefore restricted to LLPs complying with UK GAAP.

Measurement

4. There are a number of standards that are relevant to the measurement of the type of financial liabilities, provisions and other financial instruments dealt with in the SORP. FRS 26 (IAS 39) *Financial Instruments: Measurement* will only be mandatory for those LLPs which prepare accounts in accordance with the fair value accounting rules for financial instruments set out in the Regulations or are otherwise required to follow FRS 26, for example due to debt securities being listed. In this respect paragraph 1B of FRS 26 provides further guidance as to when the fair value accounting rules and thus FRS 26 would apply.

5. On the assumption that FRS 26 is not applied by an LLP, then the relevant measurement standards include:

    (a) For provisions recognised in accordance with FRS 12 *Provisions, Contingent Liabilities and Contingent Assets* that standard itself contains appropriate measurement principles (see paragraph 86 below for those FRS 12 obligations for which the measurement approach in FRS 17 *Retirement Benefits* is appropriate).

    (b) For equity instruments and financial liabilities within the scope of FRS 25 *Financial Instruments: Presentation* then the relevant measurement literature would generally be either (i) FRS 4 *Capital Instruments* for financial liabilities that meet the definition of a capital instrument or (ii) the general provisions of the Companies Act/GAAP for equity instruments and all other liabilities. In this respect, as explained in paragraph 81 below, where such a liability is of uncertain timing or amount, then it is likely that the measurement principles in FRS 12 will be relevant.

    The guidance given in these standards is considered comprehensive enough that no further guidance is necessary in the SORP.

Format and terminology

6. All the material in this Statement is an integral part of the SORP. However, the central principles are printed in bold in order to distinguish them from explanatory paragraphs.

7. For simplicity, the term 'profits' has been used rather than 'profits or losses' where circumstances allow. Similarly, the term 'year' has been used rather than 'period'.

Definitions

8. The following definitions apply within this SORP.

Allocated profit

9. Profits (after deducting members' remuneration charged as an expense) that have been allocated during the year as a result of the members deciding on a division of profits.[1]

Automatic division of profits

10. An automatic division of profits is one where a member has an entitlement to a share of future profit without the need for any further decision by the members on the division of those profits. Such a pre-agreed automatic division of profits could be in respect either of the entire profits for the year or a portion or fixed amount thereof. If the automatic division does not relate to the entire profits for the year, the fact that the actual amount allocated to the member is contingent on the existence of profits in the first place does not negate the member's unconditional entitlement to those profits nor the LLP's unconditional obligation in respect of those profits.

Designated members

11. Designated members are those members specified as such in the incorporation document or otherwise in accordance with an agreement with the other members, as required under the 2000 Act. Designated members perform certain duties in relation to the legal administration of an LLP that would, for a company, be performed by the secretary or directors. If there would otherwise be no designated members, or only one, all members are deemed to be designated members.

Drawings

12. The payment in cash (or kind) of amounts to members. Drawings may consist of regular monthly payments or *ad hoc* payments; for example, in respect of current year's and/or prior years' remuneration (as defined).

---

[1] The decision to divide profits, which gives rise to a liability in respect of allocated profits, must be distinguished from the arrangements for profit sharing. A provision in an agreement between the members which sets out the profit shares of the members does not of itself constitute an agreement for the division of profits. It merely sets out the respective profit shares of the members that will apply to those profits that the members decide to divide among themselves. Accordingly, the default rule that is applied by virtue of Regulation 7(1) of the Limited Liability Partnerships Regulations 2001 (which provides for the members of an LLP to share equally in the capital and profits of an LLP in the absence of agreement to the contrary) does not constitute a default rule as to the automatic division of profits between the members. (As explained further in paragraph 48, where the agreement between the members provides for the automatic division of profits, those divided profits will form part of members' remuneration charged as an expense and will be credited directly to the current accounts of the members without being first shown under the balance sheet heading 'Other reserves'.) Allocated profits are debts due to members which, unless otherwise agreed by the members, rank *pari passu* with ordinary creditors in the event of a winding up. The total amount of profit allocated following a decision to divide may be less (or more) than the amount of profit earned by the LLP in the relevant year.

Limited liability partnership (LLP)

13. A limited liability partnership incorporated in Great Britain under the Limited Liability Partnerships Act 2000.

Loans and other debts due to members

14. Members' interests that are debts of the LLP and are included in balance sheet item J in the accounts formats set out in the Regulations.

Members

15. On incorporation, the members of an LLP are the persons who subscribe their names to the incorporation document. Persons may become or cease to be members in accordance with an agreement between existing members.

Members' agreement

16. Any agreement express or implied between an LLP and its members that determines the mutual rights and duties of the members in their capacity as such and their rights and duties in relation to the LLP. An agreement between the members, to which the LLP is not party - for example, an agreement to guarantee a minimum or specified remuneration for a particular member - does not constitute a members' agreement for the purposes of the SORP.

Members' capital

17. Amounts subscribed or otherwise contributed by members that are classified as capital by the constitutional arrangements of the LLP. Such amounts will require analysis as to whether they are considered equity or debt in accordance with FRS 25 (IAS 32) and UITF Abstract 39 *Members' Shares in Co-operative Entities and Similar Instruments.* Members' capital is a component of 'Members' other interests' or 'Loans and other debts due to members' depending on its classification under FRS 25 and UITF 39.

Members' other interests

18. Members' interests other than debt due to them by the LLP, which constitute equity in the LLP and are included in balance sheet item K in the accounts formats set out in the Regulations. Members' other interests include 'Members' capital' that is classified as equity in accordance with FRS 25 and UITF 39, 'Revaluation reserve' and 'Other reserves'.

19. *Members' participation rights*

    All the rights of a member against the LLP that arise under the members' agreement (for example, in respect of amounts subscribed or otherwise contributed, remuneration and profits).

Members' remuneration

20. Any outflow of benefits to a member. It may include or comprise, but is not limited to, one or more of the following elements: salary, interest, bonus, risk premium and allocated share of profits. The form that remuneration takes will be a matter of agreement between the members.

Members' remuneration charged as an expense

21.   Remuneration that is payable to a member, which falls to be treated as a charge
against profits and not an allocation of profits. The treatment of members'
remuneration in the profit and loss account is determined by reference to the
nature of the participation rights that give rise to the remuneration. If the
members' remuneration gives rise to a liability in accordance with FRS 25 and
UITF 39, then it is charged as an expense. Members' remuneration charged as
an expense is not restricted to amounts that are payable by the LLP regardless of
the existence or extent of profits; it also includes, for example, any profits that
are automatically divided between members by virtue of a members' agreement.
Members' remuneration charged as an expense may in some exceptional
circumstances be a negative amount. A member can also legally be an
employee of an LLP - in this case, there will be a contract of employment
between the two parties - and such remuneration covered by the employment
contract is classified as members' remuneration charged as an expense,
including amounts relating to pension obligations.

Post-retirement payments to members

22.   Any post-retirement payments, whether in cash, in kind or any other benefits,
including annuities and payments for goodwill, payable by the LLP as principal
to former members of the LLP, other than where the payments are properly
made in return for post-retirement services performed by the recipient for the
LLP's benefit. Members who retire by or at the balance sheet date are regarded
as former members. Such post-retirement payments include, but are not limited
to, amounts payable to, for example, spouses, children and the estates of former
members. In this context, former members may include former partners in a
predecessor partnership of the LLP, where the LLP assumes responsibility for
the post-retirement payments to the former partners.

Puttable instrument

23.   The definition of 'puttable instrument' is contained in FRS 25. A puttable
instrument is a financial instrument that gives the holder the right to put the
instrument back to the issuer for cash or another financial asset or is
automatically put back to the issuer on the occurrence of an uncertain future
event or the death or retirement of the instrument holder (paragraph 11 of FRS
25, as amended in August 2008.) In practice for LLPs, puttable instruments may
include certain types of capital or members loans which carry rights for the
member (or other holder) to obtain repayment from the LLP.

Unallocated profit

24.   Profits of the LLP (after deducting members' remuneration charged as an
expense) that have been ascertained but which are not yet divided among the
members. After the profits have been ascertained, in the absence of any
agreement between members to the contrary, the balance on profit and loss
account will be unallocated profit and will need to be shown under 'Other
reserves' on the balance sheet, pending a decision to divide the profits among
the members. It is open to the members of an LLP to agree that all, or a
proportion of, the profits of the LLP shall be automatically divided between the
members after they have been ascertained; in that event, the LLP will not have
an unconditional right to avoid delivering cash or other assets to a member in

respect of those amounts. This is a matter of construction of the members' agreement. Where this is the case, any amounts automatically divided will form part of members' remuneration charged as an expense, i.e. they will be deducted in arriving at retained profit or loss for the financial year available for discretionary division among members. Accordingly, where all the profits are automatically divided, a nil amount will be reported as retained profit or loss for the financial year available for discretionary division among members, and there will be no unallocated profits.[2]

THE CONTENTS OF THE ANNUAL REPORT AND FINANCIAL STATEMENTS

25. **The Annual Report should comprise:**

   - **the financial statements;**
   - **a statement of members' responsibilities in relation to the production of financial statements;**
   - **a report on the financial statements by a registered auditor, if required by the Regulations; and**
   - **a report to the members (the Members' Report).**

26. **The financial statements, as defined by the Regulations and accounting standards, should, subject to the exemptions for small and medium-sized entities, comprise:**

   - **a profit and loss account, consolidated in the case of a group preparing consolidated accounts;**
   - **a statement of total recognised gains and losses (STRGL) in accordance with FRS 3** *Reporting Financial Performance,* **consolidated in the case of a group preparing consolidated accounts;**
   - **a cash flow statement in accordance with FRS 1** *Cash Flow Statements,* **consolidated in the case of a group preparing consolidated accounts;**
   - **a balance sheet for the LLP and, if it prepares group accounts, a consolidated balance sheet; and**
   - **notes to the above financial statements.**

Accounting by smaller LLPs

27. Exemptions from disclosure are likely to apply in cases where an LLP is eligible to apply the FRSSE (interpreted as appropriate for LLPs).

28. As noted in paragraph 2 above, in the event of conflicting requirements, those in the Regulations or accounting standards (including the FRSSE) should take precedence over this SORP. The SORP should not be interpreted as removing or not permitting exemptions for certain smaller entities in legislation or

---

[2] See the legal opinion in Appendix 5.

accounting standards, including those from the need to prepare group accounts or cash flow statements.

29.   On other matters the SORP sometimes includes references to specific accounting standards. Those preparing financial statements in accordance with the FRSSE should interpret these as referring to the related requirements that are generally included in the FRSSE (which includes as appendices tables of derivations and simplifications from other accounting standards). In particular, LLPs entitled to use the FRSSE should note that while the main part of the requirements of FRS 25 have not been incorporated into the 2008 version of the FRSSE, the definition of financial liabilities and a requirement to present those separately from equity (paragraph 12.1 of the FRSSE) have been included and these are important for the accounting for members' participation rights. (See also paragraph 45 below.) The ASB has advised that at this time it does not intend to amend the FRSSE to reflect the August 2008 changes made to FRS 25.

30.   The Members' Report should disclose the following information:

- **the principal activities of the LLP and its subsidiary undertakings, indicating any significant changes during the year;**
- **an indication of the existence of any branches[3] outside the UK;**
- **the identity of anyone who was a designated member during the year; and**
- **the policy of the LLP regarding members' drawings and the subscription and repayment of amounts subscribed or otherwise contributed by members (see paragraph 69 below).**

31.   The financial statements and related notes cannot on their own describe in full the financial performance of an LLP, nor by definition will they encompass non-financial performance matters that some LLPs will wish to communicate to the users of the Annual Report. Although not a statutory requirement, the Members' Report offers a vehicle for such communication, with the disclosures listed in paragraph 30 above required as a minimum.

---

[3]   As defined by s 1046(3) CA 2006.

THE APPLICATION OF GENERALLY ACCEPTED ACCOUNTING PRACTICE TO LIMITED LIABILITY PARTNERSHIPS

MEMBERS' REMUNERATION AND INTERESTS

Analysing members' participation rights

32. **Members' participation rights in the earnings or assets of an LLP should be analysed between those that give rise to, from the LLP's perspective, either a financial liability or equity, in accordance with FRS 25 and UITF Abstract 39. Members' different participation rights should be analysed separately into liability and equity elements. Depending on the terms of the members' agreement, members' participation rights may give rise to equity or liabilities or both.**

33. Under FRS 25 and UITF 39, a critical feature in differentiating a financial liability from an equity instrument is the existence of a contractual obligation of one party to deliver either cash or another financial asset to another party. Critical, therefore, to determining whether the LLP has a financial liability to a member, or alternatively the member holds equity in the LLP, is whether there exists a contractual obligation on the part of the LLP to deliver cash (or other financial assets) to the member - for example, on the member retiring from or otherwise leaving the LLP. Generally, a member's participation right will result in a liability unless either the LLP has an unconditional right to avoid delivering cash or other assets to the member (i.e. the right to any payment or repayment is discretionary on the part of the LLP) or certain conditions are met for puttable instruments and amounts payable on liquidation. Following the amendment to FRS 25 in August 2008 (the 'puttables amendment' – see paragraph 40 below), where the conditions are met for puttable instruments and amounts payable on liquidation, such instruments will be classified partly or wholly as equity even though the LLP does not have an unconditional right to avoid delivering cash or other assets to the member. The amendment to FRS 25 does not require rights which have been classified as members' equity to be reclassified as a financial liability of the LLP in any circumstances. The flowcharts included in Appendix 3 form part of the SORP and are intended to set out the various tests to be applied to members' interests in order to ascertain whether they fall to be treated as liabilities or equity.

34. Participation rights in respect of amounts subscribed or otherwise contributed should be analysed separately from participation rights in respect of remuneration (which may include, inter alia, salary, interest, bonus, risk premium and allocated share of profits), except where the remuneration, or part thereof, is clearly identifiable as a return on amounts subscribed or otherwise contributed. To the extent that remuneration cannot be clearly identified as a return on amounts subscribed it is regarded, for accounting purposes, as separate from the instrument that consists of the amount subscribed and return thereon. For example, profit share payable at the discretion of the LLP would be accounted for as an equity interest, even if the member's capital is treated as a liability. Where remuneration, or part thereof, is clearly identifiable as a return on the amounts subscribed – for example, non-discretionary interest payments –

rather than a return for the services provided by the members, then the amounts subscribed and that part of the remuneration that is clearly identifiable as a return on the amounts subscribed would be analysed together for accounting purposes. This important principle also has particular relevance when considering the impact of the puttables amendment. This is discussed further in paragraph 41 below and more detailed guidance on its application is given in Appendix 2.

35. **Non-discretionary amounts becoming due to members in respect of participation rights in the profits of the LLP for the financial year that give rise to liabilities should be presented as an expense within the profit and loss account (within the heading 'Members' remuneration charged as an expense').**

36. **Amounts becoming due to members in respect of equity participation rights, following a discretionary division of profits, should be debited directly to equity in the year in which the division occurs. Such amounts should not be presented as an expense within the profit and loss account. A discretionary division of profits that takes place after the balance sheet date is a non-adjusting event under FRS 21** *Events after the Balance Sheet Date.*

37. Guidance on how to apply the principles set out above is given in paragraphs 38 to 50 below. Some examples of the practical effects of analysing participation rights separately are given in Appendix 2.

Amounts contributed by members and returns thereon

38. For some LLPs, the terms of the members' agreement may result in all members' participation rights being classified as giving rise to financial liabilities, i.e. not equity participation rights. This may be the case if, for example, all profits are automatically divided between members (see paragraph 48 below), and if individual members have the right to demand payment of amounts subscribed or otherwise contributed to the LLP. The ability of a member to exercise a contractual right may be conditional on a future event; for example, a member may only be able to demand amounts subscribed or otherwise contributed on retirement. Despite the fact that the member's right is conditional on a future event, the LLP does not have an unconditional right to avoid making the payment, so, unless the conditions for puttable instruments are met, a financial liability exists.

39. If the LLP has an unconditional right to refuse repayment to members of amounts subscribed or otherwise contributed by them then, providing there is no obligation to pay a return on those amounts, such amounts will be classed as equity. If the LLP does not have an unconditional right to refuse repayment and the conditions for puttable instruments have not been satisfied, such amounts will be classed as liabilities and included within loans and other debts due to members. However, if the LLP has an unconditional right to refuse repayment of members' capital, but interest is mandatorily payable on members' capital, then because the interest would be a clearly identifiable return on that capital

(see paragraph 34 above) it should be accounted for under paragraph AG.26 of FRS 25. A liability will be recognised on subscription reflecting the present value of minimum non-discretionary outflows. In many cases, this will be the same as the relevant amount of members' capital. Such a liability will not qualify for classification as equity under the puttables amendment because of the contractual obligation to pay interest. Following the principle set out in paragraph 34, any other remuneration (salary, bonus, risk premium and allocated share of profits etc) would fall to be accounted for separately.

Puttable instruments

40.   The amendment made to FRS 25 in August 2008 affects the treatment of puttable financial instruments and obligations arising on liquidation. In certain limited circumstances rights of members which have been classified as a liability of the LLP under the original version of FRS 25 will fall to be classified as equity under the amended standard. The amendment to FRS 25 does not require rights which previously fell to be classified as members' equity to be reclassified as a financial liability of the LLP. Reclassification from liability to equity is only possible where members receive an 'equity-like' return in respect of those rights. If the LLP has other instruments that receive a variable return, with the effect that the return to members is substantially restricted or fixed, the criteria for reclassification in respect of those rights will not be met.

41.   In considering whether members' participation rights require further analysis under the provisions of the puttables amendment it is first necessary to consider how the principles set out in paragraph 34 are being applied. For example, if all remuneration is being considered separately from capital as there is no clearly identifiable return on the amount subscribed then the remuneration and the capital would also be considered separately for the purposes of the puttables amendment.[4] For LLPs where members provide services, it is unlikely that the amendment will have a significant, if any, impact. Appendix 3 contains two flowcharts and Appendix 2 some additional guidance and a number of examples designed to demonstrate the impact of the puttables amendment in various scenarios.

42.   The amendments to FRS 25 are drafted so as to apply to individual classes of financial instrument. Depending on the structure of an LLP, members' interests may consist of one or more classes of financial instrument, which themselves may comprise one or more 'components'. For example, members may invest in the capital of an LLP and may also be required to make loans to the LLP. If those loans are legally a separate financial instrument from the capital, then the LLP will have two classes of instrument with members. Under the amended Standard, reclassification is only possible for the class of instruments that is subordinate to all other instruments. Accordingly, where members' interests include more than one class of instrument, reclassification is only possible for

---

[4] In such circumstances, the puttables amendment will have no effect, because the remuneration will itself be a separate instrument or contract that has 'total cash flows based substantially on the profit or loss' of the entity and substantially restricts or fixes the return to the holders of capital. Accordingly, the test in paragraph 16B of FRS 25 would seem not to be met.

the class of instrument that is subordinate to all others. For convenience, the flowcharts refer to this most subordinate class of financial instruments as 'members' residual interests'. Frequently, members' residual interests will be members' capital, though this need not necessarily be the case.

43.   The amendments are applied differently depending on whether members' residual interests may be put (i.e. redeemed at the option of the member) (i) without the LLP being liquidated or (ii) only on liquidation. In the former case, any reclassification can only be of the entire balance of members' residual interests, i.e. it is not possible to reclassify a component of members' residual interests. Where members' residual interests may be put or redeemed only on liquidation, it is possible to reclassify a component of members' residual interests without reclassifying the entire balance.

44.   Where reclassifications arise under the amended requirements, these are mandatory rather than voluntary. Accordingly, all LLPs (other than, for the reasons set out in paragraph 45, those that apply the FRSSE) will need to consider whether they are affected by the amended requirements.

45.   The amendments to FRS 25 apply for accounting periods beginning on or after 1 January 2010. Earlier application is permitted only for accounting periods beginning on or after 1 January 2009. At the time of writing, no changes have been made or proposed to the FRSSE. Accordingly, the requirements described in Appendix 3 do not apply to LLPs that have adopted the FRSSE. Such LLPs should continue to comply with the requirements of the FRSSE in respect of liabilities and equity, which are essentially consistent with those of FRS 25 before it was amended in August 2008.

Division of profits

46.   Amounts becoming due to members in respect of participation rights in the profits of the LLP for the year that give rise to a liability might include, for example, salary, interest on capital balances and any automatic division of profits, to the extent that the LLP does not have an unconditional right to avoid delivering cash or other assets to a member in respect of such amounts.

47.   Where there are no equity participation rights in the profits for the year, it follows that all amounts becoming due to members in respect of those profits will be presented within members' remuneration charged as an expense. In these circumstances, LLPs should refer to the presentational guidance given in paragraph 51 below and the illustrative examples in Appendix 1.

48.   Where profits are automatically divided as they arise or are determined, so that the LLP does not have an unconditional right to refuse payment, the amounts arising that are due to members are in the nature of liabilities. They should therefore be treated as an expense in the profit and loss account in the relevant year and, to the extent they remain unpaid at the year end, they should be shown as liabilities in the balance sheet. Conversely, where there is no automatic

division of profits the LLP has an unconditional right[5] to refuse payment of the profits of a particular year unless and until those profits are divided by a decision taken by the members (or a committee of the members to which the authority to divide profits has been delegated); and accordingly, following such a division, those profits are classed as an appropriation of equity rather than as an expense. They are therefore shown as a residual amount available for appropriation in the profit and loss account. Once profits are divided, the amount of the divided profits is treated as an appropriation which is deducted from equity, and, to the extent that any divided profits remain unpaid at the year end, the amount unpaid will be recorded as a liability.

49. It is possible that a combination of these circumstances may arise, for example if 50% of profits are automatically divided, but the remaining profits are only divided at the discretion of the LLP, then the former will be treated as an expense/liability and the latter as an appropriation/equity.

50. Paragraph 3 of the Legal Opinion in Appendix 5 addresses the division of profits and may be helpful in determining whether payments are discretionary.

Members' remuneration: presentation and disclosure

51. **The Regulations require the profit and loss account to disclose a total, being 'Profit or loss for the financial year before members' remuneration and profit shares'. The total of 'Members' remuneration charged as an expense', as defined in paragraph 21 above, should be disclosed separately and deducted from this balance. Disclosure on the face of the profit and loss account should be as follows:**

Profit or loss for the financial year before members' remuneration and profit shares	X
Members' remuneration charged as an expense	(X)
Profit or loss for the financial year available for discretionary division among members	X

52. **The basis on which each element of remuneration (as defined) has been treated in the accounts should be disclosed and explained by note.**

53. 'Members' remuneration charged as an expense' is defined in paragraph 21 above. The Regulations require disclosure on the face of the profit and loss account of a sub-total 'Profit or loss for the financial year before members' remuneration and profit shares'. Therefore, after the sub-total required by the Regulations, a line item described as 'Members' remuneration charged as an

---

5   As it is the members who make decisions on behalf of the LLP, the members have the power to divide the profits of the LLP. However, until the members take a decision to divide the profits, the LLP has an unconditional right to refuse to pay the profits to individual members.

expense' should be deducted as an additional expense. This includes any related employment costs.

54. The treatment of members' remuneration in the profit and loss account is summarised in the following table.

Nature of element of a member's remuneration:	Treat as:
Remuneration that is paid under an employment contract	Expense, described as 'Members' remuneration charged as an expense', and deducted after arriving at 'Profit for the financial year before members' remuneration and profit shares'
Other payments, arising from components of members' participation rights in the profits for the year that give rise to liabilities in accordance with FRS 25 and UITF 39, such as mandatory interest payments	
Automatic division of profits	
Any share of profits arising from a division of profits that is discretionary on the part of the LLP (i.e. where the decision to divide the profits is taken after the profits have been made).	Allocation of profit

Where it is considered that it will assist an understanding of the financial performance of the LLP, members' remuneration charged as an expense should be further analysed within the notes to the financial statements, for example, between that which is paid under a contract of employment and that which relates to amounts arising from participation rights that give rise to a liability. In the case of a group, members' remuneration from all entities in the group that are consolidated into the parent LLP's group accounts should be considered.

Members' interests: presentation and disclosure

55. **'Loans and other debts due to members' (balance sheet item J) and 'Members' other interests' (balance sheet item K) should be disclosed separately on the face of the balance sheet. Balance sheet item J includes 'Loans and other debts due to members' and 'Members' capital' in so far as it is classified as a liability. Balance sheet item K includes 'Members' capital', 'Revaluation reserve' and 'Other reserves', in so far as they are classified as equity, which are also each required to be disclosed separately on the face of the balance sheet.**

56.   All amounts due to members that are classified as liabilities in accordance with FRS 25 and UITF 39 should be presented within 'Loans and other debts due to members'. This heading will include any unpaid element of 'Members' remuneration charged as an expense' together with any unpaid allocated profits arising from a discretionary division of profits made during the year. It will also include members' capital classified as a liability.

57.   Equity should not include members' capital that is classified as a liability in accordance with FRS 25 and UITF 39. For some LLPs, the terms of the members' agreement may result in all 'capital' subscribed by members being presented as financial liabilities. Except where the conditions described in Appendix 3 are met, this will be the case where individual members have the right to demand repayment of such balances (for example, on retirement) and the LLP does not have the unconditional right to refuse such repayment.

58.   **The face of the balance sheet should show the net assets attributable to members of the LLP (that is, the sum of items B to I). In addition, 'Total members' interests', being the total of items J and K less any amounts due from members in debtors, should be disclosed as a memorandum item on the face of the balance sheet.**

59.   **'Loans and other debts due to members' (balance sheet item J), while in substance liabilities of the LLP, do not form part of the external financing of the LLP. Consequently, these amounts should be shown separately in the analysis of changes in net debt required by FRS 1.**

60.   **Disclosure should be made under 'Members' other interests' and 'Loans and other debts due to members' of the amount brought forward from the previous year, the changes arising in the financial year and the balance carried forward at the end of the year. Disclosure should be in the following format (although additional categories of members' interests or types of movements should be disclosed where this aids clarity or circumstances require it):**

	Members' Other Interests [6]				Loans and other debts due to members less any amounts due from members in debtors [7]	Total 2XX1	Total 2XX0
	Members' Capital (Classified as equity)	Revaluation Reserve	Other Reserves	Total			
Amounts due to members Amounts due from members					X (X)		
Balance at [start of the period]	X	X	X	X	X	X	X
Members' remuneration charged as an expense, including employment and retirement benefit costs					X	X	X
Profit / (loss) for the financial year available for discretionary division among members			X	X		X	X
Members' interests after profit/(loss) for the year	X	X	X	X	X	X	X
Other divisions of profits / (losses)			(X)	(X)	X		
Surplus arising on revaluation of fixed assets		X		X		X	X
Introduced by members	X			X	X	X	X
Repayments of capital	(X)			(X)		(X)	(X)
Repayments of debt (including members' capital classified as a liability)					(X)	(X)	(X)
Drawings					(X)	(X)	(X)
Other movements	X	X	X	X	X	X	X
Amounts due to members Amounts due from members					X (X)		
Balance at [end of the period]	X	X	X	X	X	X	X

61. **Any unallocated profits should appear under 'Other reserves' (balance sheet item K). Where the LLP makes a loss for the financial year that is**

---

[6]   Balance sheet item K.

[7]   Balance sheet item J less any amounts due from members in debtors. 'Loans and other debts due to members' would include any members' capital classified as a liability. The analysis of amounts due to members is required in order to comply with the Regulations.

not allocated to the members, the amount should be deducted from 'Other reserves'.

62. The members of the LLP may agree to allocate to the members a sum different from the amount shown as profit or loss for the financial year available for division among members. Amounts may, for example, be retained in the business as unallocated profits.

63. **The notes to the accounts should explain where amounts in 'Loans and other debts due to members' (balance sheet item J) would rank in relation to other creditors who are unsecured in the event of a winding up. Details of any protection afforded to creditors in such an event which is legally enforceable and cannot be revoked at will by the members should be included in a note to the accounts. Where no such protection is afforded in respect of items shown under balance sheet item K, that fact should be disclosed.**

64. The capital (whether classified as a liability or equity) of an LLP may be reduced by agreement of the members either by repayment or by the conversion of equity capital into liability capital or other debt.[8] In the absence of agreement to the contrary, unsecured debt due to members will rank equally with debts due to other unsecured creditors in a winding up. For these reasons, some LLPs may, in order to facilitate the obtaining of credit, decide to invest their capital with a degree of permanence by subordinating debt due to members to other creditors in a winding up.

65. **The Regulations require disclosure of the amount of loans and other debts due to members falling due after more than one year.**

66. **The Regulations require separate disclosure of the aggregate amount of money advanced by members by way of loan, the aggregate amount of money owed to members in respect of profits and any other amounts.**

67. **The amount of debts owing to the LLP by members should be disclosed.**

68. Amounts owing to and from members should not be offset in the financial statements, except where they are in respect of the same member and the conditions set out in paragraph 42 of FRS 25 are met. Debits on members' balances (where, for example, drawings were made during the year in anticipation of profits) should be reviewed for recoverability and shown separately in debtors.

Other disclosures

69. **LLPs should disclose in the Members' Report the overall policy followed in relation to members' drawings, including an indication of the policy**

---

[8] Neither the Companies Act 2006 nor the Regulations contain any provisions in relation to capital maintenance of an LLP, such as those in the Companies Act for limited liability companies.

applicable where the cash requirements of the business compete with the need to allow cash drawings by members. Such disclosures should include any transfers of members' interests from equity to debt (and vice versa) during the year and up to the date the accounts are approved. The policy under which members contribute or subscribe amounts to the LLP by way of equity or debt and the policy under which their contributions and subscriptions are repayable by the LLP, should also be disclosed.

70.   In the case of large and medium-sized LLPs, the Regulations require disclosure of the average number of members in the financial year. This is determined by dividing the aggregate number of members of the LLP for each month or part thereof in the financial year by the number of months in the financial year (rounded to the nearest whole number).

71.   In the case of large and medium-sized LLPs, the Regulations also require disclosure of the profit (including remuneration) that is attributable to the member with the largest entitlement to profit (including remuneration) where the amount of the profit of the LLP for the financial year before members' remuneration and profit shares exceeds £200,000. The identity of this member need not be disclosed.

72.   When determining the disclosable amount, the LLP should take account of all the relevant factors and disclose the policy by which the amount was arrived at, as the Regulations do not provide specific guidance as to how the disclosable amount should be determined. A consistent policy should be applied. Where the LLP has an unconditional right to avoid paying an amount of remuneration or profit, the policy for determining the disclosable amount should be disclosed and should explain how current year unallocated profits and current year allocations of both current and prior year profits are treated.

73.   Where LLPs choose to disclose average members' remuneration, this should be calculated by dividing the 'Profit before members' remuneration and profit shares' by the average number of members (as discussed in paragraph 70 above), these being the two items that are required to be disclosed by the Regulations. If any other figure for average members' remuneration is given, it should be reconciled to the figure calculated in accordance with this paragraph.

Cash flow statement presentation

74.   In the cash flow statement of the LLP, in place of the line item 'Equity dividends paid' required by FRS 1, the following should be shown as a minimum:

Transactions with members and former members

Payments to members	X
Contributions by members	X
Post-retirement payments to former members*	<u>X</u>
	X

* See the following section

RETIREMENT BENEFITS

Retirement benefits of employees and members

75. Retirement benefits provided for employees of the LLP should be accounted for as required by FRS 17 *Retirement Benefits*. This will include retirement benefits payable to members that are based on any salary paid to the member under an employment contract.

Other post-retirement payments to members: recognition and measurement

76. LLPs should analyse their contractual or constructive obligations (including any relating to early retirement options) to make payments to members at and after the point of their ceasing to be members of the LLP between:

(a) those that give rise to financial liabilities falling within the scope of FRS 25; and

(b) those that give rise to liabilities of uncertain timing and amount falling within the scope of FRS 12.

In the case of a contractual liability to deliver cash or other financial assets, this will give rise to a financial liability under FRS 25 unless outside the scope of that standard (see paragraph 80 below).

In the case of contractual liabilities scoped out of FRS 25 or a constructive obligation of uncertain timing or amount, these will fall within the scope of FRS 12.

In the case of a constructive obligation of certain timing and amount, this will fall to be accounted for as a liability under the general provisions of the Companies Act/GAAP.

77. Payments by an LLP to members after they have retired, often referred to as annuities, can take many different forms. It will be necessary to examine the nature of the contractual or constructive obligations in order to determine the governing accounting standard.

78. Annuity payments may be either 'pre-determined' or 'profit-dependent'.

   (a) Pre-determined annuity payments are amounts payable that are fixed at the time of retirement; for example, by reference to historical earnings (such as a percentage of the final year's profit share) or fixed at an amount, which may be index-linked or linked to a measure independent of the LLP's future profit. The period for which they are payable may or may not be pre-determined. The payment of the retirement benefit is thus not dependent on the LLP earning profits in the post-retirement period.

   (b) Profit-dependent annuity payments are amounts payable to former members that are, in effect, a share of the LLP's ongoing profits, by way of a preferential first share, profit-points, profit-dependent bonus or some other mechanism. Many different arrangements exist, and there may be no amount payable in a year in which no or insufficient profits are earned.

79. An annuity meets the definition of a financial liability under FRS 25 if there is a contractual obligation for the LLP to deliver cash or a financial asset to a member. An example of an annuity dealt with under FRS 25 might be where a former member is to be paid a fixed annual amount for a fixed term beginning on the first anniversary of his retirement; if he were to die, an amount representing the present value of the future payments would be paid to his estate.

80. Annuities are likely in many cases to be subject to uncertainties. This will be the case, for example, where the member has a choice of retirement dates, the payments are dependent on future profits or there is significant mortality risk. In this respect, an annuity that carries a life-contingent element (i.e. a mortality risk) is outside the scope of FRS 25 because it meets the definition of an insurance contract under FRS 25. Such annuities therefore fall within the scope of FRS 12.

81. It should be noted that uncertainty of timing or amount per se is not the boundary between FRS 25 and 12 since the former envisages situations where financial liabilities within the scope of that standard will be of uncertain timing or amount. Nevertheless, in the case of such a liability within the scope of FRS 25 it is likely that, for measurement purposes, the principles of measurement contained within FRS 12 will still be the most relevant. Accordingly, in most cases, where the liability is of uncertain timing or amount, whether within the scope of FRS 25 or 12, the measurement principles of the latter standard will apply.

82.   A liability in respect of an annuity is recognised when a member obtains an actual or constructive right to the annuity, which the LLP has no discretion to withhold.

83.   **If the rights to an annuity are earned over a period, then costs should be recognised over that period.[9] This accords with FRS 25, as a liability for the annuity arises in the LLP as service is rendered by the member; and with FRS 12, under which the LLP has either an obligation or a constructive obligation to pay the annuity which builds up over time.**

84.   Often, a member of an LLP will obtain absolute entitlement to an annuity only on reaching a specific milestone, such as reaching a particular age or achieving a specified number of years' service. A member choosing to leave before reaching the milestone will not be entitled to an annuity. On reaching the milestone while remaining a member of the LLP, the member will be entitled to an annuity based on past service. The LLP cannot avoid the liability that is accruing through the service period through its own actions without the agreement of the member (unless it had the right to terminate his or her membership without compensation for the loss of annuity rights, which is unlikely to be the case). In these circumstances, therefore, a liability should be built up over the period of service rather than just recognised at the date on which the milestone is reached.

85.   **If the liability falls within the scope of FRS 12 the LLP should assess the probability of a future cash outflow using the principles of paragraphs 23 and 24 of that standard. Any liability for post-retirement payments to members earned to date and therefore recognised in the accounts should reflect the latest expectations in respect of:**

        (a)   the likely date of ceasing to be a member; and

        (b)   the amounts likely to be payable from that date.

86.   The value of the liability should be based on the best estimate of the current value of future cash flows. In practice, it will often be appropriate to value the liability on an actuarial basis consistent with the principles of FRS 17 for the measurement of pension liabilities. Where, because of their nature and/or complexity, the arrangements are such that it is appropriate to apply the guidance in FRS 17, then that guidance should be applied in arriving at the measurement of the liability. In the case of profit-dependent payments, it will be necessary for the LLP to make a best estimate of the level of future profits of the LLP. Only in extremely rare cases will no reliable estimate be capable of being made. In these extremely rare cases, if accounting for the liability under FRS 12, then a liability exists that cannot be recognised. This is disclosed as a contingent liability.

---

[9]   This is similar to the approach in FRS 17.

87. The liability should be recalculated annually to take account of changes in membership, eligibility for post-retirement payments, financial estimates and actuarial assumptions.

Post-retirement payments to members: presentation

88. **Amounts recognised in respect of current members should be charged to the profit and loss account within 'Members' remuneration charged as an expense'. The recognition of and changes in the liability for post-retirement payments to or in respect of current members and to or in respect of former members should be shown separately. The change in the liability in respect of former members should be expensed in the relevant expense item (that is, not in members' remuneration) in the profit and loss account. The change in the liability in respect of current members should be charged to the profit and loss account within 'Members' remuneration charged as an expense'.**

89. **The liability for post-retirement payments to or in respect of current members and to or in respect of former members should be shown separately. The liability in respect of former members should be shown in the balance sheet under 'Provisions for liabilities' or 'Creditors', as appropriate, as 'Post-retirement payments to former members'. The liability in respect of current members should be shown separately, if material, as a component of 'Loans and other debts due to members'. In the year in which a member retires, a transfer should be made between the balance in respect of current members and the balance in respect of former members.**

90. **Where the liability has been discounted (for example, as required by FRS 12 where the effect is material), the unwinding of the discount should be presented next to the interest cost line in the profit and loss account, to the extent that it relates to former members. Where it relates to current members it should be included in 'Members' remuneration charged as an expense'.**

91. **Additional annuities granted after the date of a member's retirement should be recognised in full in the profit and loss account within operating profit as soon as the award is granted to the former member.**

Post-retirement payments to members: disclosure

92. **The LLP's accounting policy note should disclose the LLP's policy in respect of post-retirement payments to members.**

On transition of a partnership or other undertaking to an LLP

93. **Where an LLP makes post-retirement payments to members of a predecessor partnership or other organisation, the extent to which the LLP has an actual or constructive liability for such payments should be considered. Where an actual or constructive liability exists, this should be**

recognised in the balance sheet of the LLP. Where there is merely recourse to the LLP in the event of a default of a third party and such default has not occurred and is not probable, this should be disclosed as a contingent liability.

94.   It is possible that an LLP which succeeds to the business of a partnership will not assume actual or constructive liability for post-retirement payments payable by the predecessor partnership or partners therein. However, it may, as agent for the members of the LLP, disburse the related cash to the former members.[10] In such circumstances, the payments to the former members represent amounts in respect of their services to the former partnership which the LLP is distributing to the former members as agent of the continuing members and do not represent liabilities of the LLP. Reference to these arrangements is encouraged where this would aid clarity.

TAXATION

95.   **Where tax (whether current or deferred) to be paid on members' remuneration is a personal liability of the members, it falls within 'Members' interests' on the balance sheet. It should not appear in the profit and loss account.**

96.   Amounts retained by an LLP in respect of a member's tax liability do not require separate disclosure. In such cases, the LLP is simply acting as agent of the member by settling the liability direct to the tax authorities. Amounts retained for tax should be included in 'Loans and other debts due to members'.

97.   Tax withheld from members who subsequently retire from membership should be dealt with as any other balance due to former members.

98.   **LLPs that are subject to tax on profits arising in jurisdictions where LLPs are taxed as corporate entities should report such taxes in their accounts as required by accounting standards.**

99.   **In the group accounts of an LLP which include entities or organisations that are not partnerships or LLPs, such as companies, the tax liabilities of such entities should be recorded in the profit and loss account under the relevant heading and any related liability carried as a creditor in the balance sheet.**

REVENUE RECOGNITION: STOCKS AND LONG-TERM CONTRACTS

100.   **In respect of stock, the cost of members' time and related overheads should be accounted for in accordance with SSAP 9 *Stocks and long-term contracts*. Contracts should be accounted for in accordance with SSAP 9, FRS 5**

---

[10]   Whether such arrangements exist will depend on the terms of the agreement between the predecessor partners and the former member, as varied by any agreements entered into at the time the LLP succeeds to the business of the predecessor partnership.

Reporting the Substance of Transactions - Application Note G: Revenue Recognition, **and UITF Abstract 40** *Revenue recognition and service contracts.*

101.   When calculating the cost of stock or work in progress in accordance with SSAP 9, the cost of members' time should be considered. The cost of members' time will include only those elements that would be expensed in the profit and loss account, i.e. 'Members' remuneration charged as an expense' as defined in paragraph 21 above. However, regardless of whether the time input by a member is a cost to be included in stock, any overhead related to that time should be included in the cost of stock or work in progress.

BUSINESS COMBINATIONS AND GROUP ACCOUNTS

Entity and group accounts

102.   **An LLP should follow the rules on the requirement to prepare group accounts (and the exemptions therefrom) and the contents of the group accounts (and on inclusion and exclusion of subsidiaries) set out in FRS 2** *Accounting for Subsidiary Undertakings* **and FRS 5, modified where necessary to comply with the Regulations.**

Accounting for business combinations

103.   **The accounting treatment for business combinations which include one or more LLPs should have regard to the substance of the combination. Application of GAAP with respect to mergers and acquisitions should be considered in the context of both the group accounts and the entity accounts of the LLP.**

104.   When two LLPs combine, there may be only one surviving LLP, or a new LLP may be created or one LLP may become a member of the other. The recommended accounting treatment may therefore apply both to the entity accounts of an LLP and, if relevant, to its group accounts.

105.   Consideration will be required to determine whether a particular business combination represents:

-    an acquisition;
-    a merger; or
-    the granting of membership to one or more individuals.

The circumstances of business combinations will vary greatly. Where a business combination is not simply the granting of membership to one or more individuals, it will be treated as either an acquisition or a merger in accordance with FRS 6 *Acquisitions and Mergers.*

Acquisition accounting

106. Acquisition accounting is required when the conditions set out in FRS 6 to use merger accounting are not met.

107. Where acquisition accounting is used, the fair value of the purchase consideration used in the calculation of goodwill arising on an acquisition should be assessed carefully. In particular, the profit share promised to the new members in the enlarged LLP should be assessed to determine whether any portion of that remuneration represents consideration for the business acquired, rather than future members' remuneration. For example, if members of the purchased entity were awarded an increased profit share for a limited period of time after the acquisition, falling back to 'normal' remuneration levels thereafter, this could indicate that the short-term excess amounts were part of the purchase consideration.

108. Where it is not possible to value the consideration given in accordance with the requirements of FRS 7 *Fair Values in Acquisition Accounting*, the best estimate of its value may be obtained by valuing the entity acquired.

109. Where the fair value of stock and work in progress used in acquisition accounting by LLPs cannot be ascertained from market value, consideration should be given to paragraphs 52 - 57 of FRS 7; in which case, the current cost would include the cost of members' time charged as an expense, as discussed in paragraph 101 above.

Merger accounting

110. Merger accounting is required when all five of the specific criteria set down in FRS 6 indicate that a merger, rather than an acquisition, has taken place.

111. When applying the five criteria to combinations involving LLPs, it may not be clear how to apply the guidance on size criteria set out in paragraph 68 of FRS 6. Accordingly, suitable alternatives for establishing relative sizes may need to be considered, such as respective revenues, number of members, profits, employees, relative voting rights, etc. Finally, the nature of the combination should be considered, to determine whether circumstances indicate that the size criterion should be rebutted.

Group reconstructions

112. The transfer of all or the majority of the assets, liabilities and business of a partnership into an LLP incorporated for that purpose should be dealt with as a group reconstruction, except where the requirements of paragraph 13 of FRS 6 are not met, after taking account of the different legal nature of an LLP. The initial 'opening' balance sheet should follow the accounting policies of the LLP.

Considerations on transition from an existing partnership

113. **Where existing undertakings are transferred into an LLP, the transfer should be accounted for as a group reconstruction, as noted in paragraph 112 above, where the conditions of paragraph 13 of FRS 6 are met.**

114. Both start-up businesses and existing undertakings, including partnerships, may choose to incorporate as LLPs. Where there is a transfer of an existing undertaking to an LLP, it will be accounted for as a group reconstruction where the conditions of FRS 6 are met.

115. **Single-entity LLPs that are formed by the transfer or incorporation of existing undertakings, including partnerships, which meet the requirements of FRS 6 to use merger accounting for the initial transfer of business, should reflect the transfer at book value at the date of transfer and disclose comparative *pro forma* amounts in the financial statements of the first period after incorporation. Where such comparative amounts are disclosed, they should be stated on the basis of the accounting policies adopted by the LLP. The initial statutory period may or may not be a 12-month period.**

116. In some cases there may be a hiatus between the formation of the LLP and the transfer of the existing undertaking. Where this occurs, the principles of merger accounting should be used, and the net assets at book values should be reflected in the accounts at the date of the transfer, and profits should be recognised for the period from the transfer to the end of the accounting period. A *pro forma* profit and loss account, including corresponding amounts, should be given for the whole of the original entity's accounting period spanning the transfer. These issues are considered in Appendix 4.

117. **The restatement of comparatives to consistent accounting policies will often result in a difference between the total interests of partners in the predecessor firm shown by its final balance sheet, and the members' interests in the opening balance sheet of the LLP. Such differences should not be dealt with in the financial statements of the LLP.**

118. The disclosures required by FRS 6 will be required; for example, those outlined in paragraph 22(e) of the standard.

119. **Existing groups that, using merger accounting under a group reconstruction, put a new LLP at the top of the group (whether in order to convert to an LLP or as part of a group reconstruction) should present corresponding amounts in the financial statements of the period of the merger, as required by FRS 6.**

PROVISIONS AND OTHER IMPLICATIONS OF FRS 12

120. FRS 12 applies in all respects to LLPs.[11]

121. While the application of FRS 12 is unlikely to present any unusual problems for LLPs, applying it fully may require a significant change in practice for existing partnerships that are incorporated as an LLP. Historically, partnership accounting has focused heavily on what was perceived as equitable between partners and different year groups of partners, since there are often different partners and/or differing profit shares in successive years. By agreement, major liabilities may have been spread over several years, often to match cash flows, rather than being fully provided immediately.

122. When considering FRS 12, an LLP should have regard to all contracts and all relevant circumstances, including side agreements and promises whether or not in writing. An example of a constructive obligation arising would be where post-retirement payments have been offered consistently to previous members at the point of, but not prior to, retirement. Where this is the case, it could be argued that this would build an expectation and, hence, a constructive obligation that all members would be offered this benefit at retirement. If so, then the point of recognition of the liability would be earlier than retirement (see paragraphs 82 et seq. above).

123. The basis of allocation of profits between members is a private matter and will usually be governed by the members' agreement referred to in the LLP legislation. There is no reason why the determination of profits to be allocated to members cannot be based on different accounting policies from those applied to the financial statements of the LLP.

124. If the LLP has entered into any guarantee or indemnity with respect to the borrowings of a member or members personally, the existence of such a guarantee or indemnity where material should either be disclosed as a note to the accounts (where it is unlikely that the guarantee or indemnity would be called) or provided for in the primary statements where there is an actual or constructive liability as defined under FRS 12 and it is probable that the guarantee or indemnity will be called.[12]

125. It is common practice within partnerships for partners to borrow to fund their capital and similar interests in a firm. Such arrangements may involve the firm entering into guarantees, indemnities or undertakings toward the lender concerned. Broadly similar arrangements may occur with regard to members of LLPs and the LLP itself.

---

[11] Professional services firms will apply FRS 12 in relation to claims against them and associated insurance reimbursements. Such matters are not specific to LLPs and so are not addressed in this SORP.

[12] LLPs applying the provisions of FRS 26 will need to follow the recognition and measurement rules for financial guarantees set out in that standard.

126. Of itself, the extent to which members' interests have been financed by lenders, who have lent funds to the member or members concerned, is not a matter for disclosure. Similarly, any undertaking that the LLP may give to act as agent for a member, in remitting funds from members' interests to a lender or other third party, need not be disclosed.

127. A provision would be required where, for example, an LLP has undertaken to repay a loan of a member, such that the LLP is under a legal or constructive obligation to ensure that the full liability to the lender is settled, and it is more likely than not that the guarantee will be called upon.[13] Where a provision of this nature has been made in relation to a member who is a related party (see paragraphs 128 - 131 below), further disclosures should be given in accordance with FRS 8 *Related Party Disclosures*.

RELATED PARTIES

128. The provisions of FRS 8, including the definition of related parties, apply to LLPs. An LLP which is under the control of another LLP, partnership, company or other entity will be a related party of that other entity. The fact that some members of an LLP are members of another LLP or another partnership does not in itself make the businesses related parties: the extent of common control and/or influence determines this. Predecessor partnerships of LLPs should be treated as related parties of the LLP.

129. The nature and extent of members' involvement in the management of the LLP should be considered, to determine whether a member is a related party.

130. In the case of smaller LLPs, where all members play a part in the management of the entity, it will frequently be the case that all members are related parties. However, in larger LLPs, it may not be appropriate for all members of an LLP to be considered as related parties. FRS 8 includes directors of companies as related parties by definition and the key management personnel of a reporting entity are also defined as related parties of that entity. Key management personnel of an LLP are those persons having authority and responsibility for planning, directing and controlling the activities of the LLP, directly or indirectly. Designated members are therefore likely to be related parties of the LLP.

131. The controlling party and ultimate controlling party of an LLP, if one exists, should be disclosed in accordance with FRS 8. This includes an individual or entity which has the ability to direct the financial and operating policies of the LLP, although that party may not be entitled to the majority of profits or have invested the majority of capital represented by equity or debt. It will also be necessary to consider the extent to which

---

[13]   The LLP will need to consider the extent to which it has the legal right to offset the aggregate 'capital' and undrawn profits of the member concerned against the outstanding debt.

members are acting in concert in such a way as to be able to exercise control or influence over the LLP.

COMPLIANCE STATEMENT

132.   The note to the financial statements which deals with accounting policies should refer to the LLP's compliance with this SORP, or detail areas of non-compliance and any reasons therefor, in accordance with FRS 18 *Accounting Policies.*

EFFECTIVE DATE

133.   The revised SORP should be applied for accounting periods beginning on or after 1 January 2010. Earlier application is permitted but, in respect of the amendments made to FRS 25 in August 2008, only for accounting periods beginning on or after 1 January 2009. The previous edition of the SORP (published in 2006) applies to earlier periods.

134.   In implementing the provisions of this SORP that relate to FRS 25, LLPs should have regard to paragraphs 96 – 97C of that standard, which deal with certain transitional and comparative issues. Any other changes in accounting policy should be dealt with in the normal way under FRS 18.

**APPENDIX 1: EXAMPLES SHOWING THE PRESENTATION OF MEMBERS'
INTERESTS AFTER APPLYING FRS 25 AND UITF 39**
(The LLP has no retirement benefit arrangements for current members in these examples)

EXHIBIT A - LLP Balance Sheet

	20X5 £'000	20X4 £'000
PRESENTATION AFTER FRS 25/UITF 39 – LLP WITH NO EQUITY		
Fixed assets		
Tangible fixed assets	9,500	8,200
Current assets		
Amounts recoverable on contracts	8,000	7,500
Trade debtors	17,500	16,000
Amounts due from members	1,500	1,200
Other debtors and prepayments	4,000	3,800
Cash at bank and in hand	6,000	4,500
Current assets	37,000	33,000
Creditors: amounts falling due within one year		
Bank overdraft and loans	3,000	2,800
Other creditors and accruals	6,500	6,000
Current liabilities	9,500	8,800
Net current assets	27,500	24,200
Total assets less current liabilities	37,000	32,400
Creditors: amounts falling due after more than one year		
Bank loans	4,000	3,200
Provisions for liabilities		
Post-retirement payments to former members	4,500	4,800
Other provisions	2,000	1,900
	6,500	6,700
NET ASSETS ATTRIBUTABLE TO MEMBERS	26,500	22,500

REPRESENTED BY:	20X5 £000	20X4 £000
Loans and other debts due to members within one year		
Members' capital classified as a liability	8,000	6,000
Other amounts	18,500	16,500
	26,500	22,500
TOTAL MEMBERS' INTERESTS		
Amounts due from members	(1,500)	(1,200)
Loans and other debts due to members	26,500	22,500
	25,000	21,300

Note: In this example, members' other interests are nil.

EXHIBIT B - LLP Balance Sheet

PRESENTATION AFTER FRS 25/UITF 39 – LLP WITH SOME EQUITY	20X5 £'000	20X4 £'000
Fixed assets		
Tangible fixed assets	9,500	8,200
Current assets		
Amounts recoverable on contracts	8,000	7,500
Trade debtors	17,500	16,000
Amounts due from members	1,500	1,200
Other debtors and prepayments	4,000	3,800
Cash at bank and in hand	6,000	4,500
Current assets	37,000	33,000
Creditors: amounts falling due within one year		
Bank overdraft and loans	3,000	2,800
Other creditors and accruals	6,500	6,000
Current liabilities	9,500	8,800
Net current assets	27,500	24,200
Total assets less current liabilities	37,000	32,400
Creditors: amounts falling due after more than one year		
Bank loans	4,000	3,200
Provisions for liabilities		
Post-retirement payments to former members	4,500	4,800
Other provisions	2,000	1,900
	6,500	6,700
NET ASSETS ATTRIBUTABLE TO MEMBERS	26,500	22,500

REPRESENTED BY:	20X5 £000	20X4 £000
Loans and other debts due to members within one year		
Members' capital classified as a liability	5,000	4,000
Other amounts	9,000	8,000
	14,000	12,000
Members' other interests		
Members' capital classified as equity	3,000	2,000
Members' other interests - other reserves classified as equity	9,500	8,500
	26,500	22,500
TOTAL MEMBERS' INTERESTS		
Amounts due from members	(1,500)	(1,200)
Loans and other debts due to members	14,000	12,000
Members' other interests	12,500	10,500
	25,000	21,300

EXHIBIT C - LLP Profit and Loss Account (Format 2)

PRESENTATION AFTER FRS 25/UITF 39 – LLP WITH AUTOMATIC DIVISION OF PROFIT EQUIVALENT TO SALARIED REMUNERATION	20X5 £'000	20X4 £'000
Turnover	55,500	49,500
Other operating income	2,500	2,000
	58,000	51,500
Other external charges	(8,500)	(7,500)
Staff costs	(21,500)	(18,500)
Depreciation	(2,000)	(2,000)
Other operating expenses	(11,000)	(9,000)
Operating profit	15,000	14,500
Profit on sale of fixed assets	1,000	-
Interest receivable and similar income	1,000	1,000
Interest payable and similar charges	(500)	(750)
Profit for the financial year before members' remuneration and profit shares	16,500	14,750
Profit for the financial year before members' remuneration and profit shares	16,500	14,750
Members' remuneration charged as an expense	(3,000)	(2,500)
Profit for the financial year available for discretionary division among members	13,500	12,250

Note: This example may apply to an LLP which has a members' agreement or other profit sharing arrangement which gives members the equivalent of a salary. It is not intended to suggest that all LLPs should impute notional salaries.

EXHIBIT D - LLP Profit and Loss Account (Format 2)

PRESENTATION AFTER FRS 25/UITF 39 – LLP WITH AUTOMATIC DIVISION OF ALL PROFITS	20X5 £'000	20X4 £'000
Turnover	55,500	49,500
Other operating income	2,500	2,000
	58,000	51,500
Other external charges	(8,500)	(7,500)
Staff costs	(21,500)	(18,500)
Depreciation	(2,000)	(2,000)
Other operating expenses	(11,000)	(9,000)
Operating profit	15,000	14,500
Profit on sale of fixed assets	1,000	-
Interest receivable and similar income	1,000	1,000
Interest payable and similar charges	(500)	(750)
Profit for the financial year before members' remuneration and profit shares	16,500	14,750
Profit for the financial year before members' remuneration and profit shares	16,500	14,750
Members' remuneration charged as an expense	(16,500)	(14,750)
Result for the financial year available for discretionary division among members	-	-

Note: This example may apply to an LLP which has a members' agreement or other profit sharing arrangement which has arrangements which automatically divide the full amount of the earned profit among members.

Appendix 3

EXHIBIT E - LLP Profit and Loss Account (Format 2)

PRESENTATION AFTER FRS 25/UITF 39 – LLP WITH NO AUTOMATIC DIVISION OF ANY PROFIT

	20X5 £'000	20X4 £'000
Turnover	55,500	49,500
Other operating income	2,500	2,000
	58,000	51,500
Other external charges	(8,500)	(7,500)
Staff costs	(21,500)	(18,500)
Depreciation	(2,000)	(2,000)
Other operating expenses	(11,000)	(9,000)
Operating profit	15,000	14,500
Profit on sale of fixed assets	1,000	-
Interest receivable and similar income	1,000	1,000
Interest payable and similar charges	(500)	(750)
Profit for the financial year before members' remuneration and profit shares available for discretionary division among members	16,500	14,750

Note: This example may apply to an LLP which has a members' agreement or other profit sharing arrangement which has no element of automatic division of profit and does not give members any rights to a share in the profits until it is divided.

APPENDIX 2:
LIABILITY AND EQUITY ELEMENTS OF MEMBERS' INTERESTS

General

The interests of members in an LLP are typically governed by the LLP's members' agreement. Compared to the memorandum and articles for limited companies, LLPs have considerable flexibility over how that agreement is drafted, and there is wide diversity in practice. The absence of standard arrangements makes it necessary to analyse each members' agreement with care so that members' equity and liability interests are properly reflected in financial statements.

The members' agreement will specify what members are expected to provide to the LLP and what they will receive in return. Depending on the nature of the LLP and what has been agreed, members may or may not provide services or expertise to the LLP; and they may or may not be required to provide cash, or other assets, as members' capital. In return, they may receive equity or liability interests in the LLP or a combination of the two. One purpose of the examples below is to illustrate that there need not be symmetry between the treatment of amounts subscribed as members' capital and the 'returns' arising. For example, a member may be able to demand repayment of capital subscribed (liability, unless the conditions for the puttables amendment are met) but the LLP may have discretion over the division of profits (equity).

It will generally be necessary, when analysing members' interests between equity and liabilities, to distinguish those rights that are only exercisable by the members as a whole from those rights that may be exercised by an individual member against the LLP. For example, where the profits are only divided if the members as a whole (or a committee of the members with the relevant authority) so decide, an individual member will not be entitled to a share of those profits unless and until a decision to divide them is taken; accordingly, the profits will constitute an equity interest so far as the profit and loss account is concerned (and will continue to do so even if a decision by the members to divide the profits is taken during the year in which the profits are earned; although, so far as the balance sheet is concerned, the taking of such a decision will convert the profits into a liability owed by the LLP to its members). By contrast, where the members have agreed to an automatic division of profits, the individual will be entitled to a share of those profits based on his percentage profit share, and accordingly his profit share will fall to be treated as an expense in the profit and loss account (and also as a liability in the balance sheet insofar as the profit remains unpaid at the balance sheet date).

Capital and remuneration

The examples set out below, which are provided for guidance only, illustrate both how the principles set out in the SORP should be applied to participation rights following the August 2008 amendment to FRS 25 on puttable instruments, and also, where applicable, how the accounting would have been different prior to that amendment. The matters set out in the following paragraphs are relevant when considering those examples.

Paragraphs 34 and BC20 to BC25 deal with the issue of when to treat remuneration and amounts subscribed (capital) separately for accounting purposes because there is no clearly identifiable return on capital and the substance of the arrangement makes it inappropriate to treat remuneration as a return on capital. This separate analysis will most often apply in situations where the members of the LLP provide services to that LLP (for example, professional services firms). As explained in BC23, in such situations remuneration and profit shares are often payable to members in return for participation in the business as well as representing a financial return on amounts invested by members and the latter element will represent a relatively insignificant proportion of total remuneration.

When considering whether a particular payment to a member is a return on capital subscribed or, for example, a payment in relation to services, an entity should apply paragraph 34 of the SORP. Accordingly:

a)   where a member provides both capital and services to an LLP and no element of the return to the member is clearly identifiable as a return on the amount subscribed or otherwise contributed, no part of the return to the member (which may include inter alia salary, bonus, risk premium and allocated share of profits) will be regarded as a return on capital;

b)   where a member provides both capital and services to an LLP but an element of the return to the member is clearly identifiable as a return on amounts subscribed or otherwise contributed, only that element will be regarded as a return on capital; and

c)   where a member provides no services to an LLP then the whole of the return to the member will be regarded as a return on capital.

Where the members of an LLP provide services to the LLP, and a separate analysis of the accounting for the capital and remuneration is appropriate, it will usually be the case that the puttables amendment does not have any significant impact on the accounting treatment. This is because the remuneration will usually be a separate instrument or contract that has 'total cash flows based substantially on the profit or loss' of the entity and substantially restricts or fixes the return to the holders of capital. In such circumstances, the test in paragraph 16B or paragraph 16D of FRS 25 would seem not to be met, and repayable capital would not be eligible for equity treatment under the puttables amendment.

In relation to the consideration of the puttables amendment paragraph AG.14H of FRS 25 is of particular relevance to LLPs whose members provide services. The paragraphs preceding AG.14H explain that only cash flows and contractual terms and conditions relating to the instrument holder as an owner of the entity should be considered. They give the scenario in which certain partners are remunerated for providing a guarantee to the entity as an example of a transaction in a role other than that of an owner, which would be disregarded for the purposes of the puttables amendment. Paragraph AG.14H states:

'Another example is a profit or loss sharing arrangement that allocates profit or loss to the instrument holders on the basis of services rendered or business generated during the current and previous years. Such arrangements are transactions with instrument holders in their role as non-owners and should not be considered when assessing the features listed in paragraph 16A or paragraph 16C. However, profit or loss sharing arrangements that allocate profit or loss to instrument holders based on the nominal amount of their instruments relative to others in the class represent transactions with the instrument holders in their roles as owners and should be considered when assessing the features listed in paragraph 16A or paragraph 16C.'

Broadly, this means that remuneration for services is a non-owner transaction and disregarded in the puttables analysis but other profit or loss sharing arrangements based on the nominal amount of the relevant instrument are transactions in the holder's role as an owner and do need to be taken into account. Again, following the principles set out above, the provisions of this particular paragraph should be considered only after establishing whether the capital and remuneration are being analysed together for the purposes of the puttables amendment or separately (paragraph 34).

To summarise, based on the analysis above, part or all of the capital subscribed by a member will be accounted for as a liability a) if the LLP is obliged to make payments to the member which are clearly identifiable as a return on that capital (e.g. interest on an annual basis) or b) there are circumstances in which the member can demand repayment of capital (e.g. on retirement) and the conditions set out in the puttables amendment are not met – for LLPs where members provide services, this would be where the remuneration is regarded separately for accounting purposes and so 'substantially restricts or fixes the return to the holders of capital'.

As discussed above, for many LLPs where the members provide services, it is unlikely that the puttables amendment will have a significant impact. However, where there could possibly be an impact and the amendment needs to be considered in more detail, the flow charts in Appendix 3 set out the criteria that will need to be met for an instrument that would otherwise be treated as a liability to be treated as equity under the amendment.

Example 1 - Equity capital and profits

The analysis in this example applies irrespective of whether the members provide services to the LLP.

An LLP has ten members. Under the terms of the members' agreement, each member subscribes £1,000 as initial capital and will receive a 10% share of any profits that are divided. Any decision to divide profits or return capital must be approved by a majority of the members.

All cash outflows to members are at the discretion of the LLP. Accordingly:

- the capital subscribed of £10,000 is presented within equity, and

- divisions of profit are reported as equity appropriations when they occur (whether during or after the end of the period).

Thus, if the LLP made profits of £500,000 before profit sharing, and £300,000 was paid out to members as drawings during the year, the profit reported for the year would be £500,000. The drawings of £300,000 would be included in debtors and the £500,000 of unallocated profits would be included within equity at the year end, assuming that at that point in time, the decision to divide profits had not been made. Once the profits are divided, the amount of drawings in debtors would be offset against the liability then created. This may be contrasted with Example 2 below.

Example 2 - Liability for capital and profits

An LLP has ten members. Members provide services to the LLP. Under the terms of the members' agreement, each member subscribes £100,000 as initial capital and has a 10% share of profits. All profits are divided automatically each year, and a member may demand the return of capital (for example, upon retirement). No element of members' remuneration is clearly identifiable as a return on amounts subscribed or otherwise contributed. Accordingly, no part of the return to the members is regarded as a return on capital.

The LLP has no discretion over cash outflows to members. In addition, the tests in the puttables amendment are not met, because the remuneration is regarded as separate from the capital subscribed for accounting purposes and substantially restricts (to zero) the return to the holders of capital (see the footnote to paragraph 41). Accordingly:

- the capital subscribed of £1,000,000 is presented within liabilities, and

- an expense is charged in the profit and loss account (under the heading 'Members' remuneration charged as an expense') and a further liability recognised equal to the amount of profits available for division. (This profit and loss account treatment is illustrated at Exhibit D in Appendix 1.)

Thus, if the LLP made profits of £500,000 before profit sharing, and £300,000 was paid out to members as drawings during the year, the profit reported for the year would be £nil. Members' remuneration charged as an expense would be £500,000 and the undrawn balance of £200,000 would be included within liabilities at the year end. This may be contrasted with Example 1 above.

Example 3 - Liability for capital, equity for profits

An LLP has ten members. Members provide services to the LLP. Under the terms of the members' agreement, each member subscribes £1,000 as initial capital and has a 10% share of profits. Any decision to divide profits must be approved by a majority of the members, but a member may demand the return of initial capital (for example, upon retirement). No element of members' remuneration is clearly identifiable as a return on amounts subscribed or otherwise contributed. Accordingly, no part of the return to the members is regarded as a return on capital.

The LLP has no discretion over cash outflows to members in respect of capital. In addition, the tests in the puttables amendment are not met, because the remuneration is regarded as separate from the capital subscribed for accounting purposes and fixes the return to the holders of capital at zero (see the footnote to paragraph 41). Accordingly:

- the capital subscribed of £10,000 is presented within liabilities, but

- divisions of profit are reported as appropriations (not an expense) when they occur (whether during or after the end of the period).

Example 4 - Equity for capital, liability for profits

An LLP has ten members. Members provide services to the LLP. Under the terms of the members' agreement, each member subscribes £1,000 as initial capital and has a 10% share of profits. All profits are divided automatically each year, but any decision to return capital must be approved by a majority of the members. No element of members' remuneration is clearly identifiable as a return on amounts subscribed or otherwise contributed. Accordingly, no part of the return to the members is regarded as a return on capital.

The LLP has discretion over the return of initial capital, but no discretion over cash outflows in respect of profits. Accordingly:

- the capital subscribed of £10,000 is presented within equity, but

- an expense is charged in the profit and loss account (under the heading 'Members' remuneration charged as an expense') and a liability recognised equal to the amount of profits.

Example 5 - Liability for capital, split treatment of profits

An LLP has ten members. Members provide services to the LLP. Under the terms of the members' agreement, each member subscribes £1,000 as initial capital and will receive a 10% share of any profits that are divided. A member may demand the return of capital. The membership agreement specifies that 50% of the profits made during a year will be divided automatically. Any decision to divide part or all of the remaining profits must be approved by a majority of the members. No element of members' remuneration is clearly identifiable as a return on amounts subscribed or otherwise contributed. Accordingly, no part of the return to the members is regarded as a return on capital.

The LLP has no discretion over cash outflows to members in respect of capital. In addition, the tests in the puttables amendment are not met, because the remuneration is regarded as separate from the capital subscribed for accounting purposes and fixes the return to the holders of capital at zero (see the footnote to paragraph 41). Accordingly:

- the capital subscribed of £10,000 is presented within liabilities,

- an expense is charged in the profit and loss account (under the heading 'Members' remuneration charged as an expense') and a further liability recognised equal to 50% of the amount of profits available for division, and

317

- any divisions out of the remaining profits are reported as equity appropriations (not an expense) when they occur (whether during or after the end of the period).

Thus, if the LLP made profits of £500,000 before profit sharing, and £300,000 was paid out to members as drawings during the year, the profit reported for the year would be £250,000. Members' remuneration charged as an expense would be £250,000 (i.e. 50% of available profits) and the additional drawings of £50,000 would be included in debtors. The unallocated balance of £250,000 would be included within equity at the year end, assuming that at that point in time, no further decision to divide profits had been made.

Example 6 - Liability for capital and interest payments, equity for remaining profits

The analysis in this example applies irrespective of whether the members provide services to the LLP.

An LLP has ten members. Under the terms of the members' agreement, each member subscribes £1,000 as initial capital and has a 10% share of any profits that are divided. A member may demand the return of capital (for example, upon retirement), and interest at a market rate of 6% is automatically payable on the capital subscribed. Any decision to divide the balance of profits must be approved by a majority of the members.

The LLP has no discretion over the return of initial capital. In addition, the tests in the puttables amendment are not met, because the payment of interest is a non-discretionary return on the capital. Cash outflows to members in respect of profits after interest, however, are at the discretion of the LLP. Accordingly:

- the capital subscribed of £10,000 is presented within liabilities, and

- interest expense of £600 is charged in the profit and loss account (within the heading 'Members' remuneration charged as an expense'), and a corresponding liability recognised, but

- any other divisions of profit are reported as an equity appropriation when they occur (whether during or after the end of the period).

Example 7 - Discretionary repayment of capital

The analysis in this example applies irrespective of whether the members provide services to the LLP.

An LLP's constitution requires that members subscribe capital to the LLP. Upon retirement, the LLP is required to pass a resolution before any capital is repaid. If no such resolution is passed, the LLP is entitled to retain the capital indefinitely. Any decision to divide profits must be approved by a majority of the members.

In this example, a positive resolution is required to repay capital, and without it the LLP has no obligation to repay the amounts. Accordingly, the capital is presented as equity.

Example 8 - Discretionary repayment of capital and non-discretionary return on capital

The analysis in this example applies irrespective of whether the members provide services to the LLP.

An LLP's constitution requires that members subscribe capital to the LLP. Upon retirement, the LLP is required to pass a resolution before any capital is repaid. If no such resolution is passed, the LLP is entitled to retain the capital indefinitely. Interest at a market rate is automatically payable on all capital subscribed. Any decision to divide the balance of profits must be approved by a majority of the members.

In this example, although a positive resolution is required to repay capital, the LLP is obliged to pay a return on that capital. Accordingly, a liability will be recognised to reflect the present value of the minimum non-discretionary outflows (see paragraph 39 of the SORP). In this case, as the return is at a market rate at the time the capital is subscribed, the entire capital will be classified as a liability. Furthermore, the tests in the puttables amendment are not met, because the payment of interest is a non-discretionary return on the capital.

Example 9 - Discretionary repayment of capital and no identifiable return on capital

An LLP's constitution requires that members subscribe capital to the LLP. Members provide services to the LLP. Upon retirement, the LLP is required to pass a resolution before any capital is repaid. If no such resolution is passed, the LLP is entitled to retain the capital indefinitely. The membership agreement specifies that all profits made during a year will be divided automatically. No element of members' remuneration is clearly identifiable as a return on amounts subscribed or otherwise contributed. Accordingly, no part of the return to the members is regarded as a return on capital and their remuneration is considered separate from the capital for accounting purposes.

In this example, a positive resolution is required to repay capital, and without it the LLP is neither obliged to repay the amounts nor to pay any return on that capital. Accordingly, the capital is presented as equity. An expense is charged in the profit and loss account (under the heading 'Members' remuneration charged as an expense') and a liability recognised equal to the amount of profits.

Example 10 - Minimum level of capital in aggregate

The analysis in this example applies irrespective of whether the members provide services to the LLP.

An LLP's constitution requires members to subscribe capital to the LLP. The LLP is required to repay any retiring member's capital unless the aggregate of the capital would otherwise fall below £1 million. The LLP has no obligation to any member to repay capital if the amount would fall below that threshold.

If the total amount of capital is greater than £1 million then, unless the tests in the puttables amendment are met in relation to members' capital, the excess would be shown as a liability and £1 million would be shown as equity. If the tests in the puttables amendment are met in relation to members' capital, or if the total amount of capital is less than £1 million, the whole amount would be shown as equity.

Example 11 - Liability for capital and profits

An LLP has ten members. Members do not provide services to the LLP. Under the terms of the members' agreement, each member subscribes £1,000,000 as initial capital and has a 10% share of profits. All profits are divided automatically each year, but any decision to return capital must be approved by a majority of the members. Accordingly, because the members do not provide services to the LLP, the whole of the return to the members is regarded as a return on capital. For accounting purposes, therefore, it is not regarded as separate from the capital but needs to be considered when determining the appropriate accounting treatment for that capital.

The LLP has discretion over the return of initial capital, but no discretion over cash outflows in respect of profits. Accordingly, because a non-discretionary return is paid on capital:

- the capital subscribed of £10,000,000 is presented within liabilities (in this example, this equates to the present value of the future non-discretionary outflows for profits), and

- an expense is charged in the profit and loss account (under the heading 'Members' remuneration charged as an expense') and a liability recognised equal to the amount of profits.

Example 12 - Equity capital and profits

An LLP has been set up as an investment vehicle, and has ten members. Members do not provide services to the LLP. The LLP's investments are managed by a third party who is not a member. Under the terms of the members' agreement, each member subscribes £1,000,000. The agreement specifies certain dates on which a member can require the LLP to repurchase his or her interest. On repurchase, the member will receive the £1,000,000 originally subscribed, adjusted for the member's share of any losses or any profits not yet divided. Any decision to divide profits must be approved by a majority of the members. On such a division, the profits are divided equally between all ten members.

The LLP has no discretion over cash outflows in respect of the repurchase of members' interests. However, it considers the tests included in the puttables amendment, and concludes that they are met in relation to the members' initial capital. Accordingly:

- the capital subscribed of £10,000,000 is presented within equity, and

- any divisions of profit are reported as equity appropriations when they occur (whether during or after the end of the period).

Thus, if the LLP made profits of £500,000 before profit sharing, of which £300,000 was paid out to members as drawings during the year, the profit reported for the year would be £500,000. Members' remuneration charged as an expense would be nil and the drawings of £300,000 would be included in debtors. The unallocated balance of £500,000 would be included within equity at the year end, assuming that at that point in time, the decision to divide profits had not been made.

Prior to the puttables amendment, the capital in this example would have been presented as a liability, because the LLP has an obligation to repurchase members' interests. However, the LLP now concludes that all the tests for equity treatment in the puttables amendment are met – for example the total cash flows attributable to the capital over its life are based substantially on the LLP's profit or loss (paragraph 16A (e) of FRS 25).

Example 13 - Equity for capital, split treatment of profits

An LLP has been set up as an investment vehicle, and has ten members. Apart from the one member noted below members do not provide services to the LLP. Under the terms of the members' agreement, each member subscribes £1,000,000. The agreement specifies certain dates on which a member can require the LLP to repurchase his or her interest. On repurchase, the member will receive the £1,000,000 originally subscribed, adjusted for the member's share of any losses or any profits not yet divided. One of the members, Company X, is responsible for managing the LLP's investments. It has been agreed that 5% of the reported profits for each period will be divided automatically to Company X, as compensation for providing these investment management services. Any decision to divide the remaining balance of profits must be approved by a majority of the members. On such a division, the balance of profits is divided equally between all ten members, ie including Company X.

The LLP has no discretion over cash outflows to Company X. In order to assess whether the capital should be presented as equity or liability, the LLP considers, as one of the tests, whether the profits payable to Company X represent remuneration for services provided. The LLP judges that the non–discretionary amounts payable to Company X each year are purely for Company X's investment management services to the LLP and of an amount that is equivalent to what would have been payable to a non-member for such services. It also considers the other tests in the puttables amendment and concludes that they are met in relation to the members' initial capital. Accordingly:

- the capital subscribed of £10,000,000 is presented within equity,

- an expense is charged in the profit and loss account (under the heading 'Members' remuneration charged as an expense') and a further liability recognised equal to the amount of profits (5%) automatically payable to Company X each year, and

- any further divisions of profit are reported as equity appropriations when they occur (whether during or after the end of the period).

Thus, if the LLP made profits of £500,000 before profit sharing, of which £25,000 (5%) was divided automatically to Company X, and a further £300,000 was paid out to members as drawings during the year, the profit reported for the year would be £475,000. Members' remuneration charged as an expense would be £25,000 (i.e. 5% of available profits) and the additional drawings of £300,000 would be included in debtors. The unallocated balance of £475,000 would be included within equity at the year end, assuming that at that point in time, the decision to divide profits had not been made.

Prior to the puttables amendment, the capital in this example would have been presented as a liability, because the LLP has an obligation to repurchase members' interests. However, the LLP now concludes that all the tests for equity treatment in the puttables amendment are met – for example the non discretionary payments to Company X are purely for its investment management services and the total cash flows attributable to the capital over its life are based substantially on the LLP's profit or loss (paragraph 16A (e) of FRS 25).

Example 14 - Equity capital and profits (limited life)

An LLP has been set up as an investment vehicle, and has ten members. Members do not provide services to the LLP. The LLP's investments are managed by a third party who is not a member. Under the terms of the members' agreement, each member subscribes £1,000,000. No member can require the LLP to repurchase his or her interest, but the LLP has been set up with a limited life of ten years, at which point it will be liquidated. On liquidation, each member will receive a pro rata share (i.e. 10%) of the LLP's net assets.

During the LLP's life, any decision to divide profits must be approved by a majority of the members. On such a division, the profits are divided equally between all ten members.

The LLP has no discretion over cash outflows on liquidation in respect of the members' interests in its net assets. However, it considers the tests included in the puttables amendment, and concludes that they are met in relation to the members' initial capital. Accordingly:

- the capital subscribed of £10,000,000 is presented within equity, and

- any divisions of profit are reported as equity appropriations when they occur (whether during or after the end of the period).

Prior to the puttables amendment, the capital in this example would have been presented as a liability, because the LLP has a limited life and an obligation to deliver a pro rata share of its net assets on liquidation.

Example 15 – Split treatment of capital and profits (limited life)

An LLP has been set up as an investment vehicle, and has ten members. Members do not provide services to the LLP. The LLP's investments are managed by a third party who is not a member. Under the terms of the members' agreement, each member subscribes £1,000,000. No member can require the LLP to repurchase his or her interest, but the LLP has been set up with a limited life of ten years, at which point it will be liquidated. On liquidation, each member will receive a pro rata share (i.e. 10%) of the LLP's net assets.

During the LLP's life, interest at a rate of 1% is automatically payable on the capital subscribed. Any decision to divide the balance of profits must be approved by a majority of the members. On such a division, the profits are divided equally between all ten members.

The LLP has no discretion over cash outflows on liquidation in respect of the members' interests in its net assets. Nor does it have discretion over cash outflows in respect of interest payable on members' interests. However, it considers the tests included in the puttables amendment, and concludes that they are met in relation to the members' initial capital. Accordingly:

- that component of the capital subscribed that corresponds to the interest payable is presented within liabilities (this will be the present value of the future interest payments – i.e. the present value of ten annual payments of £100,000),

- the remaining balance of the capital subscribed is presented within equity,

- each year, an expense is charged in the profit and loss account (under the heading 'Members' remuneration charged as an expense') and a liability recognised equal to the unwinding of the discount on the liability component, and

- any further divisions of profit are reported as equity appropriations when they occur (whether during or after the end of the period).

Prior to the puttables amendment, the capital in this example would have been presented entirely as a liability, because the LLP has a limited life and an obligation to deliver a pro rata share of its net assets on liquidation.

APPENDIX 3:
FLOWCHARTS FOR ANALYSING PUTTABLE INSTRUMENTS FOR LLPS
(THIS APPENDIX FORMS PART OF THE SORP)

The flowcharts below are intended to assist LLPs in applying the revised requirements of FRS 25, as amended in August 2008, in respect of puttable financial instruments and obligations arising on liquidation.

These flowcharts should be read in conjunction with the SORP and are not intended to be a substitute for applying the detailed requirements as set out in the amended standard. The flowcharts are not intended to cover every possible arrangement and judgement will need to be applied in assessing whether the requirements of the standard have been met.

Depending on the structure of an LLP, members' interests may consist of one or more classes of financial instrument, which themselves may comprise one or more 'components'. For example, members may invest in the capital of an LLP and may also be required to make loans to the LLP. If those loans are legally a separate financial instrument from the capital, then the LLP will have two classes of instrument with members. Under the amended Standard, reclassification is only possible for the class of instruments that is subordinate to all other instruments. Accordingly, where members' interests include more than one class of instrument, reclassification is only possible for the class of instrument that is subordinate to all others. For convenience, the flowcharts refer to this most subordinate class of financial instruments as "members' residual interests". Frequently, members' residual interests will be members' capital, though this need not necessarily be the case.

> Note: It may be helpful to read the guidance at the start of Appendix 2 before seeking to apply the flowcharts. In addition, some of the questions in the flowcharts below may be more straightforward to answer than others. Before addressing the more difficult questions, it may be advisable to check whether the responses to the more straightforward questions are such as to confirm that the amendment to FRS 25 will have no impact.

Flowchart 1: Repayment or redemption of members' residual interests without liquidation of the LLP (puttable financial instruments and obligations arising on liquidation)

NB: All LLPs should begin at the start of this flowchart. An LLP will only proceed to Flowchart 2 if it is directed there from Flowchart 1.

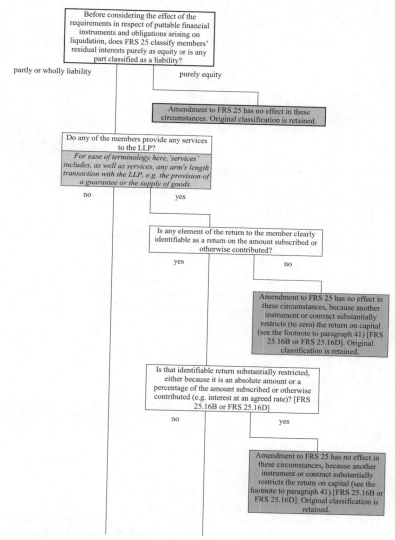

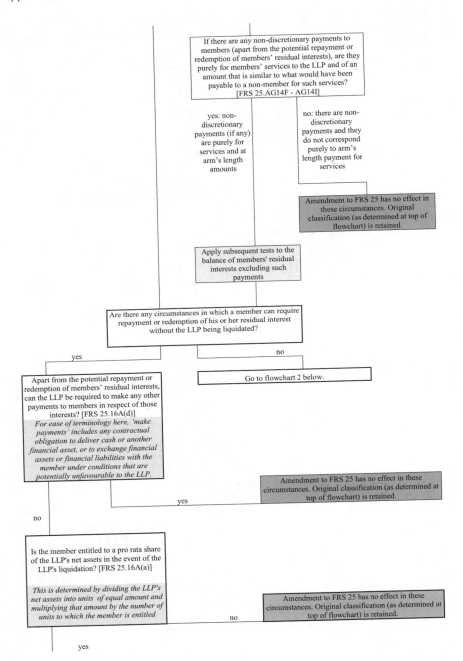

If there are any non-discretionary payments to members (apart from the potential repayment or redemption of members' residual interests), are they purely for members' services to the LLP and of an amount that is similar to what would have been payable to a non-member for such services? [FRS 25.AG14F - AG14I]

yes: non-discretionary payments (if any) are purely for services and at arm's length amounts

no: there are non-discretionary payments and they do not correspond purely to arm's length payment for services

Amendment to FRS 25 has no effect in these circumstances. Original classification (as determined at top of flowchart) is retained.

Apply subsequent tests to the balance of members' residual interests excluding such payments

Are there any circumstances in which a member can require repayment or redemption of his or her residual interest without the LLP being liquidated?

yes

no

Apart from the potential repayment or redemption of members' residual interests, can the LLP be required to make any other payments to members in respect of those interests? [FRS 25.16A(d)]
For ease of terminology here, 'make payments' includes any contractual obligation to deliver cash or another financial asset, or to exchange financial assets or financial liabilities with the member under conditions that are potentially unfavourable to the LLP.

Go to flowchart 2 below.

yes

Amendment to FRS 25 has no effect in these circumstances. Original classification (as determined at top of flowchart) is retained.

no

Is the member entitled to a pro rata share of the LLP's net assets in the event of the LLP's liquidation? [FRS 25.16A(a)]

This is determined by dividing the LLP's net assets into units of equal amount and multiplying that amount by the number of units to which the member is entitled

no

Amendment to FRS 25 has no effect in these circumstances. Original classification (as determined at top of flowchart) is retained.

yes

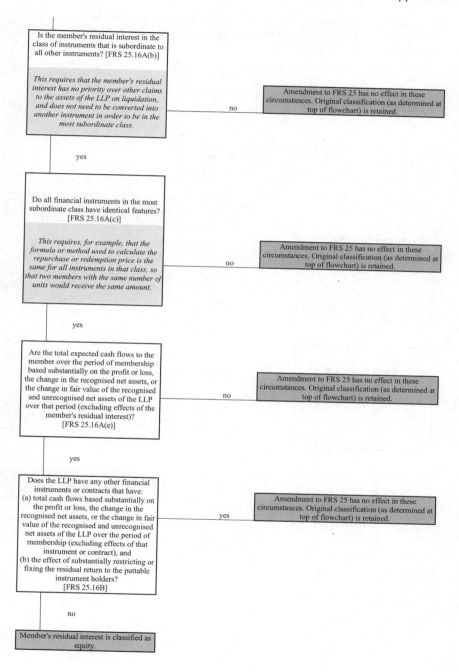

Is the member's residual interest in the class of instruments that is subordinate to all other instruments? [FRS 25.16A(b)]

This requires that the member's residual interest has no priority over other claims to the assets of the LLP on liquidation, and does not need to be converted into another instrument in order to be in the most subordinate class.

no → Amendment to FRS 25 has no effect in these circumstances. Original classification (as determined at top of flowchart) is retained.

yes

Do all financial instruments in the most subordinate class have identical features? [FRS 25.16A(c)]

This requires, for example, that the formula or method used to calculate the repurchase or redemption price is the same for all instruments in that class, so that two members with the same number of units would receive the same amount.

no → Amendment to FRS 25 has no effect in these circumstances. Original classification (as determined at top of flowchart) is retained.

yes

Are the total expected cash flows to the member over the period of membership based substantially on the profit or loss, the change in the recognised net assets, or the change in fair value of the recognised and unrecognised net assets of the LLP over that period (excluding effects of the member's residual interest)? [FRS 25.16A(e)]

no → Amendment to FRS 25 has no effect in these circumstances. Original classification (as determined at top of flowchart) is retained.

yes

Does the LLP have any other financial instruments or contracts that have:
(a) total cash flows based substantially on the profit or loss, the change in the recognised net assets, or the change in fair value of the recognised and unrecognised net assets of the LLP over the period of membership (excluding effects of that instrument or contract), and
(b) the effect of substantially restricting or fixing the residual return to the puttable instrument holders? [FRS 25.16B]

yes → Amendment to FRS 25 has no effect in these circumstances. Original classification (as determined at top of flowchart) is retained.

no

Member's residual interest is classified as equity.

327

Flowchart 2: Repayment or redemption of members' residual interests on liquidation of the LLP (puttable financial instruments and obligations arising on liquidation)

NB: All LLPs should begin at the start of Flowchart 1. An LLP will only proceed to Flowchart 2 if it is directed there from Flowchart 1.

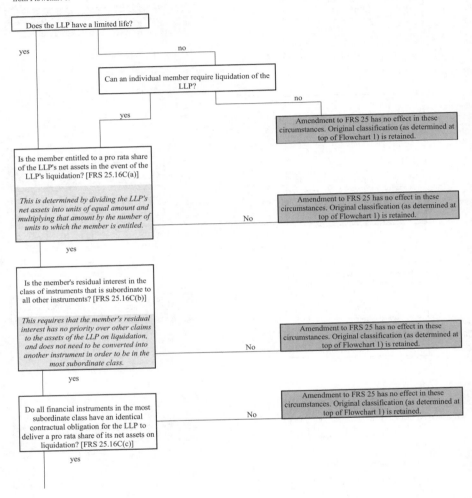

Does the LLP have any other financial
instruments or contracts that have:
(a) total cash flows based substantially on
the profit or loss, the change in the
recognised net assets, or the change in fair
value of the recognised and unrecognised
net assets of the LLP over the period of
membership (excluding
effects of that instrument or contract),
and
(b) the effect of substantially restricting or
fixing the residual return to the instrument
holders?
[FRS 25.16D]

Yes

Amendment to FRS 25 has no effect in these
circumstances. Original classification (as determined at
top of Flowchart 1) is retained.

no

Any component of member's residual
interest that can be repaid only on
liquidation is classified as equity.

APPENDIX 4:
MERGER ACCOUNTING ON INITIAL TRANSITION OF AN EXISTING UNDERTAKING TO A SINGLE-ENTITY LLP FORMED FOR THE PURPOSE

Introduction

1. This note explains how the SORP applies FRS 6 in certain special circumstances that arise when merger accounting is adopted on initial transition of an existing undertaking to a single-entity LLP formed for the purpose.

2. Paragraph 115 of the SORP states that a single-entity LLP formed by the transfer or incorporation of existing undertakings should present corresponding *pro forma* amounts.

3. Paragraph 116 of the SORP deals with a situation that is common in LLP incorporations, where the undertaking is transferred to the LLP part way though an accounting period and the LLP is not itself a parent undertaking. Paragraph 116 states that where there is a hiatus between formation of the LLP and the transfer, the net assets at book values should be reflected in the accounts at the date of the transfer, and profits should be recognised for the period from the transfer to the end of the accounting period. This is the commonly adopted practice.

4. Paragraph 116 also suggests that a *pro forma* profit and loss account, including corresponding amounts, should be given for the whole of the original entity's accounting period spanning the transfer.

Illustrative scenario and analysis

5. Entity A establishes an LLP on 1 April and transfers its trade and assets to the LLP on 1 July in exchange for an equity member's stake in the LLP. The LLP has a 31 December year end and prepares entity-only accounts. Assuming that the LLP meets the conditions for merger-accounting the transfer of the trade and assets under FRS 6 as a group reconstruction, there are potentially two alternative ways of presenting its results:

   (a) Bring in the net asset book values at the date of the transfer of trade and assets and only recognise profits arising in the LLP from the date of incorporation - 1 April, which will, in effect, only include transactions from 1 July - 31 December, since the LLP had no trade before the date of transfer.

   (b) Bring in the net asset book values at 1 January and recognise profits for the 12 month period 1 January - 31 December, to be consistent and comparable with entity A's reporting period.

6. FRS 6 is written in terms of consolidated accounts, where a subsidiary is acquired by a parent company. However, paragraphs 4 and 15 of FRS 6 state that the standard also applies to other arrangements that achieve similar results, which includes the scenario outlined above. Hence, although the rules for merger accounting in Schedule 6 to the Large and Medium-sized Companies

and Groups (Accounts and Reports) Regulations 2008 (SI 2008/410) only apply to group accounts, technically under FRS 6 they also apply to the transfer of trade and assets in entity-only accounts. Thus the merger accounting principles of reflecting the transfer at book value set out in paragraph 16 of FRS 6 should be applied to the entity-only accounts of the LLP in the scenario.

7.   From a statutory viewpoint, the accounting period being reported on is for the nine months to 31 December and therefore profits and losses relating to the period before that should not be recognised in the LLP's first statutory accounts.

8.   In addition, for companies combining with a trade and assets, common practice is to adopt option (a) and only bring in profits from the date of the transfer of trade. One rationale for this is that Schedule 1 paragraph 13(a) of SI 2008/410 only permits profits realised at the balance sheet date to be included in the profit and loss account. For companies, the pre-transfer profits are not profits, and certainly not realised profits, of the company and therefore should not be included in the entity profit and loss account.

9.   On that basis the CCAB sees no reason for the accounting in LLP entity accounts to be any different. Schedule 1 paragraph 13(a) of SI 2008/410 also applies to LLPs under the Regulations, even though the concept of realised and unrealised profits is not relevant for LLPs.

10.   However, paragraph 17 of FRS 6 states that the results of all the combining entities should be brought into the financial statements of the combined entity from the beginning of the financial year in which the combination occurred. This implies that (b) is the more appropriate presentation, assuming that the 'financial year' is the accounting period of the underlying business.

11.   Furthermore, on the basis that Schedule 1 paragraph 13(a) of SI 2008/410 is irrelevant to LLPs and that paragraphs 16 - 19 of FRS 6 should be complied with, then the commonsense approach would be to present the results for the 12 months to 31 December, with 12-month comparatives - i.e. option (b) above. This is one of the common approaches in consolidated accounts in the equivalent group scenario.

Recommended practice

12.   In view of the above considerations, the SORP recommends that LLPs should present alternative (a) as the statutory profit and loss set out in paragraph 5 above. The SORP also suggests disclosure of the 12-month profit and loss (i.e. option (b)) and comparatives as *pro forma* numbers. This approach is in line with the general requirement of FRS 6 to present such transactions as group reconstructions. It clarifies the original intention of the SORP, that merger accounting would be generally expected regardless of the date of transfer of the business. LLPs in their first accounting period may choose to use a three column profit and loss account format, or include the statutory profit and loss account in the form of alternative (a) as set out in paragraph 5 above as a separate statement for legal reasons, but give prominence to the non-statutory version.

APPENDIX 5: LEGAL OPINION

In June 2001, before the issue of FRS 25 and UITF 39, the Consultative Committee of Accountancy Bodies consulted Robin Potts QC on certain matters relating to the profits of a limited liability partnership, and received the following advice.

1. The profits of a limited liability partnership (LLP) are only converted into a debt due to its members when the members have agreed to divide the profits among themselves. The division of profits is a matter of the internal management of the LLP, as it is in the case of a company and a partnership (*Stevens v South Devon Railway Company [1851] 9 Hare 313* and *21 LJ Ch 816* and *Burland v Earle [1902] AC 83*).

2. The Limited Liability Partnership Regulations do not provide for an LLP (unlike a company) to include in its balance sheet the balance on its profit and loss account under the separate heading of 'Profit and loss account'. Accordingly, after the profits have been ascertained and in the absence of any agreement between the members to the contrary, the balance on profit and loss account would need to be included under the balance sheet heading 'Other reserves' pending an agreement to divide the profits among the members. The heading of 'Other reserves' is wide enough to encompass the balance on profit and loss account.

3. It is open to the members of an LLP to agree that the profits of the LLP shall be automatically divided between the members after they have been ascertained. Whether or not an agreement between the members has this effect is a matter of construction. The division of profits must be distinguished from the arrangements for profit sharing. A provision in an agreement between the members which sets out the profit shares of the members does not of itself constitute an agreement for the division of profits. It merely sets out the respective profit shares of the members which will apply to profits after the members have decided to divide them among themselves. Accordingly the default rule which is applied by virtue of Regulation 7 (1) of the Limited Liability Partnerships Regulations 2001 (which provides for the members of an LLP to share equally in the capital and profits of an LLP in the absence of agreement to the contrary) does not constitute a default rule as to the automatic division of profits between the members.

4. If the members agree to the automatic division of profits, then albeit that there is a scintilla of time between the ascertainment of the profits and their division among the members and notwithstanding that the balance sheet is contemporaneous with the profit and loss account, it would be acceptable to credit the profits directly to the current accounts of the members without first including the profits under the balance sheet heading 'Other reserves'.

5. An LLP could only have a revaluation reserve if there was no agreement between the members for the automatic division of profit. This is because the old common law rules regarding distributions would apply to LLPs and under these rules a revaluation reserve was distributable.

6.   Whether a contribution made by the members to an LLP constituted capital or debt was a matter of construction of the intention of the members. For a contribution to constitute capital it must clearly be designated as capital. Otherwise the presumption will be that it constitutes debt.

7.   Where the members make a contribution of capital to an LLP, they can subsequently convert the capital into debt by agreement. What constitutes an agreement between the members and in particular what majority is required to convert capital into debt is a matter of construction of the agreement between the members.

8.   On an insolvency of an LLP amounts credited to capital and reserves in its books immediately prior to the commencement of the winding up would disappear and would not constitute debt which could be proved for in the winding up.

Robin Potts, QC
27 June 2001

Note: The above opinion was given prior to the introduction of FRS 25 and UITF 39. In paragraphs 6 and 7, the opinion deals with the distinction between capital and debt. In FRS 25 and UITF 39 the equivalent accounting distinction is between equity and financial liability. Although the test for distinguishing between the two is somewhat different, the references in the above opinion to the fact that it is the division of profits, automatic or otherwise, that converts profits into debt, are nevertheless consistent with the general principles of the amended SORP and specifically those in paragraph 24.

APPENDIX 6: BASIS FOR CONCLUSIONS

INTRODUCTION

BC1.   This Basis for Conclusions summarises the Consultative Committee of Accountancy Bodies' considerations in reaching its conclusions on revising the Statement of Recommended Practice (SORP) *Accounting by Limited Liability Partnerships* in both 2006 and 2010. The Basis for Conclusions has been updated to reflect the deliberations for both revisions.

BC2.   The first edition of the SORP was published on 29 May 2002 ('SORP 2002'). In accordance with the ASB's Code of Practice, the CCAB reviews the SORP annually for changes in accounting practice and new developments. UK GAAP advanced in a number of areas to the point where the CCAB concluded that a revision of the SORP was desirable in 2005. In September 2005 the CCAB published its proposals in an exposure draft of a revised SORP ('ED SORP 2005'), with a comment deadline of 31 December 2005. The CCAB received 12 letters of comment on the exposure draft.

BC3.   Set out below is an analysis of the main changes proposed in ED SORP 2005, together with the conclusions reached in the light of comments received and in discussions with the ASB's Financial Sector and Other Special Industries Committee (FSOSIC). A revised SORP was published in March 2006 ('SORP 2006'). The subsequent, albeit less wide ranging, changes made to SORP 2006 as a result of the amendment to FRS 25 in 2008 (the puttables amendment) are also referred to in the text below where appropriate and, in particular, in BC15–19. The amended SORP was issued in March 2010 (SORP 2010).

The distinction between debt and equity

BC4.   ED SORP 2005 proposed that members' participation rights in the assets of an LLP should be analysed between those that are, from the LLP's perspective, either a financial liability or equity, in accordance with FRS 25 (IAS 32) *Financial Instruments: Disclosure and Presentation* and UITF Abstract 39 *Members' Shares in Co-operative Entities and Similar Instruments*. The accounting implications of this requirement, as set out in the SORP, are considered in paragraphs BC5 - BC11 below. The majority of respondents to ED SORP 2005 who considered this issue agreed that a revision of the SORP was required and that the proposals were consistent with the standards.

BC5.   SORP 2002 distinguished between debt due to members and 'Members' interests other than debt due to them by the LLP, which constitute equity in the LLP'. 'Members' capital' is a subset of 'Members' other interests', comprising 'amounts subscribed or otherwise contributed by members for longer-term retention in the business'. The term 'Members' capital' is used in the relevant legislation. This distinction was considered no longer appropriate in the light of FRS 25 and UITF 39, but applying these standards to LLPs is not straightforward. The constitutions and capital structures of LLPs can vary significantly. Amounts subscribed or contributed by members as 'capital' of an LLP may be withdrawn or converted to debt by agreement between the

334

members. Accordingly, whether or not an instrument is debt or equity will depend entirely on the specific terms of the members' agreement.

BC6. The basis for the accounting required in the SORP is that the members' agreement, in dealing with the financial arrangements between an LLP and its members (for example, in respect of amounts subscribed or otherwise contributed and remuneration (discussed in paragraphs BC20 et seq. below)), will give rise to rights against the LLP. Such members' rights against the LLP are referred to for the purpose of this analysis as 'participation rights'. Participation rights may meet the definition in FRS 25 of a financial instrument: that is, 'a contract that gives rise to a financial asset of one entity and a financial liability or equity instrument of another entity'. Participation rights that are financial instruments will be within the scope of FRS 25 and, by extension, UITF 39.

BC7. Under FRS 25 and UITF 39, prior to any consideration of the amendment made to FRS 25 in August 2008 dealing with puttable instruments ('the puttables amendment'), members' shares would be equity only 'if the entity has an unconditional right to refuse redemption of the members' shares' (paragraph 7 of UITF 39). The implication of this for LLPs is that, subject to consideration of the impact of the puttables amendment, members' interests will always be debts of the LLP unless the LLP has an unconditional right to refuse to pay the related amount. (There are also implications for the profit and loss account, including remuneration and profit shares, discussed in paragraphs BC20 et seq. below.) There may be instances, therefore, where members will have no interests classified as equity in the LLP.

BC8. Following the above analysis, the SORP requires members' participation rights in the assets of an LLP to be analysed between those that are, from the LLP's perspective, either a financial liability or equity, in accordance with FRS 25 and UITF 39. For the purpose of this analysis, the SORP requires participation rights in respect of amounts subscribed or otherwise contributed and remuneration (which may include salary, interest, bonus, risk premium and allocated share of profits) to be analysed separately, except where the remuneration is clearly identifiable as a return on amounts subscribed or otherwise contributed - for example, non-discretionary interest payments (see paragraph 39 of the SORP). As set out in the SORP, this means that, for example, a profit share payable at the discretion of the LLP would be accounted for as an equity appropriation even if the member's capital is treated as a liability because the LLP cannot refuse repayment of that capital (and the tests for equity treatment in the puttables amendment are not met). This reflects the reality that in many cases members' remuneration is based on participation in the activity of the business rather than providing a return on the capital invested (see paragraph BC23 below). Unless the tests for equity treatment in the puttables amendment are met, a member's participation rights will result in a liability of the LLP, except to the extent that the right to any payment or repayment is discretionary on the part of the LLP. This will depend on the construction of the members' agreement and, in respect of profits earned, the policy and mechanism for the LLP to divide profits.

BC9. ED SORP 2005 suggested *pro forma* balance sheets for use by LLPs, based on examples in FRS 25. This format was intended to allow LLPs to designate balances with members correctly as debt or equity, but also encourages presentation in a manner that provides useful information regarding the members' net interests in the LLP at the balance sheet date. Respondents to ED SORP 2005 welcomed this presentation, which was retained in SORP 2006.

BC10. The classification of capital and other members' interests in an LLP is not straightforward and will differ from one LLP to another. The CCAB believes it is likely, however, that many 'traditional' LLPs will need to classify capital as a liability. This issue has been complicated further following the amendment to FRS 25 in August 2008 (see BC15 to BC19 below).

BC11. Applying the principles of FRS 25 and UITF 39, a critical issue is whether or not the LLP retains discretion to withhold some or all of the profits to members, irrespective of whether it intends to, and invariably does, allocate all the profits to members. The CCAB accepts that any amounts that the LLP has no discretion to withhold should be classified as liabilities, unless the tests for equity treatment in the puttables amendment are met. It is possible, therefore, that undistributed profits may be shown as liabilities in an LLP balance sheet, where the members' agreement provides for profits to be automatically divided.

BC12. Although some respondents to ED SORP 2005 expressed concern at the outcomes set out in paragraphs BC10 and BC11, the CCAB concluded that they followed inevitably from applying FRS 25 and UITF 39 to LLPs.

BC13. There was some concern that the distinction drawn in ED SORP 2005 between debt and equity is spurious, because members of the LLP control the LLP and can therefore control whether or not the LLP has discretion to make payments to members. According to this view, members' interests would always be equity interests. However, this ignores the fact that, unlike a partnership, an LLP is a legal entity separated from its members by a 'corporate veil'. It is therefore correct to impute discretion to the LLP, even though this can be countermanded by the members.

BC14. Some respondents to ED SORP 2005 felt that the SORP should deal with FRS 26 *Financial Instruments: Measurement.* Given that FRS 26 is not mandatory in many cases and that the standard itself contains a significant amount of implementation guidance, the CCAB concluded that the SORP should not deal with this standard in any detail. However, paragraphs 4 and 5 have been included to provide guidance on which accounting standard is relevant when considering how to measure the type of financial liabilities, provisions and other financial instruments dealt with in the SORP.

BC15. One of the more difficult aspects of applying UK GAAP to LLPs is accounting for the interests of members in the profit or loss of the LLP and of the members' interests in the assets and liabilities of the entity. For the purposes of the guidance provided by the SORP, these interests are described as 'participation rights'. The analysis of members' interests in the assets and liabilities of a LLP needs to be reassessed as a result of the revisions to FRS 25 effective for accounting periods commencing on or after 1 January 2010. The amendment was made following a similar amendment to the equivalent International Financial Reporting Standard which arose following comments that certain types of entity may, under the previous version, have no equity shown in their balance sheet. The result of applying the amendment to LLPs may mean that certain members' interests which would otherwise have been classified as liabilities will now be classified as equity, particularly in situations where members do not provide services to the LLP. This may affect LLPs which would otherwise not have any equity interests in their balance sheets and may also result in other LLPs showing a greater level of equity than would otherwise have been the case. However, the criteria for reclassification are detailed and complex. In practice, the CCAB concluded that it would be likely that many LLPs will not be affected by the amendment.

BC16. The exposure draft of a revised SORP published on 29 July 2009 ('ED SORP 2009') contained further guidance on the application of the amended FRS 25 in the context of classification of members' interests as debt or equity, together with a flowchart and examples to illustrate some, but not all, possible scenarios.

BC17. The number of responses to ED SORP 2009 was small. A theme of some of the responses was that the guidance in the SORP was highly technical, and was for some considered difficult to interpret and use in a practical sense. The CCAB has a great deal of sympathy with this view, but was ultimately constrained by the highly technical and complex underlying amendment to FRS 25 which is itself not simple to understand or apply in practice. However, the role of the SORP is to apply that standard to UK LLPs and a degree of technical analysis is inevitable. The two most substantive responses focused on the same issue: a potential inconsistency between the principles in the SORP on members' participation rights, in particular paragraph 34, and the approach to analysing the members' interests in an LLP as financial instruments.

BC18. A member of an LLP can interact with the LLP in a number of capacities, and throughout the development of the SORP there has been a consistent principle that those different capacities (for example, service provider, investor, lender) should, where appropriate, be viewed separately and the accounting for any resulting transactions should follow the capacity in which the member acts. Respondents to ED SORP 2009 felt that some of the material on puttable financial instruments, particularly in some of the examples in Appendix 2, contradicted this principle and had sought to treat, for example, a members' agreement as a single financial instrument. The CCAB debated these responses and agreed that this underlying principle should still apply, i.e. participation rights in respect of amounts subscribed or otherwise contributed should be analysed separately from participation rights in respect of remuneration except where the remuneration, or part thereof, is clearly identifiable as a return on amounts subscribed or otherwise contributed.

BC19. The final SORP published on 31 March 2010 ('SORP 2010') therefore makes it much clearer that the interests of a member in an LLP are likely in many cases to be viewed as more than one 'instrument'. This is particularly likely in, for example, professional services LLPs where members are not simply investors or funders of the business, but also work in the business and provide services. Accordingly, SORP 2010 requires the remuneration to members in respect of services provided to be viewed separately from the remuneration in respect of capital or funding provided except where the remuneration, or part thereof, is clearly identifiable as a return on amounts subscribed or otherwise contributed. This approach is in many respects simpler and avoids a number of potentially complex accounting issues such as compound instrument accounting for amounts subscribed. It will in many cases (particularly for professional services LLPs) lead to there being no change in the designation of capital from liability to equity as a result of the puttables amendment. Given that the main change from ED SORP 2009 is to align more closely the examples and flowcharts with the principles set out in the body of the ED and that the expected result of SORP 2010 would be less change in some cases than previously expected, the Steering Group concluded it was not necessary to submit the revised SORP to a further exposure period.

Profit and loss account implications

BC20. ED SORP 2005 recommended that the treatment of the members' remuneration element in the profit and loss account should be based on the same principles as are used for determining debt and equity in the balance sheet. This means that participation rights in respect of amounts subscribed or otherwise contributed should be analysed separately from participation rights in respect of remuneration except where the remuneration is clearly identifiable as a return on amounts subscribed or otherwise contributed. Members' remuneration is 'any outflow of benefits to a member', and may include or comprise, inter alia, salary, interest, bonus, risk premium and allocated share of profits. This principle set out in ED SORP 2005 would mean that remuneration comprising a profit share payable at the discretion of the LLP should be accounted for as an equity appropriation even if the member's capital is treated as a liability. Respondents to ED SORP 2005 broadly agreed with this approach as a practical solution to a difficult problem, in line with the analysis set out below.

BC21. Some respondents to ED SORP 2005 felt there should be a closer link between the balance sheet classification of the capital instrument (debt or equity) and the way in which members' remuneration is dealt with in the profit and loss account. This is akin in the corporate situation to the linkage of a debt instrument with interest in the profit and loss account and an equity instrument with dividend payments. In addition some respondents to ED SORP 2005 felt that members' participation rights had certain features of compound instruments.

BC22. However, it is extremely difficult to apply to an LLP the provisions in FRS 25 on compound financial instruments (paragraphs 28 - 32) and 'interests, dividends, losses and gains' (paragraphs 35 - 36). The relationship between capital introduced and remuneration in an LLP is very different to that in a company, where there would normally be a clearly identifiable relationship between return on the investment and the investment itself. At one extreme, for example, there may be LLPs that have no members' capital, being entirely funded from external sources, in which case the profit and loss account treatment of remuneration must be assessed in isolation from any balance sheet amount.

BC23. In this respect, paragraph 36 of FRS 25 states that the classification of a financial instrument as a financial liability or an equity instrument determines whether interest, dividends, losses and gains relating to that instrument are recognised as income or expense in profit or loss. However, while it may be possible to consider that the remuneration and profit shares of members amount to 'interest, dividends, losses and gains' as a result of the amounts invested by members in an LLP, in many or most cases this does not reflect the substance of the arrangements in LLPs. Remuneration and profit shares are often payable to members in return for participation in the business, as well as representing a financial return on amounts invested by members. In many LLPs, the latter will represent a relatively insignificant proportion of the total remuneration.

BC24. Because, in many cases, members' remuneration constitutes a share of profits based on participation in the activity of the business, and given the difficulty of identifying the specific capital to which participation rights might attach, the CCAB considers that to treat all shares of profit in an LLP as some form of return on a financial instrument, even where the share of profit is a financial liability of the LLP once divided, would result in misleading and inappropriate accounting presentation. Accordingly, the CCAB decided to retain the principle that participation rights in respect of amounts subscribed or otherwise contributed should be analysed separately from participation rights in respect of remuneration, except where an element of the remuneration is clearly identifiable as a return of capital (see paragraph 39). As a result of comments received on ED SORP 2009, this principle has continued to be applied subsequently to the puttables amendment to FRS 25.

BC25. With regard to compound instrument accounting, while members' participation rights might include both equity and liability elements, and thus be thought of as 'compound instruments' under FRS 25, it will often be impossible to ascribe these rights to identifiable elements of members' capital, which itself will vary over time.

BC26. A minority of respondents to ED SORP 2005 expressed concern at the line taken in the ED with regard to automatic division of profits. The view was expressed that automatic division is, in effect, dependent on the agreement of the members, and so it is not correct to charge it as an expense. However, the CCAB continues to believe that an agreement for automatic division of profits does have the substance of establishing profits of the LLP as debts due to the members as they accrue. Although the members could agree among themselves to terminate the agreement, the accounting must be on the basis of the agreement that is in fact in force at the time which would be binding on the parties unless and until terminated or varied.

BC27. The position whereby a LLP had no agreement for the automatic division of profits, but had divided some of the profits during the accounting year was considered. Some views had been expressed that since at the time the accounts were drawn up the LLP had already divided the profit, it was therefore no longer discretionary and should be accounted for in the same way as an automatic division of profit. The CCAB is of the view that this is not the correct position. The position is no different in principle from that of a limited company declaring an interim dividend on ordinary shares. Accordingly, the CCAB considers that the discretionary division of profit during the year that is not clearly identifiable as a return on capital should be accounted for as an appropriation of profit in the year in which it occurs - in line with the treatment of an interim dividend paid by the company on its ordinary shares.

BC28. Appendix 1 to the SORP sets out example balance sheets and profit and loss accounts for an LLP, showing the changes that will result from applying the principles in the SORP. Appendix 2 provides illustrations of how the principles set out in the SORP would be applied to some simple LLP membership arrangements. These examples have been updated to reflect FRS 25 and the subsequent puttables amendment.

BC29. Some respondents to ED SORP 2005 suggested that FRS 20 *Share-based Payment* is applicable to members' remuneration because any share of profits a member receives is at least in part consideration for services rendered to the LLP. While the SORP cannot cover all remuneration arrangements, and it may be that in some circumstances FRS 20 is relevant, the CCAB concluded that typically members' remuneration arrangements would be outside the scope of FRS 20. The standard defines a share-based payment as 'a transaction in which the entity receives goods or services as consideration for equity instruments of the entity (including shares or share options), or acquires goods or services by incurring liabilities to the supplier of those goods or services for amounts that are based on the price of an entity's shares or other equity instruments of the entity'. The CCAB believes that what the member receives in exchange for any services given, i.e. typically a share of one year's profits, does not meet the definition of an equity instrument, which is 'a contract that evidences a residual interest in the assets of an entity after deducting all of its liabilities'. In this respect, an equity instrument is representative of the total value of the entity (for example, the price of an equity share in a corporate entity is representative of both the value of the existing assets and also of future cash flows). Accordingly, the CCAB believes that a share of one year's profits does not meet the definition of an equity instrument because it reflects only one year's earnings rather than a share in the overall value of the entity.

Post-retirement payments to members ('Annuities')

BC30. SORP 2002 required the present value of the best estimate of the expected liability for or in respect of payment to a former member to be provided in the accounts at the date of the member's retirement, in accordance with FRS 12 *Provisions, Contingent Liabilities and Contingent Assets*. (Such post-retirement payments are often described as 'annuities'.)

BC31. The introduction of FRS 25 has led to developments in the thinking behind the treatment of annuities by LLPs. The previous treatment, of recognising a liability only on the retirement of the member, was consistent with the principle of not reflecting transactions with members in the profit and loss account (except in the limited instance of salaried remuneration). However, FRS 25 has brought members' remuneration within the scope of the profit and loss account, and it would be inconsistent to treat annuities differently. Furthermore, an annuity to which a member has a contractual entitlement is a contractual obligation to deliver cash or another financial asset to another entity, and so meets the definition of a financial liability under FRS 25, although if it contains a life-contingent element it is scoped out of FRS 25 and would fall to be accounted for under FRS 12, as would annuities in respect of which the LLP only has a constructive obligation. Whichever is the relevant standard, the obligation in respect of the annuity should be accounted for at the time the member becomes entitled to a future payment that the LLP has no discretion to withhold (in line with the distinction between discretionary and non-discretionary participation rights, discussed in paragraphs BC7 et seq. above). As regards an unconditional annuity right, the granting thereof is the obligating event and it will normally be correct to recognise a liability at the time of such grant. As regards a conditional annuity obligation (for example, conditional on continuing future service), this should be accrued as the rights to that annuity accrue (whereas SORP 2002 required the liability to be crystallised at the time of the member's retirement).

BC32. As noted in the above paragraph, there may be cases in which the LLP considers that the right to an annuity meets the definition of a financial instrument under FRS 25. Note that a life-contingent annuity is likely to be an insurance contract and outside the scope of FRS 25 (see paragraph 4(d) of FRS 25 and Appendix C paragraph 24(d) of FRS 26. In this respect, the SORP deals in paragraphs 76 to 81 with the relationship and boundaries between FRS 12 and FRS 25. These explain that the technical boundary is one of scoping but point out that, whether in FRS 12 or 25, where the liability is of uncertain timing or amount, the measurement principles are likely to be the same.

BC33. FRS 17 explicitly defines retirement benefits as 'consideration given by an employer in exchange for services rendered by employees ...'. It is thus designed to deal with employer-employee relationships and how the costs of a pension liability for a defined benefit scheme should be reflected in an entity's accounts. However, the relationship between an LLP and a member is not generally an employer-employee relationship, and it therefore requires a distinct accounting treatment. Furthermore, the amount of post-retirement annuity payable is not likely to be based on a proportion of final 'salary' that is 'earned' over time, but, in the case of profit-dependent annuities at least, is normally measured in relation to events and profits arising after the retirement date. For these reasons, the CCAB believes that these types of arrangement of post-retirement payments paid by LLPs to former members fall outside the scope of FRS 17.

BC34. However, measurement of the liability raises a number of issues. Although the CCAB is of the view that FRS 17 is not the governing standard, where, because of their nature and/or complexity, the arrangements are such that it is appropriate to apply the guidance in FRS 17, then that guidance should be applied in arriving at the measurement of the liability. In order to arrive at the best estimate of the expected liability (i.e. just for measurement purposes), the

CCAB believes that it will often be necessary to adopt actuarial principles and techniques.

BC35. However, where a member of an LLP is also an employee and receives retirement benefits under his or her employment contract, then FRS 17 will be applied in full, as reflected in the SORP.

Merger accounting on initial transition of an existing undertaking

BC36. Appendix 4 to the SORP explains the reasoning behind the treatment the SORP adopts for applying FRS 6 *Acquisitions and Mergers* in certain special circumstances that arise when merger accounting is adopted on initial transition of an existing undertaking to a single-entity LLP formed for the purpose. Commentators on ED SORP 2005 generally welcomed this approach.

Revenue recognition

BC37. Paragraph 65A of ED SORP 2005, which stated that revenue on service contracts should be recognised in accordance with UITF Abstract 40 *Revenue recognition and service contracts*, was deleted, on the ground that it was not specific to LLPs.

Losses

BC38. Certain commentators on ED SORP 2005 requested guidance on the accounting treatment of losses. This was felt to be impracticable, as the treatment will vary depending on the precise provisions of the members' agreement.

The revised Statement of Recommended Practice (SORP) on accounting by Limited Liability Partnerships (LLP) has been reproduced by kind permission of the Consultative Committee for Accounting Bodies. For further information please visit www.ccab.org.uk

Precedents

Members' agreement for use on conversion from a partnership[1]

THIS AGREEMENT is made the ... day of ...

BETWEEN

    (1) Those persons whose names and addresses are set out in Schedule 1 ('Initial Members'); and

    (2) [   ] LLP [(Registered Number: [   ])] whose registered office is [at] [intended to be at] [   ] ('LLP').

WHEREBY IT IS AGREED as follows:

1 Definitions and interpretation

In this Agreement:

1.1 The following expressions have the following meanings:

2001 Regulations	the Limited Liability Partnership Regulations 2001 (SI 2001/1090);
Accountants	the Initial Accountants or such other accountants as may from time to time be appointed in accordance with the provisions of this Agreement;
Accounts Date[2]	the *(date)* in each year or such other date as may be determined in accordance with the provisions hereof as the date upon which an Accounting Period is to end;
Accounting Period	a year or other period ending on an Accounts Date being the period for which the accounts of the LLP shall be made up;

Accounting Standards	all standards from time to time accepted by the accountancy profession as relevant to the preparation of the accounts of a limited liability partnership including in particular, but without limitation, the Generally Accepted Accounting Principles, all Statements of Standard Accounting Practice, all Financial Reporting Standards and all Statements of Recommended Practice;[3]
Act	the Limited Liability Partnerships Act 2000;
Allocated Profits and Losses	profits and losses of the LLP that have been allocated to the Members in accordance with this Agreement and 'Allocated Profits' and 'Allocated Losses' shall be construed accordingly;
Auditor	[the Initial Accountants] [name] or such other auditors as may be appointed in accordance with this Agreement;
Bank	the Initial Bank or such other bank as may from time to time be appointed as the lead bank of the LLP in accordance with this Agreement;
Business	the profession and practice of *(insert nature of profession)* to be carried on by the LLP in succession to the Former Practice;
Capital Account	in relation to a Member, the capital account which shall be opened and maintained in accordance with this Agreement;
Cessation Date	in respect of any Member the date of the death, retirement, deemed retirement or expulsion of that Member;
Commencement Date[4]	(insert date);
Companies Act	the Companies Act 2006 as applied to limited liability partnerships;
Contribution	any money paid into the accounts of the LLP by a Member as capital, less any liabilities attaching to such money which shall be assumed by the LLP in substitution for him;[5]
Designated Members[6]	[all of the Members *(or)* such of the Members as shall from time to time be designated in accordance with the provisions of this Agreement];
Drawings	sums drawn by any Member on account of any anticipated profits of the LLP[7] and any other sums paid or the monetary equivalent of any assets applied for the personal benefit of any Member by the LLP (other than for any such expenses as shall be provided for in this Agreement);

Family Leave	leave to be taken by Members in the event of family emergencies in accordance with clause 16 and being analogous to that afforded to employees;
Former Practice	the practice known as *(insert name)* carried on by the Initial Members;[8]
Holiday Leave	leave to be taken by Members in accordance with clause 14;
Holiday Weeks	*(insert number of weeks' holiday)* per year;
Initial Accountants[9]	*(insert name and address of Initial Accountants);*
Initial Bank	*(insert name and address of Initial Bank);*
Initial Members	all those persons whose names and addresses are set out in Schedule 1;
Initial Property	*(insert address)* which is to be occupied by the LLP for the purposes of the Business;[10]
Intellectual Property	means patents, rights to inventions, copyright and related rights, including, but not limited to, moral rights and performing rights, trade marks and services marks, logos, trade names and domain names, rights in get-up, goodwill and the right to sue for passing off and unfair competition, rights in designs, rights in computer software, database rights, utility models, rights to preserve the confidentiality of information (including know-how and trade secrets) and any other intellectual property rights, in each case whether registered or unregistered, including all applications for (and rights to apply for and be granted), renewals or extensions of, and rights to claim priority from, such rights and all similar or equivalent rights or forms of protection which subsist or will subsist, now or in the future, in any part of the world;
Interest Rate	a rate [of ...% [above] *(or)* [equivalent to] the base rate for the time being of the Bank;
Know-how	means any non-patented information, resulting from experience and testing, which is secret, substantial and identified. For this purpose, 'secret' means that the information is not generally known or easily accessible, 'substantial' means that the information is significant and useful for the production of goods and/or services and 'identified' means that the information is described in a sufficiently comprehensive manner so as to make it possible to verify that it fulfils the criteria of secrecy and substantiality;

Leave	any or all of Family Leave, Holiday Leave, Maternity Leave, Parental Leave or Paternity Leave;
Limit of Authority[11]	(insert amount);
Loan	a loan made by any Member to the LLP in accordance with the provisions of this Agreement;
Maternity Leave	leave to be taken by Members in accordance with clause 15;
Members	the Initial Members and/or such other or additional persons as may from time to time be admitted as a member of the LLP in accordance with the provisions of this Agreement in each case until he becomes an Outgoing Member;
Members' Accounts[12]	the accounts of Members with the LLP to be kept in accordance with clause 9;
Minimum Insurance Sum[13]	the sum of £...;
Name	*(insert name)* LLP or such other name as shall from time to time be registered by the LLP at Companies House as its name;
Notice Period[14]	a period of *(insert number of months)*;
Outgoing Member	as defined at clause 25.1;
Parental Leave	leave to be taken by Members during the first 5 years of their children's lives in accordance with clause 16 and being analogous to that afforded to employees;
Paternity Leave	leave to be taken by Members at the time of the birth or adoption of any child in accordance with clause 16 and being analogous to that afforded to employees;
Payment Date	unless otherwise agreed, the last day in each month or if the same shall not be a Working Day then the Working Day immediately preceding the same;
Property	the Initial Property and/or such additional or replacement property or properties as may from time to time be owned or occupied by the LLP for the purpose of the Business;
Quorum	[two thirds of the Members or Designated Members (as the case may be)[15]];
Radius	a radius of *(insert distance)* from any Property;[16]

Registered Office[17]	the address as shall from time to time be registered by the LLP at Companies House as its registered office;
Relevant Institution[18]	*(insert name of appropriate body)*;
Retirement Age[19]	the age of *(insert age)*;
Transfer Agreement	the agreement for the transfer of the Business [of even date with this Agreement] and made between the Initial Members and the LLP setting out the terms on which it was agreed that [certain of] the assets and liabilities of the Former Practice should be transferred to the LLP;
Unallocated Profits and Losses	profits and losses of the LLP which are not Allocated Profits and Losses;
Working Day	any day from Monday to Friday inclusive save for any such day which is a bank or statutory holiday [and any day between Christmas Day and New Year's Day when the office is not open for business];

1.3 Reference to the death of a Member shall in the case of a Member being a body corporate include reference to the winding up, dissolution, or striking of the register of that Member unless the context otherwise requires.

1.4 Reference to any statute or statutory provision includes a reference to that statute or provision as from time to time amended, extended, re-enacted or consolidated and to all statutory instruments or orders made under it.

1.5 Words denoting only the singular number include the plural and vice versa.

1.6 Words denoting any gender include all genders and words denoting persons include firms and corporations and vice versa.

1.7 Unless the context otherwise requires reference to any clause, paragraph or schedule is to a clause, paragraph or schedule (as the case may be) of or to this Agreement.

1.8 The headings in this document are inserted for convenience only and shall not affect the construction or interpretation of this Agreement.

1.9 Any reference to a percentage or fraction of the Members shall if appropriate be rounded up to the nearest whole number.

1.10 A person includes any person, individual, company, firm, corporation, government, state or agency of a state or any undertaking or organisation (whether or not having separate legal personality and irrespective of the jurisdiction in or under the law of which it was incorporated or exists).

1.11 Unless the context provides otherwise, any reference to profits or losses of the LLP includes a reference to profits and losses of a capital nature.

2 Incorporation, commencement and duration

2.1 The certificate of registration of the LLP issued under the Act shall be kept at the Registered Office.

2.2 The provisions of this Agreement shall [take effect *(or)* be deemed to have taken effect] on the Commencement Date.

2.3 The LLP shall carry on the Business and/or carry on such other or additional trade, profession or business as the Members shall from time to time determine.

2.4 The LLP shall subsist until wound up in accordance with the provisions of the Act.

2.5 [From and including the Commencement Date none of the default provisions set out in Regulations 7 and 8 of the 2001 Regulations (or any other such provision as is mentioned in section 5(1)(b) of the Act) shall apply to the LLP.] [20]

3 Admission of Members

3.1 A person may be admitted as a new Member of the LLP in accordance with a resolution of the Members pursuant to clause 17.8 of this Agreement only if the provisions of clause 3.2 have been complied with.

3.2 A memorandum of any such appointment as is referred to in clause 3.1 shall be drawn up and signed by not less than 2 Members on behalf of the LLP and by the new Member who by his signature shall be deemed to have agreed to incorporate into the terms of his membership the provisions of this Agreement and to become a party to this Agreement.

3.3 Any such memorandum as is referred to at clause 3.2 shall also contain details of:

3.3.1 the remuneration and profit provisions applicable to that Member;

3.3.2 the amount of the Contribution to be made by the Member; and

3.3.3 if applicable, the amount of any Loan to be made by the Member.

4 Name and registered office

4.1 The Members may from time to time determine upon a change in the Name and/or the Registered Office.

4.2 Upon any change in the Name and/or the Registered Office it shall be the responsibility of the Designated Members to notify Companies House of any such change in accordance with the Act.

5 Property and place of business

5.1 The Business shall be carried on by the LLP from the Property.

5.2 In the event that any property from time to time comprised within the Property or any term of years in respect thereof shall be vested in any one or more of the Members (or any nominees for them), then those Members (or nominees):

5.2.1 shall be deemed to hold such Property in trust for the LLP (unless there shall be specific written agreement to the contrary[21]) and the LLP shall indemnify them and their respective estates and effects against all liability in respect of that Property; and

5.2.2 shall upon service upon them of any notice requesting them to do so and on receipt of any necessary mortgagee's and/or landlord's consents permitting them to do so, convey, transfer or assign the same to the LLP at the cost of the LLP and upon the LLP indemnifying them and their respective estates and effects against all future liability in respect of that Property after the date of conveyance, transfer or assignment, provided that for the purposes of this clause liability shall include in particular, but without limitation, all liability in respect of any outgoings payable in respect of the relevant Property, any restrictive covenants relating to it, any rent falling due in respect of it, and the performance and observance of any lessee's covenants relating to it.

5.3 Subject to the above, the Property, the Intellectual Property and all computers and ancillary equipment, office equipment, furniture, books, stationery and other property and equipment in or about the Property and used for the purposes of the Business shall be the property of the LLP.

6 Accounts

6.1 The LLP shall ensure that proper books of account as to the affairs of the LLP (which shall for the avoidance of doubt be deemed to include any computerised accounting system(s) from time to time used by the LLP) shall be kept properly posted.

6.2 Such books of account (including the data held on any such computerised system as is referred to in clause 6.1) shall be:

6.2.1 kept at the Registered Office or at such other place as the Members may from time to time determine; and

6.2.2 open to inspection by the Members.

6.3 Where the LLP is required to have its accounts audited in accordance with the provision of the Companies Act, the Designated Members and the Members (as the case may be) shall have such rights as to the appointment and removal and the fixing of the remuneration of the Auditor as shall be set out in the Companies Act.

6.5 The Members may from time to time determine to amend the Accounts Date.

6.6 A profit and loss account shall be taken in every year on the Accounts Date and a balance sheet [taking no account of goodwill other than purchased goodwill[22]] shall be prepared in accordance with the then current Accounting Standards and in such format and giving such information, notes and disclosure of the interests of the Members in the LLP as may be required by the Companies Act.

6.7 The LLP accounts prepared in accordance with clause 6.6 shall be:

6.7.1 audited by the Auditors in accordance with the Companies Act (unless the LLP is exempt by that Act from the requirement for its accounts to be audited);

6.7.2 approved by the Members in accordance with the Companies Act;[23]

6.7.3 binding on all Members after approval save that any Member may request the rectification of any manifest error discovered in any such accounts within 3 months of receipt of the same;

6.7.4 distributed to all Members (and to the holders of any debentures which may have been issued by the LLP) as required by the Companies Act; and

6.7.5 delivered, together with the auditor's report (where applicable), to the registrar of limited liability partnerships.

7 Banking arrangements

7.1 The Bank shall be the Initial Bank and/or such other bank as the LLP may from time to time determine.

7.2 All money, cheques and drafts received by or on behalf of the LLP shall be paid promptly into the bank account of the LLP and all securities for money shall be promptly deposited in the name of the LLP with the Bank.

[7.3 The LLP shall open a separate client account or accounts with the Bank and:

7.3.1 all money, cheques and drafts received by or on behalf of clients or third parties shall be paid promptly into such client account(s) and all securities for money shall be promptly deposited in the name of the clients or third parties with the Bank; and

7.3.2 any such account or accounts shall at all times be operated by the LLP strictly in accordance with any rules or regulations of any professional or regulatory body which may exercise relevant jurisdiction over the LLP and/or any Members.[24]]

7.4 All cheques drawn on or instructions for the electronic transfer of money from any such account as is mentioned in this clause 7 shall be in the Name and may be drawn or given by any [two] Member[s] or by anyone else approved from time to time by the LLP and included in any mandate given to the Bank (subject to any limitations expressed in that mandate).[25]

8 Capital

8.1 Each of the Initial Members shall at the Commencement Date [make *(or)* be deemed to have made] a Contribution equal to the amount of capital (if any) shown to his credit in the balance sheet prepared for the Former Practice in respect of the last day before the Commencement Date.[26]

8.2 For the avoidance of doubt the LLP shall have no power to require any Member to make a Contribution after the date hereof save:

8.2.1 with the agreement of the Member in question; or

8.2.2 where the Members determine in accordance with clause 17.8 that an additional Contribution is required from each Member to meet the requirements of the LLP. In which case, any such requirements shall be on the basis that the Members contribute such additional Contribution in the same proportions in which they are entitled to share [capital] [residual] profits at the time of the determination, such additional Contribution to be paid to the LLP within [3] months of the date of which such determination is made.

8.3 [No interest shall be paid or payable by the LLP upon any Contribution, or upon any amount whether of income or capital profits allocated to any Member but not yet distributed to it.]

or

[The LLP shall pay interest on a Member's Contribution at the Interest Rate.]

8.4 No Member may withdraw any amount standing to the credit of his Capital Account from time to time without the unanimous consent of the other Members.

8.5 An individual Capital Account will be maintained for each Member and all amounts of capital which have been contributed or withdrawn by a Member will be credited or debited (as the case may be) to that Member's Capital.

8.6 The capital profits of the LLP shall belong to the Members in the proportions [to which they are at that time entitled to the [residual] profits of the LLP in accordance with clause 11.8 *(or)* which the amounts of their respective Contributions bore to each other at the time of such payment].[27]

9 Members' Accounts[28]

9.1 Accounts shall be kept in respect of each of the Members showing the amounts of:

9.1.1 profit or loss to be credited or debited to them in accordance with clause 11; and

9.1.2 any Drawings debited to them.

9.2 Upon the approval or deemed approval of the LLP accounts in respect of any Accounting Period:

9.2.1 any credit balance of any Member's Account for that Accounting Period shall be payable to the appropriate Member by the LLP unless otherwise determined by the Members; or

9.2.2 any debit balance of any Member's Account for that Accounting Period shall be refunded immediately together with interest at the Interest Rate upon the amount of the deficit from the date of such approval to the date of repayment, unless otherwise determined by the Members.

10 Drawings[29]

10.1 On the Payment Date in each month there shall be paid to or for the benefit of each of the Members such sums in respect of Drawings as the Members may from time to time determine.[30]

10.2 No Drawings shall, however, be taken if the Members shall at any time determine that there is insufficient money in the bank accounts of the LLP available for that purpose or there are insufficient banking facilities available for that purpose taking into account such sums required for the expenses of the LLP as are known or can reasonably be foreseen at the relevant time.

10.3 No Member shall be entitled to any Drawings at any time when his right to share in the profits of the LLP shall have been suspended in accordance with clause 11.11.

11   Profits and losses[31]

11.1   References to sums being credited or debited to Members in this clause or to profits and losses being allocated to Members shall be construed in accordance with the following provisions:

11.1.1   all sums to be credited to a Member shall be credited to his Member's Account;

11.1.2   all sums to be debited against a Member shall be debited against his Member's Account;

11.1.3   if any sums shall fall to be debited against a Member at any time when his Member's Account shall have been exhausted, then, for the avoidance of doubt:

11.1.3.1   the LLP shall have the power (if the Members so resolve) to transfer monies from that Member's Capital Account in or towards satisfaction of the debit balance on that Member's Account; and

11.1.3.2   the Member may be required to repay to the LLP the whole of the debit balance on his Member's Account (or, if appropriate, such part thereof as has not been satisfied by any transfer effected in accordance with clause 11.1.3.1) at such time and in such manner as the Members may require.[32]

11.2   The Members may at any time determine in accordance with clause 17.8 to allocate at such time as they may specify all or any part of any profits earned by the LLP in respect of any Accounting Period.[33]

11.3   All sums shown in the accounts of the LLP as profits in respect of any Accounting Period shall (save in so far as they may already have been credited or debited in accordance with clause 11.2 and also subject to clause 11.4) be [reviewed immediately before the approval of the accounts for that Accounting Period in accordance with clause 6.7 and the Members shall at that time determine in accordance with clause 17.8 whether to allocate by way of division amongst the Members all or any of those profits][automatically allocated to the Members upon approval of the accounts for that Accounting Period in accordance with clause 6.7][34]

11.4   In the event that any profits which are of a capital nature shall have been credited to the Members' Accounts in any Accounting Period then the Members may determine in accordance with clause 17.8 that those sums shall:

11.4.1   be distributed as profits payable under clause 11.3; or

11.4.2   be deemed to augment the appropriate Members' Capital Account,

but in default of any such determination they shall remain in the Members' Accounts.

11.5   Losses shall be borne by the LLP but, subject to clause 11.6 below, the Members may resolve in accordance with clause 17.8 whether to allocate some or all of such losses to the Members, or require Members to increase their Contributions to meet that deficiency and any such resolutions shall bind the Members.

11.6   For the avoidance of doubt the Members shall before resolving to allocate any losses of the LLP consider whether it would be more appropriate for such losses to be the subject of a reserve provision in the LLP accounts than for them to be allocated at that time or at all.[35]

11.7   In the event that at any time at which the LLP is required to submit a computation of the profits and losses of the LLP for income tax purposes there shall be any Unallocated Profits and Losses then for the purposes of that return those profits and losses shall be deemed to have been divided in accordance with clause 11.8 or in such other proportions as the Members shall unanimously agree.[36]

11.8   The Allocated Profits of the LLP for any Accounting Period shall (unless the Members shall determine otherwise in accordance with clause 17.8) be credited to the Members [equally] (or) [set out method of division] [as follows:

   11.8.1 as a first charge on profits, interest at the Interest Rate (calculated as accruing on a daily basis) on the amount held during the Accounting Period of that Member's Capital Account;[37]

   11.8.2 all residual profits [after payment of all sums due in accordance with clause 11.8.1] shall be distributed between the Members [equally *(or)* [set out method of division]].[38]

[11.9   In the event that there are insufficient Allocated Profits to discharge in full the category of profits set out in clause 11.8.1 then:

   11.9.1 the amount payable in respect of that category shall be payable to such Members as are entitled to that category of profits and the sums payable to each of them shall abate rateably; and

   11.9.2 no sums shall be due in respect of the subsequent category of profits.]

11.10   Any Allocated Losses of the LLP for any Accounting Period shall (unless the Members determine otherwise in accordance with clause 17.8) be debited to each Member in the same proportions as [residual] profits are distributed in accordance with clause 11.8.

11.11   If in any Accounting Period any Member is absent from the Business for any reason other than authorised Leave or illness then (unless the Members shall determine otherwise) that Member shall [after 10 Working Days of such absence][39] cease to be entitled to share in any profits of the LLP for that Accounting Period (the amount in question to be apportioned on a time basis for the relevant Accounting Period) without affecting their liability for the losses of the LLP in accordance with clause 11.5 and the amount of profits equivalent to what would otherwise have been the absent Member's share of profits shall be divided amongst the other Members in the ratios which their entitlements to [residual] profits under clause 11.2 bear to each other.

12 Members' obligations and duties

12.1 Each Member shall at all times devote to the Business [his full time and attention *(or)* such time and attention as may from time to time be agreed between him and the [Designated] Members as being the number of hours per week which is to be worked as a minimum in respect of any Accounting Period (provided that in default of agreement the number of such hours per week shall be deemed to be 35)][40] (and in the event of any breach of this clause the Member shall account to the LLP for any profit derived by him from any activity giving rise to such breach) save that no such commitment shall apply to any Member during any period of authorised Leave or incapacity due to illness, injury or other substantial cause.

12.2 No Member shall without the consent of the Members engage in any business other than the Business or accept any office or appointment including in particular, but without limitation, any appointment as a member of any governmental or public authority or any agency of any such body or a director of a limited company or a member of a limited liability partnership or a partner in a partnership or a limited partnership or a trustee of a trust and in the event of any breach of this clause 12.2, the Member shall account to the LLP for any profit derived by him from the business, office or appointment in question [provided however that such consent shall be deemed to have been given to *(insert or schedule permitted offices for each Member)*].[41]

12.3 No Member shall without the consent of the Members derive any benefit from the use of the Name or the Property or the business connection of the LLP (and in the event of any breach of this clause the Member shall account to the LLP for any profit derived by him from the use in question).

12.4 All Members shall:

12.4.1 conduct themselves in a proper and responsible manner and use their best skill and endeavour to promote the Business; and

12.4.2 comply with all statutes, regulations, professional standards and other provisions as may from time to time govern the conduct of the Business or be determined by the LLP as standards to be voluntarily applied by the LLP to the Business or as otherwise set out in this Agreement;

12.4.3 promptly provide to the Designated Members details of any change to his personal circumstances which are required to be notified by the Act to the registrar of limited liability partnerships;[42] and

[12.4.3 *insert here any further specific duties to be imposed on Members ie duty of good faith etc in relation to their dealings with the LLP and, if applicable, with each other*].

[12.5 For the avoidance of doubt:

12.5.1 the Members shall not owe fiduciary duties[43] to each other [or to the LLP] (save for such fiduciary duties to the LLP as are expressed in this Agreement [or are implied by their status as agents]);

[12.5.2 any Member shall be entitled to retain for his own benefit any legacy bequeathed to him by any client or former client of the LLP or the Former Practice[44]].]

13   Limitations on Members' powers as agents

Limitations on the powers of any individual Member to act as an agent of the LLP or otherwise shall apply so that no Member shall without the consent of the Members:

13.1   pledge the credit of the LLP or incur any liability except in the ordinary course of the business of the LLP and for its benefit;

13.2   give any guarantee or undertaking on behalf of the LLP [except in the ordinary course of the business of the LLP and for its benefit];

13.3   procure that the LLP shall enter into any bond or become bail or surety for any person;

13.4   knowingly cause or permit or suffer to be done anything whereby the property of the LLP may be taken in execution or otherwise endangered;

13.5   assign, mortgage or charge his share in the capital or income profits of the LLP or any other interest in the LLP that he may have;

13.6   have any dealings with any person, with whom or which the LLP has previously resolved not to deal;

13.7   draw any cheque on any account of the LLP which is not in accordance with the then current mandate in respect of that account;

13.8   decline to accept appointment as a Designated Member if so required by the Members in accordance with this Agreement;

13.9 divulge to any person any trade secret or other confidential information concerning the business, investments or affairs of the LLP or any of its customers or clients unless such divulgence shall be within his normal or actual delegated authority or unless such information or secret shall already be within the public domain;

13.10 compromise or compound or (except on payment in full) release, defer for more than 30 days, or discharge any debt or connected debts [amounting in the aggregate to more than the Limit of Authority] due to the LLP;

13.11 engage or dismiss any employee of the LLP;[45]

13.12 buy or contract for any goods, services, or property on behalf of the LLP [amounting in the aggregate to more than the Limit of Authority];

13.13 lend any money or give credit on behalf of the LLP [amounting in the aggregate to more than the Limit of Authority];

13.14 borrow any money in the name of and on behalf of the LLP [amounting in the aggregate to more than the Limit of Authority]; [or

13.15 hold or deal in any stocks shares or debentures or other securities of or relating to any company or limited liability partnership which is or has been a client of the LLP or the Former Practice unless he does so in the capacity of a trustee (either alone or jointly with others) in respect of a trust of which he is not a beneficiary.[46]]

14 Holiday leave

14.1 Each Member shall be entitled in each calendar year to such Holiday Leave (in addition to statutory or public holidays) as shall be equal to the number of Holiday Weeks or to such other period as the Members may from time to time determine.[47]

14.2 Each Member shall give notice to the LLP of his intended dates of Holiday Leave and shall be responsible for ensuring that those dates do not conflict with the dates of any form of Leave already notified to the LLP by such other Members or senior employees of the LLP as may be appropriate having regard to the work undertaken by the Member.

[14.3 Not more than 2 weeks' Holiday Leave shall be taken consecutively (ignoring statutory or public holidays) without the consent of the Members.]

15 Maternity leave

15.1 A female Member shall be entitled to such time off for ante-natal care as may be reasonable and to Maternity Leave in accordance with the provisions of this clause.

15.2 [Maternity Leave shall be available for such periods as would be applicable were the Member in question an employee of the LLP with over a year's continuous service with the LLP.] [A Member shall be entitled to maternity leave for a period of [40] weeks which shall commence not more than [ ] weeks before the expected week of confinement]]

15.3 The Member in question shall use her best endeavours to notify the LLP in writing of:

15.3.1 the date upon which she intends to commence Maternity Leave not less than 3 months before that date; and

15.3.2 the date upon which she intends to return from Maternity Leave not less than 6 weeks before that date.

15.4 During Maternity Leave the profit share of the Member in question shall be ascertained as follows:[48]

15.4.1 for the first [13] weeks of Maternity Leave her profit share shall be as normal;

15.4.2 for the [14th to 22nd] weeks (inclusive) of the period of Maternity Leave her share of any [residual] profits distributable under sub-clause 11.8 shall be reduced by one half;

15.4.3 for the [23rd to 39th] weeks (inclusive) of the period of Maternity Leave her share of any [residual] profits distributable under sub-clause 11.8 shall be reduced by three quarters;

15.4.4 from the [40th] week onwards of the period of Maternity Leave she shall have no entitlement to any share of any [residual] profits distributable under sub-clause 11.8.

15.5 In the event that clause 15.4.2 or 15.4.3 may at any time be operative:

15.5.1 the Members may award a higher share of profits than that clause prescribes.

15.5.2 the amount of [residual] profits equivalent to the difference between the share of [residual] profits actually payable to the absent Member and what would have been her share of [residual] profits but for her absence, shall be divided amongst the other Members in the ratios which their entitlements to [residual] profits under clause 11.8 bear to each other;

15.5.3 the liabilities of the absent Member in accordance with this Agreement shall not be altered during any period of Maternity Leave.

16 Paternity, parental and family leave

Each Member shall be entitled to such Paternity Leave, Parental Leave and Family Leave as he would be if he were an employee of the LLP having more than one year's continuous service with the LLP upon the following terms:

16.1 During any such period of Leave the Member shall be entitled to his normal share of the [residual] profits of the LLP;[49] and

16.2 Each Member shall give notice to the LLP of his intended dates of such Leave and shall be responsible so far as possible for ensuring that those dates do not conflict with the dates of any form of Leave already notified to the LLP by such other Members or senior employees of the LLP as may be appropriate having regard to the work undertaken by the Member.

17 Management

17.1 Meetings of the Members may be convened by any [two] Member[s] (or by any liquidator of the LLP appointed under the Insolvency Act 1986).

17.2 In the normal course of events meetings of the Members shall be held at least [quarterly] or at such other intervals as the Members may determine.[50]

17.3 Not less than [5] Working Days' notice of any such meeting shall be given to all Members provided that any decision made at a meeting of which shorter notice or no notice has been given shall be deemed to have been duly made if all those Members entitled to attend were in fact present or if all of them consent in writing to short notice or it is afterwards ratified by the required majority of Members at a duly convened meeting.

17.4 All such meetings shall be chaired by such Member as shall be appointed for the purpose by those present at the meeting [but he shall not be entitled to a casting vote by reason of being chairman].

17.5 Any matters which are by reason of the Act or by this Agreement reserved for the decision of the Designated Members shall be determined by them by a simple majority at a meeting convened by any Designated Member in accordance with provisions similar to those contained in this clause 17.

17.6 No business shall be conducted at a meeting of the Members unless the Quorum shall be present in person within one hour of the time appointed for the start of the meeting and if the Quorum is not present within the stated period then:

17.6.1 the meeting shall be adjourned until the same time 7 days thereafter and at the same place; and

17.6.2 in the event of any adjourned meeting being held in accordance with clause 17.6.1 then the same may proceed if [two thirds] [   ]% of the Members are present in person within one hour of the time set for commencement, but if this requirement is not fulfilled then the meeting shall be cancelled.

17.7   At any meeting of the Members:

17.7.1 each of them who is present[51] shall, subject to clauses 17.7.2 and 17.10, have one vote;[52] and

17.7.2 a Member who has been required to retire by the LLP under clause 22.2.2 or who has served notice to retire as a Member under clause 22.1 shall not be eligible to vote for any purpose [PROVIDED THAT no decision may adversely affect his interests without his written consent unless it applies [fairly] to all Members]; and

17.7.3 all decisions and agreements shall be determined by a simple majority, save as required by clause 17.8.

17.8   A vote of [all *(or)* 75%] of the Members [present and voting at a meeting][53] shall be required for any of the following purposes:

17.8.1 the admission to membership of the LLP of any person and the terms of membership of such person;

17.8.2 the appointment of any Member as a Designated Member or the revocation of any such appointment;

17.8.3 the appointment of all Members for the time being as Designated Members or any reversal of any such resolution;

17.8.4 [any amendments to this Agreement;]

17.8.5 the requirement for Members to make an additional Contribution;

17.8.6 the making of any Loan or the terms of repayment of any Loan;

17.8.7 any determination in respect of a Member's Account in accordance with either of clauses 9.2.1 and 9.2.2;

17.8.8 the allocation of any profits or losses to the Members;

17.8.9 the alterations of the proportions of [residual] profits and losses provided for in clauses 11.8 and 11.10;

17.8.10 the holding of any office in accordance with clause 12.2;

17.8.11 any agreement that the LLP shall borrow or enter into any contract whereby it shall have an aggregate liability in excess of the Limit of Authority;

17.8.12 the deemed retirement of any Member or the withdrawal of such deemed retirement notice in accordance with clause 22.2.2;

17.8.13 the compulsory retirement of any Member in accordance with clause 22.2.3;

17.8.14 the suspension of any Member in accordance with clauses 22.3;

17.8.15 the expulsion of any Member in accordance with clauses 23.2 or 23.9;

17.8.16 the confirmation or rejection in accordance with clause 23.6 of a notice served in accordance with clause 23.2;

17.8.17 any decision to reduce, in accordance with clause 26.8.2, the burden of any of the provisions of clause 26;

17.8.18 the opening or closing of any place of business of the LLP;

17.8.19 any material change in the nature of the Business or the commencement of any new Business by the Company;

17.8.20 any determination to be made under the Insolvency Act 1986 including in particular, but without limitation, any determination to propose for a voluntary arrangement in respect of or a voluntary winding up of the LLP;

17.8.21 any decision to appoint any Member(s) as delegates empowered on behalf of the LLP to approve or reject under the Insolvency Act 1986 Section 4(5A) any modifications to any proposed voluntary arrangement in respect of the LLP;

17.8.22 any decision to appoint remove or fill a vacancy in the office of a liquidator of the LLP;

17.8.23 any decision to give or withhold any sanction required under the Insolvency Act 1986 including in particular, but without limitation, any sanction under the Insolvency Act 1986 Section 110(3) or Section 165(2);

17.8.24 any determination to wind up the LLP;

17.8.25 any determination to acquire, merge with or be acquired by any other person, firm, limited liability partnership or company; and

17.8.26 [*others*].

17.9 A resolution in writing as to a matter which is subject to the approval of the Members or the Designated Members and which is signed by all the Members or Designated Members shall be as valid and effectual as if it had been passed at a meeting of the Members or Designated Members (as the case may be).

17.10 Except as specified in clause 17.8 the Members may from time to time delegate (or revoke the delegation of) any of their powers of managing or conducting the affairs of the LLP to such persons as are appointed in the appropriate Members' decision provided that such delegation may be made subject to such conditions as the Members may prescribe.

17.11 For the purposes of any vote on a decision in relation to a particular Member, the Member who is the subject of the decision shall not be entitled to vote.

18 Unfair prejudice

[Each Member agrees and accepts that for so long as the LLP is in existence, the rights conferred on the Members by Section 994 of the Companies Act shall be excluded in relation to the LLP.][54]

19 Indemnity and expenses

19.1 The LLP shall indemnify each Member from and against any claims, costs and demands arising out of payments made by him or liabilities incurred by him in the performance by him of his duties as a Member in the normal course of the operation of the Business or in respect of anything necessarily done by him for the preservation of the Business or the property of the LLP.

19.2 Each Member shall be entitled to charge and be refunded all out-of-pocket expenses properly incurred by him in connection with the Business provided that:

19.2.1 all expenses shall be vouched by an appropriate receipt and VAT invoice where appropriate;

19.2.2 if the LLP shall provide a credit card for the use of a Member for such expenses he shall provide to the LLP the original vouchers for all expenditure charged to such card; and

19.2.3 the LLP may from time to time resolve to place upper limits on any category or categories of expenses of which reimbursement may be claimed by Members.

19.3[55] The LLP shall pay for each Member (or reimburse to the Member as appropriate) the cost of:

19.3.1 all calls made on his mobile telephone [whether] for [business *(or)* personal] use [only]; and

19.3.2 all calls made on his home telephone [whether] for [business *(or)* personal] use [only] (including for the avoidance of doubt the land line rental).]

[20 Cars[56]

20.1 Each Member shall provide a suitable car for the performance of his duties as a Member.

20.2 Each Member shall be entitled to be reimbursed by the LLP for the cost of maintaining, repairing, insuring and taxing the car referred to above including vehicle excise duty and VAT.

20.3 Each Member shall be entitled to be fully reimbursed by the LLP for the cost of all fuel used by the car referred to above including fuel duty and VAT.]

21 Insurance[57]

21.1 The LLP shall maintain policies of insurance for such respective amounts as it may from time to time determine with reputable insurers in respect of:

21.1.1 loss, damage or theft (including consequent loss of profit by reason of such loss, damage or theft) in relation to:

21.1.1.1 the Property; and

21.1.1.2 all plant, equipment and other chattels belonging to or used by the LLP (and in the case of any computers or ancillary equipment, such insurance shall cover risks relating to any virus and relating to any corruption or loss of any software or data);

21.1.2 employers' liability;

21.1.3 public liability;

21.1.4 professional negligence (such insurance to be for not less than the Minimum Insurance Sum).

21.2[58] The LLP may at its expense effect and maintain for its own benefit such life insurance and/or critical illness policies in such sums on the lives of such of the Members as the LLP shall from time to time determine and Members shall co-operate in the obtaining of such policies and in particular, but without limitation, shall undergo such medical examination(s) in respect thereof as shall be reasonable.

21.3 For the avoidance of doubt the premiums in respect of all policies of insurance provided for in this clause 21 shall be paid by the LLP and shall for accounting purposes be treated as an expense of the LLP generally.[59]

22 Retirement

22.1 If any Member shall give to the LLP notice of his intention to retire from the LLP, provided that any such notice shall be of a duration not less than the Notice Period, the notice shall take effect and the Member serving it shall retire from the LLP on [the later of:

22.1.1] the expiry of the notice; [or

22.1.2 if, at the time of service of such notice, there was another similar notice which had previously been served by another Member or other Members, then upon the expiry of a period equal in length to the Notice Period and commencing on the day after the retirement of that other Member or the last of the other Members (as the case may be)].[60]

22.2 A Member shall be deemed to retire from the LLP:

22.2.1 on the last day of the Accounting Period in which the birthday upon which he attains the Retirement Age[61]occurs (or if before that birthday the Members shall have determined and shall have agreed with the Member in question to substitute a later date, then upon that date);

22.2.2 on the expiry of not less than 3 months' notice requiring him to retire given to him by the Members following a determination by the Members in accordance with clause 17.8 that the recipient of the notice has by reason of illness, injury or other cause been unable to perform his duties as a Member throughout the period of at least [6] months immediately preceding the service of the notice or for an aggregate period of at least [6] months during the period of [18] months immediately preceding such service provided that:

22.2.2.1 there shall be excepted from the calculation of any such period any period(s) of Leave; and

22.2.2.2 a notice under this clause shall be of no effect if before it expires the Member upon whom it has been served resumes his duties as a Member to the satisfaction of the Members and the Members accordingly resolve to withdraw the notice;

22.2.3 forthwith on the service upon him of notice in writing requiring him to retire given to him by the LLP following a determination by the Members in accordance with clause 17.8 at any time after he has become a patient within the meaning of the Mental Health Act 1983 Section 94(2) or Section 145(1).

22.3[62] In the event of a Member serving a notice to retire in accordance with clause 22.1 or being given a notice of expulsion in accordance with clauses 23.2 or 23.9 then the Members may determine in accordance with clause 17.8 that the LLP shall until the expiry of that notice suspend the Member in question so that without affecting the right of the other Members to continue the management of the Business the Member in question shall be prevented from doing any of the following (without the consent of the LLP) namely:

22.3.1 entering the Property or any part of it;

22.3.2 contacting or having any other communication with any:

22.3.2.1 client of the Business;

22.3.2.2 employee of the LLP; or

22.3.2.3 referrer of work to the Business;

22.3.3 attending or receiving notice of any meeting of the LLP or its Members.

23 Expulsion

23.1 Notwithstanding clause 17.3:

23.1.1 no motion for the expulsion of any Member under this clause 23 shall be capable of being passed other than at a properly convened and conducted meeting of the Members of which not less than [5] Working Days' written notice stating the proposal for expulsion has been given to all Members;

23.1.2 if the Member whose expulsion is being proposed would normally be entitled to attend such a meeting then he must be given normal notice as in clause 23.1.1 and shall have the right to attend and speak at that meeting.

23.2 If any Member shall:

23.2.1 commit any grave breach or persistent breaches of this Agreement;

23.2.2 have a bankruptcy order made against him;

23.2.3 fail to pay any monies owing by him to the LLP within 30 days of being requested in writing by the LLP so to do;

23.2.4 be guilty of any conduct likely to have a serious adverse effect upon the Business;

23.2.5 cease to hold any professional qualification or certification required for the normal performance of his duties as a Member of the LLP; or

23.2.6 absent himself from the business of the LLP without proper cause for more than [10 Working Days] in any period of 12 months;

23.2.7 [*others*]

then the Members may determine in accordance with clause 17.8 that the LLP shall serve notice in writing upon him to expel him forthwith or upon such subsequent date as may be specified.

23.3[63] Any notice to be served under clause 23.2 shall give sufficient details of the alleged breach or breaches to enable the same to be properly identified.

23.4 If the Member on whom such notice is served (the 'Recipient') shall within [10] Working Days of the date of service of the said notice serve on the LLP a counter-notice denying the allegations and shall within the said period of [10] Working Days refer the dispute for determination under clause 30 the operation of the said notice shall be suspended.

23.5 Such a period of suspension as is referred to in clause 22.3 shall be ended by either:

23.5.1 written notice of acceptance served by the Recipient on the LLP; or

23.5.2 the successful conclusion of the process of mediation; or

23.5.3 the notification to all parties of the decision of an arbitrator appointed in accordance with clause 30.6.

23.6 The Recipient and the LLP may agree as part of the process of mediation referred to in clause 23.5.2 to confirm or reject the notice served under clause 23.2 and in the latter instance the notice shall be treated as never having been served.

23.7 Any such arbitrator as is mentioned in clause 23.5.3 may take into account all matters which may be drawn to his attention whether or not they were within the knowledge of the Members at the time of service of the notice under clause 23.2 and shall confirm or reject that notice and in the latter instance the notice shall be treated as never having been served.

23.8 Any reference in this Agreement to a date consequent upon a notice served under clause 23.3 shall if a counter-notice is served under clause 23.4 be deemed to be a reference to the date of the ending of the period of suspension pursuant to that clause.

23.9[64] If the Members [acting in good faith] shall determine in accordance with clause 17.8 that it is in the best interests of the LLP to expel any Member (regardless of the fact that the Member in question may not be in breach of any provision of this Agreement) it shall be entitled to do so by notice served upon that Member which notice shall take effect so that the Member in question shall be deemed to retire either:

23.9.1 on the date set out in such notice; or

23.9.2 if the Member who has received the notice gives notice in writing to the LLP of any determination by him that he shall retire earlier, then upon the date he so determines.

24 Provisions relating to death, retirement, deemed retirement or expulsion

24.1 In the event that, in respect of any Member, that member's Cessation Date shall be, a date other than an Accounts Date, then:

24.1.1 he shall not be entitled to receive any share of the profit of the LLP from the Cessation Date; and

24.1.2 the LLP shall not prepare any accounts other than the accounts which would normally be prepared as at the next Accounts Date (for the purposes of this clause, the 'Cessation Accounts') and for the purpose of ascertaining the amount of the Member's Account of the Member in question the profits and losses of the LLP in such LLP accounts shall be apportioned on a time basis in respect of the periods up to and including and after the Cessation Date.[65]

24.2 In the event of the death, retirement, deemed retirement or expulsion of any Member:

24.2.1 the balance standing to the credit of his Member's Account and Capital Account shall be as shown in the Cessation Accounts; and

24.2.2 for the avoidance of doubt there shall be no goodwill payable to him and there shall be no revaluation of the LLP's work in progress other than in the normal course of the preparation of the Cessation Accounts according to such principles as would have applied to such accounts in any event.[66]

24.3 The Outgoing Member's share and interest in any allocation of profits as determined in accordance with this Agreement as at the Cessation Date shall accrue rateably to the Contributions of the Members.[67]

25 Payments following death, retirement, deemed retirement or expulsion

25.1 In the event of the death, retirement, deemed retirement or expulsion of any Member (an 'Outgoing Member') the balance standing to the credit of his Member's Account shall be paid to him (or his personal representatives) within one month of the approval of the Cessation Accounts [or the date being 6 months after the relevant Accounts Date which ever is earlier].[68]

25.2 The LLP will pay the Outgoing Member a sum equal to the balance, if any standing to the credit of the Outgoing Member's Capital Account [together with the balance of any Loan] less, if any, the debit balance on his Member's Account ('Net Sum'), such payment be made as follows:

25.2.1 one third [plus interest at the Interest Rate] will be paid [12] months after the Outgoing Member's Cessation Date;

25.2.2 one third [plus interest at the Interest Rate] will be paid [18] months after the Outgoing Member's Cessation Date; and

25.2.3 one third [plus interest at the Interest Rate] will be paid [24] months after the Outgoing Member's Cessation Date. [69]

[25.3 If payment of any instalment referred to in clause 25.2 shall not be made within 10 Working Days of the date upon which it is payable then the whole of the Net Sum or the balance thereof then outstanding together with interest due thereon shall become immediately due and payable.]

25.4 For the avoidance of doubt if the LLP shall wish to make any payment referred to in this clause 25 at an earlier time than it is obliged to then it shall be at liberty to do so.

26 Other provisions following death, retirement, deemed retirement or expulsion

26.1 For the purposes of this clause 26 the following expressions shall have the following meanings:

'directly or indirectly' means the Outgoing Member acting alone or through or jointly with or on behalf of any other person whether as proprietor, principal, partner, manager, employee, agent, contractor, director, consultant, investor or otherwise;

'Relevant Period' means the period of 12 months immediately prior to the Cessation Date;

'Protected Client' means any person which is or has been a customer or client of the LLP at any time during the Relevant Period and with whom the Outgoing Member has had personal contact during the Relevant Period;

'Protected Employee' means any person who is or has been an employee of the LLP in a fee earning or managerial position at any time in the Relevant Period;

'Restricted Area' means the area within the Radius;

'Restricted Period' means a period of [one year] beginning with the Cessation Date;[70]

'Restricted Services' means [legal and other services] of the kind provided by the LLP during the Restricted Period.

26.2 Where the context so allows reference in this clause 26 to the LLP during the Relevant Period shall include references to the Former Practice.

26.3 Any Outgoing Member who shall have retired or been deemed to retire or been expelled shall not at any time during the Restricted Period, whether directly or indirectly:

26.3.1 solicit business from, or canvass instructions to supply goods or services to or for any Protected Client;

26.3.2 solicit business from, or canvass instructions to supply goods or services to or for any person, firm, limited liability partnership, company, organisation or body with whom the Outgoing Member has had personal contact during the Relevant Period and who, to the knowledge of the Outgoing Member, had at any time during the Relevant Period:

26.3.2.1 approached the LLP with a view to becoming a client of it; or

26.3.2.2 been approached by the LLP with a view to their becoming a client of it; or

26.3.2.3 been a referrer of work to the LLP; or

26.3.2.4 approached the LLP with a view to becoming such a referrer; or

26.3.2.5 been approached by the LLP with a view to their becoming such a referrer;

26.3.3 solicit or endeavour to entice away from the LLP any supplier or referrer of the LLP;

26.3.4 offer employment to or endeavour to entice away from the LLP any Protected Employee;

26.3.5 supply Restricted Services to:

26.3.5.1 any Protected Client;

26.3.5.2 any person, firm, limited liability partnership, company, organisation or body with whom the Outgoing Member has had personal contact during the Relevant Period, and who had, to the knowledge of the Outgoing Member, at any time during the Relevant Period:

(a) approached the LLP with a view to becoming a client of it; or

(b) been approached by the LLP with a view to their becoming a client of it; or

(c) been a referrer of work to the LLP;

26.3.5.3 any person, firm, limited liability partnership, company, organisation or body referred to the Outgoing Member by any person, firm, limited liability partnership, company, organisation or body with whom the Outgoing Member has had personal contact during the Relevant Period, and who had, to the knowledge of the Outgoing Member, at any time during the Relevant Period:

(a) approached the LLP with a view to becoming a referrer of work to it; or

(b) been approached by the LLP with a view to their becoming a referrer of work to it;

26.3.5.4 engage in a business which provides or intends to provide any of the Restricted Services in the Restricted Area.

26.4 The Restricted Period shall be reduced by a period equal in length to any period for which the Outgoing Member is suspended in accordance with clause 22.3.

26.5 None of the restrictions in this clause 26 shall prevent an Outgoing Member supplying Restricted Services to any person to whom he is related by blood, marriage or civil registration or any limited liability partnership or company controlled by such a person.

26.6 The Outgoing Member shall not at any time after the Cessation Date:

26.6.1 use or disclose any confidential information relating to:

26.6.1.1 the Business or the LLP;

26.6.1.2 any clients of the LLP; or

26.6.1.3 any referrers of work to the LLP;

26.6.2 represent himself as being in any way connected with or interested in the Business;

26.6.3 interfere or seek to interfere with the continuance of supplies to the Business or the LLP (or the terms of such supplies) from any suppliers who have during the Relevant Period supplied any products materials or services to the LLP;

26.6.4 interfere or seek to interfere with referrals of work to the LLP (or the terms of such referrals) from anyone who has during the Relevant Period made such referrals to the LLP;

26.6.5 carry on business under the Name or any other practising or trading name from time to time used by the LLP or any name which may sound or appear similar to any of the foregoing.

26.7 The restrictions contained in clauses 26.1 to 26.6 inclusive (on which all Members have had the opportunity to take independent advice) are:

26.7.1 considered by all parties to be reasonable in terms of time, area and subject matter in order to protect the special trade and practising connections and business secrets of the LLP but if any such restriction is subsequently held to be invalid or ineffective but would be valid or effective if some part or parts of it were deleted or amended by changing any specified period, area or service type then such restriction shall be so amended and effective accordingly;

26.7.2 considered by all parties to be appropriate as at the date of this Agreement to protect the LLP's legitimate interests but may be made less onerous by the Members determining to reduce their impact and serving notice upon the Outgoing Member of such determination at any time;

26.7.3 (and each of their sub-clauses are) separate and independent restriction so that if one or more of them are held to be invalid for any reason whatever then the remaining Clauses and/or sub-clauses (as the case may be) shall nonetheless be valid;

26.7.4 to be in addition to and not to derogate from or be in substitution for any duty or obligation which the Outgoing Member may at any time have by virtue of any statute or rule of common law or equity.

26.8 An Outgoing Member or (as the case may be) his personal representatives shall, forthwith upon receipt at any time after the Cessation Date of a notice from the LLP requiring him (or them) so to do, pay into the LLP's bank account all sums due from him to the LLP and any sums not so paid shall be recoverable by the LLP from him as a debt.

26.9 An Outgoing Member or (as the case may be) the personal representatives, trustee in bankruptcy or liquidator of the Outgoing Member shall:

26.9.1 deliver to the LLP forthwith upon request and at the expense of that Member:

26.9.1.1 all such property belonging to the LLP as is or was in the Outgoing Member's possession and in the case of any computers or similar equipment that shall include all software, data and files held upon the same and no such data and files shall be wiped from the computer before its return; and

26.9.1.2 all such books of account, records, letters and other documents relating to the LLP as are or were in the Outgoing Member's possession and as may be required for the continuing conduct of the Business but during any subsequent period in which there shall still be moneys owed by the LLP to the Outgoing Member then inspection by appointment by the Outgoing Member or his duly authorised agents shall be permitted of the books of account, records, letters and other documents of the LLP in so far as they relate to any period preceding the Cessation Date; and

26.9.2 sign, execute and do all such documents, deeds, acts and things as the LLP may reasonably request for the purpose of conveying, assigning or transferring to them any Property or assets which immediately prior to the Cessation Date were vested in the Outgoing Member as nominee for or in trust for the LLP;

26.9.3 assist the LLP to recover and get in the book debts of the LLP including attending any court proceedings that may be needed for that purpose;

26.9.4 if so required execute any deed for retirement and appointment of new trustees reasonably required in respect of any trust of which the Outgoing Member is a trustee or any will of which he is an executor if the administration of that trust or will forms part of the Business and the trust or will do not relate to any member of the family by blood, marriage or civil registration of the Outgoing Member.

[26.10 From and after any Cessation Date the LLP shall:

26.10.1 maintain and pay all necessary premiums for professional negligence indemnity insurance for at least the Minimum Insurance Sum against any claims for negligence or any other wrongful act or omission covered by a normal professional negligence policy and in accordance with the normal practice of the LLP and ensure [so far as is possible] that such policy shall cover any claims made against the Outgoing Member or his estate and effects; and

26.10.2 upon a Members' voluntary winding-up of the LLP within 15 years of the Cessation Date use its best endeavours to take out run-off cover to afford the Outgoing Member such protection until the expiry of the said period of 15 years unless the circumstances are such that there is a successor practice whose insurance cover will protect the Outgoing Member against such claims and which agrees to enter into a similar covenant for the benefit of the Outgoing Member as that contained in this clause.[71]]

27 Winding up

27.1 No Member has agreed with the other Members or with the LLP that he shall in the event of the winding up of the LLP contribute in any way to the assets of the LLP in accordance with the Insolvency Act 1986 Section 74.[72]

27.2 In the event of the winding up of the LLP, then any surplus of assets of the LLP over its liabilities (which liabilities shall for the avoidance of doubt include any amounts owing to Members on their Members' Accounts or in respect of Loans) remaining at the conclusion of the winding up after payment of all money due to the creditors of the LLP and all expenses of the winding up shall be payable to the Members in such proportions as their respective [residual] shares of profits payable under clause 11.2 shall have borne to each other on the day before the commencement of the winding up.[73]

28 Guarantees and indemnities

28.1 In the event that any Member shall have given any guarantee[74] on behalf of the LLP and (if so required by clause 13.2) obtained the necessary consent for that, then:

28.1.1 if any guarantee so given shall be called upon by the person to whom it has been given, then upon making any payment properly due under that guarantee, the Member in question shall be entitled (in addition to the indemnity contained in clause 19.1) to be indemnified forthwith by the Members or the others of them in such manner that the amount or aggregate amounts payable in accordance with the said guarantee shall (after all the Members have had the benefit of the indemnity contained in clause 19.1) be borne by the Members in the proportions which their respective entitlements to [residual] profits in accordance with clause 11.2 then bear to each other (unless unanimously agreed otherwise); and

28.1.2 upon the death, dissolution, retirement, deemed or required retirement or expulsion of that Member, the Members or the others of them shall:

28.1.2.1 use their best endeavours to procure that the person having the benefit of the guarantee shall release that Member (or his estate) from the guarantee;

28.1.2.2 provide a substitute guarantor if required by that person as a condition of release; and

28.1.2.3 jointly and severally indemnify the Member in question or his estate from and against any liability under the guarantee arising after the Cessation Date relating to that Member.

28.2 For the avoidance of doubt, nothing in this clause 28 shall require any Member to indemnify any other Member against any claim or liability resulting from the negligent act or omission of that other whether such claim is brought by the LLP itself or by any third party and whether the other Member is solely liable or is co-extensively liable with the LLP.[75]

29 Notices

29.1 Any notice herein referred to shall be in writing and shall be sufficiently given to or served on the person to whom it is addressed if it is:

29.1.1 handed to that person;

29.1.2 delivered to or sent in a prepaid first class letter by recorded mail addressed (in the case of notice to the LLP) to its

Registered Office or (in the case of notice to any Member) to him at his residential address as entered in the register of members of the LLP (and in such case the notice shall subject to confirmation of earlier delivery, be deemed to have been delivered at 9am on the second working day after posting);

[29.1.3[76] sent by facsimile transmission to a number notified by a Member as being one at which he is prepared to accept service of notices (and in such case the notice shall be deemed to have been served on the day of transmission or if sent after 4pm then upon the next following Working Day);

(or)

29.1.4 sent by electronic mail to an address notified by a Member as being one at which he is prepared to accept service of notices (and in such case the notice shall be deemed to have been served on the day of transmission or if sent after 4pm then upon the next following Working Day)].

29.2 For the purposes of this Agreement any notice shall be deemed to have been given to the personal representatives of a deceased Member notwithstanding that no grant of representation has been made in respect of his estate in England if the notice is addressed to the deceased Member by name or to his personal representatives by title and is sent by prepaid letter by recorded mail to the residential address as entered in the register of members of the LLP.

[29.3 Faxed and emailed notices are not valid for the purposes of this Agreement.]

30 Determination of disputes[77]

In the event of any dispute relating to the LLP between it and any of the Members or between any of the Members under or arising out of this Agreement:

30.1 The LLP and the Members shall take the matter before an independent mediator in accordance with the procedures of [the Alternative Dispute Resolution Group, London],[77] with the intention that the matter shall if possible be resolved by mediation.

30.2 The mediator shall be agreed by the parties, or failing such agreement within 15 Working Days of one party requesting the appointment of a mediator, shall be appointed on the application of either party in accordance with clause 30.7.

30.3 Unless otherwise agreed the costs of the mediation shall be an expense of the business but any Member who may incur any additional personal costs shall be responsible for them.

30.4 The doctrines of laches, waiver or estoppel shall not be considered in any such mediation.

30.5 Notwithstanding any such mediation the LLP or any Member may seek a preliminary injunction or other relief to prevent what they consider to be further damage.

30.6 In the event that the mediator appointed as above shall certify in writing his opinion that the dispute is not capable of resolution by mediation, or that the mediation has not been concluded within 60 Working Days of the agreement of the parties as to the appointment of the mediator or a request by either party for such an appointment, then it shall be referred in accordance with the Arbitration Act 1996 to a single arbitrator to be appointed, in default of agreement, upon the request of either party in accordance with clause 30.7, and the decision of the arbitrator (including any decision as to costs) shall be final and binding on all parties.

30.7 An appointment of a mediator or arbitrator shall be made upon the request of any party by the president or other chief officer for the time being of the Relevant Institution or any deputy duly authorised by the Relevant Institution in that regard.

31 Entire Agreement

31.1 This Agreement, and the Transfer Agreement, constitute the whole of the agreement between the Initial Members and the LLP relating to the subject matter of the Agreement and supersedes any prior agreement or arrangements between the parties in relation to the subject matter hereto.

31.2 It is expressly declared that no variations to this Agreement shall be effective unless made in writing, dated and signed by the parties for the time being to this Agreement.

32 Third Parties

No person who is not a party for the time being to this Agreement shall have any right under the Contracts (Rights of Third Parties) Act 1999 to enforce any term of this Agreement.

33 Counterparts

This Agreement may be executed in any number of counterparts each of which when executed and delivered is an original but all the counterparts together shall constitute the same document.

34   Governing Law

This Agreement and any dispute, controversy, proceedings or claim of whatever nature arising out of or in any way relating to this Agreement or its formation shall be governed by and construed in accordance with the laws of England and Wales.

AS WITNESS etc

SCHEDULE

Initial Members' Details

(signatures of (or on behalf of) the Members and LLP)

1.   This agreement is intended for use when a business is converting from a partnership to a limited liability partnership. This will most commonly be a professional services business and the agreement reflects this. The agreement provides for only one category of member.

2.   LLPs have accounting reference dates in just the same way as companies. The same date should be chosen for this purpose.

3.   As to the many elements of the accounting treatment of LLPs, see further the Statement of Recommended Practice for Limited Liability Partnerships (SORP), which was last revised in March 20010 (Appendix 3).

4.   This agreement assumes that it is to be entered into after the LLP has been incorporated, but before it takes over the business.

5.   An example of such a contribution would be if a freehold property is introduced to the LLP by a Member, upon terms that the LLP takes over the liability for a mortgage on it from him.

6.   The LLP may either regard all Members as Designated Members, or only certain specified and nominated individuals. There must always be at least two Designated Members. Certain tasks (and therefore penalties for failure to perform those tasks) fall only upon the Designated Members. The LLP may wish to delegate other tasks to them. In many smaller LLPs, it is not unusual to find that all Members also become Designated Members to ensure equal allocation of the duties and responsibilities involved.

7.   Note that drawings are effectively a loan from the LLP to the Member in question until the LLP has allocated profits equivalent to such sum to that Member. See note 33 above.

8.   This definition may need to be adjusted if either some partners in the Former Practice are not joining the LLP or if there are some Initial Members who were not previously partners.

9. Many small LLPs will be exempt from the requirement to have their accounts audited in accordance with the *Companies Act 2006, s 477*. Therefore, they do not have to choose as their accountants those who are also qualified to act as auditors. However, they may well wish to appoint initial accountants in anticipation of the day when they grow out of the small exemption's cover, or because such accountants may be more familiar with preparing accounts in accordance with the *Companies Act 2006* and the accompanying regulations as required for all LLPs, whatever their size.

10. This agreement assumes there is only one office for the firm. If there are more, it may be easier to deal with them by scheduling them.

11. This limit gives the opportunity for the LLP to set a cap on the amount which any one Member can spend or contract for on the LLP's behalf.

12. These are the equivalent of a partnership's current account, ie they will broadly be credited with their profit share allocation and debited with drawings and, if applicable, any payments for tax reserves. The agreement is drafted on the basis that they will be zeroed at the end of each Accounting Period, once the figures are known, either by paying the balance of undrawn profits to the Members or by formally capitalising them. This avoids the accidental build up of large balances in such accounts.

13. This is the minimum level of professional indemnity insurance which the LLP will undertake to maintain. This is for the benefit of Outgoing Members. Some professional regulators may impose minimum levels of insurance, eg the Solicitors Regulation Authority currently prescribes £3 million as minimum cover for solicitors' LLPs.

14. This is the period of notice which a Member needs to give to resign. An LLP may wish to provide that Members can only retire at the end of an Accounting Period. If so, appropriate amendments will need to be made to clause 22.

15. The Members can change the quorum as they see appropriate. This agreement assumes that the same quorum requirements will apply to meetings of both the Member and the Designated Members. This does not have to be the case and this clause can be adapted to reflect the individual circumstances of each LLP.

16. The radius is that to be applied to a restrictive covenant. The chosen radius should not be so large as to render the clause unfair and unenforceable. In *Allan Janes LLP v Johal*, [2006] EWHC 286, [2006] IRLR 599, Ch D it was held that a radius of six miles from the LLP's office in High Wycombe was too extensive in relation to a covenant not to practise as a solicitor, especially in the light of the built up nature of the area.

17.   Unlike partnerships, LLPs are required to have registered offices just as companies are. The address does not have to be a trading or practising address, although some professional rules may require this, eg for solicitors.

18.   This is intended to be the professional body that regulates the business, eg the Solicitors Regulation Authority, the Institute of Chartered Accountants in England and Wales, the Royal Institution of Chartered Surveyors etc.

19.   See further clause 22.2.1 of this agreement and the note to it.

20.   It is of course open for the Members to disapply any or all of the default regulations. If the default provisions are not excluded from applying to the LLP then there is a risk that even with a members' agreement, they will still apply ie if the members' agreement fails to address whether the majority of Members have the right to expel a member, then regulation 8 will prevent such expulsion unless it can be shown that express agreement has been reached otherwise (one would argue that it would be difficult to prove this if not incorporated into the members' agreement itself or otherwise reduced to writing). See the case of *Eaton v Caulfield and Others [2011] All ER (D) 63 (Feb).]*

21.   Many firms have the situation where properties are owned by only some of the partners or former partners or their estates often on an entirely informal basis with nothing in writing governing the terms of occupation. Where possible, such terms should be formalised and an appropriate lease granted. However, the heavy imposition of stamp duty land tax and the fact that the dutiable amount relates to a multiple of the rent may act as a major disincentive for such formalisation. If that is so, this clause may need amending to give maximum clarity without causing stamp duty land tax problems.

22.   This phrase should be omitted in the (increasingly rare) case of a business which does have goodwill in its accounts.

23.   Just as all Members are given the statutory responsibility of having proper accounts preserved, so the approval of those accounts is the responsibility of all, and all must be given a copy of them.

24.   Most professional services firms will be required to operate a client account.

25.   This is a simple version of a clause governing signatures for cheques. Some may prefer to be more specific eg if provisions differ for client and office accounts or according to the level of funds being committed. The only drawback with that may be the necessity to alter the agreement if practical circumstances dictate a change in such arrangements. Note that the reference to operating accounts in accordance with regulations in clause 7.3.2 of this agreement takes care of any limitations on who may be professionally eligible to sign cheques.

26. This assumes that all that is shown in the former practice's books as capital is to be introduced in a similar capacity to the LLP. The actual amount will not be known until later when the accounts are prepared for the last period of the former practice. This may need to be amended if either the accounts of the former practice failed to distinguish properly between capital and current accounts or if not all the capital is to be brought across as such eg because part is either to be repaid to parties or retained to meet any liabilities excluded from the Transfer Agreement and retained by the partners or which will to be brought in as a loan rather than capital. It will also need to be adapted if a minimum capital contribution is required with an obligation on the Members to top up the amount of the contribution if it falls below this fixed sum.

27. Two fundamental options are offered here for the ultimate division of the capital. Such a surplus might exist, for instance, if there was a freehold property which proved to have a higher value than that shown in the accounts upon the basis of which the shares had been calculated. The first option is to divide according to residual income profit-sharing ratios and the second is to divide according to the ratios of capital contributed.

28. Members' accounts are broadly the same as current accounts.

29. This agreement does not specifically provide for separate drawings to be made for the purposes of creating a tax reserve. The LLP is not itself a taxable party and any liability to pay tax rests with the Members individually. It is not uncommon, however, for firms to create such a reserve in which case the LLP has to consider whether to do this by means of an account in the LLP's name (in which case it is available as fall-back working capital, but vulnerable to claims by creditors) or by creating separate accounts in the names of Members as trustees for each other. The latter is clearly more cumbersome administratively, but ultimately safer. Any such arrangements could be recorded in this agreement but if trust accounts are to be used it may be better dealt with by separate documentation. Pragmatic alterations in those arrangements will not then require amendments to this agreement.

30. Some firms will prefer to specify in this agreement the levels of drawings appropriate at the time. This might be by means of a schedule or a table inserted at this point of the agreement.

31. Reference has already been made to the principle of the allocation of profits and losses which is a quite different concept from that of the division of profits.

32. This clause gives the LLP discretion as to whether it wishes to recoup the shortfall that was described in the note above, by transferring part of the Member's Contribution or whether it prefers to leave that intact to preserve the overall level of funds, and call upon the

Member to make good the shortfall. No Member is going to welcome any such recoupment and so it is important that drawings should be set at a level which minimises the risk of overdrawing in this way.

33. Some LLPs will want to make interim allocations eg on a monthly basis to cover drawings and some will prefer to wait until the annual accounts are prepared, and make a single allocation for the appropriate accounting period. If interim allocations are required to cover drawings as a matter of course (without requiring a resolution of the Members as set out at clause 11.1.4) then the agreement will need to be adapted to allow for this although see Chapter 11 for the risks associated with this approach. There is no difference in cash terms, but there will be a large difference as far as the balance sheet is concerned and the Members' position in the interim. Lenders and other interested third parties may need an explanation as to which policy is to be adopted. This clause and the next, taken together, allow freedom of choice and variation of that choice, as to which method is followed.

34. The first option at this clause again provides for the Members to determine upon the allocation of profits to be made. This requires a positive step to be taken by the Members which, if not taken, could put at risk any subsequent allocation of monies to the Members. An alternative provision as provided for in the second option would be to have the automatic allocation of some or all profits upon the approval of the accounts although this removes the ability to use the discretion as currently provided for in this clause but provides certainty for the Members.

35. Just as with profits, LLPs have a discretion as to whether to allocate any or all of any losses which have been made. If they are not allocated at all, they will remain losses of the corporate LLP and cannot add to the personal liability of the Members. The concept of a negative reserve may be one which is difficult to understand, but which may be very useful in practice. It seems that there is no point in allocating losses as it simply creates a debt from the Member to the LLP which goes against the whole point of seeking the limitation of liability that LLPs offer.

36. Members are of course taxed on profits earned, not profits distributed. If the LLP decides not to allocate any profits or losses, that cannot alter Members' tax liability and so there has to be a notional allocation of all profits or losses for tax purposes.

37. It is possible to differentiate between rates of interest applicable to Contribution and loans. It is not here suggested that interest should be paid on balances on Members' Accounts (ie current accounts).

38. There are numerous ways in which residual profits may be distributed by firms. Note however that the *Employment Equality (Age) Regulations 2006, SI 2006/1031* which came into force on 1 October 2006, will

mean that LLPs and partnerships cannot discriminate by age in their chosen form of remuneration split. Thus, progressive methods such as lockstep which reward long service may not be possible without the risk of claim. Reference in this agreement to 'residual profits' means profits other than Allocated Profits and the interest payments in accordance with clause 11.8.1 and so its use is only applicable if interest is payable.

39. Some LLPs may prefer to have a threshold of wilful absence before the suspension of profits kicks in. This has been provided for in this clause. In this agreement the period is the same as that which gives rise to the ability to expel for unauthorised absence: see clause 22.2.6 of this agreement.

40. It is an increasing trend for Members to be allowed, perhaps for a set period, to work less than a traditional full week. Almost certainly this will be reflected in the remuneration package. If this is to be the case, it is suggested that the minimum acceptable should be carefully specified as otherwise disputes could easily arise.

41. Increasingly, outside involvements are viewed with suspicion by firms for two reasons. First, attention to external posts may diminish a Member's input to the business. Second, the increased responsibility which is being placed upon trustees may lead to claims, or adverse reputational problems affecting Members. Against that, however, many professional service firms like to make a contribution to their communities and it would be rare to find a firm where no Member held any such posts. It is suggested therefore that care be given to what offices should be accepted and that where there are existing appointments they should be recorded.

42. This clause makes it obligatory for each Member to comply not only with legal and regulatory matters but also with external standards voluntarily adopted by the LLP such as ISO 9001, Investors In People, or the Law Society's Lexcel scheme.

43. When the LLP legislation was passing through Parliament, the government did not specify whether Members would owe any fiduciary duties to each other (as distinct from duties owed to the LLP). They indicated that it would be for the courts to find any such duties. This creates highly undesirable uncertainty. Therefore, the members' agreement should provide clearly for the duties that the Members agree should be owed between themselves. In addition, as a result of the the case of *F&C Investments*, (see 6.9 of Chapter 6 above), it is also essential that the members' agreement provides for the duties that the Members will owe to the LLP itself as it is now clear that the assumption that a Member will be bound by duties as an agent of the LLP, will not necessarily apply to all actions taken by a Member. This is an area on which it is recommended that legal advice is sought to ensure that all parties understand and agree the nature of their relationship with the other Members and the LLP itself.

44. This is a suggestion only. Some firms, especially solicitors, may prefer to specify that all legacies should go to the LLP unless they are notional ones for acting as executor or emanate from the Member's own family.

45. This may need amending if for example the power to hire and fire is to be delegated to certain Members or if all Members are to have such power in respect of junior staff. It is suggested that it is much more desirable to concentrate the responsibility for this in the hands of a few well trained Members or managers.

46. Some firms may wish to expand their conflict of interest provisions so as to include this final clause.

47. If it is the business' practice to close between Christmas and New Year, this should be clearly set out and it should be clear whether this is a compulsory part of the allowance of holiday leave or is in effect, extra to it.

48. The pattern suggested here is illustrative only and each LLP will arrive at its own formula. Such a formula must not however be discriminatory. Generally, it is recommended that the benefit/profit level to be receivable should be no less than an employee would receive. In many cases it will be much higher. Many LLPs will not apply such reductions to the entitlement to interest on capital and the clause has been drafted on that basis.

49. It is suggested that it would generally be inappropriate to reduce or suspend profit entitlement for such relatively short periods of Leave.

50. These provisions are merely illustrative of the sort of issues which need to be considered in the light of the complete absence in the *Limited Liability Partnerships Act 2000* of any provisions governing meetings. This is likely to require particular attention as the concept of defining meetings in this manner may be alien to former partners. There is no statutory requirement to do so, but failure to do so will leave a large vacuum and scope for disagreement when a meeting is needed in possibly difficult or contentions circumstances.

51. This draft does not allow for proxy voting. This can be inserted if required although it would be usual in the case of smaller LLPs for the proxy to be restricted to another Member.

52. Voting rights are often contentious. This draft assumes the most simple profile. Another option is for votes to vary with capital, eg a minimum of one vote but then an extra vote for each £10,000 held as in a Member's Capital Account.

53. Members need to consider whether the approval needed in accordance with this clause is of the requisite percentage of all Members or only those who have attended the relevant meeting at which the matter is being considered. Note that this clause contains an extensive list of examples for which such approval may be required. The list is not

definitive and can be added to, or deleted, as applicable. It is possible to separate out the matters as to different levels of authority ie 60%, 75% or 85% etc approval required.

54. The statutory provision referred to will apply to LLPs unless disapplied. If allowed to remain available, it will afford a disaffected Member the right to apply to the court for a range of discretionary remedies if he can show that unfair prejudice has been caused to him. It is suggested that where, as is the case with this agreement, a clear framework is being established for what should happen in the event of dispute and/ or expulsion and resignation, it is undesirable to allow the uncertainty of such a discretionary overlay. See *Eaton v Caulfield* for the application of these provisions to an LLP which did not have a written members' agreement and *F&C Investments* where the parties did have a properly drafted members' agreement but which did unusually not exclude the provisions of *s 994* of the *Companies Act 2006*.

55. Many businesses will now provide mobile phones for all or some of their Members. The calls paid for may be all or simply business calls. Other facilities for which similar provisions might need to be made would be communication devices such as personal digital assistant, laptop or home computers. It is not essential to document arrangements for such facilities in the agreement, but some LLPs will prefer to do so.

56. Cars are often a vexed subject and this clause offers only a very illustrative simple approach to them. Amongst the subjects to be covered are; whether the Member or the LLP is to provide the car; if the latter, what cost limits are to apply; and will the LLP pay for all motoring or only business mileage. Draftsmen are encouraged not to over complicate these provisions because the arrangements in practice may well change fairly frequently and enshrining complex provisions in the agreement can necessitate frequent amendments. If no provision at all for direct payment of car related expenses is to be made, then the whole of this clause could be omitted and a provision for business mileage at a set rate per mile could be added to the previous clause on expenses generally.

57. One form of insurance not provided for in this clause is permanent health insurance, ie insurance to provide an income for a Member if he suffers long-term illness. If this is a device used by the LLP, then the responsibility for premiums (the LLP as a trading expense, or Members as individuals) will need to be resolved. Further, it would then be normal to provide that after the threshold period required to trigger such payments from the insurer (eg six months), the ill Member's share of profit (other than interest) should either cease or abate by the amount of the insurance payment. If so, clause 11 of this agreement should then be amended accordingly.

58. If the LLP takes out any such insurance as this, it will need to consider carefully the wording of any trust clauses, to avoid the situation

where for example the death of one member increases the overall asset base of the LLP, to which the other Members would be entitled. Some LLPs may seek to amend the terms of existing trusts on such policies, taken out in the days of the former practice, so as to benefit the LLP or its Members. Expert tax advice should be taken.

59. Some types of insurance may be regarded as being for the benefit of the Members as individuals in which case the premiums, if actually paid by the LLP, should be regarded as drawings and debited to the appropriate individual Members. Expert tax advice should be taken.

60. The words in square brackets offer a chance to stagger early retirements so that two or more Members are not leaving at the same time. Other variations could provide for even more of a pause between the effective dates of resignation. In very small LLPs, it may be appropriate to provide that if one member chooses to resign, the other(s) can, if they feel they cannot carry on the business, opt to go for a winding up of the LLP and accordingly nullify the resignation notice so that one member does not get a better deal than the other(s).

61. The *Employment Equality (Age) Regulations 2006, SI 2006/1031* which came into force on 1 October 2006 will apply to LLPs – see 6.8 of Chapter 6 as to the issues relating to including a compulsory retirement age.

     This agreement includes a retirement age. If the LLP does not think it can justify the provision by objective reference to the contribution of a Member, then it should probably omit this sub-clause and its associated definition. If that course is taken, it may be that the LLP will feel it needs to specify in much greater detail what is expected of a member so that failure to attain the relevant standard can give the right to expel for breach of agreement.

62. This is a simple version of a clause giving the LLP the power to require a Member to take 'garden leave' eg to cut him off from the business if he resigns to protect the interests of the business.

63. Clauses 23.4 to 23.9 of this agreement effectively give a right of appeal against expulsion for cause. If this is not desired they should be omitted. Such a right is deliberately not given in respect of expulsion without cause under clause 23.9 of this agreement as it would be impossible for a third party to undertake the same subjective exercise as the Members may choose to.

64. This clause allows the LLP to compel a Member to retire and in effect is a 'no-fault' expulsion clause. It may not be appropriate for smaller LLPs but is becoming more frequently used by the larger LLPs. Note that the default provisions do not allow for the expulsion of a Member unless there is express agreement between the Members. See *Eaton v Caulfield* for the difficulty of proving express agreement in the absence of a written members' agreement.

65. The agreement is drafted on the basis that retirement accounts will not be prepared and, instead, the entitlement of the Outgoing Member will be calculated in accordance with the usual year-end accounts, with an apportionment of profits to reflect the period during which that financial year the Outgoing Member was a Member. Consideration needs to be given to whether controls should be placed on the preparation of those accounts ie to ensure that they are prepared on a consistent basis as previous year's accounts.

66. If there is any extant goodwill in the accounts (eg if any has been put in as a consequence of a previous merger) it might be prudent to mention this. Equally, if there is to be any revaluation eg in respect of a freehold property which is being carried in the accounts at historic cost, and whose real value is known to be markedly different, this should be specified. It used to be the case that some businesses felt it appropriate to revalue work in progress when a Member left, but this should no longer be necessary in view of the changes to the tax rules on the recognition of revenue: see further Application Note G to Financial Reporting Standard 5 (FRS5) which was issued by the Accounting Standards Board on 13 November 2003 and UITF Abstract 40 *'Revenue recognition and service contracts'*.

67. HMRC have confirmed that generally business property relief will be available when an agreement between Members provides that the deceased Member's interest passes to the survivors who in turn are required to pay the personal representatives a particular price (see *HMRC Bulletin* IHTM25292). Care should be taken though if any additional payment (ie goodwill) is made, and in that case specialist tax advice should be sought.

68. The words in square brackets may be inserted as a precaution against deliberate undue delay on the part of the Members in finalising the termination accounts. The accountants should be consulted as to the adequacy of the suggested six-month period.

69. No attempt is made here to provide differing payment regimes for different circumstances ie the suggested three-year payment pattern does not change whether the outgoing member has died, resigned, or been expelled. It is of course possible to provide for such differences.

70. This period should only be for as long as is absolutely necessary for the protection of the LLP. If it is thus restrained, it stands a good chance of being held reasonable and hence enforceable. It would be possible to apply different lengths of time to the different limbs of clause 26.3 of this agreement.

71. The long period for which this clause is designed to operate obviously makes it onerous and increases the possibility of later breach, but firms may consider it prudent in view of the *Latent Damage Act 1986*. Firms should check with their insurers how long a run-off period may be available. It may be felt that in view of the limited

circumstances in which a Member (as distinct from the corporate LLP) could be personally liable for negligence, it is unnecessary and should be deleted.

72.   This may seem obvious, but the provision referred to does specify that Members may make such an agreement. The only likely reasons seem to be to secure the status of a contributory in a winding up or to give a general guarantee in favour of the whole body of creditors in order to persuade them to trade with the LLP. Neither seems likely to be frequently desirable.

73.   See further clause 8.6 of this agreement and the note to it.

74.   The giving of personal guarantees should be resisted where possible, but some may be inevitable and, where possible should be given preferably for fixed amounts. They may not of course be given by all Members or if so given, the creditor may call upon a guarantee from an ostensibly wealthy Member and not bother with a seemingly more impecunious one.

This clause aims to spread the load of such guarantees between the Members. Any individual Member called upon to make a payment to the creditor can of course first attempt to recover the outlay from the LLP, but if that fails (as may be likely) then he has recourse to the other Members. The proportions in which they will ultimately bear the responsibility is, in this example, spread according to residual profit shares.

75.   This will probably appear more controversial than it really is. It is in rare cases possible for an individual to be co-extensively liable with the LLP for negligence, but he will normally be covered by the same professional indemnity policy as the LLP. If so, then the only circumstances in which there would appear to be ultimate personal responsibility would be if the insurance cover, aggregated with all the assets of the LLP, is less than the amount of the claim; or if the insurers are able to refuse cover for some reason such as fraud; or if the uninsured excess is not covered by the LLP's assets. Those events might of course arise in which case an individual may suffer. It is suggested that this is the price payable for the shield of limitation afforded to the other Members and that it is not desirable effectively to remove that shield by getting them to cross indemnify each other.

76.   This clause 29.1.3 and 29.1.4 may be omitted if desired.

77.   The idea is that there should be mediation first and foremost but that if that does not succeed in resolving the dispute, there can be reference to a binding arbitration.

Agreement for the transfer of a business from a partnership to a limited liability partnership[1]

THIS AGREEMENT IS MADE the ...... day of ......

BETWEEN:

(1) *(insert personal names of transferring partners)* of *(address)* (the 'Sellers')
and

(2) *(insert name of transferee Limited Liability Partnership)* [with registered
number: [   ]²] whose registered office is [intended to be]³
at *(insert registered office address)* ('the Buyer')

RECITAL

(A) The Sellers currently carry on the Business in partnership [by way
of a partnership agreement dated [   ].

(B) The Sellers wish to convert the Business into a limited liability
partnership and [have incorporated] [have applied for
incorporation of] the LLP for this purpose.⁴

(C) The Sellers intend to contribute the Business to the LLP on,
and subject to, the terms of this Agreement with effect from the
Transfer Date.

NOW IT IS AGREED as follows:

1   Definitions and interpretation

For the purposes of this Agreement:

1.1   The following expressions shall have the following meanings:

  1.1.1 'Actual Completion Date' shall mean the day upon which the
transfers from the Sellers to the Buyer which this Agreement
provides for are actually completed

  1.1.2 'Assets' means the assets, contracts and rights owned by the
Sellers and used in connection with the Business as more
particularly described at clause 2.1

  1.1.3 'Book Debts' means all amounts of money due or payable
to the Sellers in relation to the Business as at the Actual
Completion Date to the extent that such amounts relate to the
period prior to the Actual Completion Date

  1.1.4 'Business' means the business of [   ] carried on by
the Sellers from the Business Premises as at the Transfer Date

  1.1.5 'Business Premises' means the freehold and/or leasehold
premises, brief particulars of which are set out in Schedule 1

  1.1.6 'Employees' means all the employees of the Business as at the
Actual Completion Date

1.1.7 'Excluded Assets' means those assets of the Business which will not be transferred to the Buyer pursuant to this Agreement being [*insert details of assets to be retained by the Sellers here*]

1.1.7 'Goodwill' means the goodwill and undertaking of the Sellers in connection with the Business including the exclusive right for the LLP to represent itself as carrying on the Business in succession to the Sellers and the right to use the Name

1.1.8 'Intellectual Property' means patents, rights to inventions, copyright and related rights, including, but not limited to, moral rights and performing rights, trade marks and services marks, logos, trade names and domain names, rights in get-up, goodwill and the right to sue for passing off and unfair competition, rights in designs, rights in computer software, database rights, utility models, rights to preserve the confidentiality of information (including know-how and trade secrets) and any other intellectual property rights, in each case whether registered or unregistered, including all applications for (and rights to apply for and be granted), renewals or extensions of, and rights to claim priority from, such rights and all similar or equivalent rights or forms of protection which subsist or will subsist, now or in the future, in any part of the world[5]

1.1.9 'Know-how' means any non-patented information, resulting from experience and testing, which is secret, substantial and identified. For this purpose, 'secret' means that the information is not generally known or easily accessible, 'substantial' means that the information is significant and useful for the production of goods and/or services and 'identified' means that the information is described in a sufficiently comprehensive manner so as to make it possible to verify that if fulfils the criteria of secrecy and substantiality

1.1.10 'Liabilities' means all debts of the Business owing by the Sellers at the Actual Completion Date and all other liabilities (of whatever nature) of the Business subsisting at that date

1.1.11 'Members' Accounts' means the accounts of each of the Sellers with the Buyer which show the interests of those persons in the Buyer in their capacity as members thereof

1.1.12 'Name' means [   ] [or any other name including
[   ]]

1.1.13 'Net Assets Value' means such sum as represents the excess of the value of the Assets over the amount of the Liabilities as recorded in the books of account of the Sellers as at the Actual Completion Date

1.1.14 'Office Equipment' means the furniture, computers and office equipment owned by the Sellers and used in connection with the Business as at the Effective Date

1.1.15 'Outstanding Agreements' means agreements entered into prior to the Actual Completion Date by or on behalf of the Sellers in connection with the Business (whether with clients for the supply of services to them by the Business or with suppliers for the purchase of goods by or the provision of services to the Business) and which remain wholly or partly to be performed as at the Actual Completion Date

1.1.16 'Transfer Date' means [   ]

1.1.17 'Work in Progress' means the work in progress of the Business at the Actual Completion Date and the right to render bills for such work and to receive all money collected as a consequence thereof

1.2   Expressions importing the masculine gender shall include the feminine and neuter and those importing the singular number shall include the plural and vice versa

1.3   Any covenants or stipulations entered into by more than one party shall be entered into jointly and severally

1.4   Unless the context otherwise requires reference to any clause, paragraph or Schedule is to a clause, paragraph or Schedule (as the case may be) of or to this Agreement

1.5   The headings in this document are inserted for convenience only and shall not affect the construction or interpretation of this Agreement

2   Sale and purchase

2.1   The Sellers agree to transfer upon the Transfer Date to the Buyer and the Buyer agrees then to accept a transfer of the Business as a going concern[6] comprising the following assets used in the conduct of the Business:

2.1.1   the Business Premises[7]

2.1.2   the Goodwill

2.1.3   the tangible assets listed in Schedule 3

2.1.4   the Work in Progress

2.1.5   the Book Debts

2.1.6   the Intellectual Property

2.1.7   the Office Equipment

2.1.8   the benefit (subject to the burden) of the Outstanding Agreements (so far as the Sellers can transfer the same)

2.1.9   all cash in hand or at bank

2.1.10 all other assets, rights and interests of the Seller used in the Business [other than the Excluded Assets]

3   The Business Premises[8]

The Business Premises shall be transferred to the Buyer in accordance with Schedule 2.

4   Title

The Buyer accepts such title as the Sellers have to the various assets to be transferred to it and shall not be entitled to make any requisitions or objections in relation to the same.

5   Liabilities and outstanding agreements

5.1   The Buyer agrees to take the transfer of the Business subject to the Liabilities and to pay satisfy and discharge all of the same and shall indemnify the Sellers against all proceedings, costs, claims and expenses in respect of the Liabilities

5.2   With effect from the Transfer Date, the Buyer shall assume the obligations of, and become entitled to the benefits of the Sellers under the Outstanding Agreements PROVIDED THAT if any such Outstanding Agreement cannot effectively be assigned except with the consent of (or by an agreement of novation with) the third party concerned then this Agreement shall not operate so as to transfer the benefit of any such agreements or any rights under such agreement and, instead, the following provisions shall apply:

5.2.1   the Sellers and the Buyer shall each use all reasonable endeavours to procure that each such Outstanding Agreement is novated or assigned at the expense of the Buyer and

5.2.2   unless and until such Outstanding Agreement is so novated or assigned:

5.2.2.1   the Buyer shall (for its own benefit and upon such terms as shall so far as possible give to the Buyer the benefit of any such agreement as if the same had been assigned to the Buyer) perform as the sub-contractor of the Sellers the obligations of the Sellers contained in that agreement and

5.2.2.2   the Sellers shall hold any benefit received under any such agreement upon trust for the Buyer absolutely

5.3   The Buyer shall indemnify the Seller against all liabilities, losses, actions, proceedings, damages, costs, claims, demands and expenses brought or made against or suffered or incurred by the Sellers in respect of the Buyer's failure to perform or comply with the terms of any of the Outstanding Agreements from the Transfer Date

6 Consideration

6.1 The consideration for the sale of the Business shall be:

6.2.1 the assumption by the Buyer of the Liabilities and the obligations of the Sellers under any Outstanding Agreements (insofar as the latter are not comprised within the Liabilities) and

6.2.2 the Net Assets Value

6.2 Such part of the said consideration as represents the Net Assets Value shall be satisfied by the crediting by the Buyer to each of the Members' Accounts of a proportion of the Net Assets Value equal to the proportion which they held as partners in the Business immediately prior to the completion of this Agreement

7 Completion

7.1 The sale of the Business shall be completed on the Transfer Date at the offices of the Sellers' solicitors when the Sellers shall execute and provide all such deeds and do all things as the Buyer considers necessary effectively to vest the Business and the Assets in the Buyer.

7.2 In the event that following Completion the Sellers shall receive any money in respect of the Book Debts or the Work In Progress they shall forthwith upon receipt pay the same to the Buyer

7.3 The Sellers shall, after Completion, give notice in writing pursuant to the Law of Property Act 1925 Section 136 to the relevant debtors of the assignment of the Book Debts and/or of the Buyer's right to render bills in respect of the Work In Progress and to collect the money due under any of the Book Debts or such bills

8 Employees

The Buyer will continue to employ all staff employed by the Sellers in connection with the Business and will indemnify the Sellers against any claims or Liabilities of whatever nature arising from the existing contracts of employment of such staff after the Actual Completion Date or from the transfer of the employment of such staff to the Buyer[9]

9 Value Added Tax

9.1 The Sellers and the Buyer consider that the Business is being transferred as a going concern

9.2 The Buyer warrants that:

9.2.1 it is registered as a taxable person for VAT purposes or will be so registered prior to the Actual Completion Date and

9.2.2   it will immediately after the transfer of the assets of the Business use those assets in the same kind of business as they were used in prior to the transfer

9.3   In the event of HM Revenue & Customs refusing to accept that the transfer of the Business is a transfer of a going concern the Buyer shall pay to the Sellers VAT on the assets transferred as assessed by HM Revenue & Customs upon the Sellers providing the Buyer with a tax invoice to support a claim by the Buyer for a recovery of the tax paid

10   Outstanding Obligations

All obligations which remain to be performed after the Actual Completion Date shall continue in full force and effect notwithstanding completion and shall not merge

11   Rights of other Parties

For the avoidance of doubt nothing in this Agreement shall confer or purport to confer upon any person, firm, limited liability partnership or limited company which is not a party to this Agreement any benefit or right to enforce any term of this Agreement pursuant to the Contracts (Rights of Third Parties) Act 1999

12   Further Assurance

The parties to this Agreement agree, at their own expense, to do or procure the doing of all such acts and/or execute or procure the execution of all such documents so as to give full meaning and effect to this Agreement, subject to any restriction or limitation in this Agreement on the extent of any party's obligations under this Agreement.

13   Governing Law and Jurisdiction

This Agreement (and any dispute, controversy, proceedings or claims are of whatever nature arising out of or in any way relating to this Agreement or its formation) shall be governed by and construed in accordance with English Law.

Each of the parties to this Agreement irrevocably agrees that the courts of England shall have exclusive jurisdiction to hear and decide any suit, action or proceedings and/or to settle any disputes, which may arise out of or in connection with this Agreement or its formation and, for these purposes, each party irrevocably submits to the jurisdiction of the courts of England.

This Agreement may be amended in whole or in part only with the written consent of all of the parties.

14 Notices

Any notice, demand or other communication given or made under or in connection with the matters contemplated by this Agreement shall be in writing and shall be delivered personally or sent by pre-paid first class post (air mail if posted to or from a place outside of the United Kingdom) to the address set out in this Agreement or such other address such party has advised. Any notice shall be deemed to have been duly given or made as follows:

14.1   If personally delivered, upon delivery at the address of the relevant party;

14.2   If sent by first class post, 2 Working Days after the date of posting; and

14.3   If sent by air mail, 5 business days after the day of posting.

Subject always to the ability to prove actual delivery and provided further that, in accordance with the above provisions, any notice, demand or other communication which would otherwise be deemed to have been given or made after 5:00pm shall be deemed to have been given or made at 9:00am on the next Working Day.

Any party may notify to the others to this Agreement change to its address for the purposes of this clause 14 provided that such notification shall only be effective on the date specified in it or if no date is specified or the date is less than 5 Working Days after the date on which the notice is given, the dates falling 5 Working Days after the date on which the notice is given.

15 Counterparts

This Agreement may be executed in any number of counterparts which together shall constitute one agreement. Any party may enter into this Agreement by executing a counterpart and this Agreement shall not take effect until it has been executed by all parties.

Schedule 1 Business Premises

Insert description here.

Schedule 2 Terms of Transfer of the Business Premises

(Insert standard commercial property conditions of sale (second addition).)

Schedule 3

3   Transfer date

(insert intended transfer date, allowing for note 2 [1648] of this Form)

SCHEDULE 2

Business premises

> *(insert sufficient detail of business premises to enable them to be correctly identified in a subsequent transfer, including title number where appropriate)*

THIRD SCHEDULE

Plant and other assets

> *(insert list in sufficient detail to enable assets to be identified)*

(signatures of (or on behalf of) the parties)

1   Ie a limited liability partnership ('LLP') formed or to be formed under the *Limited Liability Partnerships Act 2000* ('the Act'). This Agreement could also be adapted for the transfer of the business of a sole trader.

2   This Agreement can be entered into before the LLP is actually incorporated, in accordance with the *Limited Liability Partnerships Act 2000, s 5(2)* in which case delete the wording in square brackets. In that event its effectiveness will depend upon incorporation actually occurring. It would not be sensible to make it operative from the date of incorporation itself, since this will be the date of issue of the incorporation certificate by Companies House, and that date may not be known for some little while thereafter. A suitable gap should thus be allowed when determining the Transfer Date.

3   Again, the wording in square brackets can be deleted if the Agreement is being entered into before the LLP is actually incorporated.

4   Details can here be inserted of any intellectual property which is not to pass to the LLP for any reason. If a balance sheet value has been attributed to any such which is retained, an adjustment will be needed to asset values.

[5   This assumes that the partners in the selling partnership and the members of the buying LLP are exactly the same people. If there are any differences, ie because some partners are retiring and not becoming members, or new people are coming in as members who were not partners, then amendment will be necessary. Where possible, such circumstances should be avoided, in order to maintain clear entitlement to the Stamp Duty exemption offered by the *Limited Liability Partnerships Act 2000, s 12* as repeated for the purposes of stamp duty land tax by *s 65* of the *Finance Act 2003.*]

6   It is assumed that this will be an outright transfer of the Business in its entirety, ie that the transferring partnership will retain neither the benefit of Book Debts and Work in Progress, nor the burden of the Liabilities to existing creditors. If it is intended that the transferring partnership will retain some or all of these assets and liabilities, then the agreement can be amended to take this into account and care is needed to ensure that the partners in partnership are clear as to how they would share the respective profits and/or losses of these retained assets and liabilities. Consideration is also required as to what protection the LLP may require should a third-party mistakenly pursue it for those liabilities. It may be that some, perhaps larger, businesses will however wish to keep a skeleton partnership operating during a pre-set run-off period, and would wish to keep these elements out of the transfer.

7   This Agreement assumes that all the Business Premises, as currently shown in the accounts of the transferring partnership, are to be transferred to the LLP. If this is not so, eg because individuals wish to retain them outside the LLP for reasons of control of their investment, then first a reduction in the balance sheet will need to be agreed, and secondly arrangements for the occupation of the property in question by the LLP will need to be implemented. If this tack is to be followed, however, consideration will need to be given as to whether there is a danger of breaching any covenant with a mortgagor or landlord against letting etc. Also, in the case of leasehold property, it is likely that the chances of renewal under the *Landlord and Tenant Act 1954* will be adversely affected, since it will be the LLP, not the tenants, which is carrying on the business at the premises.

8   The transfer of the interest in the Business Premises, from the transferring partners or those holding as nominees or trustees, will require to be perfected later by a Transfer or Assignment. Any requisite consents, from mortgagees or landlords, should have been obtained in the normal way, and it would be prudent to do so before this Agreement is entered into. In the case of complex properties, it might be desirable to annex a draft Transfer or Assignment to this Agreement. Care should be taken to ensure that the title is passed within the period of 12 months from the date of incorporation of the LLP, so as to gain the benefit of the exemption from Stamp Duty contained in the *Limited Liability Partnerships Act 2000, s 12* as repeated for the purposes of stamp duty land tax by *s 65* of the *Finance Act 2003*.

9   This very general and simple clause assumes that the same people will in practice be controlling the staff conditions both before and after transfer, so that it is not necessary to attempt to apportion pre- and post-transfer liabilities, or to delineate more precisely those employment liabilities which the purchaser of a business at arm's length might expect to take on.

Novation agreement for use on transfer of business to a limited liability partnership[1]

THIS NOVATION AGREEMENT is made the ... day of ...

BETWEEN:

(1) *(personal name(s) of transferring sole trader or partners)* trading [together] as *(business name of transferor business)* of *(address)* ('the Transferor')

(2) *(name of transferee limited liability partnership)* whose registered office is at *(address)* ('the LLP') and

(3) *(name of other party to contract)* of *(address)* ('the Third Party')

NOW IT IS AGREED as follows:

1 Definitions and interpretation

For the purposes of this Agreement:

1.1 The following expressions shall have the following meanings:

1.1.1 'the Contract Date' means the date appearing in the Schedule paragraph 1

1.1.2 'the Contract' means the contract made upon the Contract Date between the Transferor and the Third Party

1.1.3 'the Business' means the business which was at the Contract Date carried on by the Transferor brief descriptive details of which appear in the Schedule paragraph 2

1.1.4 'the Transfer Date' means the date upon which the Business was or is intended to be transferred to the LLP by agreement between the Transferor and the LLP and which appears in the Schedule paragraph 3

1.2 Expressions importing the masculine gender shall include the feminine and neuter and those importing the singular number shall include the plural and vice versa

1.3 Any covenants or stipulations entered into by more than one party shall be entered into jointly and severally

1.4 Unless the context otherwise requires reference to any clause, paragraph or Schedule is to a clause, paragraph or Schedule (as the case may be) of or to this Agreement

1.5 The headings in this document are inserted for convenience only and shall not affect the construction or interpretation of this Agreement

2 Recitals

2.1 The Business [is to be] [was] transferred by the Transferor to the LLP upon the Transfer Date

2.2 The Contract was entered into by the Transferor in the course of the operation of the Business

2.3 The Transferor wishes to be released and discharged from the Contract

2.4 The LLP has asked the Third Party to agree to such a release and discharge

2.5 The Third Party has agreed to release and discharge the Transferor from the Contract in return for the LLP's undertaking contained in Clause 3

3 Limited liability partnership's undertaking

In consideration of the release by the Transferor contained in Clause 4 the LLP undertakes to perform the Contract as from the Transfer Date and after that date to be bound by the terms of the Contract (in lieu of the Transferor) in every way as if it were a party to the Contract

4 Release of the transferor

In consideration of the undertaking on the part of the LLP contained in Clause 3:

4.1 The Third Party releases and discharges the Transferor from all claims and demands whatever in respect of the Contract and accepts in lieu of the Transferor the liability of the LLP under the Contract in respect of all claims, demands and liabilities arising from the Transfer Date onwards

4.2 The Third Party agrees to be bound by the Contract in respect of all obligations accruing from the Transfer Date onwards in every way as if the LLP were named in the Contract as a party in place of the Transferor

5 Rights of other parties

For the avoidance of doubt nothing in this Agreement shall confer or purport to confer upon any person, firm, limited liability partnership or limited company which is not a party to this Agreement any benefit or right to enforce any term of this Agreement or of the Contract pursuant to the Contracts (Rights of Third Parties) Act 1999

AS WITNESS etc

SCHEDULE

1 Contract date

(date upon which the Contract was made)

2 Business

(insert brief descriptive details of the nature of the Business)

3 Transfer date

(date upon which the transfer of the Business was or will become effective)

(signatures of (or on behalf of) the parties)

1   This agreement is intended to be usable for a variety of novations which will be needed upon the transfer of a business to the entity of a limited liability partnership incorporated under the *Limited Liability Partnerships Act 2000* (32 *Halsbury's Statutes* (4th Edn) PARTNERSHIP). It is suitable for use whether or not the earlier business was that of a sole trader or, as will in practice more usually be the case, a partnership. It is not particularly intended for use in the (presumably rare) circumstances where a limited company is transferring its business to an LLP, though it should be capable of adaptation for that purpose. The agreement for the transfer of the business should provide for the circumstances where it is not possible to obtain a novation, and so the Transferor has to hold the agreement on trust for the LLP in return for an indemnity.

Index

[All references are to paragraph numbers.]

Index